World Upside Down

World Upside Down

Reading Acts in the Graeco-Roman Age

C. KAVIN ROWE

OXFORD
UNIVERSITY PRESS
2010

OXFORD
UNIVERSITY PRESS

Oxford University Press, Inc., publishes works that further
Oxford University's objective of excellence
in research, scholarship, and education.

Oxford   New York
Auckland   Cape Town   Dar es Salaam   Hong Kong   Karachi
Kuala Lumpur   Madrid   Melbourne   Mexico City   Nairobi
New Delhi   Shanghai   Taipei   Toronto

With offices in
Argentina   Austria   Brazil   Chile   Czech Republic   France   Greece
Guatemala   Hungary   Italy   Japan   Poland   Portugal   Singapore
South Korea   Switzerland   Thailand   Turkey   Ukraine   Vietnam

First published by Oxford University Press, Inc., 2009
198 Madison Avenue, New York, New York 10016

www.oup.com

First issued as an Oxford University Press paperback, 2010

Oxford is a registered trademark of Oxford University Press

Library of Congress Cataloging-in-Publication Data

Rowe, Christopher Kavin, 1974–
World upside down : reading Acts in the Graeco-Roman age / Kavin Rowe.
   p. cm.
Includes bibliographical references and indexes.
ISBN 978-0-19-976761-8
1. Bible. N.T. Acts—Criticism, interpretation, etc.   I. Title.
BS2625.52.R69 2009
226.6'067—dc22   2008054873

Printed in the United States of America
on acid-free paper

For Isaac and Gabrielle (once again)

Acknowledgments

Because virtually every aspect of a book's production involves substantial contribution from others, writing a book is synonymous with the accumulation of personal debts. This is as true of the provision of the daily (or nightly) space needed for research, reading, and reflection as it is of the incredibly time-consuming labor of formatting, checking of references, and creation of indices. In my particular case, the required sustenance for daily life is such that I have far too many people to thank. Therefore, other than my parents (Tom and Betty Rowe), who are more than one could hope for in loving parents and whom I would especially like to honor and thank, and my parents-in-law (Joe and Pam Ponzi), for whom the same applies, I shall simply list those on the local scene who by their active help, conversation, encouragement, friendship, or sheer stamina in care have allowed the writing of this book: Richard Hays, Moody Smith, Greg Jones, Douglas Campbell, Joel Marcus, Susan Eastman, Stanley Hauerwas, Paul Griffiths, Randy Maddox, Stephen Chapman, Ellen Davis, Grant Wacker, Warren Smith, Geoffrey Wainwright, Reinhard Huetter, Allen Verhey, David Toole, Laceye Warner, Allan Poole, Betsy Poole, Margaret Frothingham, Samantha Fisher, the Tonn family, Jeff and Susan McSwain, Rachel Campbell, Carrie Pothoven, Cheryl Blake, Steve Larson, Chip Denton, Megan Wright, Pam Holland, Gini Osborne, Rich and Dick Jarman, T. J. Lang, Scott Ryan, Anne Weston, Diane Decker, and last but in no wise least, Susan E. Bond. These are people—some of whom don't even know it—who make our daily lives possible. Beyond this, my debt to friends and colleagues across the globe expands exponentially.

No matter how well supported, daily life while teaching does not always grant the time needed to write. To that end, my profound thanks are due to two organizations and their officers that created an extended time for me to think and write: the Lilly Endowment (for a Faculty Fellowship), and the Louisville Institute (for a Christian Faith and Life grant).

My editor at Oxford, Cynthia Read, has been exemplary, as has the production staff. Without them, of course, there would be no book to read. Portions of chapter 2 were previously published as "The Book of Acts and the Cultural Explication of the Identity of God," in *The Word Leaps the Gap: Essays on Scripture and Theology in Honor of Richard B. Hays,* edited by J. Ross Wagner et al. (Grand Rapids, MI: Eerdmans, 2008). These portions are reprinted by permission of the publisher, all rights reserved.

Finally, I know of no way to thank my wife and son, since they are in a very real sense my daily life, and so I simply dedicate the book to them as a gesture toward the kind of deep hope and—perhaps above all—silliness that goes into the richness of our life together.

Contents

World Upside Down

I

Reading Acts

At its most basic intellectual level, this book is about the inextricable connection between an irreducibly particular way of knowing and a total way of life. But—being a work of New Testament scholarship—the discussion herein is not a philosophical reflection on the importance of practical reason or an academic manifesto that proclaims the end of the false dichotomies that plague modern thought. Instead, the argument about these matters is conducted via a historicized discussion of one New Testament text—the one that, in my judgment, best encompasses the difficulties and promises of thinking through the particularity of Christian theological knowledge and its embeddedness in a comprehensive pattern of life: the Acts of the Apostles.

The Project

For almost three hundred years—since C. A. Heumann's article of 1720—the dominant trend in New Testament interpretation has been to read the Acts of the Apostles as a document that argues for the political possibility of harmonious existence between Rome and the early Christian movement (e.g., Heumann, Cadbury, Haenchen, Conzelmann, Tajra, Sterling, Heusler, and Meiser). The few challenges to this view that have arisen amount to little more than adjustments to the basic premise (e.g., Walaskay) or exegetically feeble denials of the dominant reading (e.g., Horsley).[1] To date there has not been a sophisticated, critically constructive reappraisal of Acts' ecclesiological vision. The time is long overdue for such a study.

The underlying reason for such stagnation in the study of Acts is that where the question of Luke's politics has been taken up, it has been thought about as though one could speak of politics *simpliciter*.[2] For Luke, however, politics is the particular, embodied shape of God's revelation to the world in the Lord of all, Jesus Christ. To understand Luke's political vision, therefore, one must examine the way Luke's narration of God's apocalypse shapes ecclesiology: theological truth claims and the pattern of life that sustains them—the core practices of Christian communities—are inextricably bound together.

Recognizing this interconnection requires a radical reassessment and rereading of Acts. No longer can Acts be seen as a simple *apologia* that articulates Christianity's harmlessness vis-à-vis Rome. Yet neither is it a direct call for liberation, a kind of theological vision that takes for granted the solidity of preexistent political arrangements. Rather, in its attempt to form communities that witness to God's apocalypse, Luke's second volume is a highly charged and theologically sophisticated political document that aims at nothing less than the construction of an alternative total way of life—a comprehensive pattern of being—one that runs counter to the life-patterns of the Graeco-Roman world. His literary work is thus, in the terms of Frances Young and others, a culture-forming narrative.[3]

In order to read Acts afresh, the body of this work unfolds in three successive chapters the profound tension that structures Luke's cultural vision: "Collision" (chapter 2) narrates the cultural explication of divine identity; "*Dikaios*" (chapter 3) develops the connection between the character of the Christian mission and the rejection of statecraft; and "World Upside Down" (chapter 4) focuses upon the practice of theological knowledge.

Chapter 2: Collision

The opening chapter argues that Luke narrates the Christian mission to the Gentiles in Acts as an apocalypse (see, e.g., Luke 2:32).[4] At its core, the Christian mission claims to be a revelation of God. Inasmuch as this revelation is carried in the formation of a people ("church")—rather than merely being a list of academic theses—it entails a necessary challenge to constitutive patterns of pagan life. Embracing the theological vision of the Christian gospel simultaneously creates a new cultural reality. That this process of revelation and formation inherently destabilizes essential assumptions and practices of Mediterranean culture emerges paradigmatically in the scenes in Lystra,

Philippi, Athens, and Ephesus (Acts 14, 16, 17, and 19, respectively). These passages, read narratively and in connection to their Graeco-Roman contexts, thus constitute the exegetical lens through which the problem of cultural destabilization is examined.

Chapter 3: Dikaios

In light of the findings of chapter 2, chapter 3 argues that the culturally destabilizing character of the Christian mission entails the potential for outsiders to construe Christianity as sedition or treason (as indeed it was so construed). In order to counter such a perception, Luke explicitly raises these and related charges and repeatedly narrates the course of events so that the Christians—here in the mold of Jesus himself—are found "innocent" by the Romans of seditious criminal activity. In the terms of Roman jurisprudence, they are *dikaios* (*iustus*). Thus does Luke bring Paul, the representative of the Christians, before the Roman state in the officials that are its living agents: Gallio, Claudius Lysias, Felix, and Festus (Acts 18; 21–23; 23–24; and 25–26, respectively). With deft narrative development and considerable jurisprudential skill, Luke moves Paul through to Rome while concurrently negating the charges of his opponents on the basis of a revisionary reading of Roman law: the Christian mission is not a bid for political liberation or a movement that stands in direct opposition to the Roman government.

When read together with the preceding chapter, the argument in chapter 3 uncovers the profound tension that lies at the heart of Luke's literary program. On the one hand, Luke narrates the movement of the Christian mission into the gentile world as a collision with culture-constructing aspects of that world. From the perspective created by this angle of vision, Christianity and pagan culture are competing realities. Inasmuch as embracing Christian theological claims necessarily involves a different way of life, basic patterns of Graeco-Roman culture are dissolved. The pagans in Lystra, Philippi, Athens, and Ephesus are understandably riled: the Christians are a real threat (chapter 2). On the other hand, Luke narrates the threat of the Christian mission in such a way as to eliminate the possibility of conceiving it as in direct competition with the Roman state. Of all forms of sedition and treason, Luke tells, Christianity is innocent. Paul may well engender considerable upheaval as a part of his mission, but repeatedly—in Corinth, Jerusalem, Caesarea, and Rome (so the reader understands)—the political authorities reject the accusations of his opponents: Paul is *dikaios*. The Christians are not out to establish Christendom, as it were (chapter 3). New culture, yes—coup, no. The tension is set.

Chapter 4: World Upside Down

Chapter 4 locates the origin of the tension created by the juxtaposition of the arguments in chapters 2 and 3 and, in so doing, argues for a way of reading Acts that derives from thinking the tension that the narrative exhibits. As a way into the argument of the chapter, the first section analyzes the narrative and political dynamics of Paul's and Silas' visit to Thessalonica (Acts 17:1–10a). More than any other, this scene encapsulates in one compressed piece of text the theological thought that expresses the tension inherent to Acts: the Christian mission is, in Luke's way of reading reality, a witness to a world that is upside down (17:6). Thus does cultural destabilization (chapter 2) appear to Roman eyes as sedition and treason but emerge in Luke's counter-narration as the light and forgiveness of God (chapter 3). The deconstructive move of the apocalypse to the gentiles—the *novum* that requires a new culture—has its reconstructive counterpart in the creation of a people who receive light in darkness, forgiveness of sins, and guidance in the way of peace (e.g., Acts 26:17–18; cf. Luke 1:79).

To read reality in this way is, from an outsider's perspective, clearly to make a radical claim. Yet in Acts, such a claim is not made at an abstract philosophical level but rather in relation to concrete forms of life. The epistemological move that sees things upside down is thus a lived way of knowing, a kind of "thick" knowledge indissolubly tied to a set of practices that are instantiations of a world turned right side up.[5]

To understand the origin of the narrative tension, therefore, is to examine the most critical practices required by Lukan epistemology. Hence, the remainder of chapter 4 focuses on the way Luke has narrativized three core ecclesial practices that generate the tension produced by the juxtaposition of chapters 2 and 3: the confession of Jesus as Lord (*Kyrios*), the active mission "to the end of the earth," and the assembly of the "Christians." These are core practices in three primary senses: other important activities of the Christian community—economic redistribution, for example—can be traced to these core practices; they are interdependent; and the narrative of Acts is fundamentally inconceivable without them.[6] Seen together, these three core practices constitute the practical-theological pattern that produces the tension inherent to Acts' apocalyptic vision.

This three-chapter sequence is thus intended not only to overcome literarily an atomistic reading of the text (the perennial peril of the modern exegete), but also to display Luke's remarkable—if offensive—claim that the culturally destabilizing power of the Christian mission is not to be construed as sedition or treason but rather as the light and forgiveness of God. The dissolution of patterns basic to Graeco-Roman culture (e.g., sacrifice to the gods) is nothing less than the necessary consequence of forming life-giving communities.

To understand Acts in this way is inconceivable without a sufficiently layered description of Graeco-Roman culture.[7] If "culture" names the inter-connections of concepts and practices that constitute a total way of life (see below), then the necessary historical task is to elucidate the interconnections that form this total way of life. Religion and politics, for example, are not two separate things in Graeco-Roman antiquity but intertwine to form a coherent pattern of life. So, too, religion and economics were not two separate spheres—corresponding, say, to modern academic departments of study—but were inseparable. Politics and economics are thus not ancillary but basic to what we say about ancient religion. Exposing this intertwining is necessary in this book precisely because the narrative power of Acts in the ancient world derives from the way its religious challenge simultaneously undoes political and economic practices.

Reading Acts as lively political theology in its time inevitably raises questions that directly relate to several crucial contemporary problems. Indeed, my argument is that engaging Acts in this way offers significant resources on which we can draw to understand conflicts that arise in light of profoundly different schemes of life. That all serious thinkers are in search of such resources today hardly requires comment. "God," "tolerance," "diversity," "culture," and "religious violence" are not only topics frequently in the news; they are also words that explicitly point to issues requiring sustained and refined reflection in the twenty-first century. Hence, after offering a condensed exposition of the reading of Acts given in chapters 2 through 4, the final chapter, "The Apocalypse of Acts and the Life of Truth," engages critical questions that attend the interrelation between universal truth claims and the politics they produce. It should thus be clear: my aim in this book is not simply to fill a gap in the scholarly discussion on Acts but admittedly is rather more ambitious: to reread an ancient text with historical knowledge and acumen precisely so that we might better understand how to think intelligently about the very real problems that face us today.

The Premises

This book is an interdisciplinary project. It requires for its exegetical execution significant interaction with scholarship on the New Testament and on Graeco-Roman antiquity as well as interaction with contemporary work in political theory, narrative criticism, and constructive theology. Of course, the danger in any interdisciplinary project is the temptation to spend too much time justifying the "poaching" in other disciplines. Though easily understandable as moves to hedge academic bets, such justifications are finally unnecessary for the simple reason that it is impossible for us to think in non-interdisciplinary ways. While it is obviously—perhaps platitudinously—true that some people will know more about some things than others,[8] it is also true that the days are gone when we may confidently inhabit one mode of thought to the exclusion of others—a "discipline" that exists with its own epistemological canons and discrete subject matter. Not only is this the case in practice—there is now simply too much secondary literature to read even within one's traditional field of study—but also in relation to thought: all thinking is done by people whose lives are not lived in discrete moments of intellectual disciplines but in the unity of one, narratively structured life.[9] That we can somehow extract our thinking from our lives and think solely in terms of a field of study is an illusion; it is in fact the modern university's social reproduction of a mind/body dualism. We think only within the lives we live, and since our lives are not made up of departments of study, neither is our thinking. Or, more simply: because we live interdisciplinary lives, we think in interdisciplinary terms.

Still, for the presentation of thought in writing, there are important ways in which we must make choices, must, that is, decide what to treat directly and what indirectly, what goes in the foreground and what in the background, what is argued for and what is assumed, and so on. It is in this light that we should understand the naming of this project as a "work of New Testament scholarship." This particular genre signifies the foreground of the book: exegesis constitutes its direct mode of thought, detailed discussion of passages its argumentative discourse.

This basic choice of what to place in the foreground of the book and in what primary language to conduct its argument necessarily involves a range of other interpretive choices and commitments. Here we shall enumerate those that best facilitate a reading of the coming material.

Acts and the Ancient World

The exegetical foreground of the book betrays my commitment to the importance of what Umberto Eco calls the cultural encyclopedia of a text, the wider cultural knowledge (tacit and explicit) assumed by the author and embedded in a text by virtue of its origin within a particular time and place in history.[10] To stay with an example invoked previously, in contrast to the cultural encyclopedia relevant to modern democracies, Luke has no idea of a basic bifurcation that many people now claim is necessary, namely, the separation of religion from politics; this distinction is simply not part of the conceptual configurations or political practices current in the first century (or anywhere in antiquity for that matter). To access the cultural encyclopedia of the text of Acts is immediately to become aware of the unity of religion and politics in one form of life.

To draw on Eco's notion is not simply to dress up a tired, old assertion about the importance of historical inquiry in flashy linguistic garb; it is, rather, to point to a more robust philosophical basis for textual interpretation in what Alasdair MacIntyre describes as "historically situated rationality," namely, the fact that patterns of reasoning appear "rational" only within the context of a larger history that has come to determine what rationality actually is.[11] To think that we could understand the patterns of Lukan reasoning as evidenced in the text of Acts without examining the wider history in which such patterns are intelligible is not only to return to a discredited nineteenth-century mode of inquiry—in which the biblical authors' "rationality" looks suspiciously like that of modern "critical" professors[12]—but also to abandon our hope for the kind of deep historical work that simply refuses to perpetuate the philosophical myth that places all thinking on a level plane. The truth is that there are not only different ways to think, but different ways to think about how to think. Religion and politics once more: Luke does not have a different opinion on the question of religion and politics from many modern thinkers, he has an entirely different question.

Taking Acts' cultural encyclopedia seriously enables us to offer a richer and more compelling account of the historically situated rationality displayed in the text. In practice, this means that the exegetical arguments of chapters 2 through 4 necessarily involve extensive interaction with various aspects of the Graeco-Roman world as a way to contextualize and thus sharpen our perception of the patterns of Lukan reasoning. In principle, seeking to give a rich account of historically situated rationality not only helps us better to understand Acts in the first century but also how to think about its interpretation today. If it is true, as Gadamer wanted to teach us, that without hermeneutical "sympathy" for the text we are reading we cannot hope for a melding of interpretive horizons, it is no less true that we cannot hope to develop a sophisticated version of such sympathy without some genuine understanding of the habits of reasoning that constitute what the horizons actually are. If this book thus rejects a two-step hermeneutical model—a kind of from-then-to-now linear movement—it nevertheless maintains that rigorous historical thickening of the biblical text helps to create the necessary hermeneutical conditions for the kind of analogical thinking required by sensitive readers of the New Testament today.

Acts and the Reader

In contrast to a strong stream of past New Testament scholarship,[13] this book assumes with Luke Johnson, Hans-Josef Klauck, and others that Acts is best read as a document intended for Christians (though this term was not yet a self-designation). Though individual elements occur that could lend support to an *apologia pro ecclesia* hypothesis, Acts is primarily concerned not with outwardly directed apologetic but with the story of God's apocalypse in the mission of the church. And although things would quickly change, Tertullian's comment near the end of the second century fits well the situation presupposed by the contents of Acts: "no one turns to our literature who is not already Christian" (*De Testimonio Animae*, 1.4).[14] The readers of Acts were not pagan "seekers" or "cultured despisers" of the gospel but Christians for whom such a story told the life of their community/ies.[15]

It follows, then, that in seeking to explore the interface of Acts and the Graeco-Roman world we are not asking about the perception of Acts within a "purely" pagan framework of thought—what pagans *qua* pagans would have made of Acts—but more about the contour of Christian life and thought inside conversion as evinced by the dialogical interrelation of Acts and pagan culture. Thus, for example, our question is not about the degree to which Stoics and Epicureans would have found Paul's speech in Acts 17:16–34 philosophically persuasive but about the effect of Acts 17:16–34 upon the theological life of pagan converts.[16]

And though the scenes discussed in the body of the book transpire in different geographical locales (Lystra, Athens, Ephesus, etc.), our analysis will not focus diachronically on what pagan converts in these particular places would have made of the scenes that touch only their immediate surroundings[17]—as if the guiding question in Acts 16:16–40, for example, is whether or not Philippian readers of Acts would have been able to relate a particular event to Luke's description of the great earthquake (σεισμός; 16:26). Geography in this book is thus taken more as a feature of theological vision, and less as a guide for mapping the concrete *Sitze im Leben* of Acts' readers. The interest, that is, is more in the constructive role local knowledge plays in the narrative and its contribution to the overall literary project.

To speak of a *literary* project is already to say that over against the tendency to think of Acts' theology in bits and pieces we reject the idea that the passages treated in the coming chapters were read in isolation.[18] As an increasing number of scholars are coming to affirm, to write a *story* is to give the hermeneutical direction, "read this as a narrative."[19] Thus is this work interested in the cumulative or total effect of the passages treated in the body of the book. Lest these scenes seem to leave portions of Acts untouched, we hasten to point out that the selected passages articulate animating convictions of Lukan theology and, precisely in this way, serve well as focal instances of the larger perspective rendered through the entire narrative.

In short—and to put it in stark terms—I take it that, aside from some basic generalities, we have no idea where Acts was written, or for whom, or at what particular time, or where it was to be sent (if indeed only one place was intended). In light of such ignorance, the proper hermeneutical posture is to practice a kind of interpretive asceticism in relation to what Acts' actual readers would have made of Acts. "Readers" in this book thus functions primarily as a placeholder for Christian readers of various kinds in the late first century and as a word that allows us to talk about the overall theological vision of the narrative of Acts. In simple terms, to "read" Acts is to think Christianly in the late first century Graeco-Roman world.

Acts and Interpretation

One of Acts' more notable younger scholars, Todd Penner, has recently written an extensive *Forschungsbericht* that catalogues the enormous methodological variety characterizing current New Testament scholarship on Acts.[20] The point here is not to offer observations about any one of the many aspects of Penner's seventy-page article but rather to step back and consider the piece as a whole: the fact is that the secondary literature on Acts is no longer full to the brim; it has now burst the dam and threatens to wash away the text of Acts in a torrent of scholarly glossolalia.[21]

Taken as a whole, the present state of Acts research thus points less to the accumulation of scholarly knowledge or a serious advance in exegetical sophistication than it does to a hermeneutical danger: the temptation to neglect a patient rereading of the text and engage in extended argument about the interpretation of the interpretation of Acts. Or, to put it slightly differently, we must beware the tendency to write more about those who write about Acts than about *Acts*. The great mass of scholarly studies should doubtless inspire hermeneutical humility, but if we are to practice New Testament interpretation, the body of secondary literature should not become the primary subject of our discourse. That place, it must be said, belongs to the New Testament texts themselves.[22]

The aim of this book is to display in detail my close readings of the passages necessary to sustain my thesis and, hence, to develop the argument by means of actual exegesis. So doing allows the reader not only to see a concentrated presentation of my interpretation of Acts—how I work with the text—but also to follow the basic dependency of this book for its constructive moves on ancient testimony outside the New Testament. To be sure, there is ample discussion of scholarly hypotheses, contested points of interpretation, problematic hermeneutical paradigms, and other standard academic fare. And for those who know well the scholarly literature, the positions I take in relation to current debates will be readily apparent. But the foreground of the argument is the text of Acts.

It is not fundamentally otherwise with the scholarly literature on, for example, the political shape of the concept of sovereignty, or the philosophical importance of practical reason, or the indispensability of narrative as an ordering mode of thought. In agreement with Hans Frei, I argued in *Early Narrative Christology* that the book would be most compelling as an actual interpretation of the Gospel of Luke if the bulk of the theoretical apparatus were largely invisible. That was hardly to say that it did not exist, but rather that it was left in the background "at the level of informing presuppositions."[23] The case is similar here. Thus, for example, running all the way through this book is the position that theology is not just ratiocination, an act of a (disembodied) thinking mind, but is a total life, a context within which thinking is what it is by means of the lives we live. This position can be reasonably contested (and defended) on a variety of grounds. But the argument of this particular book is not really as much about *that* as it is about *Acts*—hence, the arguments for the epistemological priority of a theological life remain in the background. Or to take one other example, in chapter 5 I assume, rather than argue for, the position that Acts is a normative text for specifically Christian reasoning and discourse. Of course, to speak of "normative" texts is to raise complex questions about intracanonical differences, varying emphases within Acts itself, the proper role of *Sachkritik,* and so forth. These are doubtless important questions, but I do not treat them directly (which, let it be said, is not the same thing as ignoring them). Instead, I simply assume that Christian communities read Acts as *scripture* and launch the inquiry from there. To defend the necessity of reading Acts as Christian scripture is an important task, but it would be a different book.

Taken as a whole, then, this book attempts to deal with the problem of secondary literature not by disregarding it but by refracting its interpretive worth through the text of Acts itself. The hermeneutical choice should thus be clear: there is more in the foreground about our reading of Acts than about our reading of the readings of Acts. This is, after all, a book about Acts.

Acts and Modern Vocabulary

Since words receive their meaning from their larger semantic context, I am somewhat skeptical of the usefulness of precise definitions: they are liable to skew the reading of sentences for the sake of words whose "definitions" are supposedly separable from the context in which they occur.[24] Still, for this study, there are a few contemporary words whose acquired connotations require us to say more or less what we mean when we use them.[25]

Culture: Raymond Williams once wrote that "culture" is "one of the two or three most complicated words in the English language."[26] How we could ever know such a thing is beyond my comprehension—but it seems right. In any event, this impression did not stop Williams from using the word in multiple publications, and neither shall it stop us. Yet we are undeterred not so much because the term "culture" is without theoretical problems[27] or is indisputably the best word to describe a comprehensive pattern of life but more because (1) I know of no better alternatives that name the interconnection of concepts and practices that comprise a total way of life (*habitus* might work, if we still wrote in Latin),[28] and (2) the word is used without definition so frequently in intellectual work of all kinds (from anthropology departments to papal encyclicals) and in the media that most of us have an intuitive grasp of what we mean—or at least what we are after.[29]

Where we could get into conceptual difficulties, in my judgment, actually has more to do with what we *cannot* mean if we are to speak intelligently about culture in a way that reflects something of the vision of Acts. Saying what we do not mean is of course hermeneutically risky business, at least in the sense that it can quickly lead to the "death of a thousand qualifications," as it were. Still, for this book, by culture we cannot mean at least three things:

(1) Culture cannot mean: a sphere of life that exists in independence from God, as if God were not the creator of all that is not God (cf. Acts 17:24, 26). In this respect, H. Richard Niebuhr's famous book *Christ and Culture* is the example *par excellence* of how not to speak of culture: in Niebuhrian grammar, Christ is one thing, culture another.[30] Whatever this teaches us about Niebuhr's thought, it is emphatically not what the word culture could mean if it is to be employed rightly in relation to the text of Acts. Indeed, to refer to a confession that will be discussed at length in chapter 4, for Luke, Jesus is Lord of all (Acts 10:36).

(2) Culture cannot mean: a piece of reality that is separable from other basic aspects of a total pattern of life (e.g., economy). When historian David Cherry, for example, writes of the effects of Roman presence in North Africa, he separates what belongs inherently together: "[t]here is in fact no evidence to show that there was any really significant measure of cultural change in the region during the period of Roman occupation. It might be supposed instead that the main consequences of the coming of the Romans were economic and social."[31] Contra Cherry, economic and social consequences are not

non-cultural consequences but are instead bound up with what it would mean to speak of cultural consequences in the first place. Precisely to the degree that the Romans affected social and economic life, they also effected cultural change.

(3) Culture cannot mean: a static backdrop to the text of Acts, as if Acts itself were somehow sealed off from and did not partake of Graeco-Roman culture[32]; or a pristine reality that Acts attempts to form, as if the new culture that Acts seeks to narrate was to retain nothing from the old. It is of course true that the "culturally fluid" situation of the late antique period bears little resemblance to the situation Acts describes.[33] But if we are to speak of culture in relation to Acts, we cannot think in terms of entirely isolated forms of life. To take only one obvious example: when the Christian community "bursts the conceptual frame" of Graeco-Roman "altruism" by engaging in radical economic redistribution (Acts 2:43–47; 4:32–37), they did not attempt to erect their own mint and strike "Christian" coins for use in the network of house churches.[34] The governor Felix hopes for Paul's collection money not for spiritual reasons but because he can use it (Acts 24:17, 23, 26).

In this book, the word "culture" is thus employed with a certain interpretive lightness of foot. Its meaning is not overly determined for the sake of what is inevitably an elusive definitional precision, but neither is the word so vacuous as to be left without substance. With all the necessary qualifications, culture nevertheless remains the word we shall employ to name the interconnections that make and sustain a total pattern of life.

Pagan: Like culture, "pagan" is a word chosen primarily because of the lack of workable alternatives. In some quarters, of course, the word could be taken to imply a denigration of non-Jews or non-Christians—a synonym for bad religion or immorality—but this is scarcely necessary, and it is certainly not the meaning invoked here. Indeed, as we will see in chapter 3, especially as we consider the narrative appropriation of Roman jurisprudence, Luke himself hardly conceives of paganism in intellectually simplistic or moralistic terms.[35] "Pagan" in this book, therefore, has rather to do with a simple way to point to the people in the ancient world who were neither Jewish nor Christian and is here employed in the same manner as we find it in the work of scholars of classical antiquity such as Peter Brown, Ramsay MacMullen, Mary Beard, Glen Bowersock, Robin Lane Fox, Fergus Millar, John North, Simon Price, and others.

The word is not, of course, intended to reduce, systematize, or smooth over the internal contestations or vast diversity of life in the Graeco-Roman world. But for the purposes of this study the term "pagan" does limit Graeco-Roman diversity in one crucial respect: the confrontation with the Christian mission. Talal Asad may be right that there are no "self-contained societies," or "autonomous civilizations," in the sense that there has always been interconnection, interaction, mutual borrowing, and so forth between what have been taken to be vastly different peoples or cultures.[36] But one does not have to endorse the intellectual fiction of complete cultural isolation, or the absence of internal diversity and contestation, to see that in fact paganism names well a contained area of life in the ancient world—at least in the profoundly significant sense that it is incapable of including a missionizing Christianity without the loss of what it would mean to be pagan.

Christian: Despite employing a plethora of terms for the early followers of Jesus, Luke studiously avoids characterizing them as "Christians." Moreover, as will be seen in chapter 4, Christian is itself a term that originated as a label given by outsiders for those who followed the man *Christus,* and it evokes from Luke a narratively crucial rejection of the word's normal meaning. Still, I know of no alternatives that are descriptively more advantageous than Christian when it comes naming the community of those who live in the Way. There are copious cumbersome alternatives and somewhat odd proposals,[37] but in my judgment, Christian remains the best word that points unambiguously to the pattern of communal life that Jews and Gentiles have together in their common confession of Jesus of Nazareth as Lord of all. The term should thus not be understood as a chronological signal that locates Acts at a definite point somewhere in the complex questions that surround the parting of the ways between Judaism and Christianity but as an effort to point clearly to the community that Acts both presupposes and seeks to create. As we use "Gospels" to talk about the texts that were later called the Gospels, so we use "Christians" to talk about the people that were later named Christians.

The Hope

This book does not depend upon or advocate a particular method. Rather, it embodies a multidimensional constructive purpose: as in a piece of music, there are discernable themes—or strands of thought—but the themes are inextricably woven together in service of a complex telos. Thus, as a composer might wish to direct attention toward particularly important themes of a work and concurrently insist that the work as a whole is the performance of these themes simultaneously, so I wish to insist that to understand this book attention must be given both to these themes and to the fact that they are played, as it were, all at once.

The reluctance to reduce the book's animating intellectual moves to a specific method does not stem from skittishness about matters methodological.

It has rather to do with the recognition that ours is a time in which there exists tangible evidence of massive and irrevocable shifts in thought and life that have occurred both on the "long march" from the Protestant Reformation to the present day, and within the last fifteen years in particular, in which the explosion of the interpretive horizon of everyday life has become a lived fact ("globalism"—the digital age, worldwide markets, market states, news media, transnational currencies, etc.).[38]

The tangible evidence of these shifts in New Testament studies is not so much the bewildering array of different methodologies for reading the New Testament or even their obvious backside, the expression of profound dissatisfaction with established modes of inquiry.[39] It is more what the whole reality of the methodological plethora portends: that we do not quite know what we are doing or how we ought to proceed, that studying the texts of the New Testament is a task requiring skills that exceed our capacity of methodological construction.[40] We are therefore learning as we go.

And, indeed, this is not surprising. Late (or post) modernity names our experience of the fact that we lost our way and must search again for how to find it. It also names, however, a time of great hope and expectation, at least in the sense that the fundamental need for creative engagement with the foundational texts of Christian discourse is widely perceived and eagerly pursued.

It is in this light that the hope that underwrites the telos of this book is best seen. If the book's aim—why I wrote it rather than something else—has most of all to do with what it means to read the New Testament at close range within a particular historically situated rationality, its hope is to display a way of thinking that is in step with the text itself. In this book, that is, our attempt to think (long) after the text is also our attempt to think with it.

2

Collision: Explicating Divine Identity

With few exceptions, New Testament scholars are not accustomed to reading Karl Barth for help with their historical and exegetical work. Yet at one point at least, it is Barth above all others in our time who has clearly seen a central theological point without which the historical dynamics involved in Christian origins are virtually unintelligible: God is the measure of all things.[1] To speak properly of God in Barth's sense is not to speak of the grandest object within our horizon but of the reality that constitutes the total horizon of all human life. God is not derivative of human culture (à la Feuerbach, Freud, et al.) but generative.

The hermeneutical corollary of Barth's insight is of momentous consequence and can be simply stated: what we think about God will determine what we think about everything else.[2] To speak of "God" is to invoke the context for all understanding, that to which all life and thought are related: to the extent that we live and think at all, therefore, we do so in light of our understanding—whether explicit or implicit—of God. Theology, that is, is never merely ideation. It is always and inherently a total way of life.

The early Christians were not Barthians. Yet, to see that the contour of their life derived from their understanding of God is to penetrate to the core of the conflict that surrounded their birth and growth. From 1 Thessalonians (1:9) through Pliny's famous epistle (10.96) to the persecution under Decius and beyond, the clash of the gods ultimately determined the shape of the collision between (emerging) Christianity and paganism.[3] There was of course confusion, diversity, difference, and complex interaction between paganism and Christianity. But the conflict as a whole and the instantiation of a new culture—for that is what it was—are utterly inconceivable apart from the clash between the exclusivity of the Christian God and the wider mode of pagan religiousness.[4] To put it slightly differently: once one grasps the primary— *sensu stricto*—importance of God for a total way of life, the conflict becomes intelligible. Converting to the God of the Christians was not merely an adjustment of this or that aspect of an otherwise unaltered basic cultural pattern; rather, worshipping the God of the Christians simultaneously involved (1) an extraction or removal from constitutive aspects of pagan culture (e.g., sacrifice to the gods), and (2) a concomitant cultural profile that rendered Christians identifiable as a group by outsiders.[5] Yet the practices that created this cultural profile were themselves dependent upon the identity of God. Christian ecclesial life, in other words, was the cultural explication of God's identity.

Taken as a whole, the narrative of the Acts of the Apostles is a rich exposition of this cultural explication of divine identity. In the book of Acts, the expansion of God's εὐαγγέλιον is coterminous with the creation of a people whom, in Luke's terms, God has taken out of the gentiles for his name's sake (Acts 15:14: ὁ θεὸς ἐπεσκέψατο λαβεῖν ἐξ ἐθνῶν λαὸν τῷ ὀνόματι αὐτοῦ).[6] The revelation of God in Christ, that is, necessarily entails the formation of a people who bear witness to God's name.[7] In this way, volume two of Luke's overall literary project displays the narrative outworking of the claim in volume one that the salvation of God comes through Jesus Christ as an apocalypse to the gentiles (Luke 2:30–32; Acts 13:47; cf. Isa 42:6; 49:9).

To elucidate these matters from the entirety of Acts would require a full-length commentary. Here we limit our focus to four especially illuminating instances in which the reconfiguration of divine identity necessitated by the witness of the early missionaries results in a collision between the expansion of the gospel and essential assumptions of ancient pagan life: the accounts of the Christian mission in Lystra (Acts 14:8–19), Philippi (Acts 16:16–24), Athens (17:16–34), and Ephesus (19:18–40).

Acts 14: Paul and Barnabas—Hermes and Zeus

> To all but a few of the highly educated, the gods were indeed a
> potential presence whom a miracle might reveal.[8]

After escaping a second straight round of persecution (first in Pisidian Antioch, then in Iconium), Paul and Barnabas make their way through

Derbe, Lystra, and the surrounding countryside preaching the gospel (εὐαγγελιζόμενοι ἦσαν, 14:7). In the Roman colony Lystra, Paul dramatically heals a cripple who had been listening to Paul preach (14:9a) and who had the πίστις to be healed (τοῦ σωθῆναι, 14:9bc).[9] The effect upon the crowds is immediate and overwhelming: they respond with religious acclamation and prepare to make a sacrificial offering to Paul and Barnabas as Hermes and Zeus respectively (14:11–13). The apostles,[10] delayed by their inability to understand Lycaonian,[11] finally rush forth to protest this pagan worship and to call for its abandonment on the basis of a reconfiguration of divine identity (14:14–18). As a result, after the arrival of some Jews from Antioch and Iconium, the crowds are persuaded to stone Paul (14:19).[12]

Though it is perhaps startling to moderns, it is hardly surprising that in the ancient world a display of power would occasion the acclamation οἱ θεοὶ ὁμοιωθέντες ἀνθρώποις κατέβησαν πρὸς ἡμᾶς (14:11; "the gods have come down to us in the likeness of human beings"). Not only was great theological importance attached to miracles,[13] but Graeco-Roman religious sensibilities had long been under the "spell of Homer,"[14] in which the appearance of the gods in human form was to be expected: "gods in the guise of strangers from afar put on all manner of shapes, and visit the cities."[15] This was no less true in various hamlets or in the interior of Asia Minor than it was in Greece itself: "Even in wretched Olbia, on the Black Sea, the wandering orator Dio (ca. 100 AD) flattered his audience on their passion for Homer and his poems."[16]

Philosophers, of course, from Xenophanes and Plato to the time of the NT and beyond were critical of Homer's anthropomorphism of the gods, crudely interpreted.[17] Only through sophisticated demythologization of the inherited mythology could Aristotle, for example, make the views of the "forefathers and earliest thinkers...intelligible" (*Metaphysics*, 12.8.18 [1074B]).[18] Among intellectuals, this criticism naturally gained considerable currency. Luke's contemporary Josephus, for example, praises "the severe censure" of the Homeric tales by the "leading thinkers" among the "admired sages of Greece."[19]

Yet, if we take our measure from material remains and from the views presupposed by the critics' criticism—as well as from the kind of data we see in Pausanias's vivid descriptions of local piety, for example—we find that "far into the second and third centuries AD, this piety of the majority survived the wit of poets and philosophers."[20] Alexander of Abonuteichos, to take but one outstanding case from the mid-second century AD, began his career

> by addressing the people from a high altar, [congratulating] the city because it was at once to receive the god [Asclepius] in visible presence.

The assembly—for almost the whole city, including women, old men, and youths, had come running—marveled, prayed and worshipped. Uttering a few meaningless words like Hebrew or Phoenician, he dazed the people, who did not know what he was saying save only that he everywhere brought in Apollo and Asclepius.[21]

After Alexander displays his divine powers by producing a small snake he had secretly prepared for the occasion, the people "at once raised a shout [and] welcomed the god."[22]

Lucian is no doubt having a bit of fun here, but in point of fact the cult in Abonuteichos was enormously successful and did center on Alexander and his pet snake. From "around 150 to the mid-170s, people flocked to this distant point where Providence seemed to have broken afresh into the world. Its god gave personal advice to Romans of the highest rank and sent an oracle to the Emperor himself."[23] If behind Lucian's satire, therefore, we glimpse a philosophically trained (Pythagorean) and religiously nimble Alexander, we must also see that his skillful charlatanry was well calculated to fit a vast, believing public.

Nor is it any surprise that in Lystra the local priest of Zeus and the crowds instantly prepare to sacrifice to Paul and Barnabas ($\theta\acute{v}\epsilon\iota\nu$, 14:13, 18), inasmuch as to worship the gods in antiquity was to sacrifice. Ovid's *Metamorphoses,* to cite a work obviously germane to Acts 14, opens its treatment of transformation with Jupiter's (Zeus's) account of his descent from Olympus "as a god disguised in human form [*deus humana ... imagine*]." After appearing at his destination in the guise of a human, says Jupiter to his divine audience, "I gave a sign that a god had come, and the common folk began to worship me" (I.200–220, LCL trans.). Ovid's tale is significant, not simply because he was still the most influential poet of Rome when it was composed (ca. AD 8), but because it reflects, with Acts 14:8–18, a common *typos,* a standard way of thinking about the appearance of the gods and the human response to them (cf. Acts 10:25–26 and 28:1–10). Indeed, if we read on in the *Metamorphoses* to Book VIII, we find the delightful account of Jupiter's and Mercury's visit—*specie mortali*—to the Phrygian countryside, where they are (finally[24]) received hospitably by the old couple Baucis and Philemon, who eventually ask to serve as priests for the gods (i.e., to guard their temple, to preside over the sacrifices, etc., lns. 707–8). The similarity to Luke's account of Paul and Barnabas in Lystra is striking, and it is not without good reason that Acts scholars have frequently drawn attention to this passage in the *Metamorphoses* as a possible basis for Luke's story.[25] Prima facie, one might easily think the Lystrans' eagerness to honor Barnabas and Paul makes excellent sense in light of their religious prehistory: Zeus and Hermes had been sighted in the interior of Asia Minor before.

Whether or not Luke knew the story in Ovid's *Metamorphoses* or a local tradition is largely indeterminable.[26] The syncretistic Jew Artapanus (second century BC), for example, tells of Egyptians who accorded Moses divine honors and designated him Hermes in response to his hermeneutical skill.[27] And Horace, too, suggests that Augustus was Mercury in human shape.[28] But that Luke shares with Ovid and other Graeco-Romans a basic understanding of the religious patterns that surround the appearance of the gods can hardly be denied. In this, as in other areas of his portrayal of paganism (see the following), Luke is simply a man of his time. As Lane Fox puts it, "Acts' author believed this response was natural."[29]

Where Luke's historical situatedness is forgotten, the critical theological edge of this carefully sketched scene is badly blunted. Haenchen, for example, asks with respect to the pagan response to Barnabas and Paul, "But is it really conceivable?" His answer is clearly that it is not:

> That the priest of Zeus would immediately believe that the two wonder-workers were Zeus and Hermes, and hasten up with the oxen and garlands, is highly improbable. . . . It is not only the priest's credulity, moreover, but that of the people which is unconvincing. The healing of the cripple was admittedly a great miracle. But surely not so great as to persuade the Lycaonians that their very gods stood in their midst.[30]

But this reading is, at best, to replace ancient religious practice with its philosophical critique, or already to adopt unawares the perspective of Paul and Barnabas. At worst, it is no less than a radical modernizing of the text, in the sense that it dismisses fundamental aspects of pagan religion as mere silliness.[31]

By contrast, to become aware of the normalcy—indeed, the religious propriety—of the pagan reaction is to become aware of the requisite background against which Luke's scene derives its critical force. For Luke's call through the mouths of Paul and Barnabas is not simply an admonition to tweak a rite or halt a ceremony. It contains, rather, the summons that simultaneously involves the destruction of an entire mode of being religious.

It is true, of course, that in a certain respect Paul and Barnabas appear "as genuine philosophers who reject such attempts at deification"[32] and, in this way, evince a joining of hands with pagan philosophical criticism.[33] Yet merely to note this connection is to reduce the import of the passage to a single point of contact with a small minority in the wider culture.

With few exceptions, principal philosophical critique was directed more against superstition (see, e.g., Plutarch's περὶ δεισιδαιμονίας[34]) and overly literal interpretation of myth than it was against cultic practice.[35] In spite of the manifest theological problems exposed by his lucid dialogue on the nature of the gods, for example, Cicero believed firmly in the necessity of traditional cultic practice (*Nat. D.*, I.ii.4) and was himself—again, despite *De Divinatione*—a member of the College of Augurs (*Nat. D.*, I.vi.14).[36] So, too, the same Plutarch who ranted against the impiety of the superstitious in his earlier years, later became a priest at Delphi with no sense of discontinuity. And the Stoics, despite Zeno's criticism of building temples to gods, "attend the mysteries in temples, go up to the Acropolis, do reverence to statues [προσκυνοῦσι . . . τὰ ἔδη], and place wreathes upon the shrines."[37] Even Epicureans, though sometimes considered atheists,[38] sacrificed to the gods.[39]

Luke's criticism, however, goes much deeper and aims at the very foundations that support the edifice of pagan religiousness in the effort to break the entire structure with a single biblical word—μάταια.[40] Accompanied by prophetic action—the rending of their clothes[41]—Paul and Barnabas characterize the whole scene as worthless, futile, or vain.[42] Though "images" (εἰκόνες/ἀγάλματα/ξόανα) are not excluded, the passage gives no indication that they are directly in view. At this point, images are not in themselves the problem. Rather, the critique reaches further, toward the entire religious complex of pagan deities and cultic sacrifice. Luke is not interested in philosophical reform or in demythologizing but in ἐπιστροφή, a conversion to a way of life incompatible with traditional pagan cults (cf. Acts 15:3, τὴν ἐπιστροφὴν τῶν ἐθνῶν; 26:20, καὶ τοῖς ἔθνεσιν ἀπήγγελλον μετανοεῖν καὶ ἐπιστρέφειν ἐπὶ τὸν θεόν).[43] Turn, say Paul and Barnabas, from these backward acclamations (the honor of mere humans as θεοί) and lifeless practices (sacrifice) to the living God.[44]

Where the pagan action would bring the human and divine almost entirely together, there is in the cry (κράζοντες) of Paul and Barnabas the explicit emphasis upon ἄνθρωποι in their sheer humanness, as it were, as an attempt to open a space between human beings and God. Καὶ ἡμεῖς . . . ἐσμεν ἄνθρωποι is emphatic and, indeed, reminds the reader of Peter's similar exclamation when confronted by a prostrate Cornelius: καὶ ἐγὼ αὐτὸς ἄνθρωπός εἰμι! (10:26).[45] In both cases, the speakers move to establish a common humanity with their audience and, hence, to drive an ontological wedge between themselves and the divine. In Acts 14:15 this attempt is further strengthened with the use of ὁμοιοπαθεῖς . . . ὑμῖν, particularly as it counterbalances ἡμεῖς . . . ἐσμεν. Ἡμεῖς ὁμοιοπαθεῖς ἐσμεν ὑμῖν ἄνθρωποι: "we" are just like "you"—human beings through and through. Ὁμοιοπαθής would of course, to the ear of the philosophically trained auditor, seal the deconstructive case: a true θεός is one without πάθος.[46] Paul and Barnabas are human.

Yet the message is not simply cease and desist. Rather, as Luke Johnson notes, the religious impulse of the crowds is received even as the official machinery is shut off. In this way, the reception of the pagan impulse involves an essential reinterpretation as to its telos—the living God. Barrett is correct that θεὸς ζῶν is "almost a proper name";[47] the potency of the name comes through in the utter contrast between death and life, the turning away from τούτων τῶν ματαίων toward θεὸν ζῶντα, the source of life itself: God "made the heaven and the earth and the sea and all that is in them" (v. 15).[48] To be the "living" God is to be Creator, to possess, that is, the life-giving power to do good and to bring rain and sustenance (v. 17).

The pagan religious impulse is thus redirected toward the living God by a sweeping criticism and the unveiling of the true divine reality behind the gifts that sustain life in the natural world. Zeus was of course seen as the giver of good things—ἐπιδιδόναι γὰρ δὴ ἀγαθὰ αὐτὸν ἀνθρώποις[49]—and, in particular, as the rain-god (Ζεὺς ʽΥέτιος/ʼΟμβρίος, etc.). In fact, these two functions could easily be linked, as Pausanias reports: "there is on Parnes another altar, and on it they make sacrifice, calling Zeus sometimes Rain-god (ὄμβριον) and some-times Averter of Ills (ἀπήμιον)."[50] In light of these well-known functions of Zeus,[51] the radical nature of the apostles' reinterpretation emerges in that it does not, in the manner of Aristobulus, for example, consist of a simple substitution of numinous realities—"that which you call Zeus is really the God of Israel."[52] It thus has no affinity with ancient pluralism (in which, e.g., divine names can be only incidental to divine realities).[53] Instead, it involves both a demolition of the pagan model *in toto* (worshipping Zeus is futile) and the call for a new construction of divine identity. Cilliers Breytenbach puts well the implicit theological ground: the God whom they preach is not only "der lebendige Gott" but "auch der *einzige* lebendige Gott."[54] At least as Luke would have it, the telos of the pagan religious impulse is not in need of a different or additional name; rather, the impulse itself requires a fundamentally new direction, from dead worship to the living God.

With such a message, it is no great wonder that the crowds, having barely (μόλις) been put off, are subsequently persuaded to attack (14:18–19).[55] This end to the episode in Lystra articulates narratively the offense caused by a collision of divine identity and the practices it entails. Contrary to much received scholarly wisdom, in Acts the gospel does not routinely meet with exuberant acceptance among the gentiles (cf., e.g., 14:2 and the careful ὅσοι formulation of 13:48).[56] It may well be that in past generations God allowed all the gentiles to walk in their own ways (v. 16, ἐν ταῖς παρῳχημέναις γενεαῖς εἴασεν πάντα τὰ ἔθνη πορεύεσθαι ταῖς ὁδοῖς αὐτῶν), but the phrase intimates that the time has now come for gentiles to turn away from their foolish ὁδοί toward the living God.[57] If idolatry is at least as much "an error about the management of society (a political error)" as it is an error of the mind,[58] it should occasion no surprise that those who would be affected by the destabilizing power of its theological critique should attempt to drive the bearers of this critique out of their community.

Acts 16: Power at Philippi

[S]treet prophets were strongly in evidence. We hear much about prophetic women, "pythonesses," as they were popularly known.[59]

After Paul's escape from Lystra, Luke narrates swiftly the passage through Derbe and Paul's eventual journey to the apostolic council (14:19–15:5). Upon approval from James and the council, Paul resumes his Mediterranean mission and soon thereafter, in response to a vision, travels to the Roman colony of Philippi. In Philippi, after the conversion of Lydia (16:14–15), the missionaries are "opposed" (ὑπαντῆσαι) by a certain παιδίσκη, who has a πνεῦμα πύθωνα by whose oracles she is able to bring to her masters (κύριοι) much economic benefit. Subsequent to their initial meeting, the mantic girl continues to follow the missionaries around crying (ἔκραζεν), "These men are slaves τοῦ θεοῦ τοῦ ὑψίστου, who proclaim to you a way of salvation" (16:17).[60] Paul, who is greatly annoyed, exorcises the spirit in the name of Jesus Christ (16:18), and, in turn, the girl's masters—with the ὄχλος and στρατηγοί (vv. 22–23)—see that Paul is removed from their midst.

The narrative force of v. 17's initial ambiguity is disclosed when we recall that ὕψιστος was a term "vague enough to suit any god treated as the supreme being."[61] Within the world of the story, that is, there exists the linguistic and chronological space—Paul was followed for "many days" (πολλὰς ἡμέρας)—for the pagan misidentification of the God of Israel with the highest god in the (local) pantheon.[62] Indeed, if Stephen Mitchell is right, there "are good grounds for thinking that the place where this confrontation occurred was a sanctuary of Theos Hypsistos. . . . [T]he cult of Theos Hypsistos is well attested epigraphically in cities of the Aegean and Propontic Thrace around the middle of the first century AD."[63] In any case, such fusion and interchangeability of the divine were of course commonplaces in Graeco-Roman antiquity, at both the popular and philosophical levels. As Celsus would later put it, "I think . . . that it makes no difference whether we call Zeus the Most High [ὕψιστον], or Zen, or Adonai, or Sabaoth, or Ammon like the Egyptians, or Papaeus like the Scythians."[64]

This is hardly to say, of course, that the proclamation ($\kappa\alpha\tau\alpha\gamma\gamma\epsilon\lambda\lambda\omega$)[65] pre-supposed by the narrative was itself polytheistic, as if Christian readers of Acts would be unaware of the specific identity of the Most High God. Rather, it is to point out that the auditor can realistically imagine that the gentile audience of Paul and his companions ($\eta\mu\epsilon\hat{\iota}s$, v. 17) would have heard the mantic's cry as a polytheistic interpretation of Christian proclamation—that is, these are the prophets of the Most High ($\H{\upsilon}\psi\iota\sigma\tau\sigma s$ $Z\epsilon\hat{\upsilon}s$) who provide healing ($\sigma\omega\tau\eta\rho\acute{\iota}\alpha$).[66] Indeed, as Klauck suggests, this conscription of God's identity by local religious tradition may well be the (implied) reason for Paul's annoyance (v. 18).[67]

The ambiguity in the phrase $\tau\sigma\hat{\upsilon}$ $\theta\epsilon\sigma\hat{\upsilon}$ $\tau\sigma\hat{\upsilon}$ $\H{\upsilon}\psi\acute{\iota}\sigma\tau\sigma\upsilon$, however, lasts only until the exorcism, at which time the identity of the Most High receives christologi-cal specification: $\acute{\delta}$ $\theta\epsilon\grave{\delta}s$ $\H{\upsilon}\psi\iota\sigma\tau\sigma s$ is not Zeus $\H{\upsilon}\psi\iota\sigma\tau\sigma s$ (or any other "supreme being") but the God who works $\sigma\omega\tau\eta\rho\acute{\iota}\alpha$ through the name of Jesus Christ (cf. Acts 4:12!). Moreover, prior to this specification, it is not clear within the world of the story that Paul's proclamation necessarily entails an attack upon pagan religiousness. But the explicit appearance of the name Jesus Christ involves a simultaneous confrontation with a pagan $\pi\nu\epsilon\hat{\upsilon}\mu\alpha$ (or $\delta\alpha\acute{\iota}\mu\omega\nu$) and the economic practices that depend upon pneumatic presence. That the citizens of Philippi find the implications of this confrontation threatening is made clear by the ensuing events, in which the power of Jesus Christ is interpreted narratively as a force of subversion for the religio-economic habits of the polis (vv. 19–24).

Such habits are represented in the character of the mantic girl. Though some scholars note the possible meaning of $\pi\acute{\upsilon}\theta\omega\nu$ as "ventriloquist,"[68] this reading would make little sense here.[69] However much the double accusative may surprise us,[70] it seems clear that the meaning is something like "a pythian/pythonic spirit."[71] The description is not of linguistic trickery but of the animat-ing spirit that is the source of the oracles ($\mu\alpha\nu\tau\epsilon\upsilon\sigma\mu\acute{\epsilon}\nu\eta$, v. 16).[72] It is this spirit of divination—in Plutarch's language, the $\delta\alpha\acute{\iota}\mu\omega\nu$[73]—that is the immediate target of Paul's exorcism. This emerges clearly in v. 18, where Luke is careful to differentiate the spirit ($\sigma\sigma\iota$) from the girl ($\dot{\alpha}\pi$' $\alpha\dot{\upsilon}\tau\hat{\eta}s$) through Paul's direct address to the $\pi\nu\epsilon\hat{\upsilon}\mu\alpha$: "I charge you in the name of Jesus Christ to come out from her."

Thus it is that the intense anger of the masters is narratively intelligible. It is not that Paul has announced the nature of a ventriloquist's linguistic trick to the wider public in order to enlighten their minds, but rather that he has destroyed the means by which the oracles were produced. The display of power through the evocation of the name Jesus Christ has removed dynamically—rather than simply epistemologically—the economic benefit derived from the possession of the girl. The masters own the $\pi\alpha\iota\delta\acute{\iota}\sigma\kappa\eta$, not the $\pi\nu\epsilon\hat{\upsilon}\mu\alpha$. The spirit has gone out (ἐξῆλθεν).[74] Indeed, the text may even suggest that this display of Jesus Christ's superior power was visible to the masters: they see (ἰδόντες) that the hope of their gain has gone out (ἐξῆλθεν).[75]

It is this dynamic character of the exorcism that is finally what is so fundamentally disruptive in Philippi. If Cicero is right, there had long been philosophical criticism of μαντική (Div., 1.3–5; Nat. D., 2.3.9), at least in its more official forms.[76] Yet, Paul's action is hardly the type of intellectual stroke that can be parried by the piety of the masses.[77] To the contrary, the vanquishing of the pythonic spirit is a tear in the basic fabric of pagan popular religion in that it demonstrates publicly the weakness of the pagan πνεῦμα in the face of the missionaries and their message. Inasmuch as such religious life was woven together with material gain,[78] such a tear means the unraveling of mantic-based economics as well (v. 19). If it is anywhere near true that "prophetic persons were to be found everywhere, in the cities, the countryside, in every cultural zone of the Empire,"[79] the economic effect could well be considerable. In this sense, the masters of the παιδίσκη perceive rightly that the power of the name Jesus Christ extends beyond one mantic; Paul and Silas are in fact "disturbing the city" (v. 19).

Verse 21 thus encapsulates the juxtaposition of perspectives present in the conflict: "they advocate customs which are not legal for us Romans to accept or practice" (καὶ καταγγέλλουσιν ἔθη ἃ οὐκ ἔξεστιν ἡμῖν παραδέχεσθαι οὐδὲ ποιεῖν 'Ρωμαίοις οὖσιν). Of course if we read from Luke's perspective and take οὐκ ἔξεστιν in v. 21 in a strictly legal sense, the charges are untrue and incapable of substantiation, as we know from the magistrates' decision to release Paul and Silas in peace (16:36, prior to their knowledge that Paul and Silas are Roman citizens). The missionaries are not calling for riotous insurrection (στάσις). Yet, read from within the perspective of the characters who utter the charges, it must be admitted that, despite their motivation (v. 19), they have witnessed in Paul's exorcism the inherently destabilizing power of Jesus Christ for the pagan way of life. The recognition of the superior power of Jesus Christ is simultaneously the invalidation of the power claims of other πνεύματα. As Ramsey MacMullen rightly notes, "The unique force of Christian wonder-working . . . lies in the fact that it destroyed belief as well as creating it—that is, if you credited it, you had then to credit the view that went with it, denying the character of god to all other divine powers whatsoever."[80] To adopt the ἔθη advocated by these missionaries, as in fact happens in the Philippian pericopae both preceding and following (Lydia and the jailer), would thus be to accept (παραδέχεσθαι) and to embody (ποιεῖν) a set of convictions that run counter to (οὐκ ἔξεστιν) the religious life of the polis. In this way, too, the ὄχλος and στρατηγοί—doubtless encouraged by the 'Ιουδαῖοι/'Ρωμαῖοι contrast[81]—are given credible motive in the logic of the narrative to join in the attack (vv. 22–23). Harbingers of economic and religious disaster rarely elicit affection. Given such a confrontational display of power, it is hardly surprising that after their beating and imprisonment, the missionaries are finally asked to leave the city (vv. 22–24, 39).

Acts 17: Athens

After leaving Philippi, Paul and Silas immediately become engaged in another disturbance, this time in Thessalonica. The two missionaries are therefore sent away by night to Beroea. After some success, the crowds are again incited against Paul, and he is sent on to Athens, the site of his famous address before the Areopagus (17:22–31).[82]

At least since Martin Dibelius's seminal analysis in 1939, this speech has been interpreted—broadly speaking—as Luke's attempt to establish common ground with the more philosophically minded of the pagans.[83] As Dibelius famously puts it, 17:30–31 contain "the only Christian sentence in the Areopagus speech." Taken as a whole, "the main ideas of the speech ... are Stoic rather than Christian."[84]

It is not difficult to see how, in general, such a conclusion could be reached. After all, it does appear on the face of it that Luke adduces an inscription and echoes well-known pagan religio-philosophical traditions in an attempt at intellectual rapprochement. Yet such a reading finally ignores the basic interpretive moves through which Luke places pagan traditions within a different hermeneutical context and thereby transforms their meaning. In order to see this transformation of meaning, we must attend first to the context of the speech before moving to an analysis of the speech itself.

Setting the Stage

Modern studies of the Areopagus speech have tended to concentrate almost exclusively on the speech proper and have, as a consequence, made use of the material surrounding the actual speech only where it is deemed immediately relevant.[85] This procedure is helpful when comparing Lukan speeches to one another. Yet, when it comes to understanding the Areopagus discourse in the narrative of Acts, Paul's speech should not be read in isolation from its surrounding context, as isolating the speech renders irrelevant a series of crucial statements that determine the way it should be heard. To interpret Acts 17:22–31 in context is thus to observe the carefully placed and explicit narrative markers in 17:16–21 that shape the reader's perception of Paul's speech.

Luke prefaces the speech with the hermeneutically significant remark in 17:16 that while Paul was waiting in Athens for Silas and Timothy, παρωξύνετο τὸ πνεῦμα αὐτοῦ ἐν αὐτῷ θεωροῦντος κατείδωλον οὖσαν τὴν πόλιν. Whether one translates παρωξύνετο as "vexed" (Barrett), "provoked" (RSV), or "exasperated" (Talbert), the general sense is clear. Paul is not moved by the city's rich philosophical or cultural heritage;[86] he is, rather, "deeply distressed" (NRSV) by what he sees in Athens.[87]

Luke's description of the cause of Paul's distress also marks the entry to the speech: κατείδωλος. Though this word turns up elsewhere only in the *Acts of John* and Georgius Syncellius (ca. AD 900), its basic meaning in its present context is readily discernable, particularly in light of the immediate connection to παρωξύνετο. Athens is a "veritable forest of idols."[88] This judgment not only coheres with what we know of the city from other ancient sources[89] but also adds narrative force to the Athenian misunderstanding of Paul's preaching: those who believe Jesus and the Resurrection to be two different divinities, Ἰησοῦς (masc.) and ἀνάστασις (fem.), have heard Paul's preaching with polytheistic ears (17:18c).[90] Or, to switch the metaphor, when refracted through interpretive lenses ground in a city full of idols (κατείδωλον οὖσαν τὴν πόλιν), the resurrection of Jesus cannot help but be fundamentally distorted and misunderstood.

No less important is the term used by the Epicurean and Stoic philosophers to denigrate Paul for his lack of sophistication, σπερμολόγος (v. 18). Demosthenes, for example, on one occasion wrote of his accuser Aeschines: "Why if my calumniator had been Aeacus, or Rhadamanthus, or Minos, instead of a mere scandal-monger, a market-place loafer [ἀλλὰ μὴ σπερμολόγος, περίτριμμ' ἀγορᾶς]...he could hardly have used such language, or equipped himself with such offensive expressions" (*De Corona*, 18.127 [269], LCL trans.). And Dio Chrysostom characterizes the Cynics as σπερμολόγοι those who post "themselves at street-corners, in alleyways, and at temple-gates...stringing together rough jokes and much tittle-tattle [πολλὴν σπερμολογίαν] and that low badinage that smacks of the market-place [τὰς ἀγοραίους ταύτας]" (*Discourse*, 32.9, LCL trans.). In a similar manner, Paul's argumentation (διελέγετο, v. 17a), so say the learned, reveals his ignorance of the primary sources (as we might put it) and simultaneously brands him as a philosophical poser. At best, his scraps of knowledge come from one of the *florilegia* circulating in the ἀγορά (v. 17);[91] at worst, from the coffee shop talk at Barnes & Noble.

Of course, by this time in the narrative of Acts, when an auditor hears Paul insulted, it arouses immediate distrust in the judgment of the insulters. Such distrust of the philosophers' judgment, in turn, accompanies the auditor through Paul's speech and shapes the perception of the speech in a crucially important way: the mention of σπερμολόγος by characters whose perspective on the matter is to be distrusted cleverly eliminates the possibility of reading Paul's citation of Aratus and allusion to pagan "poets" as evidence of his superficiality.[92] Frontloading the σπερμολόγος charge gets this objection out of the way, as it were, while concurrently positioning the auditor against the philosophers' accusation. When the subsequent allusions and citations are made, the auditor thus understands that Paul (Luke) is no σπερμολόγος and is thereby encouraged to discern the import of these "scraps" of gentile philosophical or religious traditions. Subtlety, implies Luke, should hardly be confused with ignorant babbling.[93]

The response to Paul's proclamation in Athens is suggested through the use of ἐπιλαμβάνομαι, the first word that describes an actual action on the part of those to whom Paul had preached (εὐηγγελίζετο, v. 18). While it is true that ἐπιλαμβάνομαι can be used with the sense "of a well-intentioned attachment,"[94] Gärtner was correct to draw attention to the other occurrences in Luke–Acts in which Luke uses the word to mean something like "to lay hold of" or "to seize" (Luke 23:26; Acts 16:19; 17:6; 18:17; 21:30, 33).[95] In particular, in Acts 16:19, as here in 17:19, Luke employs ἐπιλαμβάνομαι with the preposition ἐπί in order to speak about Paul and Silas's appearance before certain authorities: "[H]aving seized [ἐπιλαβόμενοι] Paul and Silas, they drug them into the agora ἐπὶ τοὺς ἄρχοντας" (cf. ἐπὶ τοὺς πολιτάρχας in 17:6). In both 16:19 and 17:19, ἐπιλαβόμενοι carries the sense of "to seize," with the intent of forcing the apprehended person to appear before the political authorities. Jerome got it right, therefore, when he translated ἐπιλαμβάνομαι here in 17:19 as *apprehendere* in the Vulgate (*et apprehensum eum ad Areopagum duxerunt*).[96] As a result of his preaching, Paul was apprehended and brought before Athenian authorities: ἡ ἐξ Ἀρείου πάγου Βουλή.[97]

THE AREOPAGUS. Of course, as is evident in this discussion, such a reading of ἐπιλαμβάνομαι is shaped in part by one's interpretation of the ensuing scene, especially the ambiguous phrase ἐπὶ τὸν Ἄρειον πάγον.[98] Many modern scholars, at least since Norden's famous book, take this phrase to mean that Paul was brought to the "hill of Ares" rather than before ἡ ἐξ Ἀρείου πάγου Βουλή. But to focus upon the hill to the exclusion of the council is highly problematic.

Given Paul's location in the agora in vv. 17–18, it makes little sense to think that he would be removed from there simply in order to be given yet another chance at getting his point across.[99] Nock saw this issue clearly when he asked,

"But why on earth should men take Paul to this hill?"[100] Moreover, excluding the council causes the allusions to the trial of Socrates (vv. 19–20, see below) to lose their narrative force entirely; indeed, the allusions become pointless: why direct so carefully the auditors' attention to Socrates' trial if it is not meant to inform their understanding of Paul's situation in Athens? So, too, both Greek and Latin patristic interpretation—in part because of the allusions to Socrates—uniformly read the scene as Paul's appearance before the Athenian tribunal.[101] Finally, though ἐν μέσῳ (in the phrase σταθεὶς δὲ Παῦλος ἐν μέσῳ) can refer in the Lukan writings to geographical location (Luke 21:21), the overwhelming sense is "amidst" (Luke 2:46; 8:7; 10:3; 22:27; 24:36; Acts 1:15; 2:22; 27:21).[102] That this is the sense of ἐν μέσῳ here is confirmed by the conclusion of the speech in which Luke writes that Paul ἐξῆλθεν ἐκ μέσου αὐτῶν.[103] Paul speaks in the midst of a group of people, that is, the Areopagus council.[104]

For these and other reasons—for example, in Acts the political authorities appear only when Christians are under (threat of) attack[105]—different scholars have taken ἐπὶ τὸν Ἄρειον πάγον to refer to the Areopagus council. Strictly speaking, as T. D. Barnes argues, this interpretation is not incompatible with the notion that Paul was led to a hill, inasmuch as (1) the council originally derived its name from its meeting place on Ares' Hill, and (2) there is no solid evidence, contra Haenchen, Cadbury, and others, that the council ever ceased to meet on this hill.[106] Thus, while Nock's question previously quoted points out the weakness of the view that excludes the council from the picture in Acts, it can also potentially be answered: Paul was taken to Ares' Hill because that is where the Areopagus council met. As Barnes puts it: "The obvious meaning of the words in Acts should be accepted: Paul was taken before the Areopagus, i.e. before the council sitting on the hill."[107] To those who might object that the hill itself was unsuitable for the gathering Luke presupposes (e.g., Haenchen, Cadbury), one could point out, as several scholars have (e.g., Dibelius), that the ridge below the hill's zenith allows room for many people to gather. In addition, the number of people presupposed is open to debate (17:34 does not necessarily imply that all those in Athens who believed were present at the Areopagus speech). The worry, therefore, that Luke did not discriminate between the two different senses of "Areopagus" actually displays well the false alternative inherent in the modern effort to separate them.[108] There is no exegetical need to distinguish clearly between the two senses of Areopagus.

Though the precise range of functions is not entirely clear, the power of the Areopagus council itself was well known in antiquity across both time and geographical locale. Lucian, for instance, presupposes the recognizable authority of the Areopagus when he stages his ingenious mock trial of various philosophies in front of the council (notably, upon the hill; *Double Indictment*, 4ff.).[109] And Diogenes Laertius writes of Stilpo's arraignment before the Areopagus for denying that Phidias's statue of Athena was a god (θεός), suggests that Theodorus either barely escaped the hemlock death penalty or received it at the hand of the Areopagus (for giving himself out as θεός), and notes that Cleanthes was hauled before the Areopagus to give account of how he sustained himself (*Lives*, 2.116; 2.101; 7.169, respectively). Inscriptions, communications between Athens and the Roman emperor, and so forth, all confirm the picture gained from the literary evidence: "In short," as T. D. Barnes has argued, "the Areopagus seems to be the effective government of Roman Athens and its chief court. As such, like the imperial Senate in Rome, it could interfere in any aspect of corporate life—education, philosophical lectures, public morality, foreign cults.... Its general constitutional position enabled it to control religion no less than any other part of the life of Athens."[110]

By writing that Paul was seized (ἐπιλαμβάνομαι) and brought before the Areopagus council, Luke thus draws on the Mediterranean cultural encyclopedia to situate Paul's speech within an overtly political context. The speech is not simply a peaceful philosophical dialogue with his curious opponents. It is, instead, so the attuned reader understands, a moment in which Christian preaching—once again—has drawn the attention of the governing authorities. That such a moment is indeed perilous for Paul is indicated by the questions and charges in vv. 19b and 20 that recall the infamous trial of Socrates.

New Testament scholars have long noted the connection of 17:19b and 17:20 to the charges brought against Socrates. Acts 17:19b reads: δυνάμεθα γνῶναι τίς ἡ καινὴ αὕτη ἡ ὑπὸ σοῦ λαλουμένη διδαχή. Contra Barrett, for example, δυνάμεθα here is stronger than a "polite request" ("may we ..."). [111] Indeed, given the authority of the Areopagus, it may well be that the sentence is more of a demand or statement of intention than a question (see the questionable punctuation of NA²⁷, NRSV, NIV, etc.): "we have the right to know ..." is probably not too strong. Δύναμαι in this reading would be closer to its meaning "to enjoy a legal right," as in Acts 25:11 or P. Oxy 899 (ln. 31; second/third centuries): δύναμαι τῆς γεωργίας ἀπηλλάχθαι.[112] That an authoritative or political reading of δύναμαι in this context captures better its semantic drift corresponds to the rest of the sentence and to v. 20a, in which ἡ καινὴ διδαχή and the participle ξενίζοντα together with εἰσφέρειν sound the bells of warning: ξενίζοντα γάρ τινα εἰσφέρεις εἰς τὰς ἀκοὰς ἡμῶν.

Embedded in the cultural memory of antiquity was the understanding that Socrates was brought to trial and received the death penalty in part for introducing "new," "strange" gods.[113] As much as Xenophon's and Plato's portrayals of Socrates may differ, both authors are agreed—almost verbatim—in their judgment about this particular charge. Xenophon, for example, begins his *Memorabilia* by stating the words of the Athenian indictment: "Socrates is guilty of rejecting the gods acknowledged by the state and of bringing in other, new deities" (1.1.1: ἀδικεῖ Σωκράτης οὓς μὲν ἡ πόλις νομίζει θεοὺς οὐ νομίζων, ἕτερα δὲ καινὰ δαιμόνια εἰσφέρων).[114] But, says Xenophon, "Socrates was no more bringing in anything new than others who acknowledge divination...augury...oracles...coincidences and sacrifices" (1.1.3: ὁ δ' οὐδὲν καινότερον εἰσέφερε).[115] In Plato's *Apology* we meet the same charge, this time through the mouth of Socrates himself: "[The charge] says: 'Socrates is guilty because...he does not acknowledge the gods that the polis acknowledges but other, new deities'" (24BC; Σωκράτη φησὶν ἀδικεῖν τοὺς... θεοὺς οὓς ἡ πόλις νομίζει οὐ νομίζοντα, ἕτερα δὲ δαιμόνια καινά).[116]

Regardless of its historical accuracy—though it is likely accurate—this memory persisted in undiluted form through the time of the NT and beyond, as Christian, pagan, and Jewish sources attest.[117] We have no evidence that Luke had read Xenophon or Plato, but the remarkable similarity of language— ξένων δαιμονίων (v. 18), ἡ καινὴ αὕτη ἡ διδαχή, ξενίζοντα, εἰσφέρεις (v. 19-20), ξένοι, καινότερον (v. 21)[118]—suggests nothing less than a conscious attempt on Luke's part to vivify the memory of Socrates' trial in the minds of his auditors and forge a connection to the Athenian reputation for enforcing the death penalty upon those who brought in new gods.[119] Once awakened, the memory of Socrates' trial reverberates with the text of Acts to create an analogy between Paul's situation and that of Socrates. The reader is therewith enjoined to discern in Paul's arraignment the potential for death.[120] Like Socrates, Paul is charged by the governing Athenian council with introducing strange, new deities (Jesus and Resurrection),[121] and, like Socrates, Paul's life may be forfeited.[122]

The transition from the demand of the Areopagus (vv. 19-20) to Paul's speech (vv. 22-31) is provided by a remark that is usually taken to reflect Luke's knowledge of yet another familiar aspect of Athens' reputation: the proverbial curiosity of its citizens (Ἀθηναῖοι...πάντες καὶ οἱ ἐπιδημοῦντες ξένοι εἰς οὐδὲν ἕτερον ηὐκαίρουν ἢ λέγειν τι ἢ ἀκούειν τι καινότερον, v. 21). At its most obvious, this reading of v. 21 is doubtless correct. Yet to say that v. 21 speaks here of Athenian curiosity in "a nonpejorative sense" or gives the "motive" of the Areopagus is to miss Luke's clever and well-placed criticism.[123]

Contra Conzelmann and others—who in essence reduce v. 21 to a needless or pedestrian comment[124]—Luke is not merely adding local color by means of stock knowledge. Through his careful use of ξένοι and καινότερον Luke creates a sense of irony in which the attentive reader can recognize Athenian hypocrisy: the council is prepared to threaten Paul with the charge of bringing in καινά/ξένα δαιμόνια, but it is the Athenians themselves who admit ξένοι into their city and together with them spend time telling and hearing something καινότερον. The force of the comparative here should not be lost,[125] as if Luke had simply written καινός (e.g., NRSV, RSV, etc.). To the contrary, καινότερον has a specific referent with which it is to be compared: the preaching of Paul. The reputation of Athens is thus turned against the city itself, as Luke makes use of common knowledge to reverse the charges brought against Paul. It is the Athenians who "do not themselves hold to legitimating tradition" but seek after even newer things.[126]

A careful reading of vv. 16–21 thus creates a distinct *Vorverständnis* with which the reader then hears Paul's speech. Instead of a romantic view of Athens as the place of university-like debate, Luke portrays the city's rampant idolatry—Paul is rightly vexed—as the context in which the Christian preaching of the resurrection of Jesus (1) is distorted and (2) results in a potentially life-threatening situation for Paul vis-à-vis the political authorities (who are themselves enmeshed in hypocrisy). Moreover, via the word σπερμολόγος and resonance with the trial of Socrates, the reader is prepared not only to encounter scraps of pagan traditions in Paul's speech but also to discern in them a wider significance than their mere occurrence initially suggests.

THE SPEECH. For our present purposes, we do not have to analyze each important element of Paul's speech.[127] We will instead focus upon five interconnected features that call for further elaboration. First, despite both Lucian and Apuleius, Acts 17:22 is widely seen by modern scholars to be an excellent example of a *captatio benevolentiae* with which ancient orators opened a speech: σταθεὶς δὲ ὁ Παῦλος ἐν μέσῳ τοῦ Ἀρείου πάγου ἔφη· ἄνδρες Ἀθηναῖοι, κατὰ πάντα ὡς δεισιδαιμονέστερους ὑμᾶς θεωρῶ.[128] This interpretation of 17:22 depends entirely upon taking δεισιδαιμονέστερος as "very religious," which of course it can well mean.[129] In this reading, Luke displays yet again his awareness of common knowledge about Athens and puts it to use in good rhetorical form.[130] Under threat, Paul attempts to flatter his audience and win their goodwill.

Conversely, other scholars note the clearly pejorative sense δεισιδαίμων could carry in the ancient world and interpret the sentence not as an adroit rhetorical move but as Paul's frontal attack on Athenian "superstition."[131] This reading, furthermore, points back to 17:16, where Luke explicitly states that Paul was exasperated at the idolatry of the city, and forward to 17:30, where Paul characterizes Athenian idolatry as ἄγνοια (cf. 17:23!)—scarcely a laudation of their piety.[132]

In fact, however, these two different readings of δεισιδαίμων are but different sides of the same coin. As Hans-Josef Klauck notes,[133] Luke actually exploits the ambiguity of δεισιδαιμονέστερος. The characters of the story, that is, hear δεισιδαιμονέστερος in a complimentary sense, while the auditors—remembering the perspective created by 17:16—hear Luke's critique of Athenian idolatry as superstition. Δεισιδαιμονέστερος is simultaneously very "religious" and "superstitious."

To eliminate the ambiguity of δεισιδαιμονέστερος, therefore, is to eliminate the dramatic irony and the sophisticated manner in which this technique negotiates between the author's historical presentation and the reader's contemporary situation.[134] By contrast, to discern the dramatic irony in the first sentence of Paul's address is to become alert to the subtlety and richness of the multilevel discourse of the speech.

Second, though such an inscription has yet to turn up, Paul asserts that he found in Athens an altar ἐν ᾧ ἐπεγέγραπτο Ἀγνώστῳ θεῷ.[135] In light of the Socratic resonance—the specific accusation of bringing in new, strange gods—it is not surprising that Luke narrates Paul's first theological move as one that attempts to deflect the charge of newness: "what therefore you worship unknowing, this I proclaim to you" (ὃ οὖν ἀγνοοῦντες εὐσεβεῖτε, τοῦτο ἐγὼ καταγγέλλω ὑμῖν). Paul's proclamation is not new, for his message in Athens is preceded there by the reality that evokes it. Indeed, Paul specifies this unknown god as "the God who made the world and everything in it," thus locating the ultimate basis of his proclamation in the origin of the cosmos.[136] To link the identity of the unknown god with creation is to undermine in the most radical way possible the charge of preaching a new divinity. Bluntly put, it can scarcely get older than this: the God about whom Paul speaks created the world in which Athens exists.

Third, Paul indicates immediately—within the same sentence—the implications that follow from God's identity as the Lord and maker of all things, namely, that the Creator/creature distinction precludes the attempt to fashion God in human terms, as if God could live in shrines and needed to receive ministrations.[137] With οὐκ ἐν χειροποιήτοις ναοῖς κατοικεῖ οὐδὲ ὑπὸ χειρῶν ἀνθρωπίνων θεραπεύεται προσδεόμενός τινος, Paul does not say anything of which the best pagan philosophy was unaware.[138] Indeed, the phrasing intentionally resonates with a wide array of philosophical traditions.

Despite the standard practice of caring for the images of the gods (washing, offerings, etc.), Greek philosophers at least since Socrates had been critical of the crude theological views that such practice presupposed. In Plato's *Euthyphro,* for example, Socrates attempts to push Euthyphro toward a better definition of holiness by asking, "What advantage could come to the gods from the gifts which they receive from us? Everybody sees what they give us. No good that we possess but that is given by them. What advantage can they gain by what they get from us? Have we so much the better of them in this commerce that we get all good things from them, and they get nothing from us?" Euthyphro takes the bait and responds, "What! Socrates. Do you suppose that the gods gain anything by what they get from us?" (14E–15A). Roman memory, too, entailed a period of 170 years of aniconic worship. Though such aniconism was likely wishful thinking, at the very least Varro knew that true gods do not need sacrifice.[139]

By Luke's time such criticism was a philosophical commonplace, particularly among Stoics. Seneca, for example, strove time and again to purify crassly material notions of divinity by sundering their tie to the practices of caring for images: "Let us forbid lamps to be lighted on the sabbath, since gods do not need light. . . . God is worshipped by those who truly know him. Let us forbid bringing towels and flesh-scrapers to Jupiter, and proffering mirrors to Juno; for God seeks no servants. Of course not."[140] And Lucian knew, as well as any Stoic, that Apollo needed no precious metals for his honor: "the god takes no interest in your gold-work," says Solon to Croesus (*Charon*, 12).[141] At least for the more sophisticated, "the anthropomorphism of Greek cult statues does not mean that the Greeks thought their gods actually were people" that required cleansing, food (i.e., sacrifices), and care.[142]

Yet we must once again be wary of projecting the philosophers' views onto the wider populus. Where modern scholars might readily sympathize with the philosophers, many—probably most—ancients took their images rather more sincerely.[143] If Lane Fox's statement that "the identification of god and image was very strong at all levels of society" is somewhat too strong, it is nevertheless broadly accurate and has the added merit of taking pagan religion seriously.[144] The citizens of Orchomenos in Boeotia, for example, vanquished a ghost by fashioning and physically restraining its ἄγαλμα:

> A ghost, say the city's inhabitants, carrying a rock was ravaging the land. When they inquired at Delphi, the god told them to discover the remains of Actaeon and bury them in the earth. He also told them to make a bronze likeness of the ghost and fasten it to a rock with iron. I have myself seen this image thus fastened. They . . . sacrifice to Actaeon as to a hero.[145]

Of course, the Orchomenians were hardly the only people to treat images as something "real." In Thasos, to take another striking example, the statue (εἰκών) of the famous athlete Theagenes was prosecuted, convicted of murder, and sentenced to be thrown into the sea. Later, however, in response to an oracle from the Pythian priestess, the Thasians wished to retrieve the statue to halt a famine. When they could not find a way to recover it, the statue placed itself into the net of some fishermen and was thereby restored to its original place. The Thasians, notes Pausanias, sacrifice to this image of Theagenes as if to a god (ἅτε θεῷ).[146]

The power of images was, moreover, hardly limited to the "supernatural" effect of an otherwise dead piece of stone or wood. Indeed, images of the gods could appear to be alive. Even Lucian, satirist and skeptic though he was, tells of a statue of Apollo that moves, sweats, spins, and leaps from one priest to another. This god, in fact, speaks "without priests or prophets."[147] Despite Lucian's silence, we may be tempted to discern trickery here or, at best, to read the events symbolically. But this is to move immediately into modern intellectual space and, hence, to work anachronistically. As one scholar put it when commenting on this particular passage, for the ancients "this image was a god, its actions were supernatural, its utterances oracular."[148] So, too, within a less explicitly public sphere, evidence remains of "secret rites which were thought to 'animate' [statues] and draw a divine 'presence' into their material."[149] Political emissaries brought images with them for assistance or had them shipped.[150] Travelers carried statuettes on their journeys.[151] Statues worked miracles, cured diseases, changed expressions, or less positively, were buried, flogged, chained, banished, defamed, lusted after, and so on.[152] In short, despite traditions of critical reflection, the practice of viewing "shrines made by human hands" as habitations of divine figures was an essential component of the larger pagan construal of reality.[153]

Thus in Acts 17:24–25 Luke aligns Paul with the broadly philosophical critique of the interface between the gods and their images. At the same time, the narrative furthers the reshaping of the readers' religious imagination by placing its theological foundation in the transcendence of the Creator God over the world of images. That such a move is conceptually similar to the statement in Acts 14:15 is not mere coincidence. Much to the contrary, the similarity points to a fundamentally important part of Luke's narrative project vis-à-vis gentile converts: to break the connection between God and the world that underwrites pagan religion. Luke's advocacy for this rupture, however, depends ultimately not on philosophically superior notions of τὸ θεῖον (17:29) but upon a biblically funded doctrine of ὁ θεός as the transcendent Creator of the cosmos (Isa 42:5: κύριος ὁ θεὸς ὁ ποιήσας τὸν οὐρανόν . . . ὁ στερεώσας τὴ γῆν καὶ τὰ ἐν αὐτῇ). To hear clearly παροξύνομαι and κατείδωλος in Acts 17:16 is to understand 17:24–25 at the narrative theological level not so much as philosophical critique as a skillfully articulated charge of idolatry.

Fourth, Luke further develops Paul's critique of Athenian idolatry by subsuming Graeco-Roman religio-philosophical knowledge into the biblical story. God's purpose in creating all ($\pi\hat{a}\nu$ $\check{\epsilon}\theta\nu os$ $\dot{a}\nu\theta\rho\dot{\omega}\pi\omega\nu$) from one ($\dot{\epsilon}\xi$ $\dot{\epsilon}\nu\acute{o}s$)[154] was so that they might seek, even grope, after God and find him (17:26–27).[155] The ground for this seeking and finding is, for Luke, ultimately biblical: "You will seek the Lord your God and you will find him, if you search after him with all your heart and with all your soul" (Deut 4:29; cf. Isa 55:6, etc.). But here he presents only the linguistic "point of contact" with pagan thinking, as he moves Paul—once again the rhetor—through a series of allusions to and citations of gentile philosophy and poetry.[156]

Paul's statement in 17:27 that God is not far ($o\dot{v}$ $\mu a\kappa\rho\acute{a}\nu$) from each one of us, if not entirely marketplace phrasing, was hardly secret wisdom. It could easily win praise from Seneca, for example, who knew that "we do not need...to beg the keeper of a temple to let us approach his image's ear, as if in this way our prayers were more likely to be heard. God is near you, he is with you, he is in you" (Ep., 41.1: prope est a te deus, tecum est, intus est). Josephus, too, as Norden recognized, reflects precisely this thought when rewriting Solomon's dedicatory prayer in 1 Kings: because of the Temple, the people should always be persuaded that God "is present and not far removed" ($\pi\acute{a}\rho\epsilon\iota$ $\kappa a\dot{\iota}$ $\mu a\kappa\rho\grave{a}\nu$ $o\dot{v}\kappa$ $\dot{a}\phi\acute{\epsilon}\sigma\tau\eta\kappa as$; AJ, 8.108).[157] And Dio Chrysostom comes still closer to Acts: "For these earlier men were not far from [$o\dot{v}$ $\mu a\kappa\rho\acute{a}\nu$] the Divine Being or beyond his borders apart by themselves [$\check{\epsilon}\xi\omega$ ... $\delta\iota\omega\kappa\iota\sigma\mu\acute{\epsilon}\nu o\iota$ $\kappa a\theta'$ $a\dot{v}\tau o\acute{v}s$], but... had remained close to him in every way" (Or., 12.28, LCL).[158]

Nor is 17:28 lacking in allusive potential. Indeed, 17:28a provides immediately the ground of 17:27 (cf. $\gamma\acute{a}\rho$) with a line that evokes further resonance with a range of theological views of divine indwelling: $\dot{\epsilon}\nu$ $a\dot{v}\tau\hat{\omega}$ $\gamma\grave{a}\rho$ $\zeta\hat{\omega}\mu\epsilon\nu$ $\kappa a\dot{\iota}$ $\kappa\iota\nu o\acute{v}\mu\epsilon\theta a$ $\kappa a\dot{\iota}$ $\dot{\epsilon}\sigma\mu\acute{\epsilon}\nu$. Scholars have attempted to derive this phrase ultimately from Plato or from the remaining fragments of Epimenides or Posidonius,[159] but—given the flexibility of the precise meaning of the formula—the wiser course is to attribute the lack of an exact verbal parallel to Luke's careful realization of the power of general allusion. By accessing a range of plausible philosophical or theological positions, Luke avoids identifying directly the God of Israel with any particular pagan construal of $\theta\epsilon\hat{\iota}os$ (e.g., the Stoic one) and thus preserves the space in which to maintain his critique of idolatry.

Though in 17:28b Luke writes $\tau\iota\nu\epsilon s$ $\tau\hat{\omega}\nu$ $\kappa a\theta'$ $\dot{v}\mu\hat{a}s$ $\pi o\iota\eta\tau\hat{\omega}\nu$, interpreters since Clement of Alexandria (Stromateis, 1.19) have recognized the ensuing statement (17:28c) as a citation of Aratus's Phaenomena, an immediately and immensely popular work translated into Latin (by Cicero, among others) and even Arabic. The opening of the work is a proem to Zeus in which Aratus writes $\tau o\hat{v}$ $\gamma\grave{a}\rho$ $\kappa a\dot{\iota}$ $\gamma\acute{\epsilon}\nu os$ $\epsilon\dot{\iota}\mu\acute{\epsilon}\nu$ (Phaen., 5).[160] Yet, as Douglas Kidd and others have suggested,[161] Aratus himself may have had in mind Cleanthes' famous hymn to Zeus, in which it is also said: "We are your offspring, and alone of all mortal creatures which are alive and tread the earth we bear a likeness to god" (*Hymn to Zeus*, 1; *SVF* ln. 4).[162] The plural ποιηταί may thus be taken seriously.

In any event, by Luke's time the general notion that humans were "sprung from the gods" was widespread and would have had no difficulties gaining a hearing. Epictetus, for example, presupposes the συγγένεια of God and humans in a discussion of its implications,[163] just as Seneca shrewdly denies the importance of pedigrees by asserting that all humans [*omnes*], "if traced back to their original source, are from the gods" (*Ep.*, 44.1). Dio Chrysostom, too, repeatedly reflects this typos: "For it is from gods . . . that the race of men is sprung" (*Or.* 30.26, LCL: τὸ τῶν ἀνθρώπων εἶναι γένος; cf. 12.27–29, 39, 43, 47, 61, 75, 77).[164] Even the Jewish philosopher Aristobulus cites the opening lines of the *Phaenomena*, though Aristobulus's primary point in so doing is theological in a strict sense: to posit an ultimate metaphysical identity between the high god of the pagans (Zeus) and the high god of the Jews (God of Israel).[165]

As noted earlier in this chapter, however, Luke's rhetorical and theological move is fundamentally different from that of Aristobulus. Whereas Aristobulus uses the Aratus text to point to the sameness of divine reality, Luke employs it to criticize the basic theological error in pagan idolatry, namely, that because human beings are the "offspring" of divinity, they can image God in their form. On Luke's construal, in other words, the pagan error is named as an error of direction: it assumes that the correspondence implied in the divine-human relation (offspring) allows humans to read "god" (τὸ θεῖον) off the face of their humanity. To the contrary, says Luke, precisely because we are the (living) offspring of (the living) God, we cannot image him.[166] The human arts and faculties are prone to ignorance (ἄγνοια) and superstition (δεισιδαιμονία) with the result that God comes to be conceived as like gold, silver, or stone—in short, a representation by human technical skill and imaginative power (17:29). As Barrett puts it: "From nature the Greeks have evolved not natural theology but natural idolatry."[167] Luke thus turns the wisdom of Aratus on its head: humanity's divine origin excludes "visual theology."[168]

In vv. 26–29, therefore, Luke incorporates aspects of gentile poetic expression and philosophical theology into the overall theological direction of the opening chapters of Genesis, from God toward humanity. By so doing Luke is able both to affirm the worth of pagan insight (we are God's offspring and do live, move, and have our being in God) and to turn it critically back upon pagan practice (we therefore cannot image God because we cannot refract the notion of divinity through our humanity).

Fifth, in 17:30–31 Luke moves immediately from his critique of pagan idolatry (τοὺς χρόνους τῆς ἀγνοίας) to God's response: now (νῦν) God commands repentance because "he has fixed a day on which he will judge the world in righteousness by a man whom he has appointed, and of this he has given assurance to all by raising him from the dead" (ἔστησεν ἡμέραν ἐν ᾗ μέλλει κρίνειν τὴν οἰκουμένην ἐν δικαιοσύνῃ ἐν ἀνδρὶ ᾧ ὥρισεν πίστιν παρασχὼν πᾶσιν ἀναστήσας αὐτὸν ἐκ νεκρῶν).[169] At this point, the radical particularity of the Christian message erupts from the universalizing scope of Paul's speech heretofore:[170] there is a particular man (ἀνήρ) upon whom and a particular day (ἡμέρα) upon which the relation of God to the entirety of the world depends.[171] Moreover, the theological intensity of this focus has been given public demonstration—πίστιν . . . πᾶσιν—in the resurrection of Jesus from the dead.[172] Indeed, it is this particular event that effected the decisive change in the human situation indicated by τὰ νῦν. Luke's move in 17:30–31 thus entails a total determination of general cosmology by a radically particularized eschatology. Whether one's interpretive structure was Platonist, Aristotelian, Epicurean, Stoic, or something else (e.g., everyday paganism), to accept Luke's construal of the importance of Jesus's resurrection for the world would mean the destruction of one's theory(ies)—tacit or acknowledged—of the origin and (non-)end of the cosmos. It is therefore hardly surprising that some sneered (χλευάζω) at Paul after hearing of the resurrection (v. 32).

That others (οἱ) wish to hear more from Paul attests to the deftness of his rhetorical strategy.[173] Whether one reads 17:32b as a statement that stems from aroused curiosity or as the decision on the part of some members of the Areopagus to postpone a verdict until the arrival of further clarification, the fact remains that Paul has given a speech that protects him from the charge of "newness"— through his effective use of the Ἀγνώστῳ θεῷ inscription, citation of Aratus, and allusions to widespread and established philosophical positions[174]—and simultaneously confronts the leading council in Athens with the proclamation of Jesus's resurrection and the truth of their coming judgment. At this point at least, Paul carefully manages to avoid the death penalty without compromising his call to bear witness to the risen Jesus before gentile authorities (cf. Acts 9:15).

CHANGING THE FRAME. In his elegant discussion of Acts 17, Luke Timothy Johnson writes, "If [Luke] does not creatively reshape Greek philosophy, he does something more important: he recognizes it as a legitimate conversation partner in the approach to God."[175] At first glance, this assessment seems obviously correct. Luke does not engage in extended dialogue with contemporary philosophical schools,[176] and his allusions to traditions of Greek thought appear to display a receptiveness to their insight. Upon closer inspection, however, Johnson's remarks miss the deep and critical transformation of pagan philosophy wrought by its incorporation into a different comprehensive story.

In point of fact, Luke constructs the scene in Athens such that the conversation with pagan philosophy takes place within two parentheses, as it were, that encompass the totality of human life: creation (17:24, 26) and consummation (17:30–31). By thus shifting the larger terms of the conversation, Luke renders hermeneutically ineffective the original intellectual structures that determined philosophically the meaning of the pagan phrases. In the Areopagus speech the line from Aratus's *Phaenomena* and other allusions are removed from their original interpretive frameworks and embedded within a different framework, one that stretches from Gen 1 through the resurrection of Jesus to the last day (ἡμέρα, v. 31).

To note this change of interpretive context is implicitly to realize the point that particular words or phrases are not in and of themselves Stoic, Epicurean, Platonist or anything else. Rather, they are "Stoic" because of the interpretive framework in which they occur, viz. "Stoicism." In a significant sense, therefore, with the change of a comprehensive hermeneutical framework the pagan philosophical phrases have *sensu stricto* ceased propounding pagan philosophy. No longer do they speak the thoughts of a system whose intellectual basis exists outside of Luke's story, whose conceptual edifice is, as Seneca once put it, *a solo excitat*.[177] To the contrary, by changing the hermeneutical context of the allusive phrases, Luke alters, even subverts, the intent of the phrases in their original interpretive structure(s). He thereby changes profoundly (and with rhetorical subtlety) their meaning: drafting pagan testimony into the service of the gospel allows pagan philosophy to speak truth not on its terms but on Luke's.

This essential shift in meaning is why it is ultimately incorrect to say that in Athens Luke is translating the gospel into pagan philosophical terms.[178] Rather than positing conceptual equivalence between the former and the latter—the sine qua non for "same-saying" or translation[179]—the Areopagus discourse articulates a rival conceptual scheme. For Luke, pagan philosophy is not Christian discourse in a different language.[180] Thus, to be "God's offspring" in *Luke's* sense is not to be the children of Zeus who can read the signs in the stars (Aratus) but is inherently to be a people that reject pagan religious practice as idolatry. To know with *Luke* that the God who might be sought is not far is not to affirm the worth of natural theology but to know that God has not been found. To embrace on *Luke's* terms that God does not live in shrines built by human hands is not to rebuke philosophically the simple-minded pagan practitioner but is to admit to the problem of gentile ignorance *in toto* and the need for repentance; it is hence to admit to the δικαιοσύνη of the God of the Jews (v. 31) and to locate the decisive event of human history in the resurrection of Jesus. To agree with the logic of the Areopagus speech in the end, therefore, is not to see the truth of the gospel in pagan philosophical terms (translation) but to abandon the old interpretive framework for the new. It is, plainly said, to become a Christian.

Thus, while Paul can avoid the specific accusation of newness, his speech is nevertheless politically charged in that it does in fact entail a call to embrace a new way of life and abandon pagan worship (cf. μετάνοια, v. 30). Indeed, the same inscription upon which Paul initially grounded his defense (Ἀγνώστῳ θεῷ) provides, by the end of the speech, a critique of the pagan religious habitus as ignorant idolatry. That the call to conversion inherent in the Christian critique was—at the very least—socially and politically dangerous emerges clearly once again in the episode in Ephesus, to which we now turn.[181]

Acts 19: Ephesus

> I think that it is still possible for [the Christian *superstitio*] to be checked
> and directed to better ends, for there is no doubt that people have begun
> to throng the temples which had been almost entirely deserted for a
> long time; the sacred rites which had been allowed to lapse are being
> performed again, and flesh of sacrificial victims is on sale everywhere,
> though up till recently scarcely anyone could be found to buy it.[182]

Having promised to revisit Ephesus—if God so willed (18:21)—Paul at last returned to the Asian metropolis and, indeed, stayed for a period of over two years, arguing with both Jews and Greeks, healing diseases, and exorcising evil spirits (19:8–12). Given Paul's lengthy stay, it is surprising that Luke does not devote more space than he does to Paul's activities in Ephesus.[183] Even so, for our purposes, we must limit the discussion to several central and interrelated aspects of the Ephesus material. These aspects emerge in 19:18–20; 23–27; and 28–41, respectively.

In 19:18–20 Luke writes of the response of πολλοί (v. 18) and ἱκανοί (v. 19) to the story of the seven sons of Sceva, which had become known "to all the Jews and even the Greeks who were in Ephesus" (v. 17, πᾶσιν Ἰουδαίοις τε καὶ Ἕλλησιν τοῖς κατοικοῦσιν τὴν Ἔφεσον; cf. 19:10).[184] It is not surprising, as we have already seen in Lystra, that a display of power should provoke a reaction among the inhabitants of the ancient world (ἐπέπεσεν φόβος ἐπὶ πάντας αὐτούς, v. 17). Nor is it surprising that in Ephesus the extolling of the name of the Lord Jesus (v. 17) leads to a clash with magical practices.

It is true of course that "the practice of magic was omnipresent in classical antiquity,"[185] but Ephesus in particular had long been known as a city with a distinguished magical pedigree. The ἐφέσια γράμματα, for example, six magical words inscribed on the cult statue of Artemis, were famous for their power from well before the imperial period.[186] Indeed, by Luke's time it was thought that the recital of these words could serve as a means of protection against the invasion of a δαίμων: "the μάγοι command those who are possessed by demons to recite and name over themselves the Ephesian letters."[187] Coins and inscriptions help to fill out the picture painted by the literary sources.[188] Ephesus may not quite have been "a *great centre* of magical practices," but it was doubtless well stocked with μάγοι and their paraphernalia.[189]

Yet, as we know from a large number of surviving papyri, as well as from formal actions taken against certain types of practice, the knowledge of magic was hardly limited to "professional" magicians, whether in Ephesus or elsewhere.[190] Romance, business, chariot races, illnesses, house vermin—virtually all aspects of human life—were dealt with by various magical amulets, voodoo dolls, tablets, and an assortment of other commonly available trinkets. Yet such things did not work by themselves.

Even a superficial study of magic in antiquity would yield the conclusion that to change, for example, a lead plate into a device that could wield power over disease, one needed the right words to say; moreover, one would need to say them in the right way. That at a popular level such spells were passed by word of mouth, old wives' tales, and so on seems obvious. But there were also books, instruction manuals in the art of magic, written guarantors of the sure connection to the powers and principalities of the numinous world. Such books are the fuel for the bonfire in Ephesus: "And a considerable number of those who practiced magic brought their books together and burned them in the sight of all" (Acts 19:19).

Whether or not Luke envisages this group of converts to represent the more professional diviner-magicians or the everyday spell-casters is impossible to say. Indeed, whatever the legal position of the larger government,[191] attempting to draw such a distinction would, from Luke's perspective, be problematic in the first place. The point, rather, is that Luke makes use of Ephesus's reputation as a home for magical arts in order to narrate the conflict between "the Lord Jesus" and the practice of magic as such. Thus it is not—as it was with Sulla's *lex Cornelia*, for example—that only certain forms of magic are condemned, say, cursing an enemy. These magical books undergo no editing for objectionable practices; nor are they simply censored. To the contrary, they all are burned.

Book burning was of course not unknown in antiquity. Often the burning was motivated by overt political concerns, such as in the early days of the empire when the Roman senate decreed that certain "republican" writings should be destroyed.[192] Less obvious but no less political were the burnings of histories, encomia, philosophical works, and other writings thought to spread dangerous ideas. Broadly "magical" books, though evidently not frequent targets, were not exempt. Livy, for example, attests to such a practice, as does Suetonius, who notes that when Augustus became *Pontifex Maximus* he "collected whatever prophetic writings of Greek or Latin origin were in circulation anonymously or under the names of authors of little repute, and burned more than two thousand of them, retaining only the Sibylline books and making a choice even among those."[193] Voluntary burnings, insofar as we know, occurred only rarely and out of the public eye; they were for the most part limited to individuals who did not want to publish or regretted publishing their own literary materials.

Luke's account, however, emphasizes that this book burning in Ephesus was both voluntary and public. The converts are not forced by the Ephesian authorities to hand over their materials for destruction; nor are they coerced by Paul or the Ephesian disciples (μαθηταί, 19:1). Rather, the logic of the narrative makes clear that their action emerges as a response to their conversion. The practitioners of magic simply gather their books and burn them. Moreover, their burning is emphatically public: it took place not in a corner but before *all* (ἐνώπιον πάντων).[194] Indeed, if the subject of συνεψήφισαν rests in the πάντων,[195] the witnesses were impressed enough to count the cost of this conversion: 50,000 pieces of silver.[196] In antiquity βίβλοι—here, scrolls—were not cheap.

It is particularly noteworthy, therefore, that the magicians do not give or throw their books away, or, for that matter, sell them for money to help widows and orphans (an obvious Lukan concern; see, e.g., Acts 6:1–2).[197] The mere existence of magic, implies Luke—not simply the practice of magic by those who now know better—is antithetical to the Christian way of life. Hence not only does the public action prevent the books from being used by others who are not similarly persuaded, it also visibly and dramatically enacts the irreversibility of the practitioners' divulgence and confession. Books once burned can never be retrieved. The termination of magical practice and the burning of the books that make such practice possible thus visibly mark and publicly proclaim the end of a way of life. The life that supports and is supported by magic has gone up in flames.

As Luke narrates it, the movement of the Way in Ephesus is one that necessarily collides with the practice of magic, as it has earlier in Samaria and

Cyprus.[198] Because "the ancient world was as tangled in a crisscross of invisible contracts ... as our modern world is entangled in radio beams,"[199] such a collision involves a rending of the web that made possible the manipulation of otherwise uncontrollable and inexplicable human experiences. No longer can one summon and command a "demon" by adjuring it with the right words (see, e.g., PGM 1.42–195), claim unrequited love with the right potion (e.g., PGM 4.1390–1495), remedy a physical malady by a carefully formulated plea (e.g., PGM 7.199–201), or put one's business revenue into the black by fashioning a beeswax doll in just the right way (PGM 4.2373–2440).[200] All such contracts are broken.

After a brief explanation of Paul's decision to remain in Asia (19:21–22), Luke tells in 19:23–27 of yet another reaction to the Way in Ephesus, a τάραχος οὐκ ὀλίγος caused by an Ephesian silversmith concerned to protect his livelihood: "Demetrius ... made silver shrines of Artemis [and] brought no little business to the craftsmen. These he gathered together, with workmen of like occupation, and said, 'Men, you know that from this business we have our wealth.... And there is danger ... that this trade of ours may come into disrepute" (19:24–27). In light of Luke's emphasis on the effective witness of the book burning—"the word of the Lord grew and prevailed mightily" (v. 20)—further collision with pagan practice should not be unexpected. Indeed, from a pagan perspective, Demetrius's actions against Paul are fully intelligible. As Pliny the Younger would also learn, Christianity can be bad for religious business.[201]

Scholars have attempted to refer Demetrius's ναοί specifically to "shrines" of Artemis, but it remains unclear what exactly these would have been. Peter Lampe, for example, notes a possible comparison with other "Tempelchen ..., die als Souvenire, Weihgeschenke oder Amulette benutzt wurden." To date, however, only terra-cotta or possibly marble "Artemistempelchen" have been found.[202] Rudolf Pesch suggests that the ναοί are actually silver shrines in which to place Artemis statuettes.[203] If he were correct, these shrines were similar to the more elaborate aediculae found in Pompeii.[204] Yet, this would restrict the buyers' market to the wealthy, rendering Demetrius's worry somewhat difficult to understand. For the majority of the populus, it is more likely that statuettes were placed not in elaborate silver shrines but in various recesses in the house, as in fact has been discovered in Ephesus.[205]

Luke's point, however, is not that this or that aspect of Demetrius's business is in peril—shrine sales slip, statuettes stay steady—but that the entire complex of idolatry-based business is breaking up as a result of the Christian mission. "And you see and hear," says Demetrius to the τεχνῖται, "that not only in Ephesus but almost throughout all Asia this Paul has persuaded and turned away a great crowd saying that the gods made with hands are not gods" (19:26).[206]

We have already seen, in the discussion of Paul's journey through Lystra and Athens, how such a statement about the images of the gods would align him with pagan philosophical criticism. But, once again in similarity to Lystra and Athens, Demetrius's accusation in Ephesus displays narratively Christianity's profound difference from philosophical criticism, namely, that to be "persuaded" by Christian missionaries necessarily involves a turning away from pagan religious practices. The turning away, that is, was not simply an epistemological act—"knowing better," as it were. Rather, the removal from pagan religious practices, so Luke tells, was a public act with economic and political consequence: "there is danger not only that this trade of ours may come into disrepute but also that the temple of the great goddess Artemis may count for nothing, and that she may even be deposed from her magnificence, she whom all Asia and the entire world worship" (19:27).

Despite our initial suspicion of hyperbole, Demetrius exaggerates only a little: Artemis of the Ephesians did in fact enjoy great renown throughout the Mediterranean world.[207] "All cities worship Artemis of the Ephesians, and people hold her in honor above all the gods," wrote Pausanias in the second century. In addition to the antiquity of the cult, he added, "three other points have contributed to her fame: the size of the temple, surpassing all human edifices, the eminence of the city of the Ephesians, and the prominence of the goddess who lives there."[208] Pausanias doubtless here reflects the perspective of the ancient city itself, as we see in an inscription from the middle of the first century: the temple of Artemis was "der Schmuck der ganzen Provinz durch die Größe des Bauwerks, durch das Alter der Verherung der Göttin und durch die Menge seiner Einkünfte."[209] And, indeed, the Artemesium was quadruple the size of the Parthenon, or, to take a contemporary example, considerably larger than the colossus cathedral in present-day Cologne.[210] Its importance in Ephesian society, furthermore, is hard to overestimate. Not only was it a temple in the strict sense of the word—a place of sacrifice and worship—but it also functioned as an arbiter in regional disputes, a bank, a place for important civic archives, and an asylum for debtors, runaway slaves, and other persons in trouble.[211] It sent its own representatives to the Olympic Games, was the beneficiary of private estates, had plenteous sacred herds, owned a considerable amount of real estate (from which it drew revenue), and so forth. In short, as Richard Oster convincingly demonstrates, Artemis of the Ephesians was "an indispensable pillar in the cultural structures and life of Asia, and was therefore a crucial factor in the lives of all...whom Christianity hoped to convert."[212]

Taking seriously the cultural role of the Ephesian Artemis cult precludes the possibility of reading Demetrius's speech cynically, as if Luke were simply exposing the cunning with which the silversmith drafted others into his effort to run Paul off and save the business. On the contrary, the words of Demetrius articulate a more radical possibility: the potential for cultural collapse. Theological criticism of the kind Paul advocates does in fact depose Artemis and, hence, removes an "indispensable pillar in the cultural structures and life of Asia." Through the mouth of Demetrius, Luke thus juxtaposes starkly the competing perspectives that form the clash of the gods: to understand rightly the Christian mission is to perceive the "danger" (κινδυνεύω) posed to Artemis of the Ephesians. It is, consequently, to witness to the prospective disintegration of religiously dependent economics.

It is on this basis that the reaction of Demetrius's compatriots is narratively intelligible: "after hearing this they were full of rage and cried out, 'Great is Artemis of the Ephesians!' And the city was filled with confusion; and they rushed into the theater, dragging Gaius and Aristarchus, Macedonians who were Paul's travel companions" (19:28–29). That those whose livelihood depends upon the Ephesian goddess should vigorously defend her greatness is only natural. Such μεγάλη acclamations, moreover, are not infrequent in the ancient world. The people of Panamara in Caria, for example, defended themselves from attack by exclaiming "Great is Zeus Panamaros" and put up an inscription to commemorate the miracle that followed.[213] In crying out μεγάλη ἡ Ἄρτεμις Ἐφεσίων, however, the craftsmen also attempt to awaken the δῆμος (v. 30) to the threat posed to the honor of Ephesus itself. As Robin Lane Fox notes, there were "keen rivalries between neighboring cities: it was shameful if a theatre or temple was left in a state much worse than the adjacent city's."[214] Indeed, the robust "civic amenities supported claims to higher status and brought greater profits from more visitors and users. Inevitably, a few cities were very much smarter and more distinguished than others."[215] As one of the "smarter" and "more distinguished" major cities in the Mediterranean, Ephesus obviously had gained much honor. It therefore had much to lose.

In truth, despite Acts and subsequent fantasizing in the *Acts of John*, Ephesus as a city did not suffer until much later.[216] But Luke's intention is not to divine the decline Ephesus would endure but to display narratively the profound incompatibility between the way of Christ and the ways of being that commonly defined pagan life, precisely as such incompatibility breaks violently into the public sphere.

It is all the more interesting, therefore, that Asiarchs are named as Paul's φίλοι (v. 31): "and some of the Asiarchs, who were Paul's friends, also sent to him and exhorted him not to venture into the theater." Though their precise function still remains somewhat hidden, the Asiarchs were clearly prominent figures in civic life.[217] That they should appear as friends who attempt to prevent Paul from being harmed illustrates well the complexity of the interface between early Christian mission and pagan culture: despite the manifest cultural destabilization that accompanies the Christian message, Luke does not preclude genuinely advantageous interaction with pagan religious and political officials.[218] Instead, he gives real depth to the problem of destabilization by placing those who would be affected by Paul's critique on the side of the Christian mission.

In the midst of the ensuing confusion of the assembly (ἡ ἐκκλησία συγκεχυμένη, v. 32), the Jews put forward Alexander: "and Alexander motioned with his hand, wishing to make a defense to the people. But when they recognized that he was a Jew, they all cried out with one voice for about two hours, 'Great is Artemis of the Ephesians!'" (vv. 33a–34). As Haenchen notes, Luke's move here has long been a *crux interpretum*.[219] On the one hand, scholars have taken Ἰουδαῖος (vv. 33, 34) at face value and seen Alexander as the Jewish spokesman, who would—were he given the chance—defend Judaism by differentiating it from Paul's messianic sect. In this way, Alexander's apologia would be an attempt to avoid a pogrom. On the other hand, scholars have suggested that the use of Ἰουδαῖος actually reflects the perspective of the gentile crowd, which could not distinguish between messianic and non-messianic Jews; Alexander is actually put forward by the Jewish *Christians* as the one to speak on their behalf (v. 33).[220] A third possibility is that Alexander is a Jewish Christian (Ἰουδαῖος, v. 34), but is *pushed* forward (προβάλλω) by non-messianic Jews (Ἰουδαῖος, v. 33) as the source of the trouble. Regardless, Alexander is not allowed a single word. Instead, we hear only the voice of the raucous ἐκκλησία: "Great is Artemis of the Ephesians!"

The length of this cry creates enough time, narratively speaking, for the Ephesian γραμματεύς to hear about the tumult and arrive at the theater to restore some order: "after he had quieted the crowd, he said 'Men of Ephesus, who is there among human beings that does not know that the city of the Ephesians is νεωκόρος of the Great Artemis and of her image which fell from the sky [τοῦ διοπετοῦς].'"[221] With his opening line, the town clerk, whom Koester calls "the most powerful Ephesian official,"[222] attempts to diffuse the θυμός and σύγχυσις (vv. 28–29, 32) in two specific ways. First, he draws attention to Ephesus's status as "temple warden" of Artemis and reminds the crowd that all is well with the cult; there is not a single person who does not know that Ephesus and Artemis are inextricably linked. The clerk thereby belies Demetrius's doom-saying by claiming that the goddess herself is responsible for the well-being of the city. Second, he reminds them that the cultic image was given by Zeus and in fact is not "made by hands" (19:26).[223] The Artemis cult in particular is not, therefore, subject to Paul's critique.[224] Once grasped in their incontrovertibility, these truths remove the reason for the crowd's anger: "seeing that these things cannot be contradicted, you should be quiet and do nothing rash" (19:36). Indeed, continues the clerk in an attempt to prevent mob violence, "you have brought these men here who are neither temple robbers nor blasphemers of our goddess" (19:37).

Having thus undermined the charges, the town clerk points to the political impropriety, perhaps illegality, of the Ephesian response to the Christian mission: "If . . . Demetrius and the craftsmen have something against anyone, the courts are open, and there are proconsuls; let them bring charges against one another. But if you seek anything further, it shall be settled in the legal assembly [τῇ ἐννόμῳ ἐκκλησίᾳ]" (19:38–39).[225] By invoking both the Roman system of government (ἀγοραῖοι . . . καὶ ἀνθύπατοι) and the proper Ephesian one (ἔννομος ἐκκλησία), the clerk's reprimand provides an outlet for the disgruntled while simultaneously upbraiding them for their present action. Moreover, to mention the Roman proconsul is immediately to call to mind another possible outcome of the unlawful assembly: the charge of στάσις. Indeed, the clerk's next (and last) line is the point to which he has been driving all along: "we are in danger of being charged with στάσις today, there being no cause we can give for this uproar" (19:40).

It is well known of course that to be charged with rioting was no small matter in the Graeco-Roman world. While there were evidently no formal rules that governed the Roman response to the unruly, what Ramsay MacMullen wrote of the second century is no less true of the late first: expressions of public disorder—riots and the like—were "checked or punished by authorities proba-bly as effective[ly] in the second century as in any European country prior to 1830, when measures developed in London began to spread more general-ly."[226] One thinks, for example, of Gaius's merciless slaughter of rowdy tax-protesters in the circus,[227] or of the decade-long revocation of Pompeii's ability to hold gladiatorial games—a severe blow to an ancient city.[228] Whatever the imagined response, the clerk's threat actually worked: "and after saying these things, he dismissed the assembly."

The standard reading of this outcome interprets the dispersing of the crowd as "evidence in favor of toleration of the Way." The town clerk's speech "identifies opposition to the Way, rather than the Way itself, as the source of trouble and the threat to the established order."[229] The Christians, in the mold of Josephus, do not "blaspheme the gods which other cities revere, nor rob foreign temples, nor take treasure that has been dedicated in the name of any god."[230] In this reading, the town clerk's words are taken as an accurate understanding of the Christian mission and should be seen to trump those of Demetrius. The Christians present no cause for concern and pose no threat to the religio-economic status quo.

Yet, it is by no means apparent that the clerk sees things more clearly than Demetrius. As Barrett has argued, the Christian mission did seem to entail a competition with Artemis; indeed, "both could not prevail. The town clerk . . . was either more tactful or less intelligent than Demetrius."[231]

Though the story in Acts 19 does not give us the town clerk's I.Q., it does present him as remarkably tactful. In fact, he appears as the consummate politician, one whose artful rhetoric has just enough truth to be able to persuade a crowd of confused people (v. 32). Yet, the clerk's "spin" does nothing whatever to address Demetrius's business worries; it merely points to his skill with a mob as a spokesman for Roman order and the status quo.[232] Demetrius, indeed, is the more honest economist and, if we may so put it, theologian.

Taken as a whole, Luke's depiction of the Way in Ephesus does not press for "toleration" of a politically innocuous group but, instead, displays the deep and often troubling cultural destabilization inherent to the early Christian mission. The burning of magical books and the uproar caused by Demetrius and the craftsmen are not two unconnected or random events but rather two different responses to the life of transformation proclaimed by Paul and the early Christians. Acts 19:18–20 and 19:23–40, that is, narrate two sides of the same, stark either/or reality. The practice of magic is incompatible with Christian life, as is the worship of Artemis and veneration of her images/shrines. In Acts, it is either magic or Christianity, either Artemis or Christ. In contrast to the understanding embodied in the smooth rhetoric of the town clerk, therefore, both the magicians and the silversmith perceive clearly that to follow the Way is to inhabit the world in a manner fundamentally disruptive to the practices inherent to the present religious order. That such disruption unfolds economically is but a necessary consequence of the inseparability of ancient religion from economics, or, to put it more along Luke's lines, the primacy of the identity of God for a comprehensive pattern of life.

Conclusion

Our investigations throughout this chapter have taken place patiently and at close range, which is to say that we have been examining the picture in fine exegetical detail. It is now necessary to step back and view the picture more comprehensively.

In an article that attempted to explore Luke's "common ground with paganism," F. G. Downing concluded that in Acts "only the persistent litera-lists are under attack."[233] Having come this far in our argument, it should now be clear that Downing's proposal falls far short of the mark. The accounts of the Christian mission in Lystra (Acts 14), Philippi (Acts 16), Athens (Acts 17), and Ephesus (Acts 19) do not merely target one particular aspect of pagan religion but display narratively the collision between two different ways of life. Taken as a whole, that is, the four passages tell the story of a profound incommensurability between the life-shape of Christianity in the Graeco-Roman world and the larger pattern of pagan religiousness.

This collision, however, is not due to the missionaries' lack of tact (though they were doubtless bold) or to a pagan propensity for rash violence (though there was doubtless bloodlust); rather, its deeper basis rests ultimately in the theological affirmation of the break between God and the cosmos. For to affirm that God has "created heaven and earth" is, in Luke's narrative, simultaneously to name the entire complex of pagan religiousness as idolatry and, thus, to assign to such religiousness the character of ignorance. Pagan religion, regard-less of the specific differences engendered by time and locale, knows only the cosmos; it does not know God.

This is not to say that Luke conceives of idolatry in a facile manner, as if it were one simple thing, an uncomplicated realm of error. Much to the contrary, the vivid particularities of the various passages in the narrative speak of a range of practices and convictions,[234] from superstition in Philippi through official cultic religion in Lystra and Ephesus to Greek philosophical theology in Athens. Nor does the naming of pagan religiousness as idolatry say of necessity that every single aspect of Mediterranean existence was opposed to the knowl-edge of God. Indeed, perhaps surprisingly, prominent pagans can appear on the side of the Christian mission (as do the Asiarchs in Ephesus, for example, or, as we will later see, various centurions). Still, at bottom, even a complex notion of idolatry and the recognition of goods within pagan life do not render the basic difference commensurable: between the affirmation and the denial of the break between God and the world there can be no rapprochement. There is finally an irreconcilable incongruity in the perception of the identity of God.

Because "religion" in antiquity was not a category separable from the rest of life—as modern usage generally implies—this difference in the perception of divine identity amounts to vastly more than a mere difference in a discrete sphere of faith and ritual (that corresponds, e.g., to the subject matter of a particular academic discipline). As both classic and more recent studies have shown, to take ancient religion seriously in its various dimensions is to see that it "ran through all [of life's] phases."[235] Ancient religion, that is to say, is a pattern of practices and beliefs inextricably interwoven with the fabric of ancient culture. Religion is not, however, just part of this fabric, ultimately passive and controlled by other more basic influences such as politics and economics, for example. Rather, religion is also constitutive of culture; it helps to construct the cultural fabric itself. Religion is, therefore, in the last resort "indistinguishable from culture."[236]

Hence, to call into question pagan religion is to critique pagan culture: tear out the threads of pagan religiousness and the cultural fabric itself comes unraveled. If it were true in Athens that "the connection of religion and politics was so close that to attack one was automatically to undermine the other,"[237] it was no less true in Ephesus that to attack religion was to undermine Ephesian economics: Artemis and Demetrius are inseparable. So, too, in Philippi did Paul's exorcism of the mantic girl put her owners out of business and elicit a beating from the crowd and the magistrates. And, indeed, in Thessalonica, as we will see in the fourth chapter, the missionaries are accused of "turning the world upside down" (Acts 17:6). Criticism of "religion" per se is a fiction. In antiquity, such criticism is inherently and thus inevitably cultural in nature.

This does not mean, of course, that each individual facet of pagan existence is directly affected by the Christian theological critique. At the very least, there remains, in Peter Brown's terms, the "neutral technology of life."[238] But the understanding of religion as a culture-constructing reality does entail the recognition that the difference between Christianity and paganism is deeper and more comprehensive than our modern linguistic habits tend to reveal. Indeed, to encounter the Christian mission from the pagan side is not as much to confront itinerant messengers with new religious ideas as it is to experience a force for cultural destabilization.

There are priests and crowds in Lystra, religious salesmen and colony magistrates in Philippi, philosophers and political authorities in Athens, magicians and craftsmen in Ephesus. Taken together these figures demolish the possibility of holding that, as Luke narrates it, the Christian mission was in its essence culturally innocuous (i.e., it was purely about εὐσέβεια/religio). To the contrary, in their social, political, and economic breadth, such persons exhibit the far-reaching and profoundly troubling effects of Christianity for pagan culture. These characters are, in fact, literary embodiments of the pagan reaction to the threat of cultural demise. In short, religion and culture are inseparable, and the difference in the perception of divine identity amounts to nothing less than a different way of life.

3

Dikaios: Rejecting Statecraft

If the previous chapter's argument for the culturally destabilizing power of Christianity's theological vision is taken seriously, it will no doubt occasion a weighty objection: does Luke not acknowledge the cultural upheaval engendered by the Christian mission precisely so that he can counter it? Luke narrates the culturally problematic history on the ground to be sure, so the critic says, but his apologetic project is actually to redescribe this history as nonproblematic for Roman order. To call the Christian mission culturally destabilizing is to identify a feature of the narrative of Acts, but to say that cultural disturbance is inherent to the identity of the movement is to endorse the perspective *against* which Luke directs his writing. For readers sensitive both to Acts and to the history of NT scholarship, therefore, the plausibility of the preceding chapter necessarily hinges upon the answer given to a question that has vexed Lukan studies for nearly 300 years: the Lukan posture vis-à-vis Rome.[1]

It is unnecessary, thankfully, to offer a detailed exposition of this long *Forschungsgeschichte*. Adequate recent surveys exist.[2] Without question, the dominant trend in NT scholarship has been to read Acts as a document that argues for the political possibility of harmonious, coeval existence between Rome and the early Christian movement.[3] This way of reading Acts extends from certain observations in Heumann's article of 1720 through the works of Johannes Weiss in 1897 and H. J. Cadbury in 1927,[4] is continued in the standard commentaries and monographs of the mid- to late-twentieth century,[5] and remains the accepted position in the essays and books of today.[6] To be sure, there are various, even extensive, disagreements between different scholarly advocates of this view. In 1983 Paul Walaskay, for example, cleverly reversed the typical line of argument by construing Christianity's political harmlessness not as Luke's *apologia pro ecclesia* to Rome but as his *apologia pro imperio* to the church.[7] But at bottom, of course, the substance of the exegetical proposal about Lukan politics is the same.[8] The reason for the substantive identity, I suggest, rests in the fact that from 1720 until the present, the advocates of this mode of interpretation have allowed similar readings of the same set of passages to control the entirety of their thinking about Lukan politics.

Prominent among these are the places in Acts where the Christian mission is on display before various Roman officials. So, for example, from the time Paul arrives in Jerusalem in Acts 21, he appears before no less than three leading Roman officials—as well as King Agrippa II, as Roman a Jew as there could be[9]—not one of whom finds Paul guilty of any crime. Indeed, Claudius Lysias, Festus, and Agrippa explicitly declare Paul innocent: "he has done nothing deserving death" (23:29; 25:25; 26:31–32). These declarations, so the standard exegesis runs, continue a theme first seen explicitly in Acts 18 in the mouth of Gallio, proconsul of Achaia and elder brother of Seneca: from the Roman perspective, the Christian mission is an intra-Jewish argument about "words, names, and...law," not a matter for Roman legal action (18:14–15; see 23:29; 25:19–20).[10] As Paul himself puts it when on trial: "I have not offended...against Caesar" (25:8). Other passages are frequently adduced as evidence, too, such as the interconnection of Acts 14:19, 17:13, and 18:12ff. where Luke is said to have pinned the cultural disruption on the Jews as a way to counter claims of a politically problematic Christianity—and the generally positive portrayal of centurions (e.g., Cornelius in Acts 10, Julius in Acts 27:1–6; cf. Luke 7:1–10 and 23:47) and other Roman dignitaries (e.g., the proconsul Sergius Paulus, "a man of intelligence," in Acts 13). But as a whole the interpretive construct of the majority view rests upon the perspective reflected in the speech of the characters that embody Roman rule.

Dissenting scholars suffer from the same limitation as their opponents; that is, aside from certain critiques of the majority exegesis,[11] their recourse is invariably to a different set of data. Again, there are differences between the particular readings of the pertinent passages, but the substance is the same: Lukan politics runs counter to Rome.

Richard Cassidy and Richard Horsley, for example, both note the remarkable social power of the "reversals" in Mary's Magnificat and see this hymn as programmatic for Lukan theology.[12] So, too, the prayer in Acts 4 upon the release of Peter and John is taken to express, via the language of Ps 2, the ineliminable opposition between the βουλή of God and human rulers, the fleshly representatives of empire:

> "Why did the Gentiles rage, and the peoples imagine vain things?
> The kings of the earth set themselves in array, and the rulers were
> gathered together, against the Lord and his Christ"—for truly in this
> city there were gathered together against your holy servant Jesus,
> whom you did anoint, both Herod and Pontius Pilate, with the
> Gentiles and the peoples of Israel, to do whatever your hand and plan
> had predestined to take place. (Acts 4:25–28)

In light of this opposition, the charges against the Christians in Acts are to be taken much more seriously for what they say about the politics of the Way: its adherents "advocate customs which it is not lawful for us Romans to accept or practice," and act "against the decrees of Caesar, saying that there is another king, Jesus" (16:21 and 17:7, respectively). Finally, such scholars ask, is it not of utmost significance that Jesus, though δίκαιος in Roman eyes (Luke 23:4, 14–16, 20, 22; 23:47),[13] was nevertheless *killed* and that the reader of Acts knows of Paul's similar fate (Acts 20:25, 38)?

What is remarkable about the exegetical basis for these diametrically opposed interpretations of Acts is that *all* the different texts to which appeal is made are part of the *same narrative*. It is difficult, therefore, to avoid the suspicion that for both the majority and minority views, a limited set of textual data is employed in service of a one-sided thesis—switch the texts, and a different picture emerges. The interpretive result of studying the *Forschungs-geschichte*, as I have previously argued,[14] is thus something of a pendulum effect, in which the reader of the scholarly literature swings to and fro between passages of putative political innocuousness and purported social disruption.

In an important sense, this pendulum effect discloses a deeper hermeneutical problem in previous NT research into our question: at least prima facie, scholarly readers are presented with a false choice in which they are forced to opt for one abstracted part of the narrative over another. So, for example, in light of the majority construal of Lukan politics, "I found he had done nothing deserving death" is read against and, hence, cancels out "these men ... advocate customs which it is not lawful for us Romans to accept or practice"—or vice versa.

But the very fact that Luke included both sets of texts in the same story should warn us against being caught in pendulum hermeneutics. Indeed, in practice opting prematurely for either the "to" or the "fro" ultimately severs Luke's narrative. But of course, dismantling the unity of the narrative is hardly the way to discern the political vision of Acts as a whole. The question is thus not so much whether we believe the owners of the pythoness in Philippi who accuse Paul, or the governor Festus who exonerates him, but how we can do interpretive justice to both kinds of passages within the same larger whole. "These men . . . advocate customs which it is not lawful for us Romans to accept or practice" must be read together with "I found he had done nothing deserving death." The hermeneutical necessity is *to think the juxtaposition.* So doing, I contend, forces us to expand and complicate considerably previous understandings of Luke's political vision and thereby, in the end, to offer a much richer account of "the culture of God."

If our last chapter explored texts that are best seen from the "to" side of the pendulum, this chapter shall focus on the most important passages that emerge on the "fro" side of the swing: Acts 18:12–17 (Gallio); 21:27–23:30 (Claudius Lysias); 24:1–27 (Felix); 25:1–26:32 (Festus). This juxtaposition will create a significant tension that goes to the heart of this book's constructive proposals, a tension that we first inhabit here and subsequently explicate in chapter 4.

Roman Officials

Everyone should agree: the exegetical instincts of the majority view are sound in the sense that if one wants to consider how Christianity is seen through a Roman lens, direct statements on this exact subject from Roman representatives are not a bad place to start. Yet, understanding the Roman pronouncements is not as simple as merely extracting them from their specific contexts and pasting them together in a list—which is then seen as *the Roman view* of Christian mission. To the contrary, the views found in the mouths of particular Roman characters are intimately bound up with their immediate textual surroundings. So, for example, as we saw in our last chapter, were we to identify Lukan politics with the words of the clerk ("these men . . . are not blasphemers of our goddess"), we would assuredly go astray.[15] Moreover, to stay with the riot in Ephesus, it is not always easy to determine whom it is that actually speaks for Roman interests. To be sure, in calming the riot the town clerk—doubtless a spokesman for Roman order more generally—secures a short-term gain (avoiding the charge of στάσις), but it is Demetrius the silversmith who actually reads the signs that portend a long-term loss.[16]

Even where such exegetical conundrums do not exist, simply identifying the speech of Luke's Roman characters with the perspective of actual non-Christian Romans is problematic. Gallio may well speak *as* a Roman proconsul would toward a Jewish delegation, but to take Luke's accuracy in "character-speech" to express the "real" legal position of the Roman provincial administration is to confuse hermeneutically the differences between irreducibly particularized perspectives. That is to say, what Acts narrates is not *Rome's* perspective of the Christian mission but Luke's *Christian* perspective of the church vis-à-vis the Roman state. In order to say that the speech of Luke's Roman characters corresponds to the self-perception of the state, we would need corroborating evidence external to Acts. Yet hard evidence of this kind does not appear until Pliny's famous exchange with Trajan (ca. AD 112); moreover, their letters display a distinctly different perception than that of the Roman administrators in Luke's narrative. In short, non-Christian Romans did not write Acts. A Christian did.

Recognizing this perspectival difference is crucial to the larger constructive task of this book. The reason is rather basic: while it may not open a window onto Roman legal policy in itself, investigating Luke's portrayal of important Roman officials in interaction with Christianity does allow us to say something about Christianity vis-à-vis the state—according to Acts. Luke's rendering of the Roman legal response to the Christian mission, that is, forms an essential part of his larger portrayal of the cultural contour of early Christianity.

Gallio

After Paul was given the space to argue and preach in the Corinthian synagogue (18:4) and elsewhere (18:5), he wore out his welcome by the Jewish community. Paul's response to his Jewish opposition—"from now on I will go to the Gentiles" (v. 6)—is intentionally more provocative than programmatic, as his first move is in fact to take up residence next door to the synagogue and convert the ἀρχισυνάγωγος (with his household).[17] Paul then stays on a further eighteen months, converting and baptizing πολλοὶ τῶν Κορινθίων (v. 8; cf. 4b). In the face of such missionary tactics and success, it is not hard to understand the irritation of the Corinthian Jews and their desire to take official action (cf. ὁμοθυμαδόν in v. 12) by bringing Paul before the βῆμα of the highest official in the province.

Since the discovery of the Gallio inscription in Delphi,[18] Acts 18:12–17 has received considerable scholarly attention for its unique importance in the effort to establish a Pauline chronology.[19] Our concern, however, is not with that specific task of reconstruction but with the implication of the Gallio pericope for the larger question of this chapter.

Ernst Haenchen was surely correct to see vv. 12–17 as the climax of the Corinthian material in Acts 18.[20] The juxtaposition of the Lord's reassuring

words to Paul in 18:10 ("I am with you, and no one shall attack you to harm you")
with the ominous note sounded by 18:12 (ἀνθύπατος, κατεφίστημι, ὁμοθυμαδόν,
βῆμα) creates a gripping tension in the narrative between the promised safety and
the actual danger that surrounds Paul. For the Christian reader of Acts, that the
Lord will make good on his promise is finally not in doubt. And yet, at this
moment Paul is standing before the tribunal of the Roman proconsul under
formal accusation: "this man incites people to worship God contrary to the
law" (παρὰ τὸν νόμον ἀναπείθει οὗτος τοὺς ἀνθρώπους σέβεσθαι τὸν θεόν).

The precise nature of this charge has long been disputed. Gerhard Schneider,
for example, attempts to relate 18:13 to the charges brought in Philippi (16:21)
and Thessalonica (17:7) and thus reads τὸν νόμον here as Roman law.[21] As in
the Roman colony Philippi and the free city Thessalonica, Paul is accused
in Corinth of a specifically legal crime against the imperial order. And, indeed,
if one recalls our last chapter, it is not difficult to conceive of crimes of which
Paul could have been accused. The new life of the baptized (v. 8) would be shaped
by practices that evidenced, as Paul the Jurist would later put it, "new sects
or religious practices . . . [that] influence the minds of men" (Sententiae,
5.21.2/12).[22]

Yet such a reading, as Jacob Jervell notes, makes it rather difficult to
understand Gallio's response, which states unambiguously to the Jews that
the issue is about "your own law" (18:15, νόμου τοῦ καθ' ὑμᾶς).[23] The νόμος of
18:13 is thus exegeted for the reader by its counterpart in 18:15: against the
"law" means against the "Jewish law" or Torah.

Moreover, the mention of "law" occurs in a series of controversial points
(ζητήματα), which are themselves characterized by Gallio as "a word and
names" (περὶ λόγου καὶ ὀνομάτων). To speak of the Jews' accusation as about a
word,[24] names, and the Torah is hardly to specify the content of their accusation as Roman law. It is, rather, to presuppose that additional explanation—not
explicitly stated in v. 13—was offered by the accusers to Gallio that unpacks in
more detail the nature of their problem with Paul. The proconsul's response is
intelligible, that is, to the extent that the reader surmises that Gallio has the
information necessary to speak accurately of an intra-Jewish theological debate. Indeed, the level of detail in the response is nonsensical apart from the
gap-filling required of a (competent) reader.[25] Hans Conzelmann errs, therefore, when he argues that pursuing the more specific nature of the legal
charge—whether Roman or Jewish—is "the result of attempting to reconstruct
history and of taking the wrong approach of asking what the Jews meant in the
actual historical circumstances."[26] To the contrary, crucial legal specificity is
not only given implicitly in but also required by the movement of the narrative
itself.

The necessity of an "interpretive addition" gains further plausibility when we remember that in the initial charge ὁ θεός is singular.[27] To speak of improper worship of ὁ θεός to a pagan official in Corinth would only beg the question, which one? But this question, of course, Gallio does not ask.[28] Paul, so says the delegation, is persuading people to worship the Jewish God—not the Roman θεοί—in ways that are contrary to the Jewish law.

But why should a Jewish group attempt to elicit a ruling from a Roman proconsul about Jewish law? This question, natural enough for interpreters who live at some remove from the workings of the Graeco-Roman world, would not necessarily have puzzled Luke's readers. The virtually absolute power of a proconsul over disorderly groups in his province was in antiquity well known.

Though for a long time in modern study it was thought that *proconsules* were subject to the senate,[29] in fact it is not until the reign of Hadrian that extant evidence appears for a proconsul's consultation of Rome for legal clarification—and this with the emperor himself rather than the senate.[30] Of course, from the time of Augustus, the emperor and the senate could issue rules and regulations that were effective empire-wide (e.g., with respect to the Jewish custom of sending money to Jerusalem). But in actual practice during the first and early second century, the proconsul was, in the words of one himself, *imperator provinciae;*[31] or, as Fergus Millar put it: "[i]n no sense whatsoever did the Senate 'control' the senatorial provinces, and the proconsuls were not 'responsible to' it."[32] Instead, "having the *imperium,* the proconsul had the total power of administration, jurisdiction, defence . . . and the maintenance of public order."[33]

Moreover, as Sherwin-White demonstrated nearly fifty years ago, the personal *cognitio* of the proconsul would allow for the hearing of cases that did not fit within established legal parameters, cases that were, in the juridical jargon of the time, outside the *ordo iudiciorum publicorum.*[34] In such *extra ordinem* situations—especially those that affected public order[35]—the court system is informally bypassed, and the proconsul as judge simply decides how best to respond to the accusations brought by the prosecuting party (punishment, further investigation, dismissal, etc.).[36] Such a process is reflected clearly, for example, in the descriptions (the legate) Pliny gives of the trials of the Christians in his correspondence with Trajan, and it is no less clear as the cultural underpinning of Luke's narrative in Acts 18:12–17 (cf. the following on Paul before Felix and Festus).

Thus to ask the question whether Jewish or Roman law with the knowledge of the proconsul's *cognitio extra ordinem* in hand is to see at once that the Jewish delegation is well aware of the broader legal situation. Arguments over the interpretation of the Torah would obviously not appear in the normal *ordo*, hence the attempt to approach Gallio directly. Yet, if it were simply a matter of halakhah, there would be no attempt to approach Gallio at all. Attending to Gallio's *cognitio*, therefore, allows a second and crucial deduction about the charge of Paul's opponents: precisely by the way in which Paul persuades people to worship the Jewish God contrary to the Torah (νόμος), they assert, he simultaneously brings them into conflict with Roman law (νόμος). The two senses of νόμος are, in the argument of the Jews, bound together in the very nature of the case. Such is the legal logic behind the initial ambiguity of νόμος in 18:13.

Paul's Jewish opponents in Corinth sense what is in fact the case elsewhere (in Lystra or Ephesus, for example), namely, that the Christian mission is potentially disruptive to gentile culture, and, as such, could bring unwanted retaliation.[37] Their strategy, therefore, is to distance themselves in the eyes of the Romans from Paul and his mission by differentiating their theological positions: Paul worships God παρὰ τὸν νόμον; what he is doing is not (true) Judaism. In this way, the Jewish delegation shrewdly seeks to avoid the (coming) blame for the practices of the newly baptized—again, πολλοὶ τῶν Κορινθίων, v. 8—and to retain the legal privileges that had long been theirs under Roman rule.[38]

If Gallio had any knowledge of the intricacies of Jewish theology, he did not show it. Instead, the highest ranking official to speak in Acts displays an anti-Judaism typical of his class (cf. εἰ ... ἂν ἀνεσχόμην ὑμῶν)[39] and summarily frustrates the legal maneuvering of the delegation. Hence does Gallio's response in 18:14–15 reject the ambiguity of νόμος in 18:13; legally speaking, there is no ἀδίκημα or ῥαδιούργημα πονηρόν.[40] The Jewish νόμος does not touch the Roman: the two senses of the word are, in Gallio's judgment, to be kept distinct.

A proconsul, of course, did not have "to enforce the principle of conformity and exclusiveness of cult within the Roman community." Gallio's final words— κριτὴς ἐγὼ τούτων οὐ βούλομαι εἶναι—are thus fully intelligible as the "precise answer of a Roman magistrate refusing to exercise his *arbitrium iudicantis* within a matter *extra ordinem*."[41] In addition to the Augustan edict from Nazareth cited by Sherwin-White to buttress this view,[42] one might also recall another statement from a slightly earlier decree issued around the time of Julius Caesar: "If any point of controversy [ζήτησις] shall arise concerning the Jews' manner of life, it is my pleasure that the judgment [κρίσις] shall rest with them."[43] Gallio's view is not dissimilar, though obviously delivered with more harshness: "and he drove them away from the tribunal" (v. 16). Christianity is off the Roman legal hook. Or so the majority has read.

Hans Conzelmann, once again, probably remains the most articulate representative of the modern trend that sees in Acts 18:12–17 "a picture of the ideal conduct of the organs of the State."[44] The Gallio incident, that is, models the legal perspective of the Roman state: Rome "should not become involved in controversies within the Jewish community involving Christians—the disputes lie outside the jurisdiction of Roman law."[45] For Conzelmann, however, this is not to say that Luke's narrative move here is made in the attempt to gain a particular legal status for Christianity akin to that of Judaism—*religio licita* and the like.[46] Rather, Acts 18:12–17 is more directly tied to Luke's conceptualization of the state as a sphere of reality distinct from the church. Gallio, as a spokesman for Luke, demarcates the proper reach of both Christianity and Roman law and thus separates them cleanly. If Conzelmann here reproduces the modern dichotomy between religion and politics—and hence works anachronistically—he nevertheless draws our attention to an undeniable feature of this passage, namely, that according to a Roman proconsul, the Christian mission in Corinth is not legally culpable.

It is precisely this feature of Acts 18:12–17 that causes the most profound difficulties for those who want to avoid the reading of the majority thesis. It is true, as Richard Cassidy has emphasized, that Gallio does not make a full investigation of the charges.[47] It is also true that he is dismissively sharp with the Jews and that his unwillingness to intervene and stop the beating of Sosthenes speaks, in Luke's view, of Gallio's poor character. But it hardly follows that "Paul survived this attack because of the manifest bias of his judge, a bias against Paul's accusers which prevented the judge from taking any interest in Paul or in the contents of his preaching."[48] Luke knew as well as any other ancient that Roman governors were a mixed lot, particularly in their attitude toward the Jews—think only of the contrast in diplomatic skill between a Petronius and a Florus, for example—but Luke also knew that their legal judgments could be correct despite their moral failings. After all, according to Luke even the notorious Pontius Pilate knew that Jesus was not ἄξιον θανάτου.[49]

Focusing on Gallio's questionable character doubtless thickens—both historically and narratively—Luke's account in 18:12–17, but, in Cassidy's analysis at least, it also has the effect of obscuring the significance of the fact that Gallio's judgment nonetheless speaks for Luke on a crucially important point: Christianity is not a bid to take over the state.[50] The Christian mission does not seek, that is, to become the new Rome by means of a direct assault upon the present polity. Rather, it claims to be a living witness to the fulfillment of God's promises to Israel and aims in Corinth simply to testify to Jews and gentiles that the Christ was Jesus and to baptize those who believe in his resurrection (18:5–8).

Conzelmann, therefore, is correct in a vital sense to discern that the "problem of Jew and Christian is not taken up in relation to the state, but, on the contrary, is deliberately excluded."[51] The state is not the arbiter in the argument over the right reading of Israel's Scriptures, as if by convicting Christians of legal infringement *extra ordinem* Rome would have settled the theological dispute over the identity of the Messiah and the occurrence of the resurrection—wielding the *imperium* does not equate to theological truth-telling. Instead, by refusing to serve as judge in a theological argument over the right construal of Jewish tradition, Gallio embodies the political truth for Luke that the state is not sovereign over the formation of the people of God.

Yet—and here we encounter a delicate distinction that must be maintained and to which I will return more fully in the next chapter—it does not strictly follow that Roman law remains unaffected by the Christian mission.[52] For Christianity, as Luke narrates it in Acts, is anything but a disembodied doce-tism in which concrete practices are elided by a purportedly higher, purer, spiritual reality. Rather, for Luke, the followers of the Way inhabit the world precisely in the practices that constitute their social and political identity—baptism is not a ruse but a way of life. And, as we saw so vividly in the last chapter, the cultural space created by this new identity simultaneously spells the possibility of pagan cultural collapse. It is to this possibility that the Roman legal system cannot remain indifferent. Of all this Gallio seems unaware.

A sensitive reader, however, would properly pose the question: But why should he be? There are no riots, no silversmiths, no τεχνῖται to tip him off. No sacrifices are prevented, no books are burned, no businesses yet lost. Such sensitivity to the narrative dynamics of Acts foregrounds the interpretive need to avoid the typical exegetical move of the majority thesis in which Gallio's response is read either as (1) Luke's view of the state *in toto,* or (2) the sum or essence of the state's response to the Christian mission.[53] Instead of reducing the political complexities of the wider narrative to a single passage, discerning the relation of the Christian mission to Rome requires a more exegetically intricate and suffi-ciently layered account that deals comprehensively with the political contours of the entire narrative. In an effort to do just this, we now turn to Claudius Lysias.

Claudius Lysias

Despite the pleading of the Christian community in Caesarea Maritima (21:8–14), Paul proceeds to Jerusalem, where he is gladly received by the resident believers (21:17). In order to reassure the Jewish Christians who are "zealots for the law" (v. 20), Paul agrees to "purify himself" and pay the expenses of four men who are under a (Nazarite) vow. Though Paul is able to give notice in the temple as to when the days of purification would be fulfilled, the week was not yet up when "the Jews from Asia, who had seen him in the Temple, stirred up the entire crowd and laid hands upon him" (21:27).

The charge of the Diaspora Jews is well aimed to excite the crowd to riot, even if, according to Luke, they were sincere in their belief in the basis for such a charge (see 21:29): "Men of Israel, help! This is the man who teaches against the people [λαός] and the law and this place to everyone everywhere [πάντας πανταχῇ]. Moreover, he even brought Greeks into the Temple and has defiled this holy place" (21:28)." Of course, as a well-known inscription now confirms, to bring gentiles into the inner courts of the Jerusalem temple would be to defile the temple.[54] It would also be to invite death for the gentile, and perhaps for the accompanying Jew as well. Indeed, if Bickerman is right, the death sentence would be carried out by the multitude apart from a formal trial by the Jewish authorities; the crowd acts, therefore, as they should.[55] "The whole city" becomes aroused and rushes upon Paul in order to seize him [ἐπιλαμβάνομαι!], drag him out of the temple, and shut the gates at once (21:30).

With a potential public killing in Jerusalem—to the Romans, a place of perennial political problems—it is hardly surprising that the next character to appear in the narrative is a military official: "And while they were seeking to kill [Paul], a report reached the tribune of the cohort that all Jerusalem was in confusion" (21:31). That the commander of close to one thousand men— χιλίαρχος translates *tribunus*—should, with some soldiers and centurions, quiet things down by his mere presence is also unsurprising.[56] Of the many words one might use to describe military action toward public disturbance in Judaea in the second half of the first century, leniency and considered hesitation would scarcely make the list (as we shall see, e.g., when considering "the Egyptian").[57] The prospect of having "to learn prudence" at the hands of the Roman military, as Josephus once put it in another context, was not a welcome one.[58] "When [the crowd] saw the tribune and the soldiers," it was thus with good reason that "they stopped beating Paul" (21:32).

The tribune was in no doubt, however, as to whom he should apprehend. Upon arriving at the scene, the tribune promptly arrested (ἐπελάβετο) Paul and bound him ἁλύσεσι δυσί (21:34).[59] New Testament scholars frequently worry over the exact manner of Paul's chaining in Acts,[60] but definite historical particulars are hard to come by here. As Rapske's thorough study shows, chaining prisoners or prisoners-to-be was virtually ubiquitous in the classical world—unless avoided by bribes[61]—and the method of chaining varied widely.

It is true of course that, in his dialogue on friendship, Lucian does mention the chaining of the hands (manacles) and neck (collar), thus presumably giving witness to a type of "two-chain" scenario that might fit Acts. Yet such precaution pertained, in striking contrast to Paul, to an already "guilty" prisoner who was in fact rotting away in prison.[62] At this point in Acts, Paul is probably either chained to a soldier on each side,[63] or both his hands and his feet are bound. The latter ambulatory inhibition fits somewhat better the flow of the narrative, in which Paul must soon be carried; he cannot, that is, walk well or quickly enough up the stairs to escape the crowd's pressure.

More significant for the readers of Acts than questions about the arrangement of his chains would be the general sense of shame and danger associated with Paul's seizure.[64] However much modern societies struggle toward the practical realization of the full dignity of every human being, for the ancient Romans, such a concept never existed. As Ramsey MacMullen has amply demonstrated, public troublemakers were "enemies" empire-wide and were to be restrained or disposed of in more or less whatever manner seemed most appropriate.[65] Indeed, according to the jurist Paul (second century), imperial *mandata* stipulated that all provincial governors "shall attend to cleansing the province of evil men; and no distinction is drawn as to where they may come from."[66]

This perception of immediate danger is contrary to that of many modern readers of Acts, for whom Paul's arrest in Acts 21 speaks already of the "protective custody" that is his after 23:23. In this line of interpretation, the tribune is read as a kind of stock hero who arrives in time to "rescue" and "save" the victim from his certain demise at the hands of the evil villains. "Lysias"—we learn his name in 23:26—"acted quickly to rescue Paul from the angry mob," had him carried "to safety inside the fortress," and thus gave Paul a chance "to catch his breath" inside the "relative quiet of the Roman fortress," where he could at last "have a calm conversation with the Roman officer in charge."[67]

It is the case of course that Paul's demise was imminent and that, in this sense, Lysias's action had the effect of rescuing Paul. But reading the tribune in such romanticizing terms, as does Walaskay for example, is possible only on a strange assumption that combines twenty-first-century democratic conceptions of justice (which are taken to apply to the first-century Roman military) and later, substantive legal developments in the Acts narrative (which are to be read back into chapter 21). If anything, however, looking ahead in the narrative would heighten the perception that Paul now faces a new danger. At this point in 21:31–32, Lysias clearly does not know of Paul's Roman citizenship. He doubtless did not think Paul was a slave; yet, *peregrini*—as good a guess as

Lysias might have had (cf. 21:39)—were hardly *cives*.[68] Moreover, depending somewhat upon the translation of 21:38 (see following), Lysias likely took Paul for a brigand, in which case his fate was all but assured.[69] This the crowd, too, seems to know: "Get rid of him!" they shout (21:36).[70]

Thus did Paul avert death at the hands of the crowd not as a result of the tribune's alleged foresight and heroism but as a by-product of Lysias's typically Roman desire to prevent a public disturbance in Jerusalem (which would itself of course call his competence into question).[71] And this Lysias does.

The removal of Paul from the threat of the crowd also creates the opportunity for him to say something the tribune can actually hear: εἰ ἔξεστίν μοι εἰπεῖν τι πρὸς σέ? Paul's question here is hardly the polite "May I say" so many translations seem to assume (RSV, etc.). Its tone, rather, is more that of a prisoner to an arresting officer: "Is it permitted . . . ?" Lysias's response, of course, is not a direct answer to Paul's query but Luke's attempt to contrast Paul, the representative of Christianity, with the leader of another public disturbance and thereby to eliminate the possibility of construing the Christian mission as a violent (Jewish) sect. "You know Greek?" says Lysias, who then continues: Οὐκ ἄρα σὺ εἶ ὁ Αἰγύπτιος ὁ πρὸ τούτων τῶν ἡμερῶν ἀναστατώσας καὶ ἐξαγαγὼν εἰς τὴν ἔρημον τοὺς τετρακισχιλίους ἄνδρας τῶν σικαρίων? (21:38).

The ambiguity of the first words of Lysias's question has long puzzled the best of Acts scholars. Like many others before him, Luke Johnson, for example, takes Lysias's question to express his sudden realization that Paul is not the notorious Egyptian: "Then you are not the Egyptian . . . ?"[72] Yet, because no one in the ancient world would be surprised to learn that Egyptians knew Greek, this translation is hard to swallow.[73] Howard Marshall more compellingly, therefore, reads Lysias's remark in the opposite manner: "Surely, then, you are the Egyptian . . . ?"[74] C. K. Barrett may well be right that Marshall is here "somewhat too positive," but the latter's translation has the advantages of clarity and dramatic flare that Barrett's more subdued alternative lacks: "So are you not the Egyptian . . . ?"[75] Moreover, Paul's response makes excellent sense as a quick and corrective contrast to the perspective of the tribune: I am a Jew from Tarsus in the province of Cilicia, *not* the Egyptian.[76]

One does not have to posit literary dependence upon Josephus to make sense of Luke's choice of the Egyptian—in contrast to the several other "rabble rousers" active during the rule of the Roman prefects and procurators[77]—as the figure with whom to contrast Paul. Despite Horsley and Hanson's strange remark that the Egyptian's movement was "not one of armed rebellion,"[78] Josephus himself takes another view entirely in the *Jewish War*: the Egyptian "false prophet . . . collected a following of about thirty thousand dupes, and led them from the desert to the mount called Olives. From there he proposed to force [βιάζεσθαι] an entrance into Jerusalem and, after overpowering the Roman garrison, to set himself up as tyrant of the people." The Roman governor Felix, who was particularly adept at violent suppression, "anticipated his attack . . . and went to meet him with the Roman heavy infantry." Predictably, the "engagement" ended when "most of [the Egyptian's] force were killed or taken prisoner." The Egyptian himself, however, managed to escape with a few of his followers (2.261–63). And, as Luke's Lysias knows as well as Josephus, he was never found. Missing troublemakers may well cause considerable consternation for the Romans (as seems to be the case for Lysias), but they also make grand narrative devices.

So, too, do the Sicarii, the backstabbing bandits (λῃσταί) known so well to us from the pages of Josephus as the drumbeaters of sedition and war. New Testament exegetes have frequently questioned the accuracy of Lysias's naming of the Sicarii as the people whom the Egyptian led into the desert. Josephus, so it is argued, thinks of them as two separate groups.[79] This may well be the case, provided that one takes πάλιν δ' οἱ λῃσταί in AJ 20.172 to indicate a shift in Josephus's narrative, a point which is certainly not beyond debate.[80] Yet Josephus clearly does associate the Egyptian's movement with that of the Sicarii, at least in the double sense that (1) when he speaks of the Egyptian, he speaks immediately also of the Sicarii in both the *Jewish War* and the *Antiquities* and (2) both groups play a causal (and blameworthy) role in the larger narrative of how the Jews came to war with Rome.[81]

Moreover, Luke's literary artistry should not be overlooked. In both Luke and Acts Roman administrators and military personnel speak like the gentiles they are.[82] Readers attentive to Luke's care in the speech of his characters, that is, would experience no surprise in hearing a gentile army officer speak with less than perfect precision about various Jewish factions. Indeed, it is just what might be expected.[83]

If the tribune somewhat confuses things, Luke's political point nevertheless remains unobscured. Claudius Lysias's perception that he has apprehended the missing insurrectionist is immediately rejected. "Indeed! I am a Jew from Tarsus in Cilicia, a citizen of no mean city."[84] The Christian mission, as it is refracted through the character of Paul, is not, like the Egyptian's movement and the Sicarii, a direct attempt to rid Palestine of Rome. It is rather, as Lysias will shortly learn, more like a Jewish theological debate. That such a debate is anything but politically irrelevant to Rome will also become clear, even if the manner in which it does so is profoundly confusing to the tribune himself.

In point of fact, the reaction to Paul's lengthy speech clearly baffles Lysias, who is unable to discern the theological problem that underlies the clamoring and dramatic display that calls for Paul's death (22:22–23).[85] If Luke here exercises his literary license in allowing Paul to address the crowd, his portrait of Lysias's response is entirely realistic. Paul's gesture and opening rhetorical move—"Brothers and fathers, hear me now as I make my defense [ἀπολογία]"—would lead Lysias to expect a typical forensic speech more or less in line with the standard conventions of legal rhetoric.[86] And, in general form at least, Paul's speech fulfills this expectation.[87] Yet, in content, Paul's *apologia* could only seem strange to Roman ears such as Lysias's. A brief story about the God of Israel's turn to the gentiles in the figure of Jesus the Nazarene[88] would be incomprehensible apart from the shared historical and theological framework of Paul and his Jewish opponents, a framework that Lysias does not share. He thus resorts to a more familiar method of gaining information: scourging. "[T]he tribune commanded [Paul] to be brought into the barracks, and ordered him to be examined by scourging, to find out why they shouted thus against him" (22:24).

Abu Ghraib and the like rightly offend us. Yet for the ancient Romans, torture was standard fare. This was true not only for convicted criminals—one thinks of the countless horrors in the theaters[89]—but also for those who were suspected of crimes and from whom certain information was desired. According to early Roman legal tradition, however, there was a major exception: *cives Romani*. As both Cicero and Livy attest, the *lex Porcia*, for example, explicitly forbade "the rod to be used on the person of any Roman citizen."[90] And the *lex Iulia de vi publica*, from the principate of Augustus,[91] confirmed and strengthened that of *Porcia* in that it prevented a Roman citizen from being beaten or bound with chains, among other brutalities: a proconsul was liable if "he puts to death or flogs a Roman citizen contrary to his [right of] appeal . . . or puts a [yoke] on his neck so that he may be tortured."[92]

As has long been recognized, this legal tradition funds the narrative power of "reversal" in the story of Paul and Silas in Philippi, in which the missionaries reveal their Roman citizenship only *after* they have been beaten publicly and thrown into prison without a trial.[93] They thereby gain the upper hand:

> And when it was day, the magistrates [οἱ στρατηγοί] sent the police [τοὺς ῥαβδούχους], saying, "Let those men go." And the jailer reported the words to Paul, saying, "The magistrates have sent to let you go; now therefore come out and go in peace." But Paul said to them, "They have beaten us publicly, uncondemned, men who are Roman citizens, and have thrown us into prison. And do they now cast us out in secret? No! Let them come themselves and take us out." The police

> reported these words to the magistrates, and they were afraid when
> they heard they were Roman citizens. So [the magistrates] came and
> apologized to them. And they took them out and asked them to leave
> the city. (Acts 16:35–39)[94]

With officials fearfully kowtowing before a pair of stubborn missionaries,
the reversal in Philippi alerts the reader to the social and legal power of
Paul's Roman citizenship and its significance for any conflict he might have
with the state.

Having purchased his own for a considerable sum (22:28), the tribune also
knows full well the advantages of Roman citizenship. Yet, unlike Acts' readers,
by this point in the narrative, he does not know that Paul, too, is a Roman
citizen. The tribune has thus summarily ordered Paul bound (21:33), but the
reader knows that the danger belongs not only to the prisoner. This tension
builds as Paul is made ready for torture at Lysias's command (22:24).

Whether or not Paul is in fact beaten here turns on the translation of the
dative τοῖς ἱμᾶσιν (v. 25). Given the use of μέλλειν in the centurion's question to
Lysias—he says τί μέλλεις ποιεῖν and not τί ποιεῖς (22:26)—it is most likely that
Paul was in the process of being stretched out *for* the thongs (i.e., his beating)
when the narrative tension is released: "While they were stretching him out to
receive the beating, Paul said to the (supervising) centurion: Is it legal [ἔξεστιν]
for you to whip a man who is a Roman and uncondemned?"[95]

The centurion, usually a decent if not admirable character in Luke–Acts,[96]
realizes the peril and warns Lysias of his potential blunder. With full justification, the tribune then becomes "afraid" upon learning that Paul is indeed a
Roman citizen (22:29).[97] Once again, Cicero says it best: "To bind a Roman
citizen is a crime, to flog him is an abomination, to slay him is almost an act of
murder" (*Verr.* 2.5.65 170).[98]

But, in truth, we should not place more weight on this and like remarks
than they can bear.[99] The privileges of Roman citizenship were far less by the
letter of the law than by the spirit of status (i.e., mammon and the upper-class
cardinal virtues of "social standing, good reputation, and prestige.")[100] Careful
students of Justinian's *Digest* and other legal materials from a wide chronological span conclude that the primary distinction operative in the avoidance of
physical brutality was not that of citizenship but of class or rank: as a whole,
and with some oversimplification, *humiliores* could be beaten, chained, and
tortured; *honestiores* could not.[101] Roman citizens occur "on both sides of the
dividing line."[102]

Yet, official policy and real life rarely go together like hand in glove, and
in practice even upper-echelon *honestiores* were not entirely safe. Seneca's

gruesome account of the pleasures of Gaius Caesar, for example, presupposes physical brutality as a means for interrogation when it tells of the needless torture of Roman senators and equites "not to extract information but for amusement" (*non quaestionis sed animi causa*).[103] Moreover, as multiple authors attest, where treason (*maiestas*) was an issue for the Romans, imperial barbarism was not. Cassius Dio's well-known remark that the reign of Claudius began with an oath that free men would not be tortured is of course arm-in-arm with his account of Claudius's torture of equestrians and senators for possible conspiracy (*Hist. Rom.*, 60.15.5–6 and 60.31.5).[104] Tacitus, too, knows of Claudius's torture of the equestrian Gnaeus Nonius (*Ann.* 11.22), and how Nero prepared to torment the senator Flavius Scaevinus and equestrian Antonius Natalis on the way to uncovering the Piso conspiracy.[105] In fact, canvassing the pages of the early Roman historians makes it easy enough to understand how the later Roman historian Ammianus Marcellinus believed that the torture of all ranks was legally permitted from the time of Sulla.[106] In this he was wrong, but it must be admitted that even in the second century— when things were generally better than in the third and fourth—an imperial decree was needed from Marcus Aurelius to prevent the flogging of decurions and *honestiores* during interrogation or as a penalty.[107] Indeed, Aurelius's law is noteworthy for another reason. It speaks to the persistence of the practice: some years earlier his predecessor Antoninus Pius had already found it necessary to issue a rescript to a similar effect.[108]

The point of these examples is hardly to say that the citizen/alien distinction was irrelevant or that the *lex Iulia* was more lip service than it was legal protection. Rather, the intent is to offer a more nuanced reading of this portion of the Acts narrative by drawing attention to the fact that Luke's readers would have known something many modern NT scholars have overlooked: Paul's mention of his citizenship is not a simple trump. The rosy picture of Roman law and administration painted by the exegetes of the *apologia pro ecclesia* thesis, with help from some classicists (see the following), blunts the narrative power of the story's unfolding. Despite the fact that he is a Roman citizen, that is, Paul's peril remains real. The prophet Agabus agrees: "Jews in Jerusalem will bind [Paul] and deliver him into the hands of the Gentiles" (Acts 21:11).[109]

Lysias does release Paul of course—as a tribune, he has no authority to try Paul formally once order is restored[110]—but he does not do so immediately, despite his fear (τῇ ἐπαύριον). Indeed, in the end, the purpose of Paul's loosing is simply to ascertain the actual foundation for the Jews' accusation (22:30). At this point in the story, readers attentive both to the story-world and to the realities of Roman rule know Paul's hope "to see Rome" (19:21) but also that his Roman citizenship would not itself guarantee the fulfillment of this hope.

Where the Romans were involved, things might still turn out as they did when Galba was governor of Tarraconensis (ca. 60–68). In an attempt to avoid his sentence of crucifixion, a convicted criminal "invoked the law and declared he was a Roman citizen." In response, Galba pretended "to lighten his punishment by some consolation and honour" and "ordered that a cross much higher than the rest and painted white be set up, and the man transferred to it."[111] Such atrocities happened in Palestine, too: around the same time Galba was crucifying in Spain, the Judaean procurator Gessius Florus decided "to scourge before his tribunal and nail to the cross men of equestrian rank, men who, if Jews by birth, were at least invested with that Roman dignity."[112]

Having summoned the Jewish leadership to help him determine Paul's crime, Lysias becomes for the second time a witness to a Jewish dispute he cannot understand. After an initial outburst at the High Priest, Luke's Paul displays considerable aplomb and cunning in discerning the move that would divide his opponents: "And knowing that one part were Sadducees and the other were Pharisees, he cried out in the council, 'Brothers, I am a Pharisee, a son of Pharisees; with respect to the hope and resurrection of the dead I am on trial'" (23:6). That Paul did not become christologically specific seems rather obvious from the response elicited by his words: "some of the scribes of the Pharisees' party stood up and contended, 'We find no evil [or crime, κακόν] in this man. What if a spirit or an angel spoke to him?'" (23:9). As Luke tells it, Paul was instead content to say nothing further and let his opponents argue with each other rather than with him. Lysias, however, with his Roman eye for disorder, understood that the developing στάσις could well mean physical trouble for Paul, and so had him returned to the barracks (23:10).

It is at this point that a substantive shift takes place in the narrative: the Lord himself appears to Paul and announces that Paul's work is finished in Jerusalem; he must now go to Rome (23:11, Luke's theological use of δεῖ).[113] In the face of a murderous plot by Paul's opponents (23:12–16, 20–21),[114] Lysias plays his part in getting Paul safely out of Jerusalem and on toward Rome. In addition to an incredible detachment of troops, his accompanying letter indicates that Paul is now in the protective custody of the Roman government (23:23–29)—at least until Felix can render judgment.

That Lysias's letter to Felix is self-serving is beyond doubt. As many Acts scholars have noted, Lysias "rearranges" some of the key details and omits others—such as the binding and near-scourging of a Roman citizen—in order to shape Felix's perception of the situation as an administratively well-handled one (see the following on the correct legal procedure).[115] Yet, to see self-interest in the letter of a Roman military officer to his provincial governor would hardly surprise ancient readers—indeed, tribunes did not always fare so well in Judaea[116]—and it should not distract us from the political importance of the letter's remarks in v. 29.[117]

After a more or less accurate statement in 23:28, Lysias informs Felix of the results of his "investigation" before the Jewish council:[118] the charges against Paul concerned only ζητημάτων τοῦ νόμου αὐτῶν. In Lysias's estimation, therefore, despite the upheaval that occurred outside of the temple and before the Jewish council, there was from the perspective of the Roman state no charge (ἔγκλημα) worthy of death or imprisonment.[119] Like Gallio before him, the tribune Claudius Lysias contrasts (implicitly) the Jewish and Roman νόμος. Issues of *their* law remain impenetrable, implies Lysias, *ours* untouched. Jewish theological dispute does not add up to brigandry or criminal activity against the Roman state. Unlike Gallio, however, Lysias is unable simply to dismiss the council and send Paul away. That time has past.

As Luke narrates it in Acts 21–23, the Christian mission in the tumultuous city of Jerusalem poses—in explicit contrast to the movements of the Egyptian and the Sicarii—no violent or insurrectionist threat to Roman rule. Belief in the resurrection may well be grounds for turbulent debate—this Lysias cannot understand—but in its Christian sense, resurrection does not entail a planned insurrection or a call to arms. That the movement of the Way out into the world does not affect Rome, however, now seems, contra Gallio and his modern followers, impossible to hold. The Roman legal machine has been turned on: under custodial escort, Paul is on his way to trial by the highest Roman administrator in the land.

Felix

Antonius (Claudius) Felix was well known in antiquity for his lack of administrative and political skill.[120] Luke's near contemporary Tacitus, for example, thought that Felix actually increased the problems in Judaea by "misconceived remedies," and heaped scorn on Felix's status—in fact, a manumitted slave—when he remembered him as a governor who "practiced every kind of cruelty and lust, wielding the power of a king with all the instincts of a slave."[121] And another of Luke's contemporaries spoke of Felix's resentment toward the High Priest Jonathan because of the latter's "frequent admonition to improve the administration of the affairs of Judaea." Indeed, Jonathan even requested that Nero "dispatch Felix as procurator of Judaea."[122] This request was not granted, though Felix was of course eventually recalled to Rome, but not before, so Luke tells, he encountered Paul.[123]

For all his known administrative bungling, Luke narrates Felix's first question in Acts as the right one, at least from the perspective of Roman jurisprudence. Upon reading the letter from Claudius Lysias, Felix questioned Paul about his ἐπαρχεία/*provincia* of origin. As the jurist Paul put it in the century after Luke: "The governor of a province has authority only over the people of his own province" (*Digest*, 1.18.3). Despite such legal practice, however, after learning that Paul's provincial home was Cilicia, Felix nonetheless decided to try him in Caesarea. Hence have exegetes and scholars attentive to the Roman legal underpinnings of Acts puzzled over Felix's supposed reluctance to extradite Paul to Cilicia.[124] Yet, as Luke knew as well as Rome's later legal scholars, "sometimes" the provincial governor "has power even in relation to non-residents, if they have taken direct part in criminal activity" (*Digest*, 1.18.3, two sentences later). Moreover, this exercise of the governor's *imperium* was particularly apropos to criminal activity that affected public order and to charges that fell outside the normal legal *ordo*.[125] The beginning of the trial scene, in striking similarity to the situation with Gallio (see previously), is thus an exemplary account of the *cognitio extra ordinem* procedure: "the facts are alleged and the governor is expected to construe them as he thinks fit."[126] So Felix: "I will hear you when your accusers arrive" (23:35).

And arrive they did: the High Priest Ananias,[127] some elders of the people, and their attorney, the only official ῥήτωρ to appear in the NT. When he was called upon to speak, Tertullus began his speech as any professionally trained rhetor would, with a *captatio benevolentiae*: "Since through you we enjoy much peace, and since by your provision, most excellent Felix, reforms are introduced on behalf of this nation, in every way and everywhere we accept this with all gratitude" (24:2–3).[128] Whether or not Luke's readers would have guffawed or gnashed their teeth at these words is an open question; that Tertullus's statement is sheer flattery is not.

Contra Haenchen and Conzelmann, both of whom overlook or minimize the role of the reader's repertoire in interpretation,[129] Luke here employs the common perception of Felix's abilities and achievements in order to shape the readers' evaluation of Tertullus's speech in a particular direction. It is slick-talking and of a perniciously clever kind. In the ancient world, as in the (post)modern, the craftiest trial lawyers did not seek to eliminate the truth altogether, but only to couch it in such terms as to recast entirely its meaning.[130] Thus in 24:5 Tertullus is not far off when he says that Paul is the leader (πρωτοστάτης) of the Nazarenes.[131] Strictly speaking, one might want to enter an argument on behalf of Peter or James, but Luke's basic concentration in Acts on the figure and mission of Paul has long been recognized.

Yet Tertullus cleverly embeds Paul's connection to the Christian mission within a set of charges that attempts to tie Paul's leadership to behavior that would alarm any provincial governor, not least that of Judaea. As is known from Claudius Caesar's surviving letter to the Alexandrians, Jewish conduct already had the potential to be construed as "stirring up a common plague throughout the world."[132] As the letter makes abundantly clear, such conduct would not be tolerated; instead, says Claudius, the imperial response would be, in a word, vengeance (ἐξέλευσις).[133] Luke's narrative, of course, does not necessarily presuppose Claudius's letter; still, there exists the extraordinary similarity between the two that helps to illumine the opening charge put by Tertullus.[134] It is a well-calculated whopper: Paul is a "plague, an activist for στάσις among all the Jews throughout the world" (24:5).[135]

Luke Johnson suggests that because στάσις here occurs with πᾶσιν τοῖς Ἰουδαίοις, it should be translated in its weak sense of "disturbance."[136] Yet surely this is to overlook the mid- to late-first-century Palestinian political situation, in which seditious disorder and sectarian violence were overwhelming problems (e.g., Barabbas the στασιαστής in Mark 15:7;[137] Eleazar ben Dinai, the Sicarii, the Egyptian, et al.—not to mention the Jewish War itself). Moreover, eliminating the charge of sedition significantly weakens Tertullus's legal position and turns the trial into something of a "police measure."[138] This the trial is not, as Mommsen and others have clearly demonstrated.[139] It is instead narrated as a proper legal trial, even if the essence of the *cognitio extra ordinem* system was itself a "legalisirte Formlosigkeit."[140] In such a venue—and in light of the similarity to the letter of Claudius—στάσις is best construed in its more robust sense as sedition.[141]

That *seditio* in the Roman Empire was treason (*maiestas*) needs no great elaboration. Tacitus is plain enough: the *lex maiestatis* had long included "seditious incitement of the populace."[142] And that *maiestas* itself was a capital charge in the first century, even for *cives Romani*, is also equally clear from the writings of Tacitus, Dio Cassius, the jurists of the *Digest*, and their modern students.[143] The actual form of the death penalty differed across time and locale, but imperial "vengeance" upon transgressors was as equally discernable in the criminal on the *crux* as it was in the mouth and claws of the *bestiae*—as both Jews and Christians knew all too well in the first and early second centuries.[144]

Tertullus's opening accusation thus creates a particular political context in which he attempts to place Paul's leadership of the "[school] of the Nazarenes."[145] The Nazarenes, so argues Tertullus, are an insurrectionist movement whose seditious activity aims to rouse the Jewish populus to riot or revolt. Were one to substitute "Sicarii" or Josephus's λῃσταί for Luke's Ναζωραῖοι, the charge would be easier for us—at this distance of remove—to recognize. The attorney's recasting of Paul's leadership is in the mold of zealotry, and the politics of his sect are characterized as a politics of sedition.[146] With such a charge, it scarcely needs to be said that the hope behind the well-crafted rhetoric is to elicit Roman "vengeance."

Tertullus's argument or spin doctoring, however, does not rest here. Indeed, he continues, this zealot "even [καί] attempted to desecrate the [Jerusalem] Temple" (24:6).[147] If there were ancient lists of the most significant locations in the empire that proved problematic or caused administrative worry in middle decades of the first century, "the famous city" of Jerusalem would consistently be near or at the top.[148] One recalls the Syrian legate Quadratus, to take only one of many possible examples, who, after dealing with all parties involved in the war between the Jews and the Samaritans,[149] hastened to Jerusalem "fearing a fresh revolution on the part of the Jewish people."[150] Despite the past incompetence of the Roman procurator Cumanus, this time there was no new revolt. But Quadratus's move was entirely logical. Indeed, as Josephus tells it, the war—in which Roman soldiers were also killed—had begun when news arrived in Jerusalem of a Samaritan killing of a Galilean (or several):[151] "When the news of the murder reached Jerusalem, the masses were profoundly stirred [τὰ πλήθη συνετάραξεν], and, abandoning the festival, they dashed off to Samaria without generals. . . . The brigands and rioters among the party had as their leaders Eleazar ben Dinai and Alexander, who . . . massacred the inhabitants of [Acrabatene]" (BJ, 2.234–35). Jerusalem, as Quadratus knew well, was a city replete with the potential for serious conflict.

Furthermore, the temple itself was without question the zenith of an already high religious sensitivity on the part of the Jews. Though, of course, they were less sensitive about certain locations in Provincia Judaea (Caesarea Maritima, for example), Jews were "extremely sensitive about Jerusalem" in particular (think only of Pilate's experience with the Roman standards[152]).[153] And such sensitivity only "increased as one got closer to the temple,"[154] as another Syrian legate, the diplomatic Petronius, learned in a moving and dramatic encounter with Jewish piety.[155] Antiochus Epiphanes had not been forgotten.[156]

Tertullus's further accusation, then, makes use of a fact well known to Roman administrators in Palestine:[157] to disrupt the Jerusalem temple was to invite στάσις. In this way, he draws upon the shared cultural encyclopedia with respect to the temple in order to demonstrate to Felix the character of Paul's leadership.[158] Acts 24:6 illustrates the truth of 24:5. One who would "desecrate" the temple is indeed an activist for στάσις among the Jews.

As important as what Tertullus says, however, is also what he does not say. Conspicuously absent is any mention of the precise way in which Paul (allegedly) polluted the temple. Most Acts scholars nevertheless assume that 24:6 makes direct and uncomplicated reference to Paul's supposed attempt to bring Trophimus beyond the Court of the gentiles (21:27ff.). Gerhard Schneider, for example, argues that Tertullus's speech presupposes

> daß der Leser die vorausgegangene Erzählung...über die Verhaftung kennt. Auf Tempelschändung stand die Todesstrafe. Die römische Regierung ist in diesem Punkt dem religiösen Empfinden des Judentums so weit entgegengekommen, daß sie die Ausführung der entsprechenden Strafbestimmung sogar gegen römische Bürger gestattete, wie JosBell VI 124–128 zeigt.[159]

But this manner of reading confuses what the accusing party knows with Tertullus's actual argument before the governor's bench.[160] Tertullus's point is not that Paul deserves the death penalty according to the Jewish law that protects the temple from gentile defilement. To such an argument Felix would have an easy reply: why did you not kill him yourself? Or, in the words Josephus gives to the future Emperor Titus, "Was it not you...who placed this balustrade before your sanctuary? Was it not you that ranged along it slabs, engraved in Greek characters and in our own, proclaiming that none may pass the barrier? And did we not permit you to put to death any who passed it, even were he a Roman citizen [κᾶν ʹΡωμαῖος]?"[161]

That Schneider made reference to this remarkable passage should have alerted him to the fact that for Tertullus to elicit a similar reply from Felix would have been to expose the Jews—rather than Paul—to the suspicion of rioting. As it stands, "we seized him" is the rhetor's effort to smother the involvement of the Jewish crowd underneath a claim for the Jews' role in preventing the στάσις Paul would have caused were it not for their restraint (ἐκρατήσαμεν).[162] Thus is Tertullus's argument much more about the extraordinary lengths to which this sectarian has gone to provoke the Jewish populus—"he *even* tried to desecrate the Temple"—than it is about Jewish law and the profanation of the temple per se. At the same time, through tacitly arguing for their actual help in staving off a riot, Tertullus enters a plea for Jewish innocence in the Jerusalem brouhaha that has landed them all before the governor. In short, as "evidence" of his zealotry, the lawyer cites Paul's potentially riotous activity with respect to the temple and juxtaposes such activity to that of the Jews as a whole, who prevented a riot with their seizure of Paul.

By this point in the Acts narrative, Paul's accusers have become much savvier. As Luke narrates it, the Jerusalem aristocracy and their professional rhetor know the legal and political landscape considerably better than do the accusers in Corinth. Whether or not Tertullus is to be seen as a Jew,[163] he obviously understands which arguments count with Roman governors and which do not. No mention is made of Paul's attempts at theological persuasion (18:13, ἀναπείθω), and no halakhic differences are discussed or explained. Much to the contrary, Tertullus takes the only tack that would educe from Felix the verdict for which the accusers hope.[164]

Since Mommsen's 1890 proposal that the persecution of Christians was due to the fact that a denial of the Roman gods was tantamount to treason (maiestas/ἀποστασία),[165] classical scholars have worried that the legal basis for Mommsen's theory is slight, or simply wanting.[166] With special reference to Pliny and Tertullian, such scholars have therefore attempted to minimize or eliminate maiestas as a factor in the early Christian encounter with Rome. But they have been too hasty and thrown the baby out, too.

Tertullus's arguments do not mention the pagan gods, but neither do they involve ambiguous or flimsy legal charges. Rather, they go for the legal jugular: seditio. Though he lived somewhat later than the dissemination of Acts, the Roman jurist Ulpian, for example, would have had no difficulty in recognizing Paul's peril: maiestas includes those who "armed with weapons or stones should be, or should assemble, within the city against the interests of the state, or should occupy places or temples." Furthermore, Ulpian continues, it was forbidden on grounds of maiestas "that there should be an assembly or gathering or that men should be called together for seditious purposes" (Digest, 48.4.1).[167]

Felix was no legal scholar, but Luke need not paint him as such. Like any provincial governor, his sense for maiestas of the sort described by Ulpian would have been well honed. A riot raiser, a ringleader of a group that assembles for seditious purposes, an occupier of a temple—these are not the things to pass Felix by. In the narrative of Acts, the articulate speech of the rhetor is thus accurately aimed to exploit the workings of Roman provincial administration: Paul is charged with behavior that constitutes maiestas; if Felix convicts him, Paul will be executed.[168]

That Tertullus's speech is effective is obvious. Unlike Gallio and Lysias, Felix does not hear Tertullus's accusations simply as "questions concerning their law" (23:29, περὶ ζητημάτων τοῦ νόμου αὐτῶν; cf. 18:15). At the very least, Felix takes the case seriously enough not to dismiss it out of hand. Indeed, he immediately summons the defendant to speak (cf. ἀπολογοῦμαι, 24:10).

As in Athens, so here in Caesarea Paul opens with a captatio benevolentiae, thereby showing that he, too, knows how to handle himself in court.[169] Yet, as many commentators have observed, his straightforward statement of fact—

Felix is κριτής over the nation—is not so much to gain goodwill as it is to establish a context within which Paul can speak of Jewish theology and practice.[170] Felix has known the ἔθνος—ἐπαρχεία is avoided—for many years.

Before turning to theological matters, however, Paul explicitly repudiates the charge of στάσις: when "I was worshipping Jerusalem," he says, "they did not find me arguing with a single soul, or inciting the mob [ἐπίστασιν ποιοῦντα ὄχλου]—not in the Temple, not in the synagogues, and not in the city!" (24:12). Indeed, the accusers "cannot prove to you the things with which they now charge me" (24:13).

In point of fact, Paul argues, that which they brand as seditious sectarianism (λέγουσιν αἵρεσιν) is Jewish through and through, which is to say that the Way is no more an insurrectionist faction than Judaism itself: "I worship the God of my fathers, believe everything that is according to Torah and written in the Prophets," and hope for that which the accusers do, too—the resurrection of all, just and unjust alike (24:14). Because of this, says Paul, "I myself endeavor to have a blameless conscience before God and all people" (24:16).

With these remarks, Luke moves Paul from a direct rebuttal of the *seditio* charge to a theological redescription of the Nazarenes as true Judaism.[171] Moreover, in v. 16 Paul implicitly chides his Jewish accusers for their dishonesty and challenges Felix to render right judgment. They, too, will be raised and should give heed to their "conscience toward God" (συνείδησις πρὸς τὸν θεόν).

As evidence for the theological redescription of the Way, Paul cites the fact that he came to give alms to *my* nation (εἰς τὸ ἔθνος μου), as well as to make offerings in the temple.[172] The mention of his travel to Jerusalem gives Paul opportunity to respond specifically to Tertullus's charge regarding the former's defilement of the temple: not only had Paul been purified—ἡγνισμένον ἐν τῷ ἱερῷ in explicit contrast to τὸ ἱερὸν ἐπείρασεν βεβηλῶσαι—but there was neither crowd nor riot (24:18).[173]

Having dispatched Tertullus's accusation about the temple, Paul is beginning to recount the story the reader knows from 21:27ff. (τινὲς δὲ ἀπὸ τῆς Ἀσίας Ἰουδαῖοι) when he abruptly halts and raises "a sound technical objection":[174] those responsible for the original allegation are absent (24:19). Such absence— *destitutio* in legal parlance—could result in the dismissal of the charges. Indeed, if the circumstances were right, the abandonment of proper prosecution could lead to a counteraccusation of "instituting false charges."[175] It is unlikely that Paul's rhetorical move is intended to lodge a countercharge, but it nevertheless displays considerable savoir-faire in angling for a dismissal of the case. Tertullus, implies Luke, is not the only legal mind in town.

Yet Paul must finally acknowledge the reality of his present accusers. He thus attempts to deflect their charges by naming the resurrection as that which has led to his arraignment. With this move, Paul both speaks the truth and reframes the trial in terms of Jewish theology rather than Roman law. In fact, it is the resurrection—of Jesus—that is the reality without which there would be no dispute. Paul and his opponents are not wrangling over whether insurrection is right or wrong but are, at bottom, divided on the question of whether or not the resurrection of the Jewish Messiah has taken place (see esp. 25:19, following). Paul's final statement—περὶ ἀναστάσεως νεκρῶν ἐγὼ κρίνομαι σήμερον ἐφ' ὑμῶν—thus poignantly and accurately describes his present circumstances in Caesarea even as it recapitulates his encounter with the Sanhedrin in Jerusalem. From first to last, the Way is about the resurrection.

"But Felix put them off. . . ." So begins the Roman response. A charitable explanation of this "prolongation" of the trial is offered by Sherwin-White, who writes: "The complication and prolongation of the trial of Paul arose from the fact that the charge was political—hence the procurators were reluctant to dismiss it out of hand—and yet the evidence was theological, hence the procurators were quite unable to understand it."[176] Whatever value this explanation might have at the level of historical reconstruction or with respect to Festus (see the following), it is near to impossible to square with the narrative of Acts at this point. The simple reason is of course that Luke clearly attributes to Felix a "rather accurate" (ἀκριβέστερον) knowledge of the Way (24:22, continuing the first sentence after Paul's speech).

A better reading, then, is that via this remark the sensitive reader is enabled to discern the reason behind Felix's reluctance to come to a verdict: he knows the charges of the Jews are inaccurate. The Way is not a seditious sect, and Paul's actions do not render him guilty of *maiestas*. Moreover, as Felix knows from Lysias's letter, Paul is a Roman citizen. It may be that Roman citizens were thrown to the beasts, burned, or buried alive, but such a move by Felix prior to any conviction or sentence would have been "illegal" and, perhaps more importantly, would risk the displeasure of Rome—something, as Luke knows well, Felix in particular could ill afford to do.

Why then does Felix not simply dismiss the case or release Paul with a verdict of not guilty? Again Sherwin-White's historicizing move is exegetically too generous: "[I]t is not surprising that Felix adjourned the case for the arrival of Lysias the tribune, the only independent witness as to the fact of any civil disturbance."[177] But such a reading makes little sense in light of the fact that Felix has already received Lysias's letter and thus knows his account of the matter.[178] As Luke narrates it, the refusal to release Paul is not motivated by his scrupulous attention to jurisprudence but is rather much more banal: Felix hoped to receive a monetary bribe (24:26). Having heard Paul's speech, Felix knew Paul had access to money (24:17) and—so the logic of the narrative—

hoped the particular type of *custodia* he imposed would allow Paul's friends to pass on the necessary money for his release (24:23).[179]

Despite measures taken from the Gracchan period on (e.g., the *Lex Repetundarum*),[180] bribery lived on in the empire. Though surely a gross exaggeration, Suetonius attributes to Vespasian a habit of extensive extortion:

> He made no bones of selling ... acquittals to men under prosecution, whether innocent or guilty. He is even believed to have had the habit of designedly advancing the most rapacious of his procurators to higher posts, that they might be the richer when he later condemned them; in fact, it was common talk that he used these men as sponges, because he, so to speak, soaked them when they were dry and squeezed them when they were wet.[181]

Court gossip aside, extortion was no doubt a viable option in the provinces, as Cicero knew in his time and Pliny, too, in his.[182] In fact, in Palestine itself, if Josephus is to be believed, bribery of Roman officials reached considerable heights during the first century. Festus's successor Albinus, for example, practiced "every form of villainy," among which the acceptance of bribes is explicitly singled out. Indeed, Josephus says, "the only persons left in jail as malefactors were those who failed to pay the price."[183]

Rather than money, however, Felix received a sermon about Jesus (24:24).[184] And despite Felix's repeated attempts at "conversation" (24:26), Paul never relented, even over a period of two years (διετία, 24:27). Whether Paul made any further impression upon Felix regarding the Way is not narrated. But one may infer from the manner of Felix's departure that his political worries were the heaviest, or at least weighed considerably more than his eschatological ones: "desiring to do the Jews a favor, Felix left Paul in prison" (24:27).[185]

Festus and Herod Agrippa II

"Now when Festus had come into his province, after three days he went up to Jerusalem from Caesarea" (Acts 25:1). While in the Judaean capital, the Jewish leadership (οἱ ἀρχιερεῖς καὶ οἱ πρῶτοι τῶν Ἰουδαίων) informed Festus of the charges against Paul. In the guise of requesting a change of venue, they attempted to have Paul sent to Jerusalem. In transit, Paul would have been vulnerable to attack, and he would have then been ambushed and killed. Festus, however, denied the request and bid the δυνατοί come to Caesarea where they could make formal charges (25:5, κατηγορείτωσαν αὐτοῦ).

After taking his seat upon the tribunal ($\beta\hat{\eta}\mu\alpha$), Festus heard the "many and weighty"—and, adds Luke, unprovable—accusations brought against Paul by his Jerusalem opponents ($\pi o\lambda\lambda\dot{a}$ $\kappa\alpha\dot{\iota}$ $\beta\alpha\rho\acute{\epsilon}\alpha$ $\alpha\dot{\iota}\tau\iota\acute{\omega}\mu\alpha\tau\alpha$, v. 7).[186] Luke is nothing if not a compelling writer, and he thus avoids stultifying repetition by omitting the specific charges levied by the Jews. Not only have Acts' readers seen Paul before Roman authorities many times, they can also learn what the charges were from Paul's *apologia* in 25:8[187] and Festus's renarration of the events in 25:18–19.

In 25:8 Paul responds to his accusers with a flat denial of his guilt: "neither against the law of the Jews, nor against the temple, nor against Caesar have I done anything wrong!" ($o\ddot{\upsilon}\tau\epsilon$ $\epsilon\dot{\iota}\varsigma$ $\tau\grave{o}\nu$ $\nu\acute{o}\mu o\nu$ $\tau\hat{\omega}\nu$ $'Io\upsilon\delta\alpha\acute{\iota}\omega\nu$ $o\ddot{\upsilon}\tau\epsilon$ $\epsilon\dot{\iota}\varsigma$ $\tau\grave{o}$ $\dot{\iota}\epsilon\rho\grave{o}\nu$ $o\ddot{\upsilon}\tau\epsilon$ $\epsilon\dot{\iota}\varsigma$ $K\alpha\acute{\iota}\sigma\alpha\rho\acute{a}$ $\tau\iota$ $\ddot{\eta}\mu\alpha\rho\tau o\nu$). Whether or not this denial responds to the charges "one by one,"[188] it certainly indicates the general congruity with the case against Paul before Gallio, Claudius Lysias, and Felix: by narrating Paul's theological construal of the Jewish $\nu\acute{o}\mu o\varsigma$ as leading to his violation of the temple, his opponents attempt to accuse him of running afoul of Roman law.

Based on Festus's remarks in 25:18–19, however, it seems that this time the Jews did not bring Tertullus along, or else that, if there, he did not display his earlier legal suavity. Festus, that is, like the tribune Lysias, cannot understand the relevance of the Jewish $\zeta\eta\tau\acute{\eta}\mu\alpha\tau\alpha$ to Roman law.[189] As he says to Agrippa II, "the accusers... brought no charge in [Paul's] case of such evils as I had supposed" (v. 18). Instead, they prattled on about matters pertaining only to their own superstition,[190] matters about which Festus is plainly at a loss ($\dot{a}\pi o\rho o\acute{\upsilon}\mu\epsilon\nu o\varsigma$ $\delta\dot{\epsilon}$ $\dot{\epsilon}\gamma\acute{\omega}$, v. 20). Yet, this much was clear: from the perspective of Roman law, Festus declares confidently, Paul "has done nothing deserving death" (Acts 25:25).

Before moving on to the further significance of Festus's statements, we must pause to delineate the hermeneutical and political importance of Paul's robust denial, as well as the significance of his appeal to Caesar. Hermeneutically, it is crucial to understand that, for Luke, Paul is a "reliable" character; indeed, he is the human protagonist of much of Acts. Thus does Paul's declaration offer an interpretive guide to the entirety of the trial and to his appearance before Roman officials. Regardless of the confusion displayed by Gallio, Lysias, Felix, and Festus, the legal reality is the same: Paul is innocent of the charges that have been brought against him. Politically, then, according to Luke, the Christian mission cannot be understood in any kind of way—whether from the perspective of the Jewish or Roman $\nu\acute{o}\mu o\varsigma$—as a takeover bid or call to sedition.[191]

If Paul is right, Festus already knows this truth when he offers Paul a change of venue. "I have done no wrong to the Jews," says Paul to Festus, "as you know very well" (25:10b). Rather than wielding the Roman *imperium* for the sake of δικαιοσύνη, the provincial governor's political strategy is focused far more upon keeping decent relations with the Jewish leadership. This strategy is understandable from the Roman point of view, of course, inasmuch as a provincial governor in the empire always had to work closely with the native aristocracy of his province. But, as the reader of Acts knows well, Jerusalem is hardly the city in which Paul would receive acquittal. Much to the contrary, in Jerusalem even the Roman governor can be subject to intense pressure from the local population, as was the *praefectus* Pontius Pilate, for example, who crucified another innocent man.[192]

That the potential for a deadly outcome in Jerusalem is not in doubt is made clear by Paul's characterization of the proposed change of venue as a "giving up" or "handing over to them": "If there is nothing in their charges . . . no one can give me up to them" (25:11, RSV etc.). When we remember that δύναμαι can approach something akin to "to enjoy a legal right," as it does on the lips of the Areopagus Council in Acts (17:19), the phrase οὐδείς με δύναται αὐτοῖς χαρίσασθαι is probably best rendered: "no one has the legal right to hand me over to them." Luke thus further stresses the highly problematic nature of Festus's suggestion, as Paul rejects the Jerusalem court and once again displays his awareness of the inside of the legal arena.[193] Yet, in practice if not also in principle,[194] the political strategy and de facto authority of the governor considerably outweigh Paul's legal point. He thus takes a gamble: Καίσαρα ἐπικαλοῦμαι—"I appeal to Caesar."

That Paul's appeal has attracted much attention from Acts scholars in the twentieth and twenty-first century needs no great comment.[195] But it was not always so: as Mommsen realized in 1901, his article on the process of appeal, if self-evident to scholars of Roman legal history, would offer much that was "nicht überflüssig" to his colleagues in the field of NT.[196] And indeed it did, setting the terms for the discussion of the legal aspects of Paul's trial through H. J. Cadbury and many others.[197]

So, too, in the main was Mommsen's hope for the "Juristen" fulfilled.[198] By and large other classicists specializing in Roman jurisprudence have found his account of Paul's appeal to be well founded, at least with respect to the two points considered here: (1) during the early empire, in the case of a capital charge against a Roman citizen the provincial governor had no choice but to send the defendant to Rome—the accused was automatically granted a right of appeal prior to the sentence (*provocatio*); and, consequently, (2) it is known that the governor could not pass sentence in a capital case against a *civis Romanus*.[199] For all his qualifications or modifications to this or that statement of Mommsen's, Sherwin-White, for example, basically accepts the German scholar's larger picture in this respect: "Cadbury suggested that the procurator had the power to disallow an appeal, and that he might himself have tried the prisoner, merely seeking confirmation of sentence if he found the man guilty. This is clean contrary to the evidence of the *lex Iulia* and of Pliny."[200] There is one ancient historian, however, who has taken Mommsen, Jones, Sherwin-White, and others to task on these exact points.

In a series of learned and perceptive publications, Peter Garnsey has demonstrated that the hard and fast distinction between an "appeal prior to sentence" (*provocatio* = early imperial period) and an "appeal subsequent to sentence" (*appellatio* = later empire) cannot be maintained.[201] There are simply no laws that allow appeal prior to a sentence.[202] This hardly means that it was not done—Paul is the star witness to the contrary—but *provocatio* and *appellatio* are not distinct names for two separate systems; rather, they are two words for the same multifaceted and complex reality of appeal. Moreover, as Garnsey has further shown, while the *lex Iulia* may certainly have prevented a provincial governor from "executing summarily" a Roman citizen, it did not prevent him from executing one "legally"—that is, with trial and sentence—save a member of the true aristocracy.[203]

Implicit in Garnsey's critique is also the point that because Jones and Sherwin-White somewhat romanticize Roman law, its actual power in the provinces is overestimated; the actions of the provincial governors that constitute "exceptions" to their theory must then be explained away.[204] Far better, argues Garnsey, to begin from the provincial evidence and simply admit "the wide discretionary power of the governor... over the whole field of provincial jurisdiction."[205] As Josephus would put it, from the time of the first Roman governor, the prefect/procurator ruled Judaea with all authority ($\tau\hat{\eta}$ $\dot{\epsilon}\pi\grave{\iota}$ $\pi\hat{a}\sigma\iota\nu$ $\dot{\epsilon}\xi o\upsilon\sigma\acute{\iota}\boldsymbol{q}$).[206] According to Luke, Paul was right to judge the courts (Jerusalem and now Caesarea) to be *iniqua* and therefore to reject them.[207] But Festus, as Luke also tells, could have refused Paul's appeal.

That he did not is narratively significant: "When [Festus] had conferred with his council, he answered, 'You have appealed to Caesar; to Caesar you shall go' " (Acts 25:12). A judge's consultation with his *consilium* ("advisory cabinet")[208] was of course commonplace in the Roman court system. In Acts, this detail provides the necessary narrative note that Festus actually considered Paul's appeal—it was not an automatic transfer—and won through to a politically ingenious solution to a highly delicate problem.

On the one hand, for Festus to acquit and release Paul would be for him to open his rule by displeasing the $\delta\upsilon\nu\alpha\tau o\acute{\iota}$ of the Jews,[209] something that he was keen not to do for reasons obviously important to the stability and governance of the province (v. 9). On the other hand, to pass sentence (cf. $\kappa\alpha\tau\alpha\delta\acute{\iota}\kappa\eta$, 25:15) and execute a Roman citizen whom he knows to have done no wrong (v. 11 passim) would be, at the very least, to raise doubts in Rome about his administrative abilities and possibly to incur a reprimand if not a recall. In short, either scenario would offer a poor way to begin his procuratorship.

By allowing the appeal, Festus avoids both these difficulties. To any complaint of the Jews, Festus could point out that Paul remains a prisoner of Rome and thereby endures the possibility of future conviction and execution. By no means has Paul been acquitted or set free. Furthermore, Festus might reply, the troublemaker is on his way out of the province. Of course, the Jerusalem Jews are not the only ones for whom Paul's absence would be a relief: by granting Paul's appeal Festus has avoided the unwanted mistake of executing an innocent Roman citizen.

For all his ingenuity, however, Festus now faces yet another administrative problem: he must refer a case to Rome that he does not understand (cf. 25:26).[210] Festus thus turns to a man well versed in translating the ways of the Jews and Romans to each other, King Agrippa II (cf. μάλιστα ἐπὶ σοῦ Βασιλεῦ Ἀγρίππα, 25:26).

If ever there were a man who could speak intelligibly to the Romans of things Jewish, it was Luke's contemporary Agrippa II.[211] Reared and educated in the court of the Emperor Claudius, friend of Vespasian and Titus, by AD 75 he had received the insignia of the praetorian rank. It is true that Josephus puts a heartfelt and lengthy speech on his lips—of which Agrippa II himself evidently approved[212]—that evidences love for the Jews and attempts to dissuade them from war with Rome (in response to the massacre by Florus).[213] Yet it is also true that, when war broke out, Agrippa II wasted no time in declaring allegiance to Rome and sending troops against the Jewish nation.[214]

He could, moreover, speak like a pagan theologian. In this case Agrippa articulates the submission of the Macedonians to the might of Rome in terms of the shifting of the goddess τύχη: "Look at the Macedonians, who still fantasize about Philip, who still have before their eyes the vision of Her who with Alexander scattered for them the seeds of the empire of the world; yet they submit to endure such a reversal of fate and bend the knee before those to whom Fortune [ἡ τύχη] has transferred Her favors."[215] If Josephus's speeches are in any way near to the wider perception of Agrippa II, readers of Acts would have found it no great wonder that Festus attempts to draw on the hermeneutical skill of the romanized Jewish king.

Indeed, Festus speaks to Agrippa II almost as if the latter were a Roman, first clarifying the legal reason why he did not simply convict Paul in Jerusalem—"it is not the custom of the Romans to hand over [ἔθος Ῥωμαίοις χαρίζεσθαι; cf. 25:11] anyone before the accused met the accusers face to face and had the opportunity to make his apologia concerning the charge laid against him" (25:16)—and then characterizing the religion of the accusers and defendant alike as δεισιδαιμονία. The points of dispute between the Jews and Paul were not about Roman legal matters but about "their own superstition" and, in particular, about "a certain Jesus who died but whom Paul was claiming to be alive" (25:19).[216]

That a gentile would deride Judaism as "superstitious" is no great surprise. From Agatharchides in the second century BC to Apuleius in the second century AD, non-Jews regularly reviled Judaism as superstition. This was no less true of Plutarch in the Greek East than it was of Tacitus in the Latin West, though the latter was much harsher: it was a shame, thought Tacitus, that Antiochus IV Epiphanes' attempt to "introduce Greek civilization" had failed to "abolish the Jewish *superstitio*" and "improve this basest of peoples."[217]

It is also not surprising, by this point in the narrative, that a Roman official would view the resurrection as Jewish quibbling. That Festus actually goes on to name Jesus specifically, however, shows that the debate in Caesarea Maritima, unlike the scene before the Sanhedrin in Jerusalem (Acts 22:30–23:10), has gotten to the heart of the matter. Paul's tactical maneuvering during his trial is far from finished, but no longer is resurrection in general that which is displayed in public as the reason for the problem. It is rather, as Festus has rightly heard, about Jesus in particular.

Yet Festus's "hearing" leads not to genuine understanding but immediately to ἀπορία (v. 20). His problem is not simply that he does not understand the intricacies of Jewish theology. It is rather a much deeper problem in that, as a pagan, he lacks the comprehensive hermeneutical framework in which to place the debate about the identity of Jesus. He is not missing bits and pieces of information, that is, but the entire context in which such information would make sense in the first place. He is literally unable to understand. The reader should not be surprised, then, at Festus's subsequent outburst during Paul's defense: "you are crazy... crazy!" (26:24).[218]

For the moment, however, Festus keeps his head and presents things to Agrippa in such a manner that the latter explicitly asks to hear Paul. "Tomorrow," says Festus, "you shall hear him" (25:22).

On the next day, King Agrippa and his sister/wife Bernice[219] came μετὰ πολλῆς φαντασίας and entered the audience hall—not a formal court—in the presence of a considerably high-profile crowd: the provincial governor, military tribunes, and prominent men of the city (25:23, σύν... χιλιάρχοις καὶ ἀνδράσιν τοῖς κατ᾽ ἐξοχήν). After Paul is brought in—no doubt as an element of show—Festus takes center stage.

His speech, if pompous, is straightforward. The "entire mob" of Jews clamored for Festus to impose the death penalty upon Paul. But the juridical investigation turned up "nothing worthy of death" (25:26). So Pilate and Jesus; so Festus and Paul.[220]

As mentioned previously, however, the granting of Paul's subsequent appeal has resulted in Festus's inability to formulate a proper letter of transfer to his κύριος (25:26). That Festus should use κύριος here is striking, and it rings as a loud and clear reminder to the assembly, not least to King Agrippa himself, of just who it is that will eventually hear this case.[221] Therefore, trumpets Festus with no little pressure, "I have brought [Paul] before you, and, especially before you King Agrippa, that, after we have examined him, I may have something to write." With such a message, Agrippa, for his part, wastes no time: "You can speak for yourself," says he immediately to Paul.

Paul, once again displaying a rhetor's ability, stretches out his hand and speaks.[222] It is true that his *captatio benevolentiae* attempts to win goodwill from Agrippa—indeed, Paul will later press him to believe—but it also does considerable interpretive work in that it shapes Paul's legal apology specifically as a defense from *within* the ἔθοι and ζητήματα of the Jews. Theology here *is* politics. Paul's appeal in the *captatio*, that is, attempts to frame the charges against him in terms of a shared theological horizon as a way to enable Agrippa to understand the political configuration of those who follow the Jewish Messiah. If Agrippa listens patiently, Paul intimates, he will hear in Paul's *apologia* the answer to Festus's political conundrum.

For readers of Acts, Paul's opening sally is familiar. He narrates his own history with particular reference to the school (αἵρεσις) well known for their belief in the resurrection, the Pharisees. And from there he attempts to redescribe the entirety of Judaism—"the twelve-tribe unit"[223]—as focused upon God's promise of resurrection (vv. 6–7) and asserts that it is this for which he is accused by the Jews. "Can you believe it?!?!," Paul implies, "put on trial for the very thing for which all Jews hope!" If God promised he would raise the dead, "why is it thought unbelievable [ἄπιστον] by you that God does raise the dead?!" (v. 8).

Paul's question is of course rhetorical, in the colloquial sense, and opens the way for him to recount his own move from ἀπιστία to πίστις. As we know from his preaching to Felix (24:24), Paul was not one to shy away from speaking christological truth to power. Indeed, as Luke sees it, this is a constitutive aspect of his vocation as a μάρτυς to the gentiles: Paul "is a chosen vessel of mine to carry my name before the gentiles and kings and the sons of Israel," says the Lord (Acts 9:15). By virtue of its obviousness, that Paul's imprisonment and trial have provided precisely such an audience can almost go unsaid. It is therefore only marginally surprising that Paul so quickly turns to "the name": Jesus of Nazareth.

In relating Jesus's appearance to him, Paul argues autobiographically for the reality of the resurrection of the dead Jesus (cf. 25:19) and, in so doing, focuses the hope of Israel christologically. This fulfillment in Jesus of the resurrection hope of Israel, contends Paul, unfolds necessarily in a universal mission of witness and proclamation to Jew and gentile alike. And it is this missionary outgrowth of the resurrection of the suffering Messiah that has led to Paul's seizure, attempted murder, and ultimately to his trial (26:16–23).[224]

That Paul should characterize the resurrection of Jesus as that which has created the possibility for gentiles to move from darkness to light and from the power of Satan to God (vv. 18, 23) implies that, absent such a move, the gentiles remain bound in darkness. It is no great wonder, then, that Festus's μανία outburst occurs precisely at the point where Paul speaks of the resurrection as "light to the people and the Gentiles" (v. 23–24). To put it differently, at this point the narrative of Acts articulates the unity of the moral and hermeneutical life. Not to repent and turn to God (μετανοεῖν καὶ ἐπιστρέφειν ἐπὶ τὸν θεόν), not to practice works worthy of repentance (ἄξια τῆς μετανοείας ἔργα πράσσοντας), is to remain in hermeneutical no less than moral darkness. Festus is not, or not yet, Sergius Paulus, ἀνὴρ συνετός (Acts 13:7; cf. 13:12). The resurrection of Jesus, so Luke through Paul, actually creates a new mode of seeing—"light." To miss the resurrection of Jesus, therefore, is to forfeit the ability to see. Μαίνῃ Παῦλε!

Yet Paul's language about light and darkness is not that of a secret society—something that would make any self-respecting Roman governor quite nervous.[225] Rather, as King Agrippa ought to know (26:26), the light has blazed forth, gone emphatically public; in Paul's own words, the witness to the resurrection has not been "in a corner" (26:26).[226] And, indeed, Agrippa does know of the "Christians." To Paul's blunt evangelism (v. 27), he responds sarcastically: "in such a short time you have persuaded me to become a Christian!" (v. 28).[227]

Luke's introduction of the word Χριστιανός into the narrative at just this moment deftly validates Paul's foregoing description of the Way as that which corresponds to public experience. Agrippa's reaction, therefore, together with Paul's speech, says to Festus and his tribunes what it means to be Christian.[228] These are a people who publicly testify to the God of Israel's resurrection of the crucified Christ, Jesus of Nazareth. Their witness is explicit and open, and their form of life is constituted by repentance and forgiveness. The Nazarenes are not a seditious sect but the concrete manifestation of God's fulfillment of the hope of all Israel.

That such theological claims appear grandiose to Agrippa is obvious; yet, with Festus and the others, he can nevertheless discern the falsity of the *maiestas* charge. "They said to one another, 'This man is doing nothing worthy of death or imprisonment' " (26:31). So Antipas and Jesus; so Agrippa and Paul.

Whether Agrippa's concluding statement is only a half-truth depends ultimately upon speculation about Festus's decision apart from the pressure of the Jews.[229] What is beyond dispute, however, is that the statement functions narratively as the final legal judgment of the authorities in Judaea vis-à-vis the accusation of insurrection and treason: "This man could have been set free if he had not appealed to Caesar" (26:32).

Conclusion

It has been said and often repeated: Luke's portrayal of the events before Gallio and the other Roman officials reveals that he is "pro-Roman to the core,"[230] or that Paul's "earthly *patria* was Rome."[231] Rome, it is argued, "ist—nach der lukanischen Darstellung—von der politischen Ungefährlichkeit von Jesus und Paulus absolut überzeugt. Der Vertreter Roms spricht sich nicht nur für ihre Loyalität aus, sondern setzt seine Auffassung auch noch in ein faires Verfahren um. Für Paulus als römischen Bürger mag dies als selbstverständlich anmuten."[232] In short, the state should not worry: "Christians make good citizens":[233] "von Jesus geht keine Gefahr für das römische Imperium aus."[234]

In light of the exegetical investigations of this and the previous chapter, such conclusions about Luke's portrait of Christianity appear at best to be simplistic generalizations about a much more complex and richly textured narrative. Yet, these caricatures are not without interpretive value in that they attempt to point, however awkwardly, to a fundamental feature common to all four passages discussed in this chapter: the Christian mission as narrated by Luke is not a counter-state. It does not, that is, seek to replace Rome, or to "take back" Palestine, Asia, or Achaia. To the contrary, such a construal of Christian politics is resolutely and repeatedly rejected. Where the tribune Lysias mistakes Paul for the Egyptian—and, by implication, a *Sicarius*—he is immediately corrected: "Indeed! I am a Jew from Cilicia!" And where Tertullus attempts to paint the Nazarenes as a pestilent and seditious sect, he is rebuffed by Paul's theological redescription of the Way as a testimony to the resurrection. So, too, with Festus: Paul and his crowd preach the resurrection of the dead Jesus, not the treasonous overthrow of Rome.

The story of Acts, therefore, raises the charge of *seditio* as *maiestas* precisely so that such an understanding of the Christian mission can be narrated out of the realm of interpretive possibility. To follow Luke's narrative is to read Christianity not as a call for insurrection but as a testimony to the reality of the resurrection.

Yet, as any number of contemporary examples might remind us—Martin Luther King Jr., to take only the most obvious—the rejection of insurrection does not simultaneously entail an endorsement of the present world order, as if the fact that Jesus was δίκαιος necessitates Luke's approval of the crucifixion. In fact, according to Acts, the refusal of statecraft could well go hand in hand with the deconstruction of mantic-based economics or with the burning of magical books (Philippi and Ephesus). Equally well would withstanding the temptation to messianic military might include, rather than preclude, the naming of traditional pagan deities as "vain things" (Lystra). Indeed, for Luke, the repudiation of sedition is no more essential to the Christian mission than its sweeping critique of the Greek world as mired in ἄγνοια (Athens). Thus if the scene before Gallio articulates narratively the conviction that the state is not equipped to discern theological truth—or, to put it in more directly political terms, is not ultimately sovereign[235]—Paul's testimony before Festus clarifies theologically why this is so. The gentiles attempt to see with closed eyes, in darkness, without light; in short, they are under the ἐξουσία of Satan (26:18).

A clearer statement than this would be hard to find, unless of course one recalls the temptation narrative of Luke's Gospel. There Luke writes,

> And the devil took Jesus up and showed him all the kingdoms of the world in a point of time. And the devil said to Jesus: "To you I will give all this ἐξουσίαν and their glory, for it has been delivered to me, and I give it to whom I will. If you, then, will worship me, it shall all be yours." And Jesus answered and said, "It is written: 'You shall worship the Lord your God and serve him alone.'" (Luke 4:5–8)

Basic, then, to Luke's portrayal of the state vis-à-vis the Christian mission is a narratively complex negotiation between the reality of the state's idolatry and blindness—its satanic power—and the necessity that the mission of light not be misunderstood as sedition. In order to circumscribe such misunderstanding, Luke must do more literarily than exhibit Paul's self-assertion of innocence (e.g., Acts 25:8). Rather, for him to make a serious political argument, the state itself must find that Jesus and his followers "have done nothing deserving death."[236] And in order to display narratively gentile blindness and idolatry, the state must kill them anyway. "I find no crime in this man," ultimately ends in "there they crucified him" (Luke 23:4, 33). So Jesus. So—the reader imagines—Paul, too.

It is doubtless the case that fruitless speculation about the ending of Acts abounds.[237] The hermeneutical task of supplying a particular ending, however, is not itself thereby rendered unnecessary; indeed, the literary dynamics of Acts actually encourage the attentive reader to complete the story of Paul's trial.[238] There are NT scholars, of course, who on (supposedly) historical grounds maintain that Paul was eventually acquitted and traveled on to Spain or elsewhere.[239] Yet the narrative of Acts seems rather clear: Paul will die in Rome as an innocent man. So Jesus (in Jerusalem). So Paul (in Rome).[240] As Charles Talbert put it with typical clarity, the narrative leads one to surmise that "(a) Paul stood before Caesar (cf. 25:12; 27:24). (b) He was innocent (23:29; 25:18–19; 26:31–32). (c) He met his death (20:25, 38)."[241] Hence does Acts carry forward and refigure imaginatively the story of Jesus in the person of Paul. In so doing Luke continues to provide the readers of Acts with the theological and imaginative resources to proclaim their own innocence and concurrently to meet death at the hands of the Roman state.

To see clearly, therefore, the profound destabilization of pagan life that accompanies the "turning from Satan to God" and "the forgiveness of sins" (chapter 2) is at once to comprehend the urgency of an ecclesiological narrative that excludes insurrection from the narration of the shape of the mission (chapter 3). To put it slightly differently: Christians do not deserve death and yet will the gentiles rage (cf. Acts 4:25–26). The tension, or dialectic, that emerges as a result of thinking the juxtaposition of chapters 2 and 3 thus illumines a central narrative task of Acts: to redescribe theologically the cultural collapse that attends the Christian mission as the light and forgiveness of God. To inhabit this tension is to dwell near the core of Luke's cultural and political vision. But to perceive Luke's coherent outworking of this tension is already to have positioned oneself hermeneutically inside the *missio Dei*—the subject of our next chapter.

4

World Upside Down: Practicing Theological Knowledge

To have followed closely the arguments of the previous chapters is to have been led into the middle of a profound tension in the interpretation of Acts. On the one hand, Luke narrates the movement of the Christian mission into the gentile world as a collision with culture-constructing aspects of that world. From the perspective created by this angle of vision, Christianity and pagan culture are competing realities. Inasmuch as embracing the Christian call to repentance necessarily involves a different way of life, basic patterns of Graeco-Roman culture are dissolved. The pagans in Lystra, Philippi, Athens, and Ephesus are understandably riled: the Christians are a real threat (chapter 2).

On the other hand, Luke narrates the threat of the Christian mission in such a way as to eliminate the possibility of conceiving it as in direct competition with the Roman government. Of all forms of sedition and treason, Luke tells, Christianity is innocent. Paul engenders considerable upheaval as a part of his mission, but time and again—in Corinth, Jerusalem, Caesarea, and Rome (so the reader understands)—the political authorities reject the accusations of his opponents: Paul is δίκαιος. The Christians are not out to establish Christendom, as it were (chapter 3). New culture, yes—coup, no. The tension is thus set.

The question then becomes what to make of this tension. If both aspects of Luke's portrayal are essential to his conception of the Christian mission, what is Christianity according to Acts? Is there something that holds the tension together, or even produces it—a more fundamental conviction, say, that would give rise to both sides of Luke's portrayal?

We will begin with a close reading of Acts 17:1–9, a passage that is remarkable for its density and concentrated outworking of the tension displayed so far. The exegesis of Paul's visit to Thessalonica leads necessarily to a thematic consideration of the three mutually interdependent ecclesial practices that ground and thus generate Luke's overall cultural vision as it is depicted in Acts: the confession of Jesus as Lord of all, the universal mission of light, and the formation of Christian communities as the tangible presence of a people set apart.[1] Though these three practices will be treated sequentially, it will be seen that they constitute a unity. And though—due to the thematic nature of the investigation—certain passages will be brought to the fore more so than others, readers of Luke's second volume should easily be able to make the connections to the texts discussed elsewhere in this book and to the narrative of Acts itself.

Another King

After leaving Philippi and passing through Amphipolis and Apollonia along the Egnatian Way, Paul and his companions arrive in Thessalonica. There Paul entered the Jewish synagogue and, "as was his custom," attempted to prove from the scriptures that it was necessary for "the Christ" to suffer and rise from the dead. Indeed, says Paul, "this Jesus, whom I proclaim to you, is the Christ" (Acts 17:1–3).

While modern scholars struggle over how best to understand Paul's christological readings of the Old Testament, a "great many pious Greeks" in Thessalonica evidently did not. Not only were they persuaded, but so, too, were "some" Jews and "not a few of the leading women." Such missionary success, however, was not well received by the local population; at the behest of the Jews, some "wicked" men from the agora gathered a crowd to rid Thessalonica of the Christian disturbers. To accomplish their task, they attacked the house of Jason—presumably the host of the Christians—and dragged him and some of the other Christians before the local magistrates alleging that "these men who have turned the world upside down have come here also, and Jason has received them; and they are all acting against the decrees of Caesar, saying that there is another king, Jesus." With such a charge, it is no great surprise that the crowd and the magistrates were sufficiently alarmed to take collateral from Jason and the rest. Reading the political signs, the Christians in Thessalonica sent Paul and Silas away by night (17:10).

Strategy of the Jews

Crucial to the interpretation of the passage is the fact that the problems that confront the Christians in Thessalonica arise as a result of actual conversions. "Some" of the Jews, writes Luke, "a great many" of the pious Greeks, and "not a few" of the leading women were persuaded by Paul's preaching and teaching. They thus "joined" the Christians (17:4). As Luke narrates it, therefore, the problem in Thessalonica is not simply a theological debate internal to the synagogue about the christological interpretation of the Jewish scriptures (v. 2) or the character and identity of the Jewish messiah (v. 3). It is, rather, a dramatically public problem whose roots lie in the social explication of the theological dispute: Jews and Greeks are joining the Christian mission.

This observation helps to understand the use of ζηλόω in 17:5, particularly in connection with the tone of the rest of the passage. Where modern exegetes interpret ζηλόω as "jealous" in the sense of feeling envious at someone else's gain or good fortune, they have good ancient ground on which to stand. Indeed, Luke himself employs ζηλόω in just this way in Acts 7:9 when he names the "patriarchs'" jealousy as the reason that they sold Joseph into Egypt. Yet here in Acts 17:5 we would be remiss not to see in the zeal of Jews their attention to the political realities created by the defection of Jews and Greeks to the Christians. We shall return to the precise nature of the charges against the Christian missionaries in 17:6–7, but for the moment it is sufficient to note that the highly political nature of the charges strongly suggests the Jews' discernment of the potential for Christian practice to bring repercussion from the local authorities. The fact that from an outsider's perspective the origins of the group of troublemakers would appear to rest in the Jewish synagogue—Paul taught there for three weeks[2]—would hardly have been lost on the Jews.

Second, attending to the possible political dimension in the Jews' fervor helps to explain the logic behind the particular manner of their attempt to rid Thessalonica of the Christian missionaries. It is certainly true that at first glance the Jews' strategy could appear misguided. As we have seen in previous chapters, creating a public θόρυβος carries with it the possibility of the charge of στάσις. This is of course a rather poor way to attract the goodwill of the local magistrates, who would doubtless worry about the Roman redress. Yet the creation of a tumult is exactly the course of action adopted by the Jews. They go to the agora—a place where, as Plutarch reminds us, loiterers who could "gather a mob and force all issues" were known to be (cf. Acts 17:17–18)[3]—and recruit some of the local ruffians to gather a crowd. As was frequently the case with the gathering of such crowds in ancient cities, the immediate effect was to set the city in an uproar.

In considering the jurisprudential aspects of this passage, Sherwin-White noticed the possible political oddity of the Jews' strategy and attempted to explain it with reference to Thessalonica's special status as a *civitas libera*. Though Sherwin-White did not well understand the nature of the charges against Paul and Silas, he rightly observed that even though Acts makes no explicit reference to Thessalonica's status, "the energetic action of the Jews against Paul and Silas might have been inspired by the knowledge that the hands of the city authorities, unlike those of Ephesus, were not directly under Roman control."[4] It is true, as A. H. M. Jones showed nearly seventy years ago, that civic "freedom" under the empire was a rather tenuous matter, and, in practice, Roman governors could more or less do what was needed to maintain the health of the empire.[5] Yet in this case Sherwin-White's observation helps to uncover (once again) not only the care Luke takes to describe provincial matters accurately[6]—at least at the more formal or constitutional *Oberstufe*, as it were—but also the way in which the Jews' strategy makes some sense on a local level: while in Ephesus such a disturbance may provoke an immediate reaction from those who are thinking of Rome (e.g., the town clerk), in Thessalonica one was technically outside the purview of direct Roman governance and, therefore, needed to worry only about convincing the local magistrates to take the right side. One could approach them directly, make accusations, and obtain a verdict.[7]

Yet such action is taken only as the proverbial "Plan B." The initial move on the part of the attackers is to bring "them"—at least Paul and Silas, but possibly also Jason and all the Christians—before the δῆμος (v. 5). Despite Sherwin-White's insistence that δῆμος "should mean the city assembly,"[8] the tenor of the passage suggests that Barrett's "mob" is closer to the mark.[9] Instead of upstanding and law-abiding citizens who join the Jews in effort to corral the city's troubles, the agora ruffians are explicitly characterized as πονηρός ("wicked"); in addition, a crowd has already been formed, the city is in an uproar, and the house of Jason is attacked. Of course in Ephesus there is both a large riot and an ἐκκλησία,[10] but here in Thessalonica the image is rather that of a crowd waiting outside Jason's house to deliver the verdict, that is, to accomplish their lynching (cf. ὄχλος in vv. 5 and 8).

But Paul and Silas are not there. Understandably riled in the face of this disappointment, the attackers drag Jason and some Christians (τινας ἀδελφούς) before the local authorities (τοὺς πολιτάρχας).[11] In so doing, the accusers display not only their resilience and determination but also their political savvy in the attempt to rid the city of the Christians. By shifting the course of action to the arena of the πολιτάρχαι, the instigators take full advantage of the fact that the court of a free city "was the one seat of jurisdiction where severe punishment could be inflicted, at least on non-Romans, *peregrini,* without invoking the governor."[12]

That "severe punishment" was the intended result for the Christians hardly needs elucidation. Yet such hope went unfulfilled. Rather than punish Jason, the officials demand instead that, as host, he vouch for his guests. Sherwin-White once again: "What is happening to Jason is clear enough: he is giving security for the good behaviour of his guests."[13] Jason and the Christians are then released.

Despite its failure to sway the officials toward harsh action, the Jews' strategy makes some good sense—at least in retrospect—in light of the particular political situation of a "free city." The creation of a tumult serves in practice to allow them a second chance at ridding the city of the Christian menace. When rousing popular sentiment against the Christian founders on the absence of Paul and Silas, the Jews are able swiftly to change course and make use of this tumult as a way to approach the city magistrates. That is to say, by the time the Jews reach the πολιτάρχαι, they have created the public evidence for the crimes of which they will accuse the Christians, and they have taken these accusations to the right authorities for such crimes.[14] That Jason and his guests are not found guilty but instead are sent forth only on probation is narratively significant. To understand such significance, however, we need first to attend with more detail to the nature of the charges.

Charges Against Christians

Having arrived with Jason and the other Christians, the accusers launch their legal attack before the politarchs with the charge that "these men who have turned the world upside down have come here, too.... They are all acting against the decrees of Caesar, proclaiming that there is another King, Jesus" (οἱ τὴν οἰκουμένην ἀναστατώσαντες οὗτοι καὶ ἐνθάδε πάρεισιν... οὗτοι πάντες ἀπέναντι τῶν δογμάτων Καίσαρος πράσσουσιν βασιλέα ἕτερον λέγοντες εἶναι Ἰησοῦν 17:6–7). Interpreters of this passage have not infrequently declared these verses difficult to understand. Sherwin-White, for example, opined that "this is the most confused of the various descriptions of charges in Acts."[15] Yet this is surely to view the charges through a narrow historicizing lens.[16] That is, when considered as a Lukan political-theological formulation intended to bring out the nature of the Christian mission—rather than as a simple attempt at objective reporting—the charges make perfect sense.[17] And in fact Sherwin-White himself moves from his declaration of their virtual incomprehensibility to a neat arrangement of three separate charges. The Christians (1) disturb the world, (2) act against the decrees of Caesar, and (3) proclaim another king.[18] As we will see, it is actually better to take these discrete elements in reverse and read them as inseparable aspects of one well-calculated charge of sedition: by proclaiming another king, the Christians act against the decrees of Caesar and thereby turn the world upside down.[19]

To say that the Christians "disturb the world"—as many translators do—is to risk obscuring the gravity of the accusation. For the charge is not simply the complaint that the Christians are a social nuisance, but rather that the Christian mission is a force for sedition in an otherwise civilized world—ἡ οἰκουμένη. As in Acts 21:38, where Luke employs ἀναστατόω to characterize the Egyptian's rebellion with the Sicarii, so here the word is used to signify seditious action that leads to revolt.[20] Thus "turned upside down" means not just disorientation but riotous upheaval. That such a charge reminds us not only of the Emperor Claudius' letter to Alexandria regarding Jewish conduct but also the series of charges leveled at the Christians throughout Acts is hardly coincidental.[21] The general point is entirely the same.

In Thessalonica, however, the accusers are not content to remain at the level of generalities. Instead, they further specify the charge in relation to the Roman emperor: all [πάντες] the Christians act contrary to the δόγματα of Caesar (17:7). Many scholars would agree with C. K. Barrett that it is "difficult to give a precise meaning to δόγματα Καίσαρος."[22] E. A. Judge, for example, prefaced his important article on this passage with the remark that "[n]o satisfactory explanation seems to have been given of the charges brought against the apostles at Thessalonica."[23] Of course Judge then went on to offer his own (presumably more satisfactory) explanation, which interpreted the δόγματα Καίσαρος in light of statements in 1 and 2 Thessalonians and in conjunction with imperial decrees preventing predictions of a change of ruler (i.e., the death of the emperor).[24]

If Cassius Dio is right, such decrees as Judge mentions had been issued from the time of Augustus, and, as we know from the *Digest*, they continued through the mid to late empire. In the third century Paulus the Jurist, for example, records a law that forbade the visiting of prophetic persons for information about the emperor: "those who consult astrologers, male or female soothsayers, or diviners, with reference to the life of the Emperor or the safety of the state, shall be punished with death, together with the party who answered their questions."[25]

Despite the intriguing nature of such decrees, it is far from clear from the Acts text itself that such predictions are in view.[26] Indeed, nothing whatsoever is said about prophets or predictions. To be fair to Judge, he does acknowledge the difficulty in connecting such decrees to Acts—1 and 2 Thessalonians seem much clearer—and attempts to overcome this problem by entering some evidence for the personal loyalty oath to the emperor as the basis on which the accusers would raise the issue of prediction.[27] From two relatively new pieces of evidence (from Cyprus and Samos), it appears that, at least in some cases, local magistrates such as the politarchs were responsible for administering this oath.[28] Such evidence has the overwhelming advantage of relating to what Acts actually says.[29]

Yet at just this point it is worth observing that, hermeneutically speaking, we must be wary of beginning our exegetical interpretation from a reconstructed conception of ancient imperial δόγματα. That is to say, the historical evidence adduced by Judge and others has inestimable importance in helping to create the background against which we might see the ruckus in Thessalonica, but such a background should not be substituted for the Acts text itself.

Indeed, the political problem in Acts' version of the events in Thessalonica is unambiguous: there is a rival King. Lest there remain any doubt, Luke's careful use of ἕτερος should remove it. In the eyes of its opponents, Christian proclamation positions a King inescapably over against Caesar. There is *another* King. Precisely in such counter-claims, argue the opponents, do the Christians run afoul of the δόγματα Καίσαρος. Surely this is really the only sensible way to take the Greek sentence: the practice against the decrees of Caesar is saying that there is a contender for the imperial throne, namely, Jesus.[30]

Hans Conzelmann, however, questions whether βασιλεύς is really meant to refer to the Roman emperor "since elsewhere [Luke] always calls the emperor Καῖσαρ."[31] Leaving aside the fact that Luke elsewhere also refers to the Roman emperor as κύριος (Acts 25:26), Conzelmann's worry might be furthered by the recollection of the widespread Roman aversion to the title *rex*. While such sentiment obviously ran deepest in the Republican period—think only of Cicero's *De Re Publica*[32]—it is significant indeed that, as Fergus Millar notes, "[n]o emperor ever used the title *rex*, or (we may confidently assume) seriously considered doing so."[33]

Yet, as Millar knows as well as anyone else, the wider historical picture is more complicated. For one thing, at least when thinking about a city like Thessalonica, it is important to note that there were no actual kings in the vicinity. It is true, of course, that Roman practice had long included establishing "client kings" on the frontier zones of the empire (e.g., the Herodians in Palestine[34]), but such figures were nowhere near the second district of Macedonia.[35] Thus the intended referent of the comparison, if not the Roman emperor, would be—to put it mildly—rather imprecise. To what βασιλεύς could Luke possibly be referring?

In fact, as Conzelmann himself actually notes with reference to the *Acta Isidori*,[36] the Roman emperor could be referred to as βασιλεύς. What Conzelmann did not notice, however, was that such a reference was not an isolated occurrence. Though it is too much to say, with Winfried Elliger, that βασιλεύς "war im Osten die offizielle Bezeichnung für den rmischen Kaiser (vgl. Joh 19,12; I Petr 2.13.17; I Clem 61,1),"[37] it is clearly the case that writers in the East could refer to the emperor as βασιλεύς. Lucian, for example, does this in his short work *The Eunuch* (3),[38] and Dio Chrysostom composed at least four— possibly five—orations for Trajan on the subject of kingship.[39] Dio's praises of the virtues of the good king are obvious references to Trajan, even as his condemnations of the vices of bad kings point directly to previous rulers. On this particular occasion, that the Emperor Nero is one of the intended comparisons with Trajan could hardly be plainer:

> One king, having become enamored with singing, spent his time warbling and wailing in the theaters and so far forgot his royal dignity that he was content to impersonate the early kings upon the stage; another fell in love with flute-playing; but the good king never makes a practice even of listening to such things.[40]

Even in the West, Seneca's treatise for Nero *De Clementia* draws repeatedly on a long tradition of philosophical reflection on kingship in order to encourage the young "prince" toward good rule.[41] Indeed, Seneca redeploys Virgil's image of a "king bee" from the *Georgics* to characterize the importance of the role Nero must play in keeping the *pax Romana*: "While their *rex* is safe, all are of one mind; when he is lost, they break their fealty."[42] It may well be that Seneca's treatise stands "alone in systematically using *rex* in a favourable sense,"[43] but it was hardly alone, as the work of Stefan Weinstock has shown, in its complex negotiation between past and present notions of kingship vis-à-vis the Roman ruler. After all, a statue of no less than Julius Caesar himself was placed on the Capitol with both the kings of Rome and L. Brutus, "who had liberated Rome from the tyranny of Tarquinius Superbus."[44]

Moreover, the fact is significant—and quite close to home, as it were—that certain Jewish revolutionaries were known to have fit the mold of "king," at least according to Josephus. Judas the Galilean's son Menahem, for example, returned as a βασιλεύς to Jerusalem from a raid on Herod's armory and promptly became the leader of the revolution.[45] And the ruthless leader of the last stages of the Jewish War, Simon bar Giora, purposefully donned the unmistakable royal purple for the dramatic scene of his capture.[46] Yet not only Jews but also pagan leaders of στάσις against Roman order could be styled as βασιλεύς, as was the principal figure in a Sicilian slave revolt.[47]

The objective here is not to pile up information to fill in a scholarly lacuna, but rather to press the point that the figure to whom King Jesus is juxtaposed is beyond doubt the Roman emperor.[48] It is therefore entirely unclear why Judge dismisses out of hand—with no more than an assertion—the charge of treason (*maiestas*) as relevant to this passage.[49] It may be that we have no extant evidence of an imperial δόγμα that says explicitly "Caesar is the only βασιλεύς; rivals to the throne will be charged with treason."[50] But this is to read δόγμα in an overly literalist manner and, further, to miss the practical connection between sedition (*seditio*) and treason (*maiestas*). As we saw in the previous chapter in relation to Paul's trials, to charge someone with *seditio* is in fact to accuse them of treason. Indeed, as in John 19:12—"everyone who claims to be a King sets himself against the Emperor"—so here in Acts the connection is actually made explicit: the Christians are seditious precisely because of their treasonous acclamation. Jesus, not Caesar, is King.

King Jesus

It is not without reason that the majority of previous interpreters have assumed—in accordance with a larger understanding of Luke's apologetic purpose—that the charges brought against the Christian missionaries in Thessalonica were false, that is, that Luke's literary project is to narrate the charge of "another King" out of the picture.[51] As we saw in the last chapter, Luke does tell of charges against the Christians precisely for the purpose of displaying the Christians' innocence of these charges. And, indeed, the politarchs' release of the Christians at the conclusion of the scene in Thessalonica exhibits narratively their innocence of sedition.

As with many passages in Acts, however, things are seldom as simple as they seem. In point of fact, it was no secret that the early Christians acclaimed Jesus as βασιλεύς. Luke was no exception.

From the very beginning of Luke's Gospel, Jesus is cast in a royal role when the angel Gabriel declares that "the Lord God will give to him the throne of his father David, and he will reign [βασιλεύσει] over the house of Jacob forever; and of his kingdom [βασιλεία] there will be no end" (Luke 1:32–33). As the narrative progresses it is thus not surprising to find Jesus himself preaching repeatedly about the βασιλεία τοῦ θεοῦ, or to observe that Luke—here changing the text of both Mark and Psalm 118—deliberately inserts βασιλεύς into his citation of Ps 118:26 as Jesus enters Jerusalem: "Blessed is he who comes—*the King*—in the name of the Lord."[52] Moreover, Luke understands well that βασιλεύς is the interpretation of χριστός that would best make sense to a Roman official. "This man," say Jesus's accusers to Pontius Pilate, "claims he is the Christ, a king" (Luke 23:2, τοῦτον ... λέγοντα ἑαυτὸν χριστὸς βασιλεὺς εἶναι). Tellingly, Pilate's response simply leaves χριστός out: "Are you, then, the βασιλεύς of the Jews?" Finally, of course, the title βασιλεύς—publicly exhibited in an inscription—signifies the political nature of Jesus's crucifixion: though innocent, Jesus is crucified as a seditious rebel (23:38).

It is true that other than here in Thessalonica Luke does not explicitly call Jesus βασιλεύς in Acts. Yet it is scarcely possible that a Christian reader of Acts in the late first or early second century would not know that Christian claims about Jesus's identity as the Christ entailed royal claims as well, or that the advent and resurrection of Jesus was the coming of the Kingdom of God. Indeed, at the very beginning of Acts, when Luke summarizes the content of Jesus's teaching to the disciples during his post-resurrection forty-day appearance, he specifies it as "the things of the Kingdom of God" (1:3). And when Philip arrives in Samaria, he preaches good news about "the Kingdom of God and the name of Jesus Christ" (8:12). Paul, too, of course preached and argued in the synagogue about the Kingdom of God (e.g., 19:8), and characterizes his own ministry as "preaching the Kingdom" (19:25). In fact, Luke's well-crafted final sentence of Acts does nothing if not make explicit the connection between the Kingdom of God and Jesus for the importance of understanding the narrative as a whole: "And he lived [in Rome] for two years ... preaching the Kingdom of God and teaching about the Lord Jesus Christ boldly and unhindered" (28:30–31).

In light of the explicit emphasis on the "royal" dimensions of Jesus's identity and Christian proclamation, we can well understand why F. F. Bruce could say of the accusation in Thessalonica that "there was just enough truth in the charge to make it plausible."[53] Jesus is King, and the reality that attends his life, death, and resurrection is named the Kingdom of God. Christian proclamation and mission entailed the announcement of this new reality, the Kingdom. It is this fact that prompts C. K. Barrett to assert that "[t]he (deliberate?) misunderstanding of Paul's message to mean that Jesus is another king (and thus a rival to Caesar) is one that must have occurred frequently. It was easy to reject, probably not so easy to dispose of."[54] That misunderstanding of the politics of Paul's message occurred frequently is doubtless correct.

Yet Barrett's remark stands in need of considerable refinement. Such a charge was *not* easy to reject, and for good reason. It is correct to say that Jesus is not a rival to Caesar in the sense that the former does not want the throne of the latter. But Luke would contest that the implication of this kind of politics is that Jesus's kingdom is entirely elsewhere than on earth (cf. John 18:36). As an example of this latter mode of thought, we may consult Eusebius, who tells of some early Christians (descendents of Jesus's brother Judas, so Eusebius thinks) that characterized the kingdom in purely spiritual terms. Having been hauled before the Emperor Domitian to give account of their practices, the Christians

> were asked concerning the Christ and his kingdom, its nature, origin, and time of appearance. They explained that was neither of the world nor earthly, but heavenly and angelic, and it would be at the end of the world, when he would come in glory to judge the living and the dead and to reward every man according to his deeds.[55]

That such a kingdom was not threatening to the imperial order is confirmed by the emperor's response to the Christians: "At this, Domitian did not condemn them at all, but despised them as simple folk, released them, and decreed an end to the persecution against the church."[56] So, too, Justin Martyr, whose mid-second century *apologia* to the Roman emperor attempted to undermine the rationale for the persecution of Christians, distinguished the Christian kingdom from Caesar's when he wrote that "when you hear we are looking for a kingdom, you unjustly suppose that we speak of a human kingdom (ἀνθρώπινον), whereas we speak of one with God (μετὰ θεοῦ)."[57]

In some contrast to the particular formulations of Eusebius and Justin, the narrative of Acts negotiates this tension between heaven and earth with much more complexity. For Luke, the kingdom is obviously not a "human kingdom" in the straightforward simplistic sense, and in this way the Christian mission does not threaten Rome as did, for example, the Parthian kingdom. Yet, against every Gnosticizing impulse, the vision in Acts is of a kingdom that is every bit as much a human presence as it is a divine work. That is, the kingdom of which Jesus is King is not simply "spiritual" but also material and social, which is to say that it takes up space in public. The very fact of the disturbance in Thessalonica—that *this* is what happens—attests to the publicly disruptive consequences of the conversions (17:4). There is no such thing, at least in Acts, as being a Christian in private.[58]

The tension that surrounds the earthly nature of the Kingdom mirrors that of the charges against the Christians in Thessalonica. For the opponents' accusations are at one and the same time both true and false. They are false in that they attempt to place Jesus in competitive relation to Caesar. Such a positioning can only lead to a politics of revolt. The accusations are true, however, in that the Christian mission entails a call to another way of life, one that is—on virtually every page of the Acts of the Apostles—turning the world upside down.

Turning to Practice

The remainder of this chapter explores the generative dynamics that underlie the narrative logic of the scene in Acts 17:1–9—in short, that make its construction as a scene intellectually possible. Inasmuch as the trouble in Thessalonica encapsulates the tension encountered in reading chapters 2 and 3 together, the following discussion is an extended argument for a way of thinking the juxtaposition of these earlier chapters.

But why, it might reasonably be asked, focus on practices? Why not simply select and discuss Lukan "theological themes"? Luke believes in A, rejects B, holds fast to C, and waffles on D—*ergo* the tension in his work.[59]

The answer is of course complex, but for the sake of letting the argument unfold through the discussion of the text of Acts itself, it will suffice at this juncture to make three principal points. (1) The tension we have been exploring is a *lived* tension, which is to say that Acts narrates the conflict that surrounds its presentation of an alternative way of life as a result of certain practices, or a pattern of life. Though Paul does once argue in the σχολή of Tyrannus (Acts 19:9),[60] the larger debate over how to read the world does not occur behind conference tables in a placid university auditorium—or in Plato's Academy—but in the rough and tumble everyday life of various cities around the Roman empire. That it does so attests not so much to Luke's snubbing of the intellectuals—indeed, he would doubtless have taken all comers—as it does to the fact that the public face of Christianity according to Acts was constituted by its practical life. To read Acts rightly, then, we must attend to the practical base of ecclesiological narration.

(2) The hermeneutical attempt with the language of "core practices" is to point to the essential importance of these particular practices for the tension we are trying to think. Remove any one of these practices from the narrative and the tension dissolves and disappears. Conversely, attending to the narrative shape of these practices according to Acts brings us to the generative locus of the tension.

Indeed, the overall narrative importance of these practices—the way in which they are actually narrativized by Luke—is deep enough that to extricate them from the story Acts tells is to unravel it altogether.[61] As important as baptism is to Acts and to Christian theology, for example, one can conceive of an Acts-like narrative without baptism or with a different "ritual" that took the

place of baptism (a "thank offering" upon entering the community, for example).[62] By stark contrast, one cannot conceive of an Acts-like narrative without
mission. Nor can one conceive of Acts' narration of cultural disruption—the
political worries, for example, of the Romans and/or Jews—without the formation of concrete communities with noticeably different patterns of life. Like
many a soapbox preacher on the streets of major U.S. cities today, there were
always "babblers" in the ancient agoras to whom no one paid any mind (cf.
Acts 17:18b). Absent the necessity to establish communities of Christians, Paul
could have hawked his strange spiritual wares without much worry. That both
mission and the formation of community are, according to Acts, the explication of Jesus's identity as the Lord of all points not only to the indispensability
of this confession for the entire narrative but also to the necessary interdepen-
dence of the three core practices: to see one is necessarily to look at the others.
Thus our focus below should not be understood as a delineation of three
formally separate practices but rather more like an attempt to direct attention
constructively toward the total practical-theological pattern that produces the
tension inherent to the vision of Acts.

(3) Reading Acts for its core practices does not mean, however, that we opt
for "doing" over "thinking." Because all practices are theory-laden, and because theorizing is itself a kind of practice that is always tied to a concrete *Sitz
im Leben*, such a doing-or-thinking dichotomy presents a false antithesis.[63] We
can never focus simply on doing. Moreover, the text of Acts embeds Christian
practices in a story and in so doing gives them a particular narrative shape.[64]
The early Christian practice of confessing Jesus as Lord, for example, is not
simply reported or repeated but is worked out narratively to make certain
claims about Jesus and the God of Israel, particularly vis-à-vis the Roman
emperor. Thus to attend to core practices in Acts is to attend to their complex
narrative shape and, hence, to elucidate the unity of thought and life that
requires us to read chapters 2 and 3 together.

Confessing Jesus as Lord of All

That the early Christians confessed Jesus as κύριος is known to every NT
scholar. What has not been seen until recently is the degree to which Luke in
particular systematically and with narrative artistry develops this confession in
his Gospel.[65] It is no different in Acts.

It would of course be a fascinating study to trace the narrative contour of
the one hundred or so times κύριος is used in Luke's second volume, but such a
book-length project cannot here be undertaken. Instead, we shall simply focus

on one passage in which the occurrence of the κύριος confession encapsulates much of what is central to our reading of Acts. From there, we shall be able to make the necessary further connections between this confession and its practical corollaries.

Cornelius the centurion is a well-known character to all attentive readers of Acts. This is not surprising: the passages within which he figures are crucial to the overall narrative movement of Acts. Moreover, as I have argued elsewhere, Acts 10:24–48 in particular is central to any serious discussion about the political shape of the larger book. Several points from my earlier article are worth reiterating for the sake of the present discussion.[66]

First, it is crucial to note the essential narrative and theological importance of Acts 10 in the overall story Acts seeks to tell. Narratively, Saul has been transformed from violent persecutor of the ecclesia to God's "elect vessel" to the gentiles (9:5). The story then moves immediately to justify theologically Paul's mission to gentiles through Peter's experience with Cornelius. This theological justification via the movement of the narrative persists through Acts 11:18 where the story returns to Saul to speak about his ministry in Antioch (11:25–26, 30; 12:25). Acts 10 thus displays the events on which the mission to the gentiles turns.

Second, the climax of Acts 10 is Peter's speech in Cornelius' house wherein the gospel is proclaimed to the gentiles for the first time. Though there is plenteous scholarly hypothesizing about earlier forms of Peter's speech, its current locus in Acts reveals remarkable care on Luke's part to set well the "Roman" stage for Peter's proclamation. The vision is given in the city founded and named for the Roman Caesar; the vision is given to a ranking member of the Roman military; the unit in which he serves had its origins and namesake in Italy; and there is at least one other soldier who is explicitly mentioned (10:7).

Furthermore, Luke heightens the readers' awareness of Cornelius' gentileness, as it were, by narrating his first response to Peter as one typical of a pious or reverential gentile. When Peter entered the centurion's house, writes Luke, "Cornelius met him and fell down at his feet and worshipped him" (10:25). It is not always easy to know how much force to assign to προσκυνεῖν, which admittedly can have a wide range of meaning in the ancient world (worship/obeisance), but in this context Peter's response leaves little room for serious debate about its breadth. "Get up!" says Peter, lifting Cornelius off the ground, "I, too, am only a human being!" Here Peter's "speech-act," like that of Paul and Barnabas in Lystra in Acts 14 (cf. esp. 14:15), marks clearly the boundary between the God of Israel and human beings. Human beings, no matter how exalted, are not to be worshipped.

Third, received by its auditors as the "word of the Lord" (cf. 10:33), Peter's speech makes a dramatic and bold christological claim. This claim is often obscured by those translations (e.g., RSV) and commentators (e.g., Barrett) that take οὗτός ἐστιν πάντων κύριος in 10:36 as a parenthetical remark. It is doubtless the case that the Greek of 10:36–37 is less than perfectly smooth and easy. But it is not so bad as to prevent a translation that draws out the force of the claim:

> You know the word which he sent to the people of Israel preaching
> peace through Jesus Christ: this one is Lord of all. You know what has
> happened throughout the whole of Judaea, beginning in Galilee after
> the baptism which John preached, as God anointed with the Holy
> Spirit and power Jesus of Nazareth, who went about benefacting and
> healing all who were oppressed by the devil, for God was with him.

As this translation illustrates, οὗτός ἐστιν πάντων κύριος is hardly peripheral to Peter's point. Indeed, the use of οὗτος makes clear that the identity of Jesus Christ as κύριος πάντων is made known in just such a way as to draw attention to its uniqueness. *This one*, and not someone else, is the Lord of all.[67]

It is a demonstrable fact, of course, that there were "many gods and many lords"—to use Paul's language—in the gentile realm. Indeed, Roscher's classic dictionary of Greek and Roman mythology devotes no less than fourteen pages to the entry on κύριος alone.[68] Yet, within the narrative of Acts, the more immediate counterpart to the οὗτος of Acts 10:36 is the Roman emperor. This is true not only because of the careful way in which Luke fashions a Roman ethos for the Cornelius scene but also because of the inner-narrative semantic link created by the use of κύριος for the emperor within Acts itself.[69]

In Acts 25 a bewildered Festus tells King Agrippa II that his confusion about Paul's appeal to Caesar is not merely intellectual. Indeed, it has the practical consequence of rendering him incapable of writing the legally necessary letter to accompany his prisoner's transfer to Rome. About Paul, says Festus with reference to the Roman emperor, "I have nothing solid to write to the lord [τῷ κυρίῳ]" (25:26).

Luke is known for his care in character speech—his characters tend to speak as their real-life counterparts should—and Festus is no exception. His reference to Nero/Domitian as κύριος reflects perfectly the posture of a state appointee.[70] Indeed, taken narratively, the appearance of this appellation in the mouth of the Roman governor verbalizes the claims of Rome: the emperor is the κύριος, just as Festus says.

Of course, this point depends on the reality that the Roman emperor was in fact called κύριος. Prior to the publication of Deissmann's illuminating *Licht vom Osten* in the first decade of the twentieth century, some German scholars had accused Luke of gross anachronism in his use of κύριος for the Roman emperor. While later Caesars were indubitably called κύριος, so ran the argument, neither the Julio-Claudians nor the Flavians were. Moreover, claimed the scholars "in Tübingen and Berlin," this fact is reflected in the NT itself: nowhere else in the entirety of the NT is the emperor referred to as κύριος. But with the publication of Deissmann's work and the accumulation in the ensuing years of new discoveries and careful rereadings of older texts, the charge of anachronism has been thoroughly laid to rest.

Not only was the Roman emperor entitled κύριος/dominus—as we now know from vast amounts of material evidence, in addition to the literary sources—but such appellations were also given universal scope. Nero κύριος, for example, was acclaimed "the Lord of all the world" (τοῦ παντὸς κόσμου κύριος Νέρων) in the public inscription from Acraephiae that celebrated his restoration of freedom to Greece.[71] And Lucan, who wrote during the reign of Nero, could speak of the victor of the much earlier civil war between Julius Caesar and Pompey as "the Lord of the world" (dominus mundi; Lucan, 9.20),[72] as could Cicero (dominus omnium gentium).[73] Indeed, the god Janus, through the literary efforts of Martial, promised a long life to Domitian, "the Lord and God of the entire earth" (omni terrarium domino deoque; Epig. 8.2.5–6; cf. 5.8.1; 10.72.3). And Arrian's records of his teacher's discourses speak of the Roman Caesar as the "Lord of all" (ὁ πάντων κύριος καῖσαρ; Epictetus, Disc, 4.1.12).

But of course the universal range of the emperor's lordship is really no surprise, at least when we remember that to the denizens of the Mediterranean basin the Romans themselves were "the Lords of the inhabited world," as Josephus once put it (οἱ κύριοι...Ῥωμαῖοι τῆς οἰκουμένης; C. Ap. 2.41; LCL "entire universe").[74] The Smyrnans, therefore, were simply following an established tradition of thought about Rome and her emperor when they acclaimed Trajan as "κύριος of all" (τῶν ὅλων κύριον; Dio Chrysostom, Or, 45.4). Insofar as the emperor was the absolute ruler of the world, he was without question the κύριος πάντων.

For this reason Luke's use of κύριος for Jesus and the Roman emperor in Acts requires the reader to think through a startling juxtaposition: both Jesus and the Roman Caesar are called κύριος; yet it is Jesus Christ, not the emperor, who is named the κύριος πάντων.[75] The universal scope of the emperor's lordship is thus implicitly denied even as it is explicitly ascribed to Jesus. In the language of the book of Revelation, it is Jesus who is the "Lord of lords" (κύριος κυρίων; cf. 1 Tim 6:15).

The startling nature of the claim in Acts goes deeper, however, than a mere denial of the emperor's ultimate lordship. Indeed, it reaches down to the foundations of what it might mean to be κύριος πάντων in the first place.

When thought about in the total context of Acts, that is, the juxtaposition of the two κύριοι does not simply reveal a substitution of names—whereas we used to think that the Roman emperor was Lord of all atop the pyramid of powers, we now know that it is actually Jesus—but instead discloses a basic contradiction in terms of the content of universal lordship.

It is not exactly a scholarly revolution to observe that the lordship of the Roman emperor had primarily to do with military prowess. It is unsurprising, for example, that the majority of the statues of the emperor we know about portray him in military dress,[76] or that a coin from Laodicea pictures an imperial temple with the word ἐπινείκιός ("warlike," "contentious") across the architrave,[77] or that the emperor was symbolically—or theologically—associated with Mars Ultor in the capital of the empire itself.[78] It really could not have been otherwise: the visual or material articulation of what it was to be the emperor of the Roman Empire was inextricably bound with the power of the Roman army. Rome's ability to lord it over its subjected peoples was precisely its ability to defeat and destroy them violently. In this sense, Rome's "foreign policy"—its political relation to the other—was not, as Susan Mattern put it in her interesting book, "a complex geopolitical chess game." It was, rather, "a competition for status" that entailed "much violent demonstration of superior prowess, aggressive posturing, and terrorization of the opponent."[79]

To belabor a point now well recognized in the study of ancient Rome: the *pax* of the pax Romana was at the very least more complex than the panegyrical remarks of Virgil, Velleius, and others would suggest. Indeed, seen from the perspective of the dominated, the pax Romana may well be rendered best—if in somewhat of an extended form—as the *pacification* of other peoples by Rome.[80] As even Tacitus was able to see, the peace of Rome was in reality little more than ruthless *domination* for those on its underside. "Today," says the British leader Calgacus in the speech Tacitus writes for him,

> the uttermost parts of Britain are laid bare; there are no other tribes
> to come; nothing but sea and cliffs and these more deadly
> Romans ... Raptors of the world, now that earth fails their all-
> devastating hands, they probe even the sea: if their enemy has wealth,
> they have greed; if he is poor, they are ambitious; neither East nor West
> has satiated them ... To plunder, butcher, and ravage—these things they
> falsely name Empire [*imperium*]: they make a desolation and call it Peace
> [*pacem*].[81]

As this remark suggests, the pacifying reality of the Roman *pax* was of course well enough understood in the ancient world, indeed, to the point that Rome's power for subjugation was routinely celebrated in public monuments. One could think immediately of the famous Arch of Titus that depicts Rome's brutal destruction of Jerusalem and humiliating victory over the Jews in AD 70. Or, to think of another prominent example, the superscription to Augustus' *Res Gestae* on the temple of Roma and Augustus in Ancyra gets right to the point: "Below is a copy of the acts of the Divine Augustus by which he subjected [*subiecit*] the entire world under the imperium of the Roman people."[82] But probably it was Lucan, himself no stranger to both the benefaction and bane of imperial politics, who best captured the irony inherent to the Roman emperor's identity as κύριος/ *dominus* of the world.

Writing about the civil war that ended the republic, Lucan asks through his character Nigidius Figulus, "And what good is it to pray to the gods for an end? *Peace will come with a Master [Cum Domino pax ista venit]*. Prolong, O Rome, a continuing series of sufferings and draw out the destruction for many ages: you will be free only as long as the civil war lasts."[83] Figulus' "prophecy" that a *dominus* was the only one who could bring peace in the midst of civil war was but Lucan's (very) thinly veiled criticism of contemporary imperial tyranny,[84] even as the reference to the impotence of the gods gestured poetically toward the overwhelming and godlike power of the sovereign ruler.[85] Sheldon Wolin may be right that Lucan's remark summarizes Augustus' principate as a whole, but we would be remiss, as Wolin knows, were we to restrict the relevance of the remark to the early empire. Indeed, precisely because Lucan grasped so clearly the political connection between a godlike *dominus* and violence that was given the name of *pax*, his remarks can serve well as "the epitaph of Roman politics."[86] To be the κύριος/*dominus* of the Roman Empire was to embody militarily the political claim to universal and ultimate authority, a claim that, in the end, can only be understood in relation to the realm of the gods.

Specifying exactly what is meant by saying that the Roman emperor was "divine" or a "god" has long entailed a complicated discussion. Not only has it been difficult to avoid "Christianizing" assumptions in the analysis of pagan conceptions of divinity, but it has also proved exceedingly difficult (1) to trace with precision the changes that occurred from one emperor to the next, (2) to draw out the probable differences in perception and evaluation of the emperor between, say, the Roman Senate and the populus, (3) to know when to prefer the *Tendenz* of one ancient writer to another, and (4) to account sufficiently for the dramatically local character of the theological construals that lie behind the diverse expressions of devotion to the emperor.[87]

Thankfully, for our purposes we do not have to sort out all the difficulties of these multifaceted problems. Instead, we may simply and, given the complexity of the topic, briefly focus on a few matters that are both constitutive of the divine identity of the emperor and relevant to the overall vision of Acts.

On any reading of the evidence, it would be difficult after the work of Paul Zanker, Simon Price, Steven Friesen, Manfred Clauss and others to overestimate the significance of the transformation of public space in the imperial period to reflect—or "construct"—the importance of the emperor. Zanker is of course correct that the material production of Rome begun under Augustus evidenced an intricately conceived centralized program geared toward the unity of the empire, but Price is no less insightful in pointing out that such a unity did not come about in a simple "top-down" manner. Instead, the provinces themselves actively participated in its creation.[88] Ephesus, for example, a city from which the remaining evidence is particularly rich, was massively remodeled during the Flavian regime, but it would be a mistake to see such a building campaign as imposed from the outside. It reflects, rather, the city's intraprovincial competition and desire to garner favor and attention from Rome. With respect to the role of the Roman emperor, the movement from Rome outward toward its provinces was mirrored, that is, by a movement from the provinces inward toward Rome. Rome and its provinces together built the reality that placed the emperor at the center of the world.

In the modern period we are tempted to read such a remarkable phenomenon as the centrality of the Roman emperor in strictly political terms (Rome was expanding and consolidating its power; to do so it obviously needed to place the emperor at the center, etc.). But a dichotomy between politics and religion gets us almost nowhere with respect to the Roman emperor. Indeed, a striking overall feature of this bidirectional move that placed the emperor at the center of the empire was that it was simultaneously religious, which is to say that the emperor was interpreted theologically. As Clifford Ando notes in his erudite book, "[T]he position of Augustus atop the empire allowed the Mediterranean world to share a deity for the first time."[89] Thus did the political practice of the "cult" carry with it—it both presupposed and produced—the understanding that the sphere of the gods was the place in which the emperor belonged.[90]

Indeed, as a whole, the Greek world showed little to no compunction in addressing the emperor, both living and dead, as θεός. Some intellectuals—at least by the time of Porphyry—worried, for example, about the precise meaning of sacrifice vis-à-vis the living emperor.[91] But the vastly more prevalent sense of the emperor is well reflected in an inscription from Cyzicus in Anatolia, which reads:

> Since the new Sun Gaius Caesar Sebastos Germanicus wanted to cast
> his own rays also on the attendant kings of his empire, so that the

greatness of his immortality should be in this matter, too, the more splendid, though the kings, even if they racked their brains, were not able to find appropriate ways of repaying their benefactions to express their gratitude to such a great god [τηλικοῦτος θεός].

"As a result of the favor of Gaius Caesar," the inscription continues a few lines later, such men "have become kings in the joint government of such great gods [εἰς συναρχίαν τηλικούτων θεῶν], and the favors of the gods [θεῶν] differ from a purely human succession as much as day differs from night and eternal from human nature."[92]

It has of course been observed on more than one occasion that the distinction in Latin between *deus* and *divus* potentially allowed for further theological refinement in the West.[93] But in fact a consistent demarcation along linguistic lines has been harder to establish than once thought, and what may be true of "official" usage (e.g., the Senate's consistent use of *divus* for the dead emperor) was not necessarily so of unofficial, popular, or even poetic usage.[94] That is, whatever the theoretical precision of the Latin language, in practice "traditional" gods could be referred to as *divus* and emperors could be called *deus*. Jupiter, Mars, Minerva, and others were not only *dei/dii* but also *divi*.[95] Pliny the Younger, for example, speaks of Jupiter Capitolinus as the *divus* who protects the *princeps*, bestows benefits, and hears prayers.[96] For the emperors, Ovid remains an obvious case in point—Augustus is repeatedly called *deus*[97]—but Suetonius could also speak of Claudius' *consecratio* as his being enrolled *in numerum deorum* (*Claudius*, 45),[98] and Seneca could say that "we believe [Augustus] to be a *deum*" (*De Clem.* 1.10.3).[99] Thus, in order not to impose overly simplistic conceptual distinctions on the evidence and to avoid backsliding into the invisible realm of "what people *really* thought," we should simply take the point that the emperor was a god. By no means did this erase the emperor's humanity.[100] But as Domitian knew well, to be *dominus* was also to be *deus*.[101] Or, to put it in the language of the NT, to be κύριος was to be θεός.[102]

And so it must be. As political and legal theorists from Carl Schmitt to Giorgio Agamben have taught us, to be the κύριος πάντων (or Sovereign) both presupposes and requires a life that transcends the normal human realm, that overcomes, as it were, the limitedness inherent to human situatedness and finitude. This kind of sovereignty entails further, if we were to try to visualize the conceptual schema, a kind of space in which the Lord stands outside of the system over which he presides or even creates, a "zone"—to use Agambem's term—in which the legal and political elements of human life are suspended and from which they are created and legitimized.[103] This does not mean that

Lord of all entirely forgoes participation within the system, but it does mean that he is the "external" founder of a total political reality.[104] In short, the κύριος πάντων must be divine (or at the very least uniquely connected to the divine).[105] Social contract advocates since Rousseau have naturally tried to dispense with this necessity—as has the modern world in general—or at least to restate it in terms of the power of "the People." But the ancients knew better. Ultimate sovereignty entails divinity. The Roman emperor was a god.

And therein lies the central, animating fact behind Luke's juxtaposition of Jesus Christ and the Roman emperor: the Christians have to deny what the Roman emperor has to be. Just because the Imperial god's declaration of ultimate lordship simultaneously demanded the practice of divine worship, it could not help but to rival the God of Israel. Where the ancient pagans would doubtless agree that "[t]he emperor's overwhelming and intrusive power had to be represented not in terms of a local hero but of a universal god," Luke would say instead, as he put it in Acts 17:24, that there is only one "Lord of heaven and earth" (οὗτος οὐρανοῦ καὶ γῆς ὑπάρχων κύριος).[106] The Roman emperor's claim to be the κύριος πάντων is at its core the usurpation by a human being of the identity that belongs to the God of Israel alone.

But could not the same be said about Jesus, a fully human being to whom Acts ascribes universal lordship? Indeed, was it not Peter himself—the one who proclaimed Jesus as κύριος πάντων—who said in Acts 5:29, "We must obey God rather than human beings"?

In contrast to the emperor, the ultimate Lordship of Jesus Christ in Acts just is the Lordship of God. Indeed, the God of Israel and Jesus Christ do not stand in competition for the designation κύριος but rather share this identity. In case there is any doubt about this, we may dispense with it by a brief recollec- tion of the use of the OT in Acts 2:16–21, where Peter counters the charge of drunkenness with a citation of Joel 3:1–5 (LXX). " 'And in the last days,' says God [ὁ θεός], 'I will pour out my Spirit ... and show wonders ... before the day of the Lord [κυρίου] comes, that great and manifest day. And it shall be that whoever calls on the name of the Lord [τὸ ὄνομα κυρίου] shall be saved."

In a way that bears a material resemblance to Paul's use of Joel 3:5 in Rom 10:13, Luke's use of Joel here involves a christological extension of the use of κύριος in the OT.[107] Whereas κύριος in the Joel text taken alone refers only to the God of Israel, in the context of Acts 2, κύριος refers both to the God of Israel and to Jesus, the only name by which there is salvation (see Acts 4:12). It is not the case, that is, that what we see in this text is a simple substitution of one κύριος for another—as if the κύριος of Joel 3:5 no longer applies to God.[108] Instead, Luke's hermeneutical appropriation of the OT reflects a rather more complex theological move, one in which the prophecy of the text of Joel is expanded—

not negated—to say that the *Lord God*'s coming is actually and really fulfilled in the appearance of the *Lord Jesus*.[109] That such a christological expansion of the identity of God does not, in the Acts of the Apostles, threaten the God of Israel is at once confirmed by taking notice of the actual speaker of the Joel text. It is God himself who proclaims that his eschatological coming is the coming of the κύριος Jesus.

The christological extension of the use of κύριος in an OT text is not limited to Joel 3. Indeed, just a few verses later, the use of ὁ κύριος in Ps 15:8 (LXX) is taken to refer to Jesus. David prophesied the resurrection of Jesus because he "foresaw the Lord forever" standing before him (προορώμην τὸν κύριον ἐνώπιόν μου διὰ παντός; Acts 2:25).[110] And the first use of ὁ κύριος in James' citation of Amos 9 in Acts 15:16–17 refers doubly, in the logic of the narrative of Acts, to the God of the OT and to Jesus. "After this," says God, "I will rebuild the dwelling of David . . . and I will set it up, that the rest of humanity may seek the Lord." Lest we be tempted to say that here κύριος should be restricted to God,[111] we should remember the beginning of the gentile mission in Cornelius' house wherein Jesus is proclaimed to the gentiles as κύριος, the Philippian jailer who is told to have faith in the κύριος Jesus (16:31), the preaching of "the word of the Lord," and so on. Throughout the gentile mission in Acts, that is, the "rest of humanity" turns to the κύριος God precisely through turning to the κύριος Jesus, or, as Paul puts it to the Ephesian elders, through "repentance toward God and faith in our κύριος Jesus" (20:21). In short, Acts 10:36 and 17:24 are not contradictory but complimentary, mutually interpreting and reinforcing. "Jesus Christ—this one is Lord of all" parallels theologically "[t]he God who made the world and everything in it—this one, [is] Lord of heaven and earth." God's universal Lordship is expressed in the Lordship of Jesus Christ.

When carried through to its political conclusion, Luke's theological move requires us to reverse the customary thought patterns about Jesus and Caesar in NT scholarship. Contra Horsley, Wright, Crossan, Reed, and others, Jesus does not challenge Caesar's status as Lord, as if Jesus were somehow originally subordinate to Caesar in the order of being. The thought—at least in its Lukan form—is rather much more radical and striking: because of the nature of his claims, it is Caesar who is the rival; and what he rivals is the Lordship of God in the person of Jesus Christ.

Yet, we would be mistaken were we to think that this rivalry takes place on a level playing field—an ontological basis, say, that is deeper than both Jesus and Caesar—as if there were two competitors playing for the same prize, the title κύριος πάντων. In this way of thinking, κύριος πάντων is something separable from Jesus himself, a trophy, as it were, that he (rather than Caesar) wins. But in Luke's way of thinking, κύριος πάντων is who "Jesus" is: Jesus is completely inseparable from his identity as the universal Lord.[112] Caesar's rivalry thus takes the form of wrongful (self-) exaltation to the sphere whose existence is exactly concomitant with the identity of God in Jesus Christ. Politics, that is, inevitably involves the question of idolatry.[113] From the perspective of the Graeco-Roman world, therefore, things are indeed upside down: Jesus's lordship is primary—ontologically and, hence, politically—not Caesar's.

In Luke's vision, the practical corollary of the primacy of God in Jesus Christ is, to employ contemporary language, the primacy of peace and service.[114] Where the lordship of the Roman emperor entailed a *pax* predicated upon pacifying strength and terror, the lordship of Jesus, so Luke believed, produced a revaluation of the world's sense of *pax*. If the Caesars could be called "peacemaker,"[115] it was not without the realization that their form of peace was tied to a still deeper possibility of military violence. As Seneca would have the young Nero to say:

> I am the arbiter of life and death for the nations; it rests in my power what each man's lot and state shall be; by my lips Fortune proclaims what gift she would bestow on each human being; from my utterance peoples and cities gather reasons for rejoicing; without my favor and grace no part of the wide world can prosper; all those many thousands of swords which my *pax* restrains will be drawn at my nod; what nations shall be utterly destroyed, which banished, which shall receive the gift of liberty, which have it taken from them, what kings shall become slaves and whose heads shall be crowned with royal honor, what cities shall fall and which shall rise—this it is mine to decree (*De Clem.* 1.1.2, LCL).

By stark contrast, in Luke and Acts, *pax* ($\epsilon i \rho \dot{\eta} \nu \eta$) is interpreted christologically, which is to say through the lens that is the life of Jesus of Nazareth. In the heart of the passage that initiated our discussion in this section—indeed, in the very sentence that leads to the $\kappa \acute{\upsilon} \rho \iota o s$ $\pi \acute{a} \nu \tau \omega \nu$ confession—Luke summarizes the gospel as the preaching of peace through Jesus Christ: "You know the word which he sent to the people of Israel preaching peace through Jesus Christ" (10:36).

Of the NT scholars who have explored the narrative theological significance of this phrase for Luke–Acts, Ulrich Mauser's concise treatment of fifteen years ago remains the most insightful.[116] The reason is rather simple. Mauser understands both the dramatic importance of this section of Acts—"much of the content of [Cornelius'] address is a thumbnail sketch of our fully developed Gospels"—and its overall relation to the rest of the Lukan corpus.[117] Such an attention span allows Mauser to see not only that for Luke *pax* is christologically shaped but also its converse, namely, that peace is the major practical category by which Luke interprets the life of Jesus: "In the Lukan writings . . . the word 'peace' comes close to becoming a theological term that captures the whole meaning of the Christ event."[118] The summary in 10:36, therefore, renders the "whole story of Jesus . . . a declaration of peace."[119]

Inasmuch as the story of Jesus is one that ends in crucifixion by the Romans—a radical subversion of the militant-triumphant (messianic) paradigm—the declaration of peace that issues forth from this life is also one of crucifixion, or subversion. Mauser is basically right of course that the book of Acts "is engaged in silent dialogue with the ideal of the Roman Peace," but Luke's side of the conversation should be seen for what it is: a subversion and rearrangement of the very notion of peace.[120]

Such a rearrangement, however, best makes sense not in isolation—as if the pax Romana were the only object of Luke's gaze—but as part of a larger conceptual field in which the Lordship of God through Jesus Christ determines theologically the practical outworking of life. Precisely because the character of the Lord is what it is in his life, the texture of peaceful Lordship turns out to be humble service. Naturally, we may think back to the beginning of Luke's Gospel where Jesus rejects Satan's tempting offer of authority over all the kingdoms of the world and the glory that comes therewith. Jesus is not that kind of King, as he makes clear in the entrance to Jerusalem (here, a King who comes to his crucifixion in the name of the κύριος and brings peace), and in his actual crucifixion ("the King of the Jews"), and as his disciples labor to reveal in Thessalonica ("another King"). But the most striking passage that pursues narratively the essential connection between Lordship and service is doubtless Jesus's admonition to his quarreling disciples.

Immediately after the Last Supper, where the disciples learn that the new covenant is made through Jesus's blood, they begin, once again, to bicker "about which one of them appeared to be the greatest" (Luke 22:24). To ears schooled by the realities of Graeco-Roman life, Jesus's response to his disciples' repeated quest for greatness would be nothing short of arresting:

> The kings of the gentiles exercise lordship over them; and those in authority over them are benefactors. But not so with you; rather let greatest among you become as the youngest, and the one who governs as the one who serves. For which is the greater, the one who reclines at the table or the one who serves? Isn't it the one who reclines? But I am in your midst as the one who serves (Luke 22:25–27).[121]

This response vividly recalls Jesus's parable in Luke 12—where the returning κύριος who finds his servants awake will serve them at table[122]—even as it adumbrates the startling moment in Peter's speech in Acts 10 where the κύριος πάντων is said "to have been put to death by hanging on a tree" (10:39).

For Luke as for Rome, to be the Lord of all is to be the "peacemaker." But the respective ways in which they construe this role could hardly be more different. For Luke and not for Rome, the *pax* of the *dominus mundi* is the kind of humble service that accepts its own suffering and death. The particular challenge entailed in the Roman emperor's claim to be the κύριος πάντων thus turns out to take the form of a violent refusal of the Lordship of Jesus Christ, the primacy of peace that is manifested in the willingness to serve God rather than humans through trial, suffering, and death.

That learning to confess Jesus as the κύριος πάντων in the way that his life demands was good practical training in suffering and death for the community that Acts seeks to form is evidenced not only in the way Luke's character "Paul" paradigmatically faces his own suffering,[123] trial, and impending death but also elsewhere in the NT and in the earliest examples of persecution against the Christians in the second century. Acts itself, of course, was not written under the same immediate firestorm as Revelation, nor was it composed in the heat of a local communal struggle of the kind we see in 1 Peter.[124] Moreover, the events that Acts relates took place significantly prior to the first records we have of Christians being brought to trial explicitly for their Christianity.[125] Indeed, there was no legal compulsion—at least in the upper strata of the juridical system—to participate in the cult of the Roman emperor until the middle of the third century under Decius. But these facts should not obscure the similarity that underlies the difference between official, systematic suppression at the highest levels and *ad hoc* persecution: as Acts relates in passage after passage, Christians were brought before provincial officials or local magistrates with the possibility of suffering and death, *ab initio*. Still less should these facts prevent us from seeing Acts' materially fundamental contribution to the rehearsal that prepared the Christians for the crises of persecution in the second century.

Precisely in learning to see Jesus Christ as the expression of the universal Lordship of the God of Israel were the Christians made ready to live the distinction drawn in Acts—in the contrasting speech of Peter and Festus— between Jesus and the Roman emperor. Where the demand would later come to worship and confess Caesar as κύριος under the threat of torture and death, those schooled by the narrative of Acts could detect the false claim of a usurper and the violent challenge to the basic priority of peace and service. That they could, further, pattern their response after that of Jesus and Paul, and hence go in peace to their own trial and death, is nothing less than the internal connection between christology and ecclesiology, or, to put it into literary terms, between Luke's first and second book.

Let me be clear: I am not arguing that Luke saw the trials of Christians and wrote a church history or character study of Paul as a response. Luke did not live next door to Pliny, and neither, it is likely, had he heard of Serennius Granianus, Minucius Fundanus, or any of the other Roman administrators who conducted official trials of the Christians vis-à-vis the κύριος Καῖσαρ. The argument, rather, is that basic to Luke's "upside down" epistemological commitments are the conviction that there really can be only one Lord of all and the corresponding sense for the necessity of a narrative whose deep structure evidences a refusal to flinch in the face of the inevitable religio-political repercussions. Polycarp, Speratus, the anonymous Christians mentioned in the *Ep. Diognetus* 7.7, Apollonius, and others may or may not have known the book of Acts. But both in their rejection of the universal Lordship of the Roman emperor and in their acceptance of its practical enforcement, they embodied a substantial portion of the theological vision that generates this text: the Lord of all is Jesus Christ.

Of course, the very existence of people who live such a confession presupposes the reality and success of Christian mission. Or, to put it another way, mission is that practice presupposed by all existing Christian communities, the fundament upon which their communal life was originally made possible. According to Acts, however, the basis for Christian mission is not internal to the notion of mission as such; rather, mission is the necessary response to the universal Lordship of God in Jesus Christ. The Lordship of God in Jesus engenders the practice of mission even as mission establishes the communities that witness to the Lord of all. To understand the universal Lordship of God in Jesus Christ we must thus turn first to mission and secondly to the Christian assembly.

Universal Mission

Inasmuch as the Acts of the Apostles is the only text in the NT actually to narrate the mission of the early church, scholars of early Christianity have long looked to Luke's second volume as the primary source with which to paint the picture of early Christian mission. This is so even where John Knox's dictum to prefer Paul over Luke when they conflict is taken as gospel truth: every scholar of history needs a narrative framework, and time and again, Acts turns out to provide much that is crucial in any particular outworking of the *Ausbreitung* of the early Christian movement.[126] The concern in this section, however, is not so much to reconstruct the historical developments that lie behind Acts as it is to focus on (1) the remarkable fact of Christian mission itself in the context of the ancient Mediterranean world, and (2) how Acts narrates this movement as the necessary explication of God's universal Lordship in Jesus. Though in fact (1) and (2) are interdependent, the latter can best be understood if seen against the background of the former. We thus begin with the significance that attends the sheer existence of Christian mission.

Because of the formative effects Christianity has had upon the entirety of Western society, it may be very difficult for us to unthink the necessity of mission as an essential element of vibrant religious life and to overcome the inevitable sense of strangeness that can accompany the encounter with pro-foundly non-missionary religion(s).[127] Yet this is precisely what we must do when thinking through the question of early Christian mission vis-à-vis the wider Graeco-Roman world around the end of the first century. To state it categorically in the words of Robin Lane Fox: exactly "none" of the pagan religions "had a strong missionary drive."[128]

Those well versed in the scholarly discussion of this matter will likely object at once that Lane Fox did not mention the ancient philosophers, those pagans whose aim it was to draw people into different "schemes of life," to recall Nock's famous phrase.[129] But even here, it would be difficult to see evidence that amounts to significantly more than attempts to add particular forms of life onto an already-existing basis.[130] To put it a little differently: including (roaming) philosophers in one's notion of mission necessarily com-mits one to a view of mission that includes almost any serious "argument" intended to provoke change (and this of quite varying degrees).[131] But this is surely too broad.

It might be noted in reply, however, that to eliminate entirely the pagan philosophers from one's conception of mission runs the risk of conceiving of "mission" too narrowly, as something that is only active solicitation, and that such a narrow conception runs the concomitant risk of overlooking or unduly minimizing the dramatic attraction that accompanies certain distinctive pat-terns of life.[132] And this reply may well have some merit, too, though in point of fact the "add on" reading of pagan philosophy would still stand: the philoso-phies we know of did not require any kind of radical or substantial break with traditional religious practice.

There is simply no good analogue to early *Christian* mission in the ancient pagan world. As Martin Goodman remarked with pointed clarity, "[n]o pagan seriously dreamed of bringing all humankind to give worship in one body to one deity."[133] And that, of course, is just what early Christian mission is according to Acts.

Students of ancient religious movements might grant this point but go on to raise questions about Jewish precursors to Christian mission. At least since

Lightfoot's work on the Talmud and the NT in the seventeenth century, most scholars—Acts exegetes included[134]—have assumed the existence of a pre-Christian Jewish mission (based not infrequently on Matt 23:15).[135] Indeed, this view has gone virtually unchallenged until relatively recently. But with the work of Martin Goodman, Scot McKnight, Will and Orrieux, and now Rainer Riesner, no longer may one toil innocently oblivious to the historical possibility raised by these scholars, viz., there was no pre-Christian Jewish mission.[136]

For our purposes we do not need to untie every knot in the debate. This is all to the good, since, as James Carleton Paget has noted in his learned article, "[t]he literature on Jewish proselytism is enormous."[137] But we should draw attention to one overarching, if not outright dominating, feature that emerges from a reading of some of the more recent work on this question. That feature is the serious problem of definition. "Mission" is notoriously defined in different ways by different scholars. The argument over the right interpretation of the data thus turns out to be an argument about the correctness of one's particular definition of "mission."

Given such a situation, it is somewhat odd that the importance of finding a "good" or "right" definition still receives such vigorous defense.[138] One might have thought that the continual spawning of ever-newer definitions to deal with basically the same evidence would have pointed rather clearly to the inadequacies of "definition" as a mode of inquiry. The conceptual problem here is, on the one hand, that the attempt to formulate a definition of "mission" that would allow one to treat particular instances (i.e., ancient religions and philosophies) under a general heading creates an intellectual construct with no corresponding reality: there is no such thing as mission in general. In this way of thinking, the real religions of the ancient world are seen as instances (or not) of something that in actual fact does not exist anywhere other than in the body of scholarly discourse (the "minds" of the researchers).

On the other hand, where scholars depart from a general view of mission, the pattern of mission of one particular religious group (usually Christianity) is often taken as what mission *really* is and thus turned into the measuring stick for all other genuine forms of mission. In this way of thinking, it is of course totally unsurprising—and intellectually unhelpful—that what does not look like (say) Christianity does not count as mission. But this is only slightly less banal than saying outright that non-Christian religious practice is not Christian.

Far better than seeking a definition with which to organize the disparate pieces of evidence is to think by means of description, which is in this context simply to say that comparison ought not to be performed by relating different entities to a scholarly construct as much as it should seek to set forth total patterns in relation to one another. When thinking in this manner through the various elements involved in the question of early Jewish/Christian mission, it becomes immediately apparent that one should not say that "there never was a Jewish mission of any kind prior to Christianity" but rather that there never was a Jewish mission of the kind we see in Acts prior to Christianity. It is doubtless the case that some Jews desired the conversion of pagans to Judaism. But it is no less the case that what we see in Acts—*taken as a whole*—finds no counterpart anywhere in the Jewish world prior to the end of the first century.

Recognizing Acts' uniqueness in the ancient world does not of course entail the denial of the importance of the Jewish synagogue for early Christian mission. The opening words of Harnack's great work remain relevant to any study of Acts: the Jewish synagogues

> formed the most important presupposition for the rise and growth of Christian communities throughout the empire. The network of the synagogues furnished the Christian mission with centers and courses for its development, and in this way the mission of the new religion, which was undertaken in the name of the God of Abraham and Moses, found a sphere already prepared for itself.[139]

Still, we must not suppose that this presupposition—confirmed by the narrative of Acts itself[140]—should lessen the impact of the point that the total picture of mission in Acts confronts us with a *novum*.

A true *novum* creates difficulties, not just for the ancient Romans, who in the end knew not what they faced in the early Christians,[141] and for the Troeltschian historicists, whose philosophical presuppositions exclude the very possibility of drastic historical newness, but also for the critics of Troeltsch who allow for radical novelty in the course of history and who therefore must craft a treatment of Christian mission that avoids narratives of evolution (a difficult task indeed in the modern world).[142] Strictly speaking, there is nothing in the socio-cultural sphere from which Christian mission evolves. It is, as Isaiah might say, a new thing (Isa 43:18–19).

What this uniqueness or newness means is that (1) mission is strictly internal to the early Christian self-understanding and not to be explained by a carefully arranged potpourri of social forces, and (2) we therefore must seek its origins and significance within its theological outworking in Acts.

Carleton Paget is right to doubt that the early Christians possessed a *Missionstheorie* if by "theory" he means a highly developed, comprehensive view of exactly what should happen.[143] In their view, the Christians were subject to the freedom and initiative of the Holy Spirit and would go where the Spirit led; indeed, the Spirit could even directly contravene their own intentions and plans (e.g., Acts 16:6–7). Yet if we take *Missionstheorie* a little more loosely and ask whether or not Acts sets forth a programmatic theological vision that both requires and initiates "worldwide" mission, then the answer is that it surely does.

Readers do not have to labor long in the book of Acts until they come across its programmatic thesis: after receiving the power of the Holy Spirit, says the risen Jesus, the disciples "shall be my witnesses in Jerusalem and in all Judaea and Samaria and to the end of the earth" (1:8).[144] As Earl Ellis and others have shown in great detail, if one thinks in geographical terms there are doubtless many ways to understand the phrase "end of the earth" (Spain, Rome, Ethiopia, etc.).[145] Regardless of the particular option one favors, however, the telos or underlying point of the outward movement imaged in the progression "Jerusalem, Judaea, Samaria, end of the earth" remains the same: the disciples are enjoined to witness to Jesus "everywhere," or universally.[146] Such a universal extension of the witness to the resurrection of Jesus is, as Barrett straightforwardly remarked, nothing less than "the content of Luke's second volume."[147]

Not only are the words of 1:8 spoken by the risen Jesus—indeed, they are his last before ascending to heaven, thus punctuating his earthly presence—the importance of the disciples' role as witnesses is continually trumpeted throughout the narrative. "Witness" (μάρτυς) and its cognates occur no less than twenty-three times in Acts.[148] In fact, the first occurrence after 1:8 comes quickly in 1:22, where the apostolic task is defined as being a "witness to [Jesus's] resurrection." The discerning reader will of course note the deeper connection between the etymology of "apostle" and the task of mission: the apostles are those who are sent out to witness (see esp. 8:25 and 13:31; cf. 4:33). Thus is Peter, the main character of the first half of the book, given to repeating this fact in his speeches to a variety of audiences: "this Jesus God raised up, and of that we are all witnesses," he says at Pentecost (2:32); God has raised up the Author of life, and "[t]o this we are witnesses" hear the people in Solomon's portico (3:15); even the High Priest and Sanhedrin learn from Peter (and the others) that "we are witnesses" to the exaltation of Jesus as Leader and Savior to the right hand of God (5:32). Cornelius and his household are no different in this respect; indeed, in this crucial passage Peter emphasizes repeatedly the essential connection between apostleship and witness:

> "And we are witnesses to all that [Jesus] did . . . [and] God raised
> him on the third day and made him manifest; not to all the people but
> to the witnesses chosen by God—that is, to us—who ate and drank
> with him after he rose from the dead. And he commanded us . . . to
> witness that he is the one ordained by God to be the Judge of the living

and the dead. To him all the prophets bear witness that everyone who believes in him receives forgiveness of sins through his name" (Acts 10:39, 41, 42, 43).

Of course Paul, the main character for the second half of Acts, is no less determined to speak about the nature of his mission with the language of "witness." Not only does he summarize his ministry for the Ephesian elders in terms of witnessing "both to Jews and Greeks" (20:21; cf. v. 24; cf. 26:22), he also repeats this essential information both times he retells the story of his calling in the voice-overs for Ananias and Jesus: Ananias tells Paul, "you will be a witness for [Jesus] to all human beings of what you have seen and heard" (22:15; cf. v. 18), and is then echoed by Jesus in 26:16, "I have appeared to you for this purpose, to appoint you to serve and to witness to the things in which you have seen me." Narratively speaking, Paul's claims are reinforced both by the narrator (18:5; 28:23) and by the voice of the Lord Jesus himself: "The following night, ὁ κύριος stood by Paul and said, 'Take courage, for as you have witnessed to me in Jerusalem, so you must witness also in Rome' " (23:11).

Such a witnessing role, however, is not limited to the apostles and Paul. Indeed, as many scholars have noticed, it is difficult to overestimate the significance of Luke's naming of Stephen as the Lord's "witness."[149] In his speech to the angry Jerusalem crowd, Paul relates how he said to the risen Jesus that "when the blood of Stephen your μάρτυς was shed, I was standing by and approving" (22:20). Whether or not Luke was here consciously forging the first explicitly verbal link between "witnessing" and becoming a "martyr" in the later Christian sense of the term,[150] the text doubtless draws clearly the line between the mission of witnessing to the risen Jesus and the reality of trial, suffering, and death. In so doing, it elevates for clear inspection what it means to be a witness in the missionary theology of Acts. It is, in fact, to reenact the life-pattern of the suffering Christ (26:23: παθητὸς ὁ χριστός), to suffer for his Name (5:41; 9:16), to be put on trial (Peter, John, the apostles, Stephen, Paul), to face the possibility of death (Peter, John, the apostles, Stephen, Paul, Jason, Alexander, etc.), and to proclaim the resurrection (e.g., 23:6; 24:21; 26:7–8!). In short, it is to embody the cruciform pattern that culminates in resurrection.

It would not be too much, in fact, to say that the resurrection of Jesus is the reason for mission. In one sense, of course, this is a platitude. Had the disciples thought that Jesus's execution was the end of the story, it is unlikely that they would have initiated a universal mission in his name. But in a more complex sense, the connection between the resurrection of Jesus and the witness to the end of the earth is essential and runs much deeper than a purely formal analysis might suggest. Briefly put, the former generates the latter. It is not only the case that, literarily speaking, Acts narrates explicitly that what the disciples witness to is the resurrection (1:22 etc. above), it is also the case that the resurrection is the fount of new reality out of which the *novum* that is Christian mission emerges. This generative power of the resurrection is in essence the point of Luke's careful literary design: both at the end of the Gospel and at the beginning of Acts, the risen Jesus himself is the origin of universal mission. Luke 24:47 is the anticipatory note—or mirror image—of Acts 1:8. And the risen Jesus, writes Luke at the conclusion of his Gospel, said to his disciples, "thus it is written, that the Christ should suffer and on the third day rise from the dead, and that repentance and forgiveness of sins should be preached in his name to all nations, beginning from Jerusalem."

Ernst Haenchen, with plain reference to Bultmann's famous essay of 1941, captures well the difficulties in thinking through the Lukan picture: "The modern reader, who imagines the Apostles and other leading figures of the early church as completely self-sufficient human beings, must again and again in Acts be struck by the way in which such 'mythical powers' as the Lord, the Spirit, an angel, the 'vision,' decisively intervene in the action."[151] Haenchen's remark is typical of German NT scholarship in the mid-twentieth century, but it is telling because it reads as his reaction to the phenomenon he describes so well in the sentences just prior:

> To Luke it is of the utmost importance that Acts should begin not
> with the disciples left to their own devices, but with the Lord who
> visits and instructs them for forty days more. In this way the Christian
> mission on which they then embark becomes not a merely human
> enterprise but a process which the Lord himself has guided on its way.[152]

Haenchen is right. However tempting it may be to the modern historian to explain it this way, Christian mission according to Acts is finally not derivative of various social forces or even of the psychological state(s) of the apostles. To seek its origin in these spheres is not to "explain" Christian mission but to reproduce the Troeltschian need for precedents and to engage in eisegesis of the text—in short, it is to misdescribe the object of inquiry and, therefore, to render it incomprehensible.[153] As difficult as it may appear to the modern mind, we must look to the resurrection of Jesus to understand the Christian mission in Acts. That is the "place" from which Christian mission begins.

For Luke the resurrection of Jesus is not a necessary consequence of his life—as if the movement of history could of itself produce life over death—but an act of God. As Peter put it early on, Jesus was "crucified and killed by the hands of lawless men, *but God* raised him up, having loosed the pangs of death" (2:23–24; cf. 2:36; 3:15: 5:30–31, etc.). And as Paul would say in Pisidian Antioch, the crucifixion led not to immortality but to the tomb. It was God who raised Jesus from the dead. "And when all things that were written about him were fulfilled, they took him down from the tree and laid him in a tomb. *But God* raised him up" (13:28–30). Thus it is that the ultimate origin of the Christian mission lies in the act of God. That is why the Christian mission is a *novum*: it does not, it cannot, arise naturally out of the mundane sphere—death is the final boundary of natural human life—but comes directly from the new life given by God to Jesus on the other side of death. The location of the origin of Christian mission according to Acts, that is, is beyond death, and in this way Christian mission exceeds dramatically all human possibilities of creation and initiation. It not only is but must be the *missio Dei*.[154] The early Christian mission in Acts is best seen, therefore, not in terms of daring initiative or social creativity but in terms of *response*. It moves on the basis of a prior reality.

Yet we would be mistaken were we to think that the mere fact of the resurrection—a kind of resurrection *qua* resurrection—engenders universal mission. (A dead man coming to life again might mean any number of things.) According to Acts, it is rather that the resurrection confirms the identity of Jesus as the Lord of all and makes this identity effective now, in the present, for the whole world. Though Luke has long been accused of toning down the eschatological fervor of the early (usually Pauline) church, the narrative of Acts is actually replete with eschatological markers that underline dramatically the radical shift in cosmic conditions that occurred with the resurrection of Jesus.[155] *Tὰ νῦν*—"But now"—says Paul to his Athenian audience (17:30). Or, as Peter famously proclaims in his Pentecost speech: "Let the whole house of Israel therefore know assuredly that God has made him both Lord and Christ, this Jesus whom you crucified" (Acts 2:36).[156]

Still, as with the resurrection, the Lordship of the Christ might in theory mean any number of things, some of which would obviously not lead to specifically Christian mission (the expulsion of the Romans from Palestine, for example: read again the disciples' question in 1:6). In the book of Acts, however, the universal Lordship of Jesus means "salvation," indeed, to the extent that Acts eliminates completely the possibility of thinking of salvation apart from Jesus. As Acts 4:12 makes clear, to think Jesus is simultaneously to think salvation, and to think salvation is simultaneously to think Jesus: "for there is no other name under heaven given to human beings by which we must be saved." God has concentrated his salvific action entirely in the person of Jesus. Simeon's praise of God in Luke 2:30 upon seeing the baby Jesus—"my eyes have seen your salvation"—thus finds its fulfillment in the confirmation of the Lordship of the Christ in the resurrection of Jesus. Jesus is not only Lord *in se*, but also *pro nobis*.

It is true, as Stenschke, Witherington, and others have demonstrated in detail, that σωτηρία and its cognates cover a wide range of meaning in the Lukan corpus.[157] But it is no less true, as Joel Green rightly observed, that these various uses of "salvation" can be seen to constitute something of a thematic unity: the incorporation into a community whose life is a testimony to the identity of the resurrected Lord of all.[158] It is not a coincidence, in other words, that in virtually the same breath Peter proclaims to the household of Cornelius both that Jesus is the κύριος πάντων and that "everyone who believes in him receives forgiveness of sins through his name" (10:36, 43), or that Paul and Silas say to the Philippian jailer "believe in the Lord Jesus and you will be saved, you and your household" (16:30–31). It is, rather, the heart of the matter. The Lordship of the Christ initiates a community of salvation. As Green puts it, forgiveness of sins, release of debts, rescue, healing—in short, salvation—are all oriented toward the creation of a "christocentric community of God's people."[159] Christian mission, then, actively socializes the salvific reality that attends Jesus's universal Lordship and in this way bears public witness to his resurrection.

Of course to say that Jesus's resurrection effects communities of salvation is necessarily to imply that there exists a prior problem, something in the human situation to which the salvation pertains. As one might expect, Lukan anthropology has long elicited complicated scholarly discussion (not least because of the alleged absence in his work of a *theologia crucis*).[160] For our purpose it is less important to adjudicate between competing positions in the debate than it is to note the correlation in Luke's work between the scope of Jesus's salvific Lordship and the range of the need for salvation: both are universal.

Though one can find scholars who argue that Luke conceives of the Jews as especially culpable actors in the drama of human sin,[161] it is largely apparent that Acts envisions a universal problem.[162] This problem gets formulated in different ways of course—ignorance, violence, bribery, idolatry, magic, superstition, avarice, and so forth—but these failings are simply different expressions of the fundamental quandary: human beings are lost, sinners, in the dark; they need new direction, forgiveness, light. Luke is careful, that is, always to cast the anthropological net as wide as it can go. Peter does indeed issue a vigorous call for Jews to repent (Acts 2:38), but he also later narrates his experience with Cornelius to the apostles and others in Jerusalem in such a way that they exclaim: "Then to the Gentiles also God has given repentance unto life!" (11:18). No different in substance is the unitary voice (ὁμοθυμαδόν) of the disciples that cries out: "truly in this city were gathered together against your holy servant Jesus . . . both Herod and Pontius Pilate with the gentiles and the peoples of Israel" (4:27). The rejection of Jesus, we are to understand, is ultimately not the responsibility of a particular people (or group thereof) but, as Herod and Pilate together illustrate, of humanity, Jew and gentile alike. That is why, as he tells King Agrippa, Paul could preach both to the Jews and "also to the Gentiles, that they should repent and turn to God and perform deeds worthy of their repentance" (26:20). The Areopagus council heard something similar: in light of the rejection and resurrection of Jesus, God now (νῦν) commands *"everyone everywhere* to repent" (17:30; on "everyone, everywhere," cf. 21:28).[163]

Unlike anything else we know of in the ancient world, the Christian mission actively envisioned its target audience as anyone or everyone. Widows and orphans, eunuchs and the lame, magicians and philosophers, centurions and local magistrates, governors and proconsuls, and high priests and kings—in short, both "small and great" (Acts 26:22)—were summoned to a community of salvation constituted by the Lord of all.[164]

Once again, because of the decisive influence of Christianity on Western consciousness, it can be difficult for modern thinkers to appreciate the sweeping nature of the early Christian missionaries' claims in the context of the ancient world. But considered from a pagan point of view—that is, any Graeco-Roman perspective outside the specifically Christian rationale for mission—the Christian mission must inevitably appear strange. It is not simply that the death of one Jew at the hands of a Roman governor would not even make the news, or the idea that all of time should be thought in relation to this Jew rather than the emperor, or his followers' belief that this Jew was alive again, or the conviction that what was "wrong with the world" was directly related to humanity's worship of the God of Israel, as strange as these things would doubtless appear.[165] It is rather, to be conceptually more precise, that there was no preexistent category or tradition of inquiry within which the phenomenon of Christian mission could be rightly perceived. Such a way of knowing simply did not exist. As we saw in the previous chapter, Festus' perplexity was not uncomplicated astonishment at the audacity of Paul's beliefs about the "Jesus who was dead" (25:20) but was the proper epistemological posture of someone who thinks the Christians are literally crazy. To understand the universal Lordship of Jesus, and, hence, the need for salvation, would be already to have moved into the space named repentance, to have seen the light that comes from the apocalypse to the gentiles (Luke 2:32). Apart from such repentance, Festus—and the gentiles—dwell in darkness. To them, the Christian mission can only appear as μανία, or, as they hear in Thessalonica, upside down.

Such judgments about the early Christian movement are but the episte-mological counterparts to its historical uniqueness. Differently said, the uniqueness of Christian mission remains a permanent historical conundrum if one is already committed to the impossibility of what the text of Acts clearly grants, namely, that its origin is to be found beyond death, or *inside* the act of God. For Luke, Jesus's identity as Lord of all is not something produced by the Christian mission, a kind of evolutionary endpoint of a naturally expanding claim about the significance of Jesus of Nazareth as the gospel penetrated ever more deeply into Mediterranean culture. It is rather the source from which mission springs. That this identity is a saving identity and that people—not just some, but *people*—need salvation are two sides of the same reality mani-fested in the dramatic sequence that was Jesus's ministry to the lost, his rejection and crucifixion, and ultimately his resurrection. That this sequence of events constitutes a turning point in the cosmos, a "fulfillment" of the plan of God to overcome salvifically the division between Jew and gentile, is not something simply to be announced—as if the early Christian missionaries were only street-corner preachers—but something to be lived, or embodied. Christian communities, as we have had occasion to say, are the sociological explication of God's universal Lordship in Jesus Christ.

Christian Assembly

It has often been thought that early Christianity was more about the internal state of a person than about public life. The "Christians aimed to reform the heart, not the social order" runs the argument.[166] While it is true that the early Christians did not attempt to populate local political councils or organize street protests in relation to particular social injustices, this way of thinking ultimately fails to grapple seriously enough with the final unity between theology and social life. At least according to Acts, the universal Lordship of Jesus is not only about the heart but also about the formation of a particular public—the two, in fact, are inseparable: repentance and salvation entail a socially noticeable way of life. Put differently, the Christian mission's proclamation of the good news was simultaneously a summons to church.

Of the many ways in which Acts narrates the public dimension of the Christian mission, the most striking ought perhaps to be its use of the name "Christian."[167] Though much scholarly ink has been spilled over the (in)accuracy of Luke's use of the term, considerably less attention has been given to what such a narratively precise usage might say about the political shape of the ἐκκλησία according to Acts.[168] But it is just here, in the cumulative effect rendered by paying close attention to the two places where "Christian" is used in the narrative, that we encounter the crystallization of an issue with which we have been wrestling throughout this entire book. We thus turn to Acts 11:26 and 26:28.

In Acts 11:19–30 Luke starts to thicken his account of the beginnings of the gentile mission and the constitution of Christian community. Because of the persecution (θλῖψις) that arose in connection with Stephen's martyrdom, many of the disciples were scattered well beyond Judaea (Phoenecia, Cyprus, and Antioch). Initially, those who had fled the persecution spoke "the word only to Jews." But upon coming to Antioch on the Orontes, one of the ancient world's largest cities, some of the believers from Cyprus and Cyrene spoke also to the Greeks.[169] In contrast to his bare-bones report about the preaching "the word" to the Jews elsewhere, Luke pauses here to linger over the beginnings of Christianity in Antioch.

> Now those who were scattered because of the persecution that arose over Stephen traveled as far as Phoenicia and Cyprus and Antioch, speaking the word only to Jews. But there were some of them, men of Cyprus and Cyrene, who on coming to Antioch spoke also to the Greeks, preaching "Jesus is/as Lord." And the hand of the Lord was with them, and a great number of those who believed turned to the Lord. News of this came to the ears of the ecclesia in Jerusalem, and they sent Barnabas to Antioch. When he came and saw the grace of God, he was glad; and he exhorted them all to remain faithful to the Lord with steadfast purpose; for he was a good man, full of the Holy Spirit and of faith. And a large company was added to the Lord. And Barnabas went to Tarsus to look for Saul, and, having found him, brought him to Antioch. For a whole year they gathered together with the ecclesia and taught a large crowd. And it was in Antioch that the disciples began to be called "Christians" (Acts 11:19–26).

Of particular interest for our interpretive project is what the disciples from Cyprus and Cyrene (presumably Hellenist Jews; 6:1) preach to the Greeks, namely, the confession that Jesus is Lord. Acts 5:42—εὐαγγελιζόμενοι τὸν χριστὸν Ἰησοῦν—reminds us that εὐαγγελιζόμενοι τὸν κύριον Ἰησοῦν in 11:20 can as reasonably be rendered "proclaiming Jesus is/as Lord" as it can "proclaiming the Lord Jesus" (cf. 18:5, 28). Of course for the readers of Acts, the substantive difference here is nonexistent. As Rudolf Pesch correctly notes, they already know from Acts 10 the confession that Jesus is the κύριος πάντων.[170] And yet, we would be remiss not to note the significance of such well-targeted proclamation.

As scholars since at least the nineteenth century have noticed, it would have made little sense to initiate evangelism to gentiles with the term χριστός.[171] Unless they were already steeped in the messianic hopes of Judaism, to hear that Jesus was the Jewish messiah would in all probability have had little effect. Even Cornelius, a pious and religiously knowledgeable gentile, heard of Jesus less in messianic terms than in cosmic ones (Judge of the living and the dead, Lord of all, etc.).[172] To proclaim τὸν κύριον Ἰησοῦν, however, would be to speak in a language intelligible even to (from a Jewish perspective) impious and religiously ignorant gentiles. As we have already remarked, there were in the ancient world many gods and many lords.

Yet, precisely because of the multiplicity of lords, such proclamation would also risk the invitation to idolatry. Jesus is not, that is, simply one more κύριος to be received into the pagan pantheon, as if—to recall our discussion of the practical contour of Christian mission—the aim of the evangelists in Antioch was to add Jesus on to a locally preexistent pattern of worship.[173] Much to the contrary, Luke quickly narrates a flatly pagan interpretation of the κύριος confession out of the picture with a literarily deft repetition of the word.

Immediately after relating the preaching of the Lord Jesus, Luke writes "and the hand of the Lord was with them, and a great number who believed turned to the Lord" (11:21). As Haenchen, Johnson et al. have noted, the expression χεὶρ κυρίου in v. 21a is OT talk, just as ἐπέστρεψεν in 21b is an OT term that names a turn or return to the God of Israel, as, for example, in Acts 15:19 "we should not trouble those Gentiles who turn [ἐπιστρέφουσιν] to God."[174] It is thus easily conceivable that the two occurrences of κύριος in 11:21 refer to God (so, for example, Gerhard Schneider).

It is also conceivable, however, that κύριος in the OT expression χεὶρ κυρίου refers to God and the one following, ἐπέστρεψεν ἐπὶ τὸν κύριον, to Jesus (so Haenchen, for example).[175] Nor can we exclude the possibility that the first use of κύριος in the Antioch scene is meant to influence hermeneutically our reading of κύριος in 11:21, that is, in such a way as to encourage us to see a reference to Jesus κύριος (vs. 20) both times in the very next sentence (v. 21ab).

What should strike any sensitive reader is the exegetical impossibility of determining which of the three interpretive options is right. Jesus-God-God is no more exegetically necessary than Jesus-God-Jesus, and this no more so than Jesus-Jesus-Jesus. Neither immediate context—Luke uses κύριος twice more, in 11:23 and 11:24[176]—nor larger Lukan usage can push us beyond doubt toward the resolution of the ambiguity.

The exegetical ambiguity, however, does not point toward linguistic imprecision but to Luke's extended narration of the unity of identity between Jesus and the God of Israel.[177] The ultimate reason we cannot resolve the ambiguity in 11:20–21, therefore, is because there are not two κύριοι but only one. Jesus and the God of Israel are—together—κύριος. To turn to the God of Israel, in a reversal of our previous formulation, is to confess Jesus as Lord. That such turning took place, according to Luke, is evidence of the hand of the Lord.

This turning of the gentiles was not mere intellectual assent or an affective awakening but something that entailed simultaneous social change. "A great number that believed turned to the Lord" conveys, that is, a concurrence between believing and turning that corresponds to James' declaration in the Jerusalem council of the theological reality behind gentile conversion: they are a people taken out (λαβεῖν ἐξ ἐθνῶν λαόν; 15:14).[178]

Though his focus is on "morality" more narrowly, Wayne Meeks describes nicely the correlative effect of such a taking out: "when people move from a community with one kind of culture into one that is quite different, very often their moral intuitions no longer match the reality around them."[179] If we think through the implications of Meeks' statement in relation to the founding of the church in Syrian Antioch, we would understand well why Luke believes the first sizable Christian community to include gentiles needs an entire year of διδαχή: the new converts in Antioch are not only "taken out" but must also be "gathered in" and "educated"—in short, resocialized—in the common practices that constitute their life as a community of repentance and salvation (συναχθῆναι ἐν τῇ ἐκκλησίᾳ καὶ διδάξαι; 11:26).[180]

Absent such resocialization—formation, that is, in the pattern of life adequate to Christian community—it is doubtful whether the name "Christian" would have ever been coined. Put positively, according to Acts, the distinctive life of Jews and gentiles together in the Antiochene community forms the public witness that calls forth the label Χριστιανός.

Despite the learned essay by Elias Bickerman,[181] it has seemed evident to most modern scholars that Χριστιανός was not a term invented by the Christians themselves but by "outsiders."[182] On this point at least, Luke would agree with the moderns, even against ancient patristic testimony.[183] It is true, as Bickerman stresses, that χρηματίσαι in 11:26 is in the active voice. Yet, not only do active voice infinitives frequently require passive meanings, χρηματίζειν is itself a word predominately stamped by its use in the realm of Roman jurisprudence, as Erik Peterson pointed out over sixty years ago.[184] Had Luke meant simply to indicate that in Antioch the followers of Jesus first took the name Christians for themselves, he could have easily used καλεῖν.[185] With χρηματίζειν, however, Luke draws on the cultural encyclopedia of the late first century and signals to his knowledgeable readers the locus of the term's origin. The "Christians" were so named in the sphere of Roman administration.[186]

Recognizing the importance of Luke's signal does not, however, preclude the possibility that the assembly of Jews and gentiles in Antioch was first noticed by the local populace. Indeed, in Acts the missionaries and their communities almost uniformly come to the attention of Roman administrators by way of a disturbance among the locals.[187] The point, rather, is that the Roman administrative sphere is where the term originated in such a way as to stick.

This is not to say, however, that we should imagine that persecutorial trials of the kind we find in Pliny lie behind the scene in Acts 11. Despite the fact that the *legatus* of Syria was headquartered in Antioch and that Roman presence in and around the city increased dramatically from the mid-70s on,[188] Luke does not speak directly in Acts 11 of anything that would lead us to presuppose such an elaborate process.[189] Contra Haenchen, the absence of such direct reference to the Romans' role in establishing the neologism is not because including it would scuttle Luke's pro-Roman agenda (indeed, Luke has no such agenda). It is rather because by the end of the first century no such direct reference was needed to ensure readers would know the standard meaning of the word. Not only does πρώτως indicate repeated use of the name,[190] insofar as the word Χριστιανοί (*Christiani*) appears in non-Christian sources with reference to events in the first century, it is uniformly a derogatory term.

Tacitus, as is well known, had no love for the "detestable superstition," the "evil" whose home was originally Judaea, and neither did the crowds about whom he wrote: to shift blame for the great fire in Rome, Nero "substituted as culprits, and punished with the utmost cruelty, a class hated for their abominations, whom the crowd called *Christiani*. *Christus*, the author of the name, underwent the extreme penalty... and the detestable superstition was checked for a moment, only to erupt once more, not merely in Judaea, the origin of this evil, but in the capital itself, where all things atrocious and shameful collect and are celebrated" (*Ann.*, 15.44; LCL alt.). Suetonius was no different. The *Christiani* were to him a "new and evil superstition" (*Nero* 16.2; *Christiani, genus hominum superstitio nova ac malefica*). And Pliny, in his correspondence with Trajan of ca. AD 112, says that the torture of two slave-women known to be Christian *ministrae* yielded only a "perverse and extravagant superstition" (*superstitionem pravam et immodicam;* 10.96).[191]

From within the NT, 1 Peter unambiguously confirms the impression created by the non-Christian sources. The "fiery ordeal" faced by the letter's addressees is explicitly said to include suffering "as a Christian" (ὡς Χριστιανός; 4:16). Close attention to 1 Peter shows not only "what the target of external criticism was... [namely,] the Christians' allegiance to Christ" but also that Χριστιανός "emerges specifically as one of a number of labels (along with "murder," "thief," etc.) that may be the direct cause of suffering." The implication "is that these labels are... attached by outsiders, as accusations."[192]

Regardless of the exact year the term was actually coined, therefore, by the time it found currency in the mid-first century, its political connotations were apparent (so, rightly, the argument of Peterson).[193] This is not to say that we know for sure, for example, that *Christiani* corresponded in every case—in Syria, say—exactly to Pliny's political society (*hetaeria*),[194] or that the *flagitia* associated with the Christians were uniformly identical in every part of the empire.[195] But it is to say that the overall impression remains the same. As Taylor notes, it is "striking that in the non-Christian 1st century sources [sic], the names Christ and Christian are invariably associated with public disorders and crimes."[196] What is certainly no less striking is that reading Acts makes this larger picture intelligible: as we saw in chapter 2, religious critique, social disorder, economic disaster, the threat of στάσις, accusations of political crimes, actual trials, and a veritable host of other public problems attend the arrival of Christian mission in the Graeco-Roman world on page after page of Luke's second volume.

It would be inaccurate, therefore, to say with Cadbury that Luke "gives no indication of the spirit in which [Χριστιανοί] was applied."[197] It is rather that he expects his readers will have little to no trouble filling in the blanks. To borrow from Pliny, the *nomen ipsum* was in this case hermeneutically sufficient. By the time Acts was read, the term would have been used repeatedly, and its disparaging connotations long been made clear. Indeed, this is likely the reason Luke never uses "Christian" in his role as narrator ("the Christians" in Iconium did this or that, for example).[198] Had the early Christians coined Χριστιανός as a constructive self-affirmation of group identity, Luke may not have restricted its use so dramatically.

In point of fact, the only other time Χριστιανός occurs in the Acts narrative is in the mouth of King Agrippa II, and here it is doubtless insulting (26:28). To Paul's most hopeful evangelistic plea—"Do you believe in the prophets, King Agrippa? I know you do believe!"—Agrippa responds derisively. Indeed, one can almost hear the laughter in the audience hall: "In such a short time," mocks Agrippa, "you have convinced me to become a Christian!"[199]

Agrippa's response is significant not only because it artfully displays the deprecatory dimension of Χριστιανός but also because it shows that the term made sense to gentiles—assuming Agrippa's demeaning joke was understood by his Roman audience[200]—as the name of a publicly identifiable group. "To become a Christian" (Χριστιανὸν ποιῆσαι) means to "become one of you people," "to join your group." In both these ways, the occurrence of Χριστιανός in Acts 26:28 confirms and extends the sense we get from examining its use in 11:26. From the perspective of an outsider, the Christians are a strange and problematic social reality.

Taking account of such a perspective in our reading of Χριστιανός in Acts enables us to see the constructive use to which the term is put. Luke not only studiously avoids characterizing the followers of Jesus as "Christians," he also skillfully structures the narrative so as to object to the pagan reading of "Christian" social reality.

Immediately after the second occurrence of Χριστιανός Paul is declared innocent. "Then the king rose, and the governor, and Bernice and those who were sitting with them. And when they had withdrawn they said to one another, 'This man is doing nothing worthy of death or imprisonment.' And Agrippa said to Festus, 'This man could have been set free if he had not appealed to Caesar'" (Acts 26:30–32). And with that Agrippa, the one who himself introduced the dangerously loaded term Χριστιανός directly into Paul's trial, suddenly and subtly shifts its connotation. Agrippa has rightly taken Paul for a missionizing Christian, but he does not read such missionizing as a direct treasonous challenge. As Agrippa clears Paul, he is simultaneously clearing the name: Paul "the Christian" is not guilty of treason and neither, we are to understand, is it the case that to be a "Christian" is to be treasonous. There exists no essential link between the revolutionary connotation of the term and the group to which it points.

The narrative logic surrounding the use of the term Christian in Acts thus exhibits *in nuce* the larger pattern of the Lukan conviction about the community of Jesus's followers. Rather than suppress the political perceptions of the ἐκκλησία in Antioch, the public visibility of the first "mixed" church and its core practices is frankly acknowledged by Luke to have earned the epithet Χριστιανοί. It would be too wooden and entirely unLukan, however, simply to object directly to such branding. True to his literary form, therefore, Luke reintroduces the term only after he has allowed his readers to understand the nature of the mission in the wider Roman world. Not before—but only after— the narrative winds its way through the turbulence in Cyprus, Pisidian Antioch, Iconium, Lystra, Derbe, Philippi, Thessalonica, Beroea, Athens, Corinth, Ephesus, Jerusalem, and elsewhere is the reader in a position to hear well the alarming cultural resonance that issues forth from the word "Christian." It is no accident that in its second occurrence in the story Χριστιανός erupts once again in the sphere of its origin, the arena of Roman administrative power; indeed, for the properly tuned ear, it bursts forth in a well-orchestrated, dramatic moment of the trial for Paul's life: Festus has declared Paul crazy, and the reader turns—as did Festus himself—to Agrippa for the verdict. Χριστιανός! And immediately the treasonous connotations are rejected: this man is δίκαιος.

Luke thus introduces Χριστιανός simultaneously with the visible entrance of gentiles into the church, withholds the word for the vast remainder of the story, and then injects it in a pivotal political moment in order to counteract its prevailing sense of meaning. Read narratively, the two uses of Χριστιανός combine to produce a conceptual pattern that both accepts and renarrates the cultural reality to which the term points. The "Christians" do indeed stand out publicly (Antioch)—they can be marked by outsiders—but they are not seditious criminals (Agrippa).[201]

We would be badly mistaken, however, were we to interpret this narrative movement as Luke's attempt to say that following *Christus* was merely a spiritual or theological matter and not a political one.[202] When, therefore, contemporary scholars such as Botermann bifurcate the interpretive options surrounding Χριστιανός into "political" and "theological"—thus implying a choice must be made between the two—they cannot help but distort the fundamental issue at stake.[203] The hermeneutical choice produced by attending to the word Χριστιανός in Acts and its *Umwelt* is not between a political or theological reading of their community but between different kinds of theological politics or political theologies, between, that is, radical perspectival differences in the overall construal of life.

That such differences in perspective correspond exactly to a particular social location vis-à-vis the church is not surprising, though it is deeply significant. "Outsiders" and "insiders" do not see things the same way. The formation of a superstitious sect bent on sedition for one is the witness to the apocalypse to the gentiles for the other. Tacitus construes "Christian" social reality one way and Luke another. Were Tacitus to agree with Luke, were Pliny or Suetonius or the officials in Syrian Antioch to have been formed hermeneutically by the narrative of Acts, they would have already made the move from outsiders to insiders, or, as Luke might put it, from darkness to light. As the ancient data stand, however, Christus and his followers exercise no constitutive formation upon the practical hermeneutics of the pagans.

The political judgments that are tied to particular social loci thus correspond to particular theological judgments. While on the surface it may appear that the quarrel over the content of "Christian" rests in a disagreement about the political shape of their common life—and there *is* a disagreement about this—both the Roman and Lukan political readings of "Christian" are themselves necessarily intertwined with, even dependent upon, a particular theological posture vis-à-vis the figure of *Christus*. No Roman administrator who came to confess that *Christus* was in fact the κύριος πάντων would have continued to view the "Christians" as maniacal, for they would now be seen as "brothers and sisters" (Acts 1:15, 16, 2:37; 6:3; 9:17, 30; 16:2, 40; 17:6, 10, etc.). What Botermann and others see as mutually exclusive interpretive options are in fact, therefore, essentially linked. The Christians appear as "Christians"

precisely because the theological conviction of Jesus's universal Lordship unfolds socially in the mission to gather Jews and gentiles into one community, a
people set apart.[204] That, and nothing else, is the basis of the disagreement
over the political contour of "Christian" and that and nothing else, is the reason
they can be seen.[205]

What is at stake, then, is not whether the Romans perceive the "Christians" as political criminals or a new religious problem—they are plainly seen
as *both*[206]—but, to put it starkly, the question of truth that accompanies the
recognition of any genuinely incommensurable positions. Attending to the
hermeneutical pressure of Acts, that is, forces the question, Whose reading is
right? Are the Christians a group of superstitious and treasonous followers of a
Christus who was himself guilty of sedition (Rome)? Or are they the peaceful
embodiment of the universal Lord's salvation of humanity, Jew and gentile
alike (Acts)? To answer these intractably theological questions—in our time no
less than in Luke's—is necessarily to be positioned socially on the inside or the
outside of the group that confesses Jesus as Lord and, hence, simultaneously to
commit to a certain political understanding of the "Christian" ἐκκλησία.

When Johannes Weiss characterized Acts 11:19–26 as a "colorless report,"
it was not his best day on the job.[207] Of course, inasmuch as reading Acts
narratively with historical sophistication was a thing of future NT scholarship,
Weiss himself is not to blame.[208] Still, his remark helps to underscore the ease
with which NT scholars can pass over the importance of Χριστιανός for Luke's
overall theological project in Acts. Haenchen, for example, who cites Weiss
approvingly, reads the scene in Syrian Antioch as an "anticlimax" after the
story about the conversion of Cornelius.[209] In reality, however, such judgments
stem less from exegetical arguments—the narrative importance of the church
in Antioch in Acts is hard to overestimate (esp. 13:1–4!)—than they do from
habits of reasoning that prioritize the importance of the individual over community and marginalize the theological interconnection between conversion
and church.[210]

While it is certainly the case that the conversion of Cornelius is of fundamental importance to the whole of Acts, it simply does not follow that the
founding of the church in Antioch is less so, as if we should think in terms of
their competition for "air time" in the narrative. "It was precisely not the
foundation of the community at Antioch . . . that [Luke] sought to present as
the epoch-making event, but the preceding conversion and baptism of Cornelius by Peter!" But surely we should say instead that for Luke the one necessarily leads to the other—not, however, as "the secondary following in the wake of
the primary" but as the essential unfolding of the Lordship of Jesus in the
social reality of mission and conversion.[211] Read narratively—"in order," as

Luke would have it—Cornelius prepares the way for Antioch. At Antioch, the church of Jews and gentiles goes public. It is there that their witness to the Lord of all becomes visible to the gentiles.[212] They are Χριστιανοί, a light to the nations.

Conclusion

Looking back through the underlying conceptual structure of the present chapter, we can perceive that the three core practices—confessing Jesus as Lord, engaging in mission to the end of the earth, forming publicly identifiable communities of Jews and gentiles—render the scene in Thessalonica politically intelligible. That is to say, the Lordship of the God of Israel in Jesus Christ and its necessary cultural correlates generate the tension that we have been trying to think. Thus, the movement of thought required by reading chapters 2 and 3 together does not yield a final or irresolvable contradiction but a complex unity whose origin lies in a still more basic and productive intellectual pattern, namely, the dialectical outworking of God's self-identification with Jesus of Nazareth as the salvific Lord of all humanity. That such an outworking of the universal, salvific significance of Jesus is, for Luke, inherently material and communal results narratively in the collision with gentile idolatry (chapter 2) and in the necessity to argue against the ensuing misconstruals of the embodied practice of Jesus's salvific Lordship (chapter 3).

That the history of Acts scholarship demonstrates an inability to tolerate the conceptual unity inherent to narratively articulated dialectical thinking seems clear from the way in which NT scholars have regularly opted for some version of one side of the dialectic or another. Whether this long-standing interpretive habit derives ultimately from the ingestion of modern dichotomies between politics and religion, or from a discipline-bound tendency to avoid protracted theological tangles, or from a complex intersection of these and other matters is uncertain (and probably unanswerable). Such complexities do not, however, prevent us from naming a more proximate hermeneutical problem, one that will help to shed light both on past interpretive habits and on the significance of the Lukan ecclesial vision.

The problem, though interpretively disabling, is also disarmingly simple. Both the traditional *apologia* advocates and their opponents have in large part adopted the Roman religio-political perspective and accepted their terms for debate. As a consequence they have written about Acts as if Luke, too, had accepted these terms and constructed his narrative within the "either/or" parameters they demand (either accommodation or liberation). But of course he did not.

The failure to perceive that Luke is not working analytically within the circumscribed area of Roman religio-political practice and reflection—as if he were somehow forced rationally to render the judgment "innocent" or "guilty" on their terms—has prevented us from seeing that the narrative of Acts offers an entirely different alternative. The alternative is not a piecemeal substitution of Christian terms for Roman ones but the refusal of the Roman premise and a construction of a different set of terms, or a whole pattern of thinking. Because he knows that Jesus is the κύριος πάντων Luke proclaims him, in contrast to the emperor, as "another King," as one whose salvific claim upon his subjects results in a new, worldwide, and publicly identifiable form of communal life. And because of the peacemaking character of Jesus's Lordship, Luke also proclaims—via the mouths of his Roman officials—that Christians are innocent of the charges of sedition and treason. The universal Lordship of God in Jesus leads neither to an *apologia* to (or for) Rome nor to an anti-Rome polemic. It is simply, but really, a different way (Acts 18:25, 26; cf. 9:2, 19:9, 23; 24:22).

Reading Acts as a document that explicates "the Way of the Lord" (Acts 18:25) thus allows us to see that Luke's redescription of cultural dissolution as the gracious act of God in bringing the pagan world out of darkness—his insistence that Christianity is not a governmental takeover but an alternative and salvific way of life—is a reading of the world in deeply and ultimately Christian terms. The epistemological *Grundstruktur* that makes for such a reading is irreducibly particular and, in the Graeco-Roman world, inevitably strange.[213] Put more bluntly, the way of knowing that underlies the perspective of Acts is that of a convert, one who inhabits a world that from the outside can only appear to be upside down.

Such an epistemological dwelling place does not mean that Luke's resultant hermeneutical moves necessarily forsake the world in which he lives—a kind of irrational (and ultimately impossible) rejection of the realities intrinsic to historical life. He writes in Greek, after all (to wit, he uses ἐκκλησία to speak of Christian community), and must have esteemed Greek philosophical ideals of friendship and community to have depicted their embodiment in the κοινωνία of the early Christian gatherings (Acts 2:42–47 and 4:32–37).[214] At a more significant level, the book of Acts avoids facile cultural caricatures and instead portrays the expansion of Christianity into the Mediterranean world in a complex and nuanced manner, one in which certain constitutive aspects of pagan culture are criticized as idolatry and others seen as relative goods—indeed, goods to be put in service of a more adequate, or even corrective, description of what it means to be disciples of Jesus. It is impossible, to take only the most striking example from chapter 3, to see Luke's narratively sophisticated utilization of the Roman legal system without appreciating his knowledge of this arena or his respect for its processes.[215]

Still, such goods do not determine normatively the narrative of Acts. Relative goods are identified and accepted but they do not dictate the terms of the conversation, shape it from the inside out—as if, to stay with our jurisprudential example, once the specifically "Christian" linguistic layers of Paul's trials were stripped away, a Graeco-Roman conceptual nucleus would be exposed. Much to the contrary, for Luke, the normative core is the Apocalypse, the Light.

It is impossible to know for sure how much of Acts Luke had already conceived when he wrote near the beginning of his Gospel that Jesus was a light for an apocalypse to the gentiles (Luke 2:32). By the time one gets to Acts 15, however, it becomes clear that this conviction works on a theologically fundamental level to describe the character of the interface between the Lord of all and the Graeco-Roman world.[216] Indeed, Jesus's revelatory light is that which goes forth from his resurrection in the form of a universal mission and creates a people set apart for the name of the resurrecting God (15:14; cf. esp. 26:23).

This is not to say that Luke was an apocalyptic thinker in the same way as the Apostle Paul (in emphasizing sin as a cosmic power, for example).[217] But the deep connection between the apocalypse of light and the basic tension inherent to the vision of Acts should not be missed: according to the logic of Acts, darkness is hermeneutically significant. Insofar, that is, as the socially embodied witness to the Lord of all is interpreted from a perspective whose foundations are in the shadows, it will of necessity be misperceived and, hence, misconstrued.

Apocalyptic is thus the name of the irreducibly particular way of knowing that is the Acts of the Apostles.[218] To write a narrative based on God's revelation as Lord in the life, death, and resurrection of Jesus of Nazareth is of course to make claims that depend on a kind of knowledge that cannot in principle be constructed from the human side of the God/creature relation. To comprehend the knowledge of God in Jesus Christ as that which gives rise to and orders productively the tension we have explored, therefore, is at once to understand that reading Acts raises crucial, even urgent, questions about theological truth and the practical intelligence it requires, or, said differently, about the total pattern of life that is bound together with the claim to truth about God.

5

The Apocalypse of Acts
and the Life of Truth

If the reading of Acts offered in this book is right, we are inescapably confronted with serious questions regarding the place of this text in religious/political thought today. In order to engage the most salient questions that Acts presses upon us, it is first necessary to draw together our extended exegetical work from the previous chapters in a focused exposition of the vision of Acts.

It would be a serious mistake, however, to read the third section of the present chapter ("The Politics of Truth") as if the hermeneutical procedure that moves us from chapters 2 through 4 to 5 were a clean, two-step process from exegesis to application, or from description to contemporary relevance. Reading in this way presumes de facto that this final section is at best an appendix to the real project. But this is not the case. Not only are our contemporary concerns inextricably bound to historical investigation—we can do no other than think with *our own* historically situated rationality—it is also a gross misunderstanding of the act of interpretation to think that we could somehow avoid, as Paul Minear once put it, the "kerygmatic intention and claim of the Book of Acts."[1] That is to say, even to begin to read Acts—for whatever purpose—is already to be confronted with the necessity of making normative evaluations about its contemporary theological impact. Far from being additional to the project, this chapter is required to complete it. It is to "follow through" in the act of interpretation as we think what it means to read Acts in the first part of the twenty-first century—which of course is the only place that *we* can read it.

Apocalypse to the Gentiles: The Lord of All

At the heart of this book's constructive proposals about how to read Acts vis-à-vis the gentile world is the argument that Acts offers a coherent vision of the apocalypse of God. Because this vision is nothing short of an alternative total way of life, the book of Acts narrates the formation of a new culture.

That such a new pattern of life was not in principle comprehensible in terms of preexistent cultural schemata helps explain Luke's "yes and no" dialectical explication of its particular shape: yes, there must be a break with idolatry; no, Christians are not guilty of στάσις; yes, Caesar challenges the Lordship of God in the King Jesus of Nazareth; no, Jesus is not after Caesar's throne; yes, the resurrection of Jesus threatens fundamentally the stability of Roman life; no, the Christians are not violent zealots. And so on.

In light of the tension generated by the necessity to say both "no" and "yes," one can see that the crucial interpretive move of this book has been to think both "yes" and "no" *together*—in literary terms, to take the dialectic as one narrative whole. The essential conceptual corollary to this interpretive move is the notion that to opt for one side of the dialectic or the other is to divide what Luke has united and, hence, to lose the ability to see from inside the distinctively Lukan hermeneutical perspective. Choosing exclusively either "yes" or "no" as a way to talk about Acts and Graeco-Roman culture, that is, signals both the adoption of an interpretive standpoint that Acts itself aims to exclude—the stark either "for" or "against" of Roman jurisprudence—and the corresponding loss of the insight that Acts narrates its alternative way precisely through its powerful juxtaposition of "yes" and "no."

Through its discussion of the Christian missionaries' encounter with constitutive aspects of pagan culture in Lystra, Philippi, Athens, and Ephesus, chapter 2 traced the profound collision between the Christian mission and the wider Graeco-Roman world that accompanies the missionaries' call to repentance, forgiveness, and communal formation. In Lystra, where Paul and Barnabas were taken as gods, the entire complex of pagan piety that entailed the divinizing of human beings and the traditional practice of sacrifice to the gods was rebuffed, criticized, and labeled "empty." In its place the Christian missionaries proclaimed the necessity for a "turn" to "the Living God." In Philippi, where Paul was repeatedly shadowed by a slave-girl with a "spirit," a conventional polytheistic interpretation of her cry "the Most High God" was rejected in a display of power that announced Jesus Christ as the bringer of "salvation" (σωτηρία) and simultaneously dismantled mantic-based economics. In Athens, a veritable "forest of idols" in which Paul was put on trial, the common practice of caring for divine images was critiqued, the philosophers and political authorities declared "unknowing" or "ignorant," and all of time determined by its relation to one man, the judge whom God has appointed. In Ephesus, recent converts to the Way publicly burned their magical books, and local artisans, recognizing Paul's missionary influence in the province of Asia, recalled the message that foretold the end of their great goddess and the businesses she sustained.

In all of these places—and in many others as well (e.g., Thessalonica, Beroea, etc.)—the end result of the collision was more or less the same: the Christians, whether missionaries or local converts, were stoned, beaten with rods, put in prison, put on trial, thrown in harm's way, harassed, mocked, or driven out. Taken as a whole, these reactions express narratively the fact that the "good news" seemed far from good to many it encountered; instead it entailed a deep threat to preexisting, foundational ways of life in the Mediterranean world. In their vivid portrayal of the pagan realization of Christianity's danger, the scenes in Lystra, Philippi, Athens, and Ephesus thus articulate the intuitive perception of a radical possibility—that of cultural collapse.

Yet, as these same passages make clear, it would be a mistake to read this aspect of Acts through the lens of "cultural criticism," as though Luke's primary aim was to confront socially problematic pagan religious and economic practices directly and only secondarily to introduce God into the picture—as a kind of theological overlay to legitimize an otherwise independent social critique. Though both volumes of his literary work reveal extraordinary concern about the power of money and its (im)proper link to religious practice, Luke was not engaged in an ancient version of Marxist criticism: insofar as the possibility for cultural collapse attends the Christian mission in Acts, it does so because of the primacy of God.

In Lystra and Philippi no less than in Athens and Ephesus, both the critiques and the reactions they evoke arise out of the identity of the God of Israel as one who is fundamentally distinct from the cosmos, or in more directly Jewish terms, who is the Creator, *not* the creation. Just as in Lystra "the Living God" forms the theological underpinning of the criticism of pagan religious vanity and the distance the missionaries put between humanity and God—"we are only human beings just like you!"—so in Athens "the God who made the world and everything in it, the Lord of heaven and earth" grounds Luke's critique of idolatry and provides the starting point for the biblically framed renarration of human history as one that culminates in the resurrection and return of Jesus. So, too, in Ephesus does the threat to the temple of Artemis emerge out of the missionaries' claim that "gods made with hands are no gods." In Philippi the substance is no different: Luke's elimination of any assimilation between "the Most High God" and the God of Israel depends on an ineliminable distinction between even the highest of pagan deities (Zeus) and the God whom Paul preaches. To grasp the narrative importance of the primacy of God over the world is thus to read Luke's basic theological criticism in terms of idolatry. As even their own poets would testify—on Luke's counter-reading of course—the pagan offspring of God know only the cosmos. God is "unknown."

Thus, according to Acts, the challenge posed by early Christianity to the cultural foundations of the pagan world is directly theological, which is to say that the possibility of cultural demise is rooted in a counter-cultural explication of the break between God and the world.[2] To speak in this way is to affirm, with Luke as well as some more contemporary theorists, the constructive or "objective" role of religion in the formation of a total culture.[3] But it is also to say more: because "God" in Luke's sense corresponds not to a particular point within the widest of human horizons but to that which constitutes—makes possible and stands over against—the entirety of the human horizon, the call to (re)turn to God carries with it an entire pattern of life. The pagan reaction to the Christian mission in Acts, therefore, encompasses vastly more than immanent worries about local businesses: more fundamentally, it has to do with the scope of the impact of an alternative way of life.

To get at the scope of the impact required by a transformation of a total horizon of life, we may draw on philosopher Charles Taylor's notion of the social imaginary.[4] By social imaginary Taylor means "something much broader and deeper than the intellectual schemes people may entertain when they think about social reality in a disengaged mode." The social imaginary is rather much more comprehensive and entails "the ways people imagine their social existence, how they fit together with others, how things go on between them and their fellows, the expectations that are normally met, and the deeper normative notions and images that underlie these expectations."

For those who confuse Taylor's idea with social theory, he explains that he employs the word "imaginary" rather than "theory" for three reasons: first, because imaginary allows him to focus on "the way ordinary people 'imagine' their social surroundings, and this is often not expressed in theoretical terms, but is carried in images, stories, and legends"; second, "theory is often the possession of a small minority, whereas ... the social imaginary is shared by large groups of people, if not the whole society"; and, third, "the social imaginary is that common understanding that makes possible common practices and a widely shared sense of legitimacy."[5]

This third reason for the use of imaginary points to a further feature of Taylor's conception that is important for our purposes: the common understanding that facilitates our collective practices is not only factual but also normative. That is to say, "we have a sense of how things usually go, but this is interwoven with an idea of how they *ought to go, of what missteps would invalidate the practice.*"[6] Moreover, such norms as exist in the social imaginary are not self-evidently valid but depend on some version of a still more basic "moral or metaphysical order" within which they make sense as norms.[7]

Of the examples Taylor offers to help concretize his notion, organizing a demonstration is particularly illustrative:

> Let's say we organize a demonstration. This means that this act is already in our repertory. We know how to assemble, pick up banners, and march. We know that this is meant to remain within certain bounds, both spatially (don't invade certain spaces), and in the way it impinges on others (this side of a threshold of aggressivity—no violence). We understand the ritual. The background understanding which makes this act possible for us is complex, but part of what makes sense of it is some picture of ourselves as speaking to others, to which we are related in a certain way—say, compatriots, or the human race.... The immediate sense of what we're doing, getting the message to the government and our fellow citizens that the cuts must stop, say, makes sense in a wider context, in which we see ourselves as standing in a continuing relation with others, in which it is appropriate to address them in this manner, and not say, by humble supplication, or by threats of armed insurrection. We can gesture quickly at all this by saying that this kind of demonstration has its normal place in a stable, ordered, democratic society.[8]

Thus the organizing of a demonstration has the sense it has because of the larger "imaginary" or, as he otherwise puts it, the "wider predicament" in which it literally makes sense to demonstrate. Taylor continues:

> We can see here how the understanding of what we're doing right now... makes the sense it does, because of our grasp of the wider predicament: how we continuingly stand, or have stood to others and to power. This in turn opens out wider perspectives on where we stand in space and time: our relation to other nations and peoples, e.g., to external models of democratic life we are trying to imitate, or of tyranny we are trying to distance ourselves from; and also of where we stand in our history, in the narrative of our becoming, whereby we recognize this capacity to demonstrate peacefully as an achievement of democracy, hard-won by our ancestors, or something we aspire to become capable of through this common action.[9]

In short, a demonstration makes sense *as a demonstration* because it "draws on our whole world, that is, our sense of our whole predicament in time and space, among others and in history."[10]

Taylor's discussion of a demonstration is important for the way in which it illuminates the interdependency of the normative notions that unavoidably accompany the making of the sense the practice makes and the moral or metaphysical order these normative notions presuppose. The practice of demonstration necessarily entails the understanding that the way things are now are not as they *ought to be* and, further, the intention to bring them in line with how they ought to be. It ought to be the case, for example, that the poor have an equal opportunity to vote, and where this norm is ignored demonstration takes place in order to change things. Demonstration is thus inescapably oriented both by and toward normative understandings—understandings of how things ought to be.

Yet normative notions of how things ought to be depend inevitably on some larger sense of *why* things ought to be the way they ought to be, why, to stay with the example, the poor should not be excluded from a properly democratic process (e.g., democratic processes that exclude people on the basis of economic status are not truly democratic, etc.). This larger sense of the why behind the ought is the moral or metaphysical order—in this case, the range of ideals signified by word "democracy."

The interdependency of practice, norms, and moral/metaphysical order helps to clarify why an invalidation of—or challenge to—a practice as basic as a demonstration can have extraordinary consequences (as of course it has in recent history—in Tibet, for example). It is because the invalidation can never be an invalidation of the practice *simpliciter,* as if the practice could exist in isolation from the context in which it derives its meaningfulness as an intelligible practice.[11] Rather, invalidating or challenging the practice will always and simultaneously involve invalidating or challenging the normative notions and moral order necessarily embedded in the sense the practice makes. If demonstrators were to say, "this demonstration stuff isn't working so well, let's break into the White House, hold the president hostage and demand reforms on behalf of the poor," they would not only have invalidated the practice of demonstration but also have challenged, whether consciously or not, the normative notions of how things ought to go or be, and behind that the moral and metaphysical order that made these notions normative in the first place. Through the invalidation of the practice, that is, democracy itself would have come under attack.

Conversely, the interdependency of practice, norms, and moral/metaphysical order also helps to explain how practices can lose their meaning, become unintelligible, and permanently disappear. While an argument for different norms (things ought to go or be *this* way rather than *that* way) on the basis of a shared moral/metaphysical order could result in the disappearance of a practice (e.g., demonstration), the more fundamental challenge to its intelligibility comes at the level of the moral/metaphysical order. Simply put, if this order is rendered invalid, then the normative notions and the practices they underwrite are, too. When the moral or metaphysical order is invalidated, a practice whose sense was made in relation to this order literally loses its sense: replacing democracy with tyranny devastates the context in which the practice of demonstration makes any sense. Thus demonstration is itself devastated and collapses. In the language of Acts, the practice has become "empty" (Acts 14:15).

Attending to Taylor's concept of the "social imaginary" allows us to offer a richer account of the collision described in chapter 2 of the present book. In Taylor's terms, the collision of the Christian mission with constitutive elements of Graeco-Roman culture occurs not only at the level of particular practices and the normative notions they embody but also at that of the moral or metaphysical order. Indeed the former collision is but the necessary and derivative outworking of the latter.

Sacrificing to the gods, soothsaying, magic, the use of household shrines, and so forth all gain their intelligibility as practices within a moral or metaphysical order that underwrites the reality in which it makes sense to do these things. The (vast) disagreement within paganism about the particular ways in which magic ought to be done, for example, or between the philosophers and the larger public on the usefulness of caring for images of the gods, points not to different moral or metaphysical orders but to the operative normative notions within a shared sense of the wider predicament.[12] These are, as it were, in-house differences.

By contrast, according to Acts, sacrificing to the gods, soothsaying, magic, and so forth, do not "make sense" for the early Christians. The reason is not hard to find: the wider predicament in which these practices made sense has disappeared. Thus the collision between the Christian mission and the larger Mediterranean world is both extraordinarily deep and "thick" for the reason that it entails multiple layers of a whole world of sense-making, that is, a social imaginary. In Lystra, for example, Paul and Barnabas' call "to turn to the Living God" states the challenge to the locals' pattern of worship and sacrifice to the gods not so much in terms of the practice itself, as if the goal were simply to get the Lystrans to substitute horn blowing for sacrificing, or in terms of the normative notions of pagan sacrifice (for it to work properly, you really ought to be doing it this way rather than that way), but in terms of a different total framework, one in which sacrifice to the gods becomes literal nonsense, or, in biblical language, idolatry. Precisely because the intelligibility of all practices depends on the understandings they necessarily carry with them, challenging the practice of pagan sacrifice—at least in the way that Acts narrates it— entailed the invalidation of a rival moral/metaphysical order and, hence, of the "whole sense of things" that made pagan sacrifice what it was.

Insofar, therefore, as the collision with the Christian mission extended to "that common understanding that makes possible common practices and a widely shared sense of legitimacy," the citizens in Lystra, Philippi, Athens, Ephesus, and elsewhere are rightly portrayed as intuiting the serious threat to their basic patterns of life that arrived with the Christian missionaries.[13] To speak of this threat as the radical possibility of cultural collapse is not an exercise in rhetorical exaggeration, a heightened or even shrill way of pointing toward the effect of Christianity over the long haul: it is, rather, what happens when a whole range of practices constitutive of pagan culture—sacrifice to the gods, manipulating reality by magic, soothsaying, temple-based economic practice, and so forth—is rendered unintelligible or obsolete by a fundamentally different moral or metaphysical order.[14]

Acts, of course, does not speak of the "moral or metaphysical order" but of "the Living God." And that is right to the point. The argument here is hardly that Luke was thinking in Charles Taylor's terms, that, after all, the notion of the social imaginary is the hermeneutical sieve through which we should strain the Acts of the Apostles.[15] Much to the contrary, the point is rather that Taylor's description of the coinherence of practices, normative notions, and a larger moral or metaphysical framework is interpretively advantageous because it helps to uncover the deeper matters that are at stake in the way Luke tells the story of the Christian mission. If one takes the narrative of Acts as a whole, that is, the reactions of the pagans in city after city are not disparate, dissociate outbursts of anger but are instead variant tremors of a still more basic quake. To see the potential of the Christian mission for cultural demise is to read it rightly. Indeed, this is but the flip side of the reality that God's identity receives new cultural explication in the formation of a community whose moral or metaphysical order requires an alternative way of life. "Abstaining from the pollutions of idols" (Acts 15:20) is essentially—not accidentally— related to the "taking out of a people for God's name (15:14)."

In light of the profound collision described in chapter 2, chapter 3 of the present book explored Acts' narratively sophisticated rejection of the most natural inference about a force for cultural disruption in the Roman world: the Christians are seditious and involved in treasonous competition with Caesar for the imperial throne. Through its discussion of the scenes involving chief Roman officials—Gallio, Claudius Lysias, Felix, Festus (and

King Agrippa II)—chapter 3 followed Luke's attempt to refuse the reading of the Christian mission as seditious and instead to redescribe it theologically as a living testimony to the resurrection of Jesus.

In Corinth, where the local Jews ingeniously tried to link the argument over the right reading of Torah (νόμος) to the Christians' disobedience to Roman law (νόμος), Gallio's response displayed narratively the fact that the state is not hermeneutically equipped to discern theological truth, that is, to settle by means of Roman jurisprudence whether or not Torah testifies to Jesus' resurrection. In refusing the suggested linkage between the debate over the right construal of Israel's heritage and the Roman legal sphere, Gallio also begins—on Luke's behalf—the argument that the Christian mission is not a zealous bid for Caesar's power and throne. It is instead, as Gallio says, a living contention for a particular construal of "a word, names, and [the Jewish] law" (18:15). Attending to further developments in the narrative, however, reveals that for all his correctness in discerning the deeply Jewish character of the Christian mission, Gallio's response should not be taken as Luke's total view of *the* state any more than it should be seen as the entirety of the Roman state's response to the Christian mission.

In Jerusalem, where the tribune Claudius Lysias mistook Paul for a missing revolutionary leader of four thousand assassins (Sicarii), Luke once again redescribes the movement Paul's character represents as a community focused on the resurrection. "With respect to the hope and the resurrection of the dead I am on trial" (23:6). Like Gallio before him, Lysias lacks the interpretive categories necessary to make judgments about the truth of the Jewish debate over resurrection and thus reads the Christian mission (i.e., "Paul") in terms of "questions about *their* law" (23:29). Yet, in contrast to the situation before Gallio, who was able simply to drive Paul and his accusers away, the Roman legal system is no longer capable of avoiding an encounter with the Christians. Though Paul has done "nothing deserving death or imprisonment"—Christianity is not brigandry—he is placed inside the sphere of Roman jurisprudence and moved to formal trial in Caesarea.

In Caesarea before Felix, "the Way" is yet again renarrated as an emphatically Jewish position on the question of the resurrection of the dead over against the trial lawyer's suavely official accusation of sedition (as στάσις) and his attempt to associate the Nazarenes with other zealous factions. As in Jerusalem, so in Caesarea: "With respect to the resurrection of the dead I am on trial before you this day" (24:21). Before Festus and King Agrippa II, things were not much different. With the absence of Tertullus' legal wit, Festus heard only points of dispute between rival members of a common superstition (25:19–20), and King Agrippa himself bore witness to the public reality and criminal innocence of the "Christians": strange and worthy of mockery they may be, but they are not a secret society—their life is not lived in a corner—and they have incited no sedition and committed no treason. They are not worthy of death.

In all of these passages, and in others as well (e.g., in Philippi), the Christian mission is blatantly branded as a movement of sedition and resolutely redescribed as a living argument for a particular construal of the Jewish law centered on the resurrection of the dead. But about this, the Roman government can make no judgment one way or the other, for its representatives lack the hermeneutical framework within which the terms of the explicitly theological debate make sense. The ability to know the truth about "Jesus, who was dead, but whom Paul claimed to be alive" does not, therefore, come with a particular function of the state or reside within the sphere of Roman administration, as if the declaration of innocence could validate Paul's claim.[16]

Yet Roman law is not for that reason without its constructive place in Luke's portrayal of the overall contour of early Christianity. Indeed, in a reversal of sorts, Luke subpoenas it to testify on behalf of the Christians. Not only in structure and detail does the narrative presuppose considerable legal knowledge—even Paul, when in a pinch, is pictured as something of a man of the court—but also, insofar as the law can speak through the officials who enforce it, it speaks correctly about the missionaries: they are not out to incite sedition, nor do they endeavor to usurp the imperial throne in the name of Jesus. Of such crimes, says the law, they are innocent. Of course in reality, as we should know by now, this is Luke's voice and not that of the *lex Romana* itself. But that is precisely the point: Acts' political strategy is vastly more than self-assertive apologia (e.g., 25:8); properly construed, it is a legal tour de force that argues for the right testimony and application of the Roman law itself. Inasmuch as law must always be mediated by human presence—law cannot interpret or apply *itself*—Luke's work stands between the Roman law and his Christian readers and reshapes the former to fit the latter.[17] *Rightly* read for the question of insurrection in the case of Christians, the law yields the verdict "innocent."

That Luke's reading is that of a legal revisionary—what would a Pliny or an Ulpian make of it?—points not to automatic argumentative defeat but, once again, to the fact that any and all attempts to construe what law is about depend unavoidably on a larger conceptual scheme. It is no great surprise that Luke's larger conceptual scheme—that which structures his reasoning about Roman law—turns out to be Christian, but the importance of this fact should not be overlooked. For it stresses the deep connection between Luke's wider theological vision and the specific legal conclusion for which Acts argues: grant the vision, and the conclusion follows. Thus what is really at stake in the legal interpretation of cultural disruption is the truth of the more comprehensive conceptual scheme within which the legal interpretation takes place. Luke reads the Roman law not as a *Roman* jurist but as a Christian one. In so doing he simultaneously validates the Roman law as politically crucial to the identity of the Christians and reappropriates it within a different hermeneutical framework that allows its legal terms to be uttered with the right inflection. Acts, it might be said, attempts to see for the gentiles who cannot and therefore crafts an argument about the political shape of Christianity on their behalf.

But this validation and specifically Christian interpretation of Roman law hardly means the text of Acts is "pro-Rome" or that the Roman state as such receives Luke's theological endorsement. To read Acts in this way, as so many interpreters have, is to miss entirely the second step, if we may so put it, of the complex negotiation with the reality of the Roman political system, namely, that it delivers the innocent up to death. Jesus was killed under Pilate. Paul will die in Rome. For Luke, that is, the Roman law may well be capable of right interpretation, but the gentiles are nevertheless blind. Their eyes are closed, and their sight is darkness.

Put categorically, Luke's "second step" means that the declaration of innocence can never be divorced from the coming death. Jesus' in Jerusalem. Paul's in Rome. So do the gentiles blindly rage. In Lukan narrative logic, therefore, the legal rendering of δίκαιος is meant neither to applaud nor to exculpate the state but simply—and clearly—to describe the political shape of the Christian mission via a particular construal of Roman law.

Taken as a whole, then, the scenes treated in chapter 3 argue narratively for the impossibility of construing the cultural disruption emanating from the Way as sedition. Luke raises the charge for the precise reason of rejecting it and thereby delineates more precisely the cultural contour of Christianity. According to Acts, the movement that testifies to Jesus' resurrection is not lived from the template of insurrection—even Roman jurisprudence can deliver the correct verdict—but grows instead from the unfolding of God's salvific apocalypse to a world that dwells in darkness.

Reading the argument of chapter 3 together with that of chapter 2 produces a dynamic tension that animates the narrative of Acts and must be thought as a whole. On the one hand, the Christian mission into the gentile world entails a collision with culture-constructing aspects of that world. In this way, Christianity and pagan culture are competing realities. Precisely because the Christian call to repentance necessarily involves a different way of life, basic patterns of Graeco-Roman culture are disrupted and face collapse. The pagans are justifiably incensed: the Christians embody cultural peril. On the other hand, the attempt to read this cultural peril as a bid for governmental power is roundly rejected. The upheaval that inevitably attends the arrival of Christian mission-aries has nothing whatever to do with sedition and treason. As we have said before, new culture, yes—coup, no.

Can such a tension possibly hold? Is there a way to account for it, to discover patterns of reasoning or narration that would produce it? *Can it be thought?* These are the questions addressed in chapter 4, which is in essence an attempt to think the juxtaposition of chapters 2 and 3, to take the "yes" and "no" together.

Through its close reading of Acts 17:1–9, chapter 4 argued that the origin of the tension created by Luke's interpretation of Christianity's cultural disrup-tion lies in a more basic conviction about how to read the world. The tension displayed in chapters 2 and 3, that is, arises out of a specific epistemological location, one whose way of knowing necessarily makes claims for the character of the world in which the Christian mission exists—namely, that the world is upside down. Bluntly stated: Luke's reading of the world is irreducibly Chris-tian—there is nothing more general or epistemologically basic than that—and the conflict with Graeco-Roman culture is not based upon this or that particu-lar point of disagreement but upon a radically different way of seeing things as a whole and, therefore, of naming the world's predicament. Is it right side up, or upside down?

As the exegesis of the charges against the Christians in Thessalonica demonstrated, fundamentally different answers to such a basic question result in drastically different construals of the same words and reality. On the one hand, the Christian proclamation of Jesus as King is interpreted as a direct rivalry to the "other king" of the people of the empire, the Roman emperor. In this way of thinking, Jesus is read as a usurper, a competitor with Caesar for the designation Βασιλεύς, and the leader of a group whose political objec-tives are directly revolutionary. On the other hand, in the (Lukan) Christian understanding of the thing, the political form of Jesus' kingship is that of crucifixion—he was, after all, publicly crucified as Βασιλεύς—and the kingdom of which he is King offers no platform for revolution but instead an alternative way of life.

Yet, precisely because this way of life is exhibited publicly, as the rumpus in Thessalonica unmistakably shows, it becomes the concrete focal point that reveals the essential epistemological conflict about how to read the world, which is to say that the public fact of the Christian mission requires a judg-ment about its testimony: Is it upside down or right side up? In the narrative of Acts, those missionaries "who have turned the world upside down have come here, too" is of course one way to answer; "the salvation of God has been sent to the Gentiles" is the other.

If we think of epistemology as something we can reflect on in abstraction from the lives we live, then the remainder of chapter 4's argument will seem less immediately related to the exegesis at its beginning than if we grasp the point that our way of reading the world is always and necessarily bound up with the lives we are living.[18] And, consequently, if we understand that epistemological location—the place, as it were, from where we see things—is coextensive with the practices that shape our sight, then the turn to the three core practices that shape the vision of Acts can be seen as the requisite hermeneutical move for the explication of the tension generated by chapters 2 and 3. This is not to say that Luke thinks his way from the tension he establishes to particular Christian practices but rather something like the reverse: the tension created by acknowledging cultural disruption and insisting on its specifically Christian interpretation emerges as a result of the attempt to write a certain kind of narrative in light of the constitutive and interdependent practices of an alternative way of life.[19] The theological vision of Acts is the outworking of a particular practical epistemology.

Jesus is the Lord of all. So says Peter. The emperor is Lord. So says Festus. Through its analysis of Acts' particular narrative shaping of the early Christian practice of confessing Jesus as κύριος, chapter 4 probed the significance of the startling juxtaposition created by the contrasting speech of Peter and Festus. The hermeneutical impact of the contrast was due not as much to the use of κύριος per se as to Luke's careful placement of its modifier πάντων ("of all"): in ascribing universal Lordship to Jesus, Acts also implicitly denied it to Caesar. Close attention to Acts' cultural encyclopedia only heightened the point: where the logic of Roman imperial rule entailed the divinity of the Roman emperor, Christian counter-logic required its rejection. There is only one *dominus mundi*.

Yet, as Luke's reading of the OT made clear, the confession of Jesus as Lord of all was not a reaction to Caesar's claims—as if preaching τόν κύριον Ἰησοῦν (11:20) was predominantly a counter-claim—but was instead the necessary constructive consequence of Jesus's relation to the God of Israel.[20] Joel 3, Amos 9, and Psalm 15 (LXX), among others, exhibited a crucial christological extension of the identity of the Lord of whom the texts originally spoke. When in Acts these OT texts speak of God as Lord, they now also speak simultaneously of Jesus. Even the scripture testifies, as Luke could have said, that Jesus does not rival God's identity as Lord of the cosmos; in fact, he expresses it. The universal Lordship of God takes shape as the life, death, and resurrection of Jesus of Nazareth. As we noted earlier, Acts 10:36 and 17:24 are complimentary and mutually interpreting: "Jesus Christ—this one is Lord of all" interprets christologically "the God who made the world and everything in it—this one, [is] Lord of heaven and earth."

Precisely because the life of Jesus exegetes concretely what it is for the God of Israel to be Lord of all, universal lordship is linked inextricably to the bringing of peace. "You know the word which God sent to Israel preaching peace through Jesus Christ—this one is Lord of all" (10:36). As Ulrich Mauser argued, Acts focuses the "whole story of Jesus" into "a declaration of peace."[21] Inasmuch as the "whole story of Jesus" is the story of the Lord of all, to be Lord in Lukan thought is not to wield the power of the sword over all who might challenge the legitimacy of his dominion—Nero's "many thousands of swords which my *pax* restrains will be drawn at my nod"—but is rather to embrace crucifixion and death and to exhibit publicly the refusal to vanquish one's enemies. That in the context of Roman imperial practice this constitutes a radical revaluation of *pax* should be as evident now as it would have been to Lucan, Tacitus, and Cassius Dio, to the pacified peoples in Judaea, Britain, North Africa, Asia, and Greece, and to all those in the empire who knew that the *pax Romana* formed on the tip of the Roman spear. If we were to try to envision universal lordship in light of such a revaluation of *pax,* our fundamental image should be built from the bottom up rather than top down. As Jesus put it in the Gospel of Luke, "I am in your midst as the one who serves" (22:27). According to Acts, "peace" names the outworking of Lordship in the total life of Jesus of Nazareth.

Realizing that this christological construal of universal lordship makes sense only in a reading of the world that from the outside appears upside down should help to facilitate a still further step in the reversal of our typical way of thinking. Where the narrative of Acts clearly rejects any hint of the notion that Jesus is a rival for Caesar's throne—that he competes with the emperor for the title κύριος πάντων—it does so on the basis of a more startling claim: Jesus, the bringer of peace, simply *is* the Lord of all, and the mode of being that is Caesar's represents a violent refusal of this universal Lordship. Differently said, *Caesar* is the challenger, not of course because Jesus wants to rule the empire,[22] but in the sense that the self-exaltation necessary to sustain Caesar's political project is inevitably idolatrous. *Dominus et deus noster* pays the imperial bill, but for the Christians it claims an allegiance—a form of devotion—that belongs only to another: the true Lord of all.

That the universal Lordship of the God of Israel in Jesus of Nazareth is *practical* theology—rather than merely cognitive or propositional play—is nowhere as strikingly evident as it is in the early Christian practice of mission. Thus does the focus of chapter 4 move from Jesus's identity as Lord of all to its socio-cultural explication: "You shall be my witnesses in Jerusalem, in all Judaea and Samaria, and to the end of the earth," says Jesus, at once punctuating his visible presence with the disciples and articulating the narrative program of the Acts of the Apostles (1:8).

If, in accordance with this narrative program, we take Acts seriously as the hermeneutical template for a description of early Christian mission, then the necessity of eschewing the temptation to fashion a general definition of mission into which Acts could fit becomes apparent: in that they require the transmutation of the *novum* that generates Christian mission into a (more or less) ordinary social phenomenon, all such attempts entail an interpretive perspective that runs counter to that of the Acts narrative itself. That is to say, in taking Christian mission as an instance of a more general type, theories of mission subsume the resurrection of Jesus by God into a more comprehensive explanatory scheme. As Acts tells it, however, the resurrection of Jesus by God is not a point within an overall larger scheme, but the fount from which mission springs.

Adequately attending to Acts' narrative program thus involves coordinating the historical fact of the uniqueness of Christian mission with a rejection of certain Troeltschian historical canons in favor of the possibility proffered—or rather proclaimed—by the narrative, namely, that Christian mission arises from God's side of death. It is no accident, in other words, that the primary grammar of mission in Acts is that of witnessing to the resurrection of Jesus.

It is after all the resurrection that confirms Jesus's identity as the Lord of all (Acts 2:36). On any reasonable account, that is, Jesus's execution at the behest of Pilate would at the very least render highly questionable the reading of his life as that of the Lord. He may well be innocent, but Lord he is not. According to Acts, however, in his resurrection God rejects the rejection of Jesus's lordship, authenticates his life—and death—as part of what it means to be the Lord of all, and extends this life into a mission of salvation in his name.

The life of the missionaries in Acts, therefore, is in essence a life of response, an alternative way of being in the world that takes as its pattern the life of the one to whom they bear witness. Differently said, Acts does not construe "witness" monothematically as the proclamation of Jesus's resurrection—preaching the word, as it were—but more comprehensively as living out the pattern of life that culminates in resurrection. Peter, Stephen, and Paul, for example, doubtless knew what to say, but such speech occurs in Acts as part of a larger narrative reality of the witnessing shape of their lives. Paul's "I am on trial for the resurrection of the dead" thus has a double significance: Jesus' and his own after his coming death. Mission in this sense is a mimetic representation of the foundational story of the Gospel of Luke: the main characters in Acts, to put it plainly, look like Jesus—and precisely in this way embody his life and carry it forth into the wider Graeco-Roman world.

That they go forth at all, of course, implies a judgment about the basic need of humanity. Acts is not content with implied theology, however, and makes the anthropological correlate to mission explicit: the resurrection of Jesus discloses publicly the need for "everyone everywhere to repent" (17:30). In short, universal Christian mission—witnessing to "the end of the earth"— practices the unity between the universal human problem and the saving significance of the universal Lord: "everyone, everywhere," corresponds to "there is no salvation in any other name" (cf. 4:12).

Despite common interpretive tendencies in contemporary American Christianity, salvation is not, according to Acts, oriented solely toward the internal aspect of the human being (soul, heart, etc.). Against all spiritualizing tendencies, Luke narrates the salvation that attends the Christian mission as something that entails necessarily the formation of a community, a public pattern of life that witnesses to the present dominion of the resurrected Lord of all. If, after the unavoidable impact of the Reformation, the Enlightenment, and our contemporary consumerist culture,[23] we have trouble grasping this point, we would do well to remember that the ancient pagans did not: the community of Jews and gentiles gathered around a new pattern of life is the sociological presupposition both of the ability to scapegoat/persecute the *Christiani* (from Nero on) and of the fact that in Acts the missionaries are perceived not so much as religious quacks as harbingers of deep cultural problems. Indeed, the name for the public community that actually stuck was no term of fondness.

Though there are multiple ways one could speak about the formation of community as a core practice for Acts, the remainder of chapter 4 argues— perhaps surprisingly—that attending to the only two occurrences of the same word would best disclose the cultural significance of this practice (at least with respect to the aims of this book). As the passages from Tacitus, Pliny, Suetonius, and 1 Peter amply demonstrated, "Christian" was from first to last a term of derision, a way in which pagan "outsiders"—Roman administrative and otherwise—could specify with a single word the problematic contour of the followers of the man *Christus*. It was, in other words, a term whose very usage presupposed a particular reading of the public reality of the Christian community.

Luke's usage of this word both confirms its public, derogatory sense and paints a counter-portrait, as it were, of Christianity's public face. His use of Χριστιανοί, that is to say, is narratively precise, and it is in attending to the cumulative effect of this precision that we come to see *in nuce* the conceptual pattern that structures much of the "yes and no" of the larger story.

Despite the multiplicity of terms he uses to characterize the followers of Jesus, in his authorial voice Luke avoids writing about this community as

"Christians." In this sense, it is true to say that Luke resists calling the Christians "Christians" and that the restriction of this term in the narrative of Acts evidences a fundamental rejection of many of the common associations the term carried.[24] Yet, this rejection is not the ham-fisted, total *Nein!* of an angry protest. Indeed, in a crucially important way, the narrative of Acts accepts—incorporates into its overall testimony—a deeply significant part of the word's current meaning. As its first use in Acts shows, Luke knew well that a community of resocialized Jews and gentiles in a Syrian metropolis—a hub, in fact, for Roman administration in the East—would provoke public interpretation (11:26). In admitting the word Christian into the narrative of the first "mixed" church's initial public appearance, Luke acknowledges, even highlights, the fact that the Christians' public witness is perceived by the wider culture as problematic and, in so doing, names the ecclesial community as a concrete instance of a conflict of interpretation. Doubtless, the Christians can be seen. But what the insiders and outsiders make of what they see is drastically different.

Thus is such acceptance of the culturally problematic reality of the Christians but the necessary prelude to the reinterpretation of that which Χριστιανοί attempts to describe. This reinterpretation, it was argued, occurs via the effect of the term's reintroduction in the mouth of Agrippa II after a long stretch of narrative in which the Christians' potential for cultural disruption is plainly seen. Paul is on trial for his life—the Roman administrative machine is full on—and Agrippa's jibe makes sense of the reality that has landed Paul there: the Χριστιανοί are publicly problematic, as by now the readers of Acts will agree. It is therefore all the more significant that Paul is immediately declared unworthy of death. The declaration, made in the face of a context that suggests entirely otherwise, reshapes the social reality to which Christian refers: the Christians are not zealots who stir the pot of revolution.

Attending to the word Christian in Acts discloses not only Luke's narratively disciplined vocabulary but also something more significant: the core practice of communal formation and the necessarily complicated negotiations that arise out of the reactions evoked by this community's public presence. ("Christian" is a public word.) It discloses, further, the depth of the interpretive problem surrounding the nature of that presence. The contrary readings of the public reality of the Christians point to the inextricable tie between hermeneutical perspective, social location, and response to the man "Christus."[25] Put more simply, how one construes what the Christians are—the shape of their common life and its public effects—will inevitably depend upon one's location inside or outside the particular community itself, and this will, in turn, depend ultimately on what one makes of the identity of Christus. To recognize his universal Lordship is, according to Acts, to be positioned within the community that witnesses publicly to this Lordship and, therefore, to judge the character of the cultural disruption that accompanies its universal mission as the inevitable outworking of the culturally determinative dialectic that is the acceptance and rejection of the Light to the gentiles.

Taken as a whole, chapter 4 thus argued for a way of knowing that arises out of the belief in Christus as the apocalypse of the God of Israel to the gentiles. This way of knowing, however, was not analyzed as a formal feature of the intellect per se but rather seen as a distinctive form of practical knowledge, one whose shape was indissolubly bound to the narrative outworking of three core ecclesial practices. To know in this way is to construe reality from a quite particular place, that is, within the community named derisively by outsiders as "Christians." Acknowledging this criticism—how else could Χριστιανός initially sound?—it is nevertheless to wager one's total perception on the insiders' reading of those who follow the Jesus who was dead. Epistemological location is thus foundational to the tension that is indelibly inscribed within the book of Acts: there is no way to narrate the conflicting claims between insider and outsider as commensurable readings of the Christian reality, especially of Christus himself. Luke must instead shape the narration of the potential for cultural collapse *Christianly,* as it were, offer an interpretation such that it is seen not as a disaster to be violently avoided but as forgiveness, deliverance, and light. To be sure, the tension between acknowledged cultural disruption and its interpretation as non-seditious "good news" holds together only in the particularity of Luke's practical epistemology. As time would show, Romans *qua* Romans would not agree with him. But that is just the point: to think well the juxtaposition of chapters 2 and 3 of this book just is to think the apocalyptic perspective of Acts.

The Politics of Truth

If this reading of the Acts of the Apostles is taken seriously, several critical questions immediately arise. Though there are many important issues with which we could deal, as a whole, the most crucial questions center on the intersection between so-called universalism and the politics it produces. Put simply, is it not the case that Luke's claim to truth necessitates a hegemonic politics, a kind of eradication of the "other" in the name of one's own truth, a political posture that is fundamentally intolerant? Is not cultural difference suppressed or destroyed in the name of one Lord? The constructive attempt in this final section is to think along with Luke about these matters, to see what we can learn from reading Acts in conversation with our own pressing questions. In short, we want to ask, how might Acts help us to particularize and refine our notions—or suspicions—about universal claims and the politics they engender?

Because these questions of political theology have been vigorously discussed over the last several centuries—frequently grouped thematically in modern discussion under the issue of "tolerance"—we obviously cannot hope to cover the full range of issues.[26] What we can do, however, is to focus our entry into a segment of this discussion via a selection of one recent thinker's particularly sharp formulation of the central problem.

Jan Assmann is perhaps not as well known in North America as he should be, not because his thinking is entirely original or necessarily compelling on our specific questions but because his historical knowledge is vast and his analyses of basic problems in the study of the impact of ancient texts through the history of Western thought are particularly clear and well stated.[27] Reading Assmann facilitates a sensitive grappling with the questions that face us because of his historically deep understanding of polytheism and its inextricable connection to, as he puts it, the issue of "cultural translation."

In the opening essay of *Moses the Egyptian*, Assmann states that his project concerns "the distinction between true and false in religion that underlies more specific distinctions such as Jews and gentiles, Christians and pagans, Muslims and unbelievers."[28] Once this fundamental "Mosaic" distinction between true and false is made

> there is no end of reentries or subdistinctions. We start with Christians and pagans and end up with Catholics and Protestants, Calvinists and Lutherans, Socinians and Latitudinarians, and a thousand more similar denominations and subdenominations. Cultural or intellectual distinctions such as these construct a universe that is not only full of meaning, identity, and orientation, but also full of conflict, intolerance, and violence. Therefore, there have always been attempts to overcome the conflict by reexamining the distinction.[29]

Readers who worry that Assmann's path will be through the well-trod debates about relativism—plainly it either exists totally, in which case we would not know it and could not argue for it, or not at all—will be pleasantly surprised that he turns not to a sophisticated version of "can't we all just get along" but in a more interesting direction, toward that of the relationship between polytheism and culture.

It is a mistake, says Assmann, to think that the true/false distinction "is as old as religion itself, though at first sight nothing might seem more plausible." Do we not all think, he asks, that "every religion quite automatically puts everything outside itself in the position of error and falsehood and look down on other religions as 'paganism'?" Do we not tend to assume that this is "quite simply the religious expression of ethnocentricity?" Is it not the case that "every religion produce[s] 'pagans' in the same way that every civilization generates 'barbarians'?" Assmann's "No" to all these questions hinges fundamentally on the conviction that "[c]ultures not only generate otherness by constructing identity, but also develop techniques of translation."[30]

By "translation" Assmann means to point to the way in which our constructions of the "other" can be deconstructed such that the differences created in the act of other-construction between "us" and "them" can be dissolved. Such deconstructions are not totalitarian or colonial annexations of the "real other" precisely because what is deconstructed is not the other but our own preconceived notions of who or what the other is.[31] Among the notions that need deconstructing—concepts that belong not to the other *in se* but only to our construction of the other—are "paganism" and "idolatry." When and where such "antagonistic" concepts do *not* exist, as in ancient polytheism, the possibility of cultural translation does. Thus does polytheism emerge in Assmann's interpretation as "a technique of translation," a way of "making more transparent the borders that were erected by cultural distinctions."[32]

Although we may still be "far from a full understanding" of polytheism,[33] it is clear in Assmann's reading that polytheism was a great ethical boon in the ancient world in that it was able to provide a religious foundation for cultural translation. By construing gods in terms of their cosmic rather than tribal function, polytheism—or "cosmotheism"—provided a way in which deities of different religions did not have to negate each other but instead could be equated or absorbed one into the other. The sun god of one region, for example, could easily be read as the sun god of another—and the necessary political treaties thus sworn to and signed: the gods were "international because they were cosmic."[34] Despite differences in language, custom, and so forth, cosmic polytheisms provided a common ground for different societies and prevented fundamental cultural collision; indeed, they rendered cultural differences "mutually transparent and compatible." Precisely because the true/false distinction "simply did not exist in the world of polytheistic religions," that is, the gods were able to function "as a means of intercultural translatability."[35]

The obverse of Assmann's theory, of course, is that where the true/false distinction obtains, cultural estrangement and potential destruction will of necessity follow. The reason is rather simple, though far reaching in its implications: "False gods cannot be translated."[36] They must instead be overcome or rendered obsolete.

The primary way in which such a counter-move is made is through the construction of a "grand narrative," a story that subsumes all other religious differences into one all-consuming reading of the world. This metanarrative then forms the basis for the retelling of the counter-move in innumerable various ways—all of which have in common the true/false distinction and, thus, the possibility for cultural rupture.

Assmann's theory becomes more complex and richer in its articulation—not least because of the range and amount of material he is able to cover (from Akhenaten to Freud)—but for our purposes its main lines are clear enough. In its conceptual configuration, there are serious, even debilitating, problems, many of which have been rightfully buried under an ever-increasing heap of philosophical/theological criticism. For instance, he reifies the intellectual construct "religion" and mistakes this for a real "thing," which of course it is not. No one believes in or practices religion in general.[37] Assmann also, to take only one more example, repeats the standard nineteenth-century German line that religion is what cultures "construct" or produce (for translation, exclusion, etc.), a claim that runs counter to those of most (all?) actual religions themselves and is therefore phenomenologically at odds with the phenomenon it seeks to describe.[38]

Despite such problems, Assmann's argument is a particularly clear example of a current way of thinking about the interface between conflicting religious claims and their cultural effects. Indeed, he is hardly the first thinker in recent times to sing "In Praise of Polytheism," to recall the title of philosopher Odo Marquard's lecture from thirty years ago.[39] Marquard's lecture makes something of a rambling essay, but the main line of thought in relation to our question is discernable: to the extent that polytheism represents a diverse thought pattern that encourages multiple rather than single (meta) narratives and tolerates difference it should be embraced. Polytheism is, after all, "the great humane principle."[40]

For both Assmann and Marquard, and perhaps for the majority of the European and North American religious studies establishment, early Christianity of the kind we meet in Acts exemplifies the problem polytheistic thinking can overcome.[41] Paul's plea for conversion, "I wish you might all become as I am" (26:29), for example, is heard in this schema as a fundamentally intolerant claim, a "universal," which counteracts difference and prevents cultural translation. Furthermore, because Paul's wish is finally only intelligible on the basis of a comprehensive narrative, one that claims to tell one story that is simultaneously everyone's story—that of the Lord of all and the salvation in his name—it renders "untrue" other narratives that seek to tell the totality of the human story and is thus at a crucial level "intolerant" of them and the lives they produce.[42] To the extent, therefore, that Acts narrates the reality of the collision between the Christian mission and constitutive aspects of pagan culture—articulates narratively, that is, the possibility of cultural collapse— and to the extent that such a collision is rooted ultimately in the universal Lordship of the God of Israel in one particular human being, Jesus of Nazareth, the Acts of the Apostles is a text whose required ethical posture is potentially problematic. Indeed, from the perspective of those thinkers for whom "tolerance" is an unquestioned ethical desideratum and for whom "difference" *as such* is a good, Acts could appear as nothing short of dangerous. After all, the "Great Light to the Nations" in the modern world was no less than Joseph Stalin.[43]

For members of the hermeneutical community that takes Acts as one of its normative texts for theological discourse, the questions raised by Assmann and others cannot go ignored. It is therefore of prima facie importance to articulate how we—I am a member of one such community—might read Acts in light of such questions. Yet because this articulation requires a rethinking of some widespread assumptions about religion and "tolerance," the following discussion should be relevant to anyone interested in giving serious thought to the cluster of issues that surround theological truth claims and their accompanying politics.

Before we deal directly with such issues, however, we need to make three preliminary remarks. First, the following discussion is not a defense of Acts, as if, in a somewhat odd twist in the history of NT scholarship, we should engage in an *apologia* for Acts in light of an (allegedly) independent and more comprehensive moral order (Tolerance). Since I do not believe that such an independent order exists, the argument below should obviously not be read as an attempt to help Acts reach the bar of modern concerns. On its simplest level, it should rather be seen as acknowledging (1) that there is an important connection between our reading of Acts and many live questions in the realm of religious/political discourse today,[44] and (2) that to think about the normative function of the scriptural texts is necessarily to cultivate an analogical conversation with contemporary modes of analysis.

Second, when I speak of truth I mean first of all not so much to point to the intricate philosophical discussions about true propositions—important though these are—as I do toward something more like what theologian Robert Jenson has called "the dumb sense" of truth.[45] Jenson's wonderful phrase tries to get at the sense of "true . . . with which we all use the word when behaving normally, and which just therefore I cannot and do not need to analyze further." Truth in this "dumb sense" or "ordinary way" has its context in everyday "normal" human life: "when we are behaving normally, we use 'true' as an adjective which attributes a presumed common characteristic . . . to certain beliefs, assertions, etc.; and we proceed so even if we are unable to analyze that characteristic further." So, for example, if my son informs me that my wife wants me to fix macaroni tonight for dinner, and I then ask my wife, "is it true that you want me to fix macaroni?" she may say "no" or "yes," but she will not say, "what do you mean by true?" Nor would I reply to a student's question, "Dr. Rowe, is it true that you were ten minutes late to lecture?" with "what is the specific theory of correspondence you're advocating when you say 'true'?" A simple "yes" or "no" (or qualification: "well, actually, only five minutes . . . ") would be the ordinary, everyday and sufficient answer, an answer that takes for granted that we know what we mean when we say "true."

But in saying that Acts is a narrative that can render "untrue" other narratives that offer substantially different schemes of life—that tell the human story in such a way as to say "your entire life should be lived in this way"—I am also attempting to point toward something more comprehensive or "thicker" than the sense we get from simple everyday occurrences of the word "true," namely, the truth of a habit of being, a kind of true total way of life whose pattern can be falsified by living in a fundamentally different way. We may call this the practical contour or shape of truth. It is the kind of truth, for example, that Dietrich Bonhoeffer presupposed when he wrote in his letter to Bishop Valdemar Ammundsen in 1934 that "only complete truth and truthfulness can help us now." Bonhoeffer's point was hardly that those who opposed the union between Christianity and Nazism needed to stop lying and become more rigorous in sticking to the truth. It was rather that the truth would be revealed, would show up as what truth is, in the coming choice "between National Socialism and Christianity"; to opt for theological union with the Nazi way of life was to live in a way that was untrue and thus to falsify practically the shape of a true life. Truth was no doubt "open speaking" but it was also "living."[46]

To put this point in a slightly different way, the sense of truth at which the narrative of Acts aims is not so much how to make a true statement as opposed to a false one but more the kind of life that forms the background of the possibility of being able to know the truth rather than the lie—a true kind of life.[47] In this way of thinking, knowing the truth does not correspond simply to a correct cognitive choice between the truth and falsehood of an individual statement (or clusters of them) but has more fundamentally to do with the alternative between an entire pattern of life in which truth is enabled to show up *as truth* and a pattern of life whose total context requires truth to show up not as truth but as something else ("craziness," for example; cf. μανία in Acts 26:24).

Insofar as Acts narrates the collision between early Christianity and paganism it does so at this deeper level, the level where it is true (or false) to say that the dead Jesus is now alive and is Lord of all. Make no mistake, for Luke the statement that "God has raised Jesus from the dead and made him both Lord and Christ" is absolutely and universally true. To see it as true, however, is to live the life in which it shows up as truth, that is, the life that has turned toward the God of Israel in repentance and for forgiveness of sins. Where such a claim about "the dead Jesus" shows up as "craziness" or as something to be "mocked" (cf. 17:32) it is not because the claim does not properly correspond to "in fact truth" or "reality" but because an entirely different pattern of life—one in which God's call to repentance is rejected (cf. Acts 14:15–18; 17:30–31, etc.)—creates a total interpretive context that prevents the knowledge of the truth about the dead Jesus.[48]

Third, and briefly, the relatively obvious implication of speaking of truth in the way it is employed here is that the term "truth claim" is to be understood as something that carries with it a way of life. At its most basic level, a truth claim in this sense points not to an isolated statement to which one gives or withholds assent but to an entire mode of being into which one enters or does not. As we stressed in chapter 4, for example, the confession "Jesus is Lord of all" is not simple parallel or rival claim to Caesar, but is instead an altogether different pattern of Lordship. Grasping this unity between truth and life renders intelligible the essential coordination between truth claims and the politics they produce.

With these three preliminary clarifications in mind, we can now turn to a consideration of Acts in light of the troubling questions raised about truth and politics in relation to its universal vision. Our discussion will unfold in five steps.

(1) *The Politics of Graeco-Roman Polytheism: Tolerance and Translation?* This broad heading frames an essential feature that begins our discussion. We may say it bluntly: the notion that polytheistic religions issue in political tolerance and cultural understanding is at best a serious distortion of the realities of the Graeco-Roman world. But for a variety of reasons, such a claim has not been self-evident.

For one thing, if one does enough digging, it is possible to uncover tolerant-sounding statements that seem to capture something of the ethos of the age, as, for example, that of Cicero in his defense of the provincial governor Flaccus: "Every people, Laelius," says Cicero to Flaccus' accuser, "has its religion, and we have ours" (*Flacc.*, 28.69). Josephus, too, knew an ancient religious version of "to each, his own," which he put on the lips of Nicolaus of Damascus, who at Herod's request petitioned Marcus Agrippa on behalf of the Jews: "The only thing which we have asked to share with others is the right to preserve our ancestral religion [τὴν πάτριον εὐσέβειαν] without hindrance. This in itself would not seem to be a cause for resentment, and is even to the advantage of those who grant this right. For if the Deity delights in being honored, it also delights in those who permit it to be honored" (AJ 16.41–42).[49]

Moreover, as we noted in chapter 2, "polyonomy"—the multiplicity or interchangeability of divine names for gods and goddesses—was a ubiquitous practice,[50] and as a whole Roman expansion and conquest led not to the eradication of vanquished gods but to their incorporation. Furthermore, some "foreign" cults such as that of Isis, Sarapis, or Atargatis spread in varying degrees around the Roman empire with little hindrance and, indeed, often much welcome.

These basic realities of the Graeco-Roman world lie behind the judgment of one of the late twentieth century's leading classicists that, aside from a few exceptions, the formation of the Roman empire issued in a period of religious tolerance. The increase of Roman power

> brought into being successively fewer but larger states that drew
> strength from the absorption of divine, as of human, resources. To
> rehearse that whole story would be to rehearse the whole of ancient
> history. The process was now over. Rome's Empire under our gaze was
> complete, and completely tolerant, in heaven as on earth.[51]

MacMullen knows of exceptions to such complete tolerance of course and was quick to say, in the very next sentence in fact, "Perhaps not quite completely: Jews off and on, Christians off an on, Druids for good and all, fell under ban...So did human sacrifice...mutilation" and so forth. But, he argues, "*humanitarian* views were the cause" of such repression "not bigotry."[52] "Tolerance in paganism operated" both in the divine and human realms, as mirrors of one another, at least "until Christianity introduced its own ideas."[53]

If one were to ask after the reason for such tolerance and humanitarian principles, MacMullen might well point to a later essay in which he wrote of the absence of "right and wrong" from pagan religion: "It was possible to be right and to be wrong in Judaism or in Christianity—very possible. Hence, many sects condemned one another. It was *not* possible in any other ancient religion, so far as I am aware." Indeed, he continues, "[t]here can be, and there ordinarily was and is, religion without right or wrong belief."[54]

MacMullen's judgments are significant not only because of his indisputably immense knowledge of ancient history, but also because he offers a reading of the religious shape of the Graeco-Roman period in terms that fit well with Jan Assmann's theoretical proposals. "Right and wrong" may not be exactly the same distinction as "true and false," but for our subject it is plenty close enough: both MacMullen and Assmann claim that absent the true/false or right/wrong distinction, polytheism engenders tolerance, cultural forbearance, and even humanitarianism. They note exceptions (Druids, etc.), but these are the kind of exceptions that prove the rule.[55]

On the face of it, if one studiously avoids the importance of the exceptions (see below), MacMullen's interpretation of the Roman empire's extraordinary diversity as the religious face of a politics of tolerance seems plausible. But it has not fared well in recent years, and with good reason.[56] The problem is not so much that in speaking of tolerance MacMullen engages in anachronism—an error of which he has been accused—since even if the specifically modern concept was missing in the classical world, the religio-political relation of one people to another has always been with us (the context in which tolerance gets its relevant meaning).[57] It is rather that the picture of polytheism is far too rosy, if not outright romantic. As Simon Price put it with respect to the Greeks in particular:

> 'Polytheism' . . . is often seen as a tolerant and open religious system. It is associated with amateur priests, who lacked authority, and with an absence of dogma, orthodoxy and heresy. Already having many gods, it is attributed the capacity to accommodate even more at any time. This romantic view of Greek religious liberalism has little to commend it. The absence of dogmas did not entail that anything was permitted, nor was the pluralism of gods open-ended.[58]

A diachronic glance at the history of Athens—not least Paul's own trial there—confirms Price's statement.[59]

It was not otherwise with the Romans. Already by 1917 had Auguste Bouché-Leclercq traced "religious intolerance" under every emperor from Augustus to the Antonines.[60] And "Rome," say Beard, North, and Price in a more recent work, was "never a religious 'free for all.'"[61] In fact, Rome was rather more adept than many at "setting boundaries between the legitimate and the illegitimate, between 'us' and 'them.'" Never was there a time in the early empire when the Romans failed to identify "a set of transgressive religious stereotypes (from horrendous witches to monstrous Christians) against whom they waged war, with the stylus and with the sword—or with wild beasts in the arena: 'Christians to the lions' was a powerful slogan." In short, argue MacMullen's critics, the "fact that there was a plurality of gods did not necessarily mean that religion had no limits, or that (apart, of course, from

Christianity) 'anything went.'" "Polytheistic systems," they say, form no real barrier against intolerance, but "can be as resistant as monotheism to innovation and foreign influence. And, although Roman religion was marked throughout its history by religious innovation of all kinds, there were, at the same time, clear and repeated signs of concern about the influence of foreign cults; there were also specifically 'religious crimes,' categories of religious transgression liable (as in the case of the unchastity of the Vestals) to public punishment."[62] Indeed, by the beginning of the third century, Cassius Dio could articulate clearly the Roman imperial policy of intolerance. "You should," says Maecenas to Octavian in a speech that ties later imperial politics to the years just prior to Octavian's accession,

> not only worship the divine everywhere and in every way in accordance with our ancestral traditions, but also force all others to honor it. Those who attempt to distort our religion with strange rites you should hate and punish, not only for the sake of the gods...but also because such people, by bringing in new divinities, persuade many folks to adopt foreign practices, which lead to conspiracies, revolts, and factions, which are entirely unsuitable for monarchy (*Hist. Rom.* 52.36.1–2; LCL altered).

Whether Dio's formulation was current in Augustus' day is of course debatable; but that the famous speech of Octavian's friend and counselor captures well the essential connection between Roman imperial strategy and religious suppression is not.[63]

The brutal repression of the Bacchic cult in 186 BC, the destruction of the Druids in the first century AD, the perennial execution of philosophers, magicians, fortune tellers and the like, the persecution of the Christians, and so on, should not be seen as exceptions that prove the rule of polytheistic tolerance. They should rather be seen in their own right for exactly what they are: the concrete reality that evokes the convictions exhibited in the speech of Maecenas and exposes the limits of polytheistic tolerance. In practice—and in principle—ancient polytheism cannot be read as religiously systemic tolerance; to do so is to engage in political fantasy. Had we thought hard enough about it, however, we might almost have known this ahead of time—indeed, in such a way as to make us expect to find something like the treatment of the Druids or the Christians. Strictly put, interpreting polytheism as system of universal or complete cultural tolerance, or ripe with the potential for such tolerance, commits not only a historical error but a critical conceptual one as well.

(2) *Tolerance and Diversity as Parasitic Concepts:* For all the attention the notions of tolerance and religious diversity have received in the West since

John Locke's famous letter of 1689, it is remarkable that so little of the talk we hear about these matters frankly acknowledges that both tolerance and diversity are *parasitic* concepts; they are entirely dependent for the range and particular shape of their meaning on larger conceptual schemes.[64] Tolerance and diversity, that is, can never of themselves produce tolerance and diversity or work as centrally organizing conceptions or principles precisely because they cannot of their own conceptual resources answer the questions, what will we not tolerate? what kind of diversity is unacceptable?[65] Answering these questions invariably requires recourse to a more comprehensive pattern of thought, one in which tolerance and diversity receive meaning and explication.

This can be seen even in the contemporary research university—among the most tolerant of contexts for diverse views—where certain things are simply out of bounds. There is not a lot of pressure, for example, to establish an Adolf Hitler Chair in Nazi Studies, or in the Practice of Racial Hierarchy. Such proposals—thanks be to God—would not be tolerated. But to realize that there are things that will not be tolerated is at once to see that "tolerance" is itself thought inside of a larger conceptual scheme, or erected on a normative conceptual base. In the case of intolerance toward the latter chair, that of the Practice of Racial Hierarchy, the concept of tolerance is presumably worked out within a larger way of thinking that includes the judgments that creating hierarchies on the basis of race is an evil to be avoided rather than just one more interesting opinion on the question of how we should group human beings, and, further, that the university's telos would be injured by cultivating this particular evil in its students. Were someone to advocate for the establishment of such a chair—on the grounds that the university was wrongly intolerant of his practices and views—the argument with such a person would not be about whether racial hierarchies were racism, since that term already carries with it the particular perspective of the moral scheme under attack, but about the larger context in which specific kinds of categorizing human beings were understood to be evils or not[66] and whether the telos of a university included allowing the practice of ordering hierarchies on the basis of race. Tolerance, that is, would not form the ground on which the debate was conducted but would instead receive its particular shape from the larger position for which one was arguing. "Yes," we should have such a chair presupposes and produces one kind of tolerance; "No," we absolutely should not, presupposes and produces another.[67] In short, the conceptual configurations of tolerance and intolerance are inescapably bound to a larger pattern that defines them.

To speak meaningfully, therefore, of tolerance, diversity, cultural translation and the like, we must speak explicitly of their relation to the larger pattern on which they depend for their meaning. Precisely because polytheism is one such larger pattern, it can never simply function as a cipher for "tolerance" or "cultural translation" in general, a kind of tolerance *simpliciter*.[68] Polytheism is rather the scheme of life that defines a *particular kind* of tolerance—the kind that places a missionizing Christianity outside its limits. In Assmann's terms, polytheism cannot translate the culture that is Christianity.[69] To attempt to do so would not be to facilitate the absorption of Christianity into a more comprehensive and tolerant hermeneutical frame, thereby creating mutual understanding, but to invite extinction of the polytheistic frame itself.

The significance of this fact should not be underestimated. From the polytheistic side of things, it is tantamount to the claim that Christianity offers a false way of being, a way of life—including, of course, its conceptual frame— that is fundamentally untrue. Seen in this light, it should be clear that polytheism is hardly an endlessly open or permanently deferring conceptual configuration; nor does it avoid or overcome the true/false distinction. It is instead just one more alternative claim—in the thick sense—to truth.

It may well be, of course, that prior to its conflict with the Christian mission, the nature of Graeco-Roman polytheism as a fundamental "regulative idea" was not readily apparent, at least to its participants for whom there were no alternatives;[70] but serious conflict of one kind or another often discloses deeper conceptual and practical commitments beneath the surface of an otherwise undisturbed way of life: in this case, the course of history, in which polytheism preexisted Christianity, should not be confused with the absence of (necessary) normative commitments that structure the range of what it could *ever* mean to be a polytheistic culture. Contra Assmann, the advent of the Christian mission does not *create* "polytheism" as a regulative mode of cultural existence, as if cultures could exist without constructive, normative rules in the first place. Rather, early Christianity exposes in an unprecedented manner what it could mean *not* to be polytheistic and, therefore, encounters the limits of what polytheism could be. So, too, though it is quite clear that in their territorial expansion polytheistic cultures may incorporate or colonize one ancestral deity after the other,[71] and that polytheist repression of certain religious groups did occur (e.g., the Druids), such moves are merely additions or exclusions within a common pattern—a pattern that to secure its own continued existence rejects that which would mean its end. In short, despite the advocacy for the remarkable openness of polytheistic culture, polytheism itself, as Charles Taylor once said of liberalism in another context, is no less than "a fighting creed."[72] The early Christians do not face intolerance because a true/false distinction somehow corrupts an otherwise entirely tolerant system but because the "creed" of polytheism intolerantly rejects the Christian claim to truth—as indeed it must.[73] As goes the creed, so goes tolerance. It is a parasitic concept.

(3) *Against Bifurcations:* It is significant that those thinkers who advocate for multiplicity, diversity, openness, and tolerance through the language of poly-theism(s) do not take their use of the term "polytheism" to mean real polythe-ism—as if their proposals were that we should return to worshipping actual numinous entities named Jupiter, Mars, Pluto, and so forth. Rather, "polytheism" names a type of intellectual pattern and concomitant politics.[74] It should go without saying that neither the pattern nor the politics are identical from proposal to proposal, but there is a remarkable similarity in the desire for "human fraterni-ty" (Rorty) and reduction of violence in the name of religious claims to truth: as Marquard put it, "enlightened polytheism" is what "we have to bet on."[75]

Of course, the new polytheists are by no means the only ones whose hope for more tolerance and less bloodshed entails serious criticism of theological—or specifically Christian—claims to a true way of life.[76] Indeed, as almost everyone knows, there is a deeply entrenched modern interpretive tradition of reading the so-called Wars of Religion as a vivid display of the political carnage that attends truth claims. They are, so the standard story goes, practical reason's greatest argument for the necessity to exile theological claims from the political arena. It is doubtless the case that this interpretive tradition stands in need of critical reorientation—the Wars of Religion may just as well be called the birth pangs of the modern nation state[77]—but it is unlikely that such reorientation will convince those who believe the true/false distinction harbors remarkable energy for a new form of "hate" that theological truth claims do not put the "religious other" at grave risk.[78]

Even if most scholars recognize that slaughter in the name of explicit theological conviction is hardly limited to Christians, whether in late antiquity or more recently, there will continue to be some who nevertheless assert that the emergence of Christian mission provides a "new theological justification, or at least latent encouragement" for religious violence, precisely because of its claim to a "new, total and universal grasp on truth."[79] And there will likely be more who will still seek tolerance and cultural diversity by holding out for a clean break or, in Mark Lilla's terms, a Great Separation between political philosophy and theology. However, as Lilla's own book powerfully shows—quite in the face of his language of "experiment" and elegant plea at the book's close—the Great Separation has never been more than an abstraction, or, perhaps more accurately, a discourse of modern eschatological hope.[80]

Unlike many other calls for tolerance, therefore, those who speak of "polytheism" rightly employ a religious vocabulary for the grammar of political life, and in this they are closer than many so-called secularists to overcoming the fiction that has afflicted political thinking at least since Rousseau—namely, that politics can get free of theology, that we can in fact successfully deny the need for an extrinsic grounding of human community and instead from our own immanent resources create a tolerant society, a fundamentally self-generated and self-sustaining political way of being. In contrast to this distinctly modern position, those thinkers who employ religious terminology in political discourse intuit—or know—something that the ancients lived and that Carl Schmitt demonstrated in his essay on "political theology." Plainly said, all political thinking is inescapably theological. Our theological judgments may of course be hidden by a limited range of vocabulary that attempts to eliminate explicit theological terms from "pure" political discourse. But after some work with a Schmittian spade, one will sooner or later get down to "the metaphysical kernel of all politics."[81] Schmitt's imagery is wrong here but the insight is not: "politics" cannot help but to take particular positions on the question of God, on God's relevance to world mechanics, on human nature, on our place in the cosmos, on the significance of our existence, on the telos of human community, and so on—in short, on the whole range of issues that must be engaged in order to think intelligently about life together.[82]

Of course, for Luke, as for the ancients in general, the idea that we should or could think politically without thinking theologically would not only be utterly strange but even perverse. Indeed, in the narrative of Acts, as we have said many times over, political life is the display of God's universal Lordship in Jesus of Nazareth. Remove the theological truth claims from this political vision and the vision ceases to exist. Moreover, as we emphasized above, the claims to universal truth in Acts are not simply cognitive propositions to be *used*, as if they could first be grasped conceptually and subsequently employed in the service of a political system that was itself independent of the "truth claim" whose labor it exploited—a kind of billystick of truth in the hands of politicians.[83] In the Lukan sense, truth claims are rather about a whole way of life. Knowing that claims breed intolerance or violence is not, therefore, a matter of simply pointing out *that* Acts is replete with claims to universal truth—as if this could close the case on the text's potential to engender religious violence—but instead entails sustained reflection on the lived pattern of the truth claim as it is displayed in the total narrative. To think along with Acts thus far is hence to reject both the bifurcation between thinking and living—that is, the thinning of truth claims down to pure cognition—and between theology and politics, the conceptual fiction offered for our consumption only in relatively recent times.

(4) *Acts and the Question of Tolerance and Bloodshed:* In at least one important respect, the critics of religious claims to universal truth are correct. Insofar as our attempt to think with Acts is relevant to the current life of the church, it will be so because of the church's commitment to "foundational texts."[84] That is to say, there is little point in the discussion above—with all its various distinctions, qualifications, nuance, and so on—if Acts itself is laced with the kind of universal truth claims that produce violent coercion. Inasmuch as Acts serves as a norm for the life of Christian communities, a text to which we continually return to (re)gain our theological bearings, if it breeds intolerance of the kind that leads to the bloodying and death of the "other," it will form us to reproduce theological violence again and again. Indeed, any tendencies toward the peaceful embodiment of truth—should they exist—would be corrected, or normed, by a text that inscribes violence into the heart of religious belief.

We should say it straightforwardly: in a crucial way, the vision of Acts is profoundly intolerant. The God of Israel is "Lord of heaven and earth, the Maker of the world and everything in it"; he commands "everyone, everywhere to repent." Jesus is "the Lord of all." "There is no other name under heaven by which human beings can be saved." "You shall be my witnesses in Jerusalem and in all Judaea and Samaria and to the end of the earth." "I wish you all might become as I am." Examples abound. In Acts, such claims obviously bear no resemblance to theological thought experiments; they are, rather, the expression of the hope for a universal conversion to the Way, the community of "Christians" that lives out these claims in a total pattern of life. Of course, Luke is enough of a realist to know that on this side of the day on which the world will be called to account (17:31) such universal conversion remains a hope rather than a reality. He speaks more concretely, therefore, of the *ekklesia*, or a "people taken out to witness to the name of God" (15:14–18; cf. Luke 1:76–79, etc.). But the underlying judgment that a universal savior corresponds to the breadth of the human predicament remains.

Indeed, when thinking about the pagan world, Luke names this problem variously as "the pollution of idols," or "darkness," or "ignorance." This language doubtless entails a moral no less than a hermeneutical valuation of the depth of human life apart from the turn to the living God. Those who remain on the outside of the community are not simply "left alone" and thought of as "alright" but are seen to be in need of the saving pattern of life that that is the proclamation of light (26:23).

Such judgments, however, are hardly self-righteous or priggish, as they may appear when pulled from the text and quoted *en masse;* for they are not restricted to the religious "other": the need for the light that comes from the apocalypse applies to everyone, including Luke himself and his Jewish heroes Peter and Paul (cf. esp. 26:20). Moreover, as I have repeatedly emphasized, Luke's reading of the world's predicament does not include a flatfooted negation of all that pagan culture could possibly offer, as if the narrative of Acts split cleanly all of reality into two monolithic blocks: the Christian community (good) and pagan culture (bad). Admittedly, Luke is not Justin Martyr, Clement of Alexandria or Origen—his literary project is more openly critical than theirs—but it would be a bizarre reading indeed that could not detect Luke's indebtedness to Roman jurisprudence, his appreciation for pagan poetry and philosophical ideals of fraternity and friendship, his note on Paul's powerful friends the Asiarchs, and his recurring praise even of certain centurions. All of these features—and there are many more—point clearly to Luke's subtle or layered evaluation of the complex reality of pagan culture. Luke is not of course interested in articulating a particular take on the nature/grace argument; nor, in this context, are we. The point is rather more simple: the language of darkness and ignorance does not, in the Lukan schema at least, emerge from a more fundamental theological and narrative grammar that would entail an in-principle dismissal of the possibility of goods within pagan culture. Indeed, on Luke's terms, one should expect to find them.

Still, the narrative logic of Acts does maintain that the overall pattern of life that constitutes pagan culture is deeply problematic. What goods there are, therefore, exist within a larger whole that stands in need of "salvation."[85] The mission to the end of earth does not erase the worth of every aspect of pagan life, but it does, in an embodied and public way, reject notions of tolerance premised on the hope for an endless diffusion of difference ("to each, his own," etc.). Luke is unwilling, that is, to restrict practically the reach of God's apocalypse to the gentiles. To do so would be to invoke a more comprehensive interpretive framework, a different and deeper truth claim, one which would enable him to know to whom God's salvation applied and to whom it did not (e.g., already-curious or pious gentiles such as Cornelius on the one hand, and run-of-the-mill idolaters such as those in Lystra or Ephesus on the other). To be sure, both the conceptual and practical configuration of "tolerance" would look different in a carefully restricted framework—perhaps more like the modern rage against "proselytizing"[86]—but it would also contradict and thus dissolve Acts' universal vision. For many and various reasons, such a move away from a universal mission may today appear desirable, but it would indubitably dispense with the normative notions in Acts. As the language of ignorance implies, the narrative of Acts consistently contends that God's revelation to the gentiles is *good for them* even though they do not know it.

Inasmuch as the communal embodiment of God's revelation involves the potential for cultural collapse, Acts' "good for them even though they don't know it" claim is startling, even offensive. To modern ears it will likely sound the warning bells of triumphalism, imperialism, and so forth. That such bells should ring, however, is largely a result of the history effected by the changes in the Roman empire in the fourth century rather than a close reading of the text. Our awareness of the warring and repressive Christian emperors, Augustine's argument for coercion in the Donatist controversy, the medieval crusades, colonialism, and many other ecclesial cancers makes it extremely difficult not to read Acts with the knowledge that Christians could eventually do great harm in the name of particular theological construals of the mission of God— and indeed, we should not attempt to bracket out such knowledge precisely because it enables us to ask necessarily pointed questions of our normative texts. Yet, there is simply no trace in Acts of the "common Christian argument that *coercing* the other will do him or her good."[87]

And on historical grounds one might rightly wonder, how could there be? The Christians in Luke's time were a tiny and randomly persecuted minority in the vast sea of the Roman empire, and they lacked entirely the machinery necessary for significant coercion. As a result, one might reasonably think that their imaginative possibilities were limited, that because they were nowhere near being able to use force against non-Christians, they could not conceive of themselves as having the power to coerce. On this reading, the absence of coercive thinking in Acts would be due primarily to the absence of the social and material presuppositions of coercion.

Yet such an explanation may be too easy, or at least too quick.[88] It is unquestionably the case that the early Christians did not have, in the parlance of the common contradiction, the material means for the forced conversion of pagans. But that historical reality would not necessarily rule out the possibility of a scriptural logic, as it were, that would turn the tables once the reins of power changed hands, a kind of biblical discourse that grounded forced conversions in a universal mission. And, indeed, ecclesial history no less than any other is rife with examples of the persecuted turned persecutor. To think along with Acts, therefore, we must think about the ethical logic of its universal truth claims rather than just about the lack of the early Christians' physical ability to force conversion. Or, to put it in the terms of this book, we must ask if the narration of cultural collapse as part of the outworking of the good that comes to the pagan world via the Christian mission leads in the logic of Acts to the coercive making of Christians "for their own good."

There is a direct answer to this question: No. The narrative logic of Acts points in another direction altogether. In contrast to much that goes for modern political theory, Acts knows of no possibilities for self-grounded communities; its vision of human life together, as this book has labored to demonstrate, is instead grounded entirely in the identity of the Lord of all. Insofar as the formation of Christian community is the cultural explication of this identity, the political vision of Acts cannot be sundered from the life of the universal Lord. Whether Luke knows the Pauline conception of the church as the "body of Christ" is open to debate, but that Acts narrates the life of the Christian mission as the embodied pattern of Jesus's own life is not. Put succinctly, according to Acts, the *missio Dei* has a christological norm.

As was emphasized in chapter 4, this norm is displayed narratively in the shape of the life of the Lord's disciples—Stephen, Peter, and Paul above all, but also the communities in Jerusalem, Iconium, Thessalonica, and elsewhere—where the pattern of a willingness to suffer even unto death is the mimetic reproduction of Jesus's own life as narrated in the Gospel of Luke and retold in the speeches of Acts. Thus the truth claim about Jesus's Lordship does not lead in Acts to a narrative blueprint for the need to coerce others for their own good but to a form of mission that rejects violence as a way to ground peaceful community and instead witnesses to the Lord's life of rejection and crucifixion by living it in publicly perceivable communities derisively called Christians. The claim to universal truth is not thin but thick, or enfleshed—shown to be what it is in the living out of the person's life about whom the claim is made. According to Acts, therefore, to be the community that claims to know the Lord of all is to be in the world in just such a way as the Lord himself was. Theologically said, ecclesiology is public Christology.[89]

The narrative logic of Acts thus cannot be read as leading to the coercion of the religious other, but in fact must be seen to oppose all such moves that would contradict the nature of Jesus's own Lordship. In this light, the text of Acts compels us to read the later development of coercive measures in the history of the church as fundamental and tragic departures from the normative witness of scripture, a turning of the ecclesial back on the foundational narrative of Christian mission.[90] If we are thinking along with Acts, we can see, furthermore, that these departures are not simply wayward moments in an otherwise forward-marching ecclesial history. Rather, recalling the thick or lived character of a truth claim, we should understand them as evidence of a much deeper problem in the Christian witness to the universal Lord: the potential to live a false life, to embody the lie that renders untrue *practically* the claim that Jesus is Lord of all.

Attending closely to the narrative logic of the Acts of the Apostles thus requires us to read both chapters 2 and 3 of the present book as equally indispensable guides to the ethical map of Lukan ecclesiology. Chapter 4 tells us why chapters 2 and 3 must thus be read—gives us, that is, the texture of the truth claim that lies at the origin of both narrative patterns—but it is chapter 2's language of cultural collapse that gets at the basic contour of Acts' intolerance and chapter 3's language of legal innocence that narrates intolerance's practical outworking as the refusal of the priority of violence. Hence does the tension that lies at the heart of Acts produce both an unavoidable conflict over the truth of a claim to a comprehensive way of life and a description of that conflict as witness rather than coercion.

(5) *The Kerygmatic Intention and Claim of the Book of Acts:* Focusing on questions of truth, tolerance, coercion, and so on, enables us to evade the fiction that our reaction to Acts could be indifference, avoidance, or "tolerance."[91] Precisely because Acts provokes a conflict over the truth of its comprehensive claims, it disallows a response that would seek to sidestep its claim as a whole. To read Acts is not only to face the question of how we shall take its claims but also to render a decision—in the lives we live no less than in the thoughts we think—about those claims. Paul Minear was right. The book of Acts has a "kerygmatic intention." In just this way, the text itself performs the fulfillment of Jesus's programmatic instruction in Acts 1:8 to carry the witness to him to the end of the earth.

Taken as a whole, Acts' mode of discourse thus sits uneasily next to—or, perhaps better, confronts—what is still the predominant epistemological paradigm in NT studies. Borrowing from Alasdair MacIntyre's Gifford lectures, we could characterize that way of knowing as "encyclopedic."[92] To put it simply, the encyclopedic way of knowing is essentially the epistemological posture that makes possible, intelligible, and compelling the notion that the vast production of studies about the NT adds to a central pool of knowledge.[93] Encyclopedic epistemology depends upon an assumption of a shared set of agreements about how to know what it is we want to know about the NT texts and what it is that one is in fact knowing—a mode of inquiry and body of information that could be summarized, say, in a still-to-be-written *Anchor Bible Encyclopedia of the New Testament (ABENT).*[94] To be sure, such a multivolume work would assume and reflect the fact that there are multiplicities of methodological approaches and almost endless differences in interpretive results. But in the encyclopedic way of knowing that underlay the *ABENT*'s existence and unity as one work, all such variety would be read as variance within a more basic or common epistemological project, that of the discovery and cataloging of knowledge about the texts of the NT.

The predecessor to our imagined *ABENT* offers a salient example of the encyclopedic way of knowing. The "Introduction" to the *Anchor Bible* Dictionary (ABD) reveals both the presumption that what is included between the covers of the six volumes is a snapshot of the progress of knowledge to the point of the *ABD*'s publication, and a remarkable confidence in the epistemological posture that would sustain the production of future encyclopedias (or encyclopedic "dictionaries"):

> Every generation needs its own Dictionary of the Bible. Within its pages one can expect to find ... the essence of critical scholarship on subjects pertaining to the Bible, as those subjects are understood by students of that generation. Thus while encyclopedic reference works provide a valuable service to their readers ... they can never transcend the limits of their own historical contexts. In time they inevitably become outdated, and after a generation or so they can hope to achieve a sort of "second shelf life" as a valuable period piece, a witness to where the field of biblical studies was at one point in its history.

In an effort to acknowledge the range of methodological debates near the end of the twentieth century, the *ABD* then reports that the "majority of the major articles found in the following pages devotes a good deal of space to the *basic epistemological question:* 'How do we know what we know about this topic?' One will be hard pressed to find here any sort of sweeping historical synthesis that presumes a scholarly consensus."[95]

What the *ABD* does not realize is that such a question is not epistemologically *basic* at all. It is seen by the editors as such, but that is because the question is asked within a larger way of knowing that is taken for granted, the one that is so clearly evident in the opening statement cited above: an epistemological framework in which the "essence of critical scholarship" corresponds to the "field of biblical studies," which itself moves forward in "history." That is to say, the answer that will be given to the editors' version of the epistemological question will, in the context of the *ABD*, be worked out within an overall way of knowing that is already presumed valid ("the field of biblical studies"—as construed by the *ABD*). To be sure, the editors would no doubt grant that the answers vary in respect to different *topics,* but it is simply assumed that whatever the variance, it is understandable within the prior, more comprehensive hermeneutical framework that makes a work like *the ABD* necessary or intelligible in the first place. To ask the epistemologically basic question, therefore, is not to ask about methodological or historical discrepancies *within* the encyclopedic way of knowing but is to question the epistemological viability of the framework itself.[96]

To read the book of Acts within the encyclopedic mode of modern inquiry is thus to read it in light of a larger interpretive pattern in which a particular construal of knowledge norms our reading of the narrative by situating its interpretation within a larger, hermeneutically determinative framework: Knowledge in General. Encyclopedic knowing thus reads Acts as an object appropriate to a certain field of inquiry, a field which is itself but one specific area of the knowledge we accumulate as our research continues to progress (in biblical studies, ancient history, history of religion, etc).

If, however, the Acts of the Apostles is anything like the text this book takes it to be, its narrative resists such interpretive capture and instead challenges encyclopedic epistemology—indeed, exposes its nonexistence as a way of knowing and thus of reading Acts.[97] Attending carefully to Acts' irreducibly particular way of knowing, that is, requires the development of an interpretive grammar of claim and conflict, which is to say that Acts' mode of discourse will inevitably yield hermeneutical negotiations of its claims in the lives of its readers. To think that our readings of Acts would produce bits and pieces of knowledge that we could, irrespective of our particular convictions or reactions, insert into some wider interpretive scheme is not to practice scholarly (or existential) deferral but is *already* to have offered a counter-reading of the world, one in which the comprehensive vision of Acts is negated in favor of a larger noetic paradigm.

To the extent that we refract the kerygmatic intention of the book of Acts through the encyclopedic lens, therefore, we *contest* hermeneutically the vision of Acts and, consequently, distort it—turn it into a fund for knowledge in the sense of a textual repository of the historical or religious materials for encyclopedias, or at least for the books and articles out of which encyclopedias are made. In opposition to the encyclopedic mode of knowing, the text of Acts calls for the kind of knowledge that is a whole way of life, a moral no less than an intellectual habitus that cannot itself be explained by a yet more comprehensive way of knowing.

The Acts of the Apostles thus puts its readers in something of a paradoxical situation. On the one hand, to reduce Acts to a more complete explanatory framework is to contest its vision by means of an alternative epistemological paradigm and, hence, to misread the text; on the other, to avoid such reduction, and hence to read the text rightly, is already to have accepted Acts' claims.[98] In the final analysis, therefore, if we are to think along *with* Acts about the pressing questions that face us today, we must think within the particular way of life it claims is necessary to know the truth of its kerygma. That this way of life is not self-grounded but derives from the apocalypse of God in the Lord of all just is the "kerygmatic intention and claim" of the book of Acts. That it could be proven is of course ridiculous. That it could be true is not.

Notes

1. Paul Walaskay, *"And so we came to Rome": The Political Perspective of St Luke* (Cambridge: Cambridge University Press, 1983); Richard A. Horsley, *The Liberation of Christmas: The Infancy Narratives in Social Context* (New York: Crossroad, 1989). Richard Cassidy, *Society and Politics in the Acts of the Apostles* (Maryknoll, NY: Orbis, 1987) is perhaps the most nuanced, but even he is unable to deal hermeneutically with Luke's juridical arguments (i.e., the preponderance of the material that will come in chap. 3 of the present work). Standard surveys exist; see, for example, Alexandru Neagoe, *The Trial of the Gospel: An Apologetic Reading of Luke's Trial Narratives* (Cambridge: Cambridge University Press, 2002); or, Steve Walton, "The State They Were In: Luke's View of the Roman Empire," in *Rome in the Bible and the Early Church*, SNTSMS 116, ed. Peter Oakes (Grand Rapids, MI: Baker Academic, 2002), 1–41.

2. An exception is Gary Gilbert, "Roman Propaganda and Christian Identity in the Worldview of Luke–Acts," in *Contextualizing Acts: Lukan Narrative and Greco-Roman Discourse*, SBJSS 20, ed. Todd Penner and Caroline Vander Stichele (Atlanta, GA: Society of Biblical Literature, 2003), 233–56.

3. Frances Young, *Biblical Exegesis and the Formation of Christian Culture* (Cambridge: Cambridge University Press, 1997).

4. It is has become readily apparent over the last thirty years that the Lukan writings are very much concerned with Judaism. Extensive studies confirm this fact; see, e.g., the work of Jacob Jervell, Joseph Tyson, et al. By comparison, only scant attention has been given to Luke's concern with gentiles and paganism. In fact, I know of only two recent attempts, the first of which is quite brief. See Hans-Josef Klauck, *Magic and Paganism in Early*

Christianity: The World of the Acts of the Apostles (Edinburgh: T. & T. Clark, 1999); and, Christoph W. Stenschke, *Luke's Portrait of the Gentiles Prior to Their Coming to Faith*, WUNT 2/108 (Tübingen: Mohr Siebeck, 1999).

5. For a discussion of thick concepts/knowledge, see Cora Diamond, "Losing Your Concepts," *Ethics* 98 (1988): 255–77, and chap. 5 of the present book.

6. Who can think of Acts without mission?

7. Cf. David Horrell's "Introduction" to the *JSNT* 27/3 (March 2005) special issue on imperial cult in which he argues that we are in serious need of a reintroduction of Graeco-Roman materials into our thinking about the NT.

8. Cf. A.N. Sherwin-White's remark about the attempt of ancient historians and New Testament scholars to work across their respective disciplines: "Scholars attempting to deal with two worlds of this magnitude need two lives. We must appear as amateurs in each other's field." (preface in *Roman Society and Roman Law in the New Testament* [Oxford: Clarendon Press, 1963]), v). Sherwin-White's language of "two lives" is of great significance. We do not have two lives, and nor can we think as if we did.

9. Alasdair MacIntyre, *After Virtue*, 3rd ed. (Notre Dame, IN: University of Notre Dame Press, 2007).

10. For the use of Eco in NT studies, see Stefan Alkier, "Intertexualität–Annäherungen an ein texttheoretisches Paradigma," in *Heiligkeit und Herrschaft: Intertextuelle Studien zu Heiligkeitsvorstellungen und zu Psalm 110*, ed. Dieter Sänger (Neukirchen-Vluyn: Neukirchener Verlag, 2003), 1–26.

11. *Three Rival Versions of Moral Enquiry: Encyclopaedia, Genealogy, and Tradition* (Notre Dame, IN: University of Notre Dame Press, 1990), 65 passim.

12. The obvious example is Schweitzer's catalog of the Liberal Jesuses, but there are many others. This is also why the biblical authors are declared unintelligible or superstitious when the thought pattern does not fit into the pattern of nineteenth-century thinking. What it means to be theologically rational is what it means to be theologically rational in the nineteenth century. When, for example, Paul's participationist language is declared theologically unintelligible, it is not because his arguments cannot be followed, but because his conception does not fit the historically situated rationality of the nineteenth century.

13. For the view that Acts is addressed to pagans, see, e.g., the classic by Johannes Weiss, *Über die Absicht und den literarischen Charakter der Apostelgeschichte* (Göttingen: Vandenhoeck & Ruprecht, 1897).

14. Tertullian is not entirely right, of course. We may think of Celsus (fl. ca. 175–180), for example, against whom Origen later wrote his *Contra Celsum* (ca. 248). Yet the exceptions in the second century were probably limited. In the first century, they may have been nonexistent. Joseph Tyson's suggestion that Acts envisions an audience of Godfearers is intriguing, but it does not seriously address the most basic question to his hypothesis: why would Godfearers even read Acts? And where would they have done this? Moreover, contrary to Tyson's speculation about Theophilus, Luke explicitly says that he has been catechized in things Christian. See "Jews and Judaism in Luke-Acts: Reading as a Godfearer," *NTS* 41 (1995): 19–38.

15. Of interest is the fact that this working assumption coheres nicely with a second-century prologue external to Luke's Gospel in which the purpose of the Gospel is said to be related to writing for gentile converts. Inasmuch as my assumption derives more from "internal" evidence, this point of contact with ancient tradition is particularly scintillating, though of course the historical reliability of this prologue is hardly established by this coherence. For a concise discussion of this prologue, see Fitzmyer, *Luke*, 1.38–39. With the majority of commentators, I assume that the Christian readers of Acts were mainly gentiles—though obviously in light of Jacob Jervell's work, we now understand better how Acts would be intelligible to Jews as well.

16. Cf. Klauck, *Magic and Paganism in Early Christianity*, 59: "Acts addresses a Christian public, and consequently the same is true of the Areopagus discourse." I take the phrase "theological life" from my colleague Geoffrey Wainwright's book, *Lesslie Newbigin: A Theological Life* (New York: Oxford University Press, 2000).

17. This is generally the path taken by those who want to ask about the "historicity" of this or that particular passage (e.g., was there really a riot in Ephesus? How would this have affected the mission there?). While I think questions of historicity are important, the focus in this work lies elsewhere—on the effect of the whole narrative on its auditors.

18. The classic example is the Areopagus speech. See n. 82 in chap. 2.

19. See, for example, the work of Joel B. Green, F. Scott Spencer, et al.

20. Todd Penner, "Madness in the Method? The Acts of the Apostles in Current Study," *CBR* 2.2 (2004): 223–93. Penner's article is excellent not only for its exhaustiveness but also for its refusal to lose sight of the hermeneutical issues involved in any discussion of Acts (whether text-critical or socio-historical or something else).

21. Indeed, according to the opening note, even Penner needed two grants to enable the work of his report. Penner sees this well: the title itself says as much (his term for the prodigality is "madness").

22. My position is not that there is no place for *Forschungsberichten* but rather that we ought to think more carefully about their proper place. We obviously need them, and I here depend on and am thankful for Penner's.

23. *Early Narrative Christology: The Lord in the Gospel of Luke*, BZNW 139 (Berlin: Walter de Gruyter, 2006), 9–10.

24. This problem continues to plague NT scholarship. See C. Kavin Rowe, "Acts 2:36 and the Continuity of Lukan Christology," NTS 53 (2007): 37–56, for an illustration of the hermeneutical problems involved in this way of thinking.

25. "More or less" not because I favor careless writing but because of the commitment to semantic context and the primary importance of use for word meaning; that is, the use of the words in this book will say what they mean.

26. Raymond Williams, *Keywords: A Vocabulary of Culture and Society* (New York: Oxford University Press, 1976), 76.

27. See Kathryn Tanner, *Theories of Culture: A New Agenda for Theology* (Minneapolis, MN: Fortress, 1997), esp. 38–58. For a helpful use of "culture" in constructive theology, see James Wm. McClendon Jr., *Systematic Theology: Witness, Volume 3* (Nashville, TN: Abingdon, 2000), esp.15–182. I read McClendon long before

I began writing this section and now—in going back to his book after writing this introductory chapter—I find that I have learned much from his way of thinking of culture in terms of witness and mission (i.e., ecclesiologically). I suspect, however, that we are both more primarily formed by Acts and that my agreement comes from further study of the biblical text rather than more definitional clarity with respect to the word "culture."

28. Or, if there were a decent English plural. Cf. McClendon, *Systematic Theology*, 3.50: "I mean by culture the set of meaningful practices, dominant attitudes, and characteristic ways of doing things that typify a community (or a society or a civilization)."

29. To jettison this shared or intuitive sense of meaning is to render unintelligible the word's extraordinary prevalence.

30. By "Christ" Niebuhr means the embodiment of absolute monotheism.

31. *Frontier and Society in Roman North Africa* (Oxford: Clarendon Press, 1998), 141. Cf. Richard Horsley, "Paul's Assembly in Corinth: An Alternative Society," in *Urban Religion in Roman Corinth: Interdisciplinary Approaches*, eds. D. N. Schowalter and S. J. Friesen, HTS 53 (Cambridge, MA: Harvard University Press, 2005), 371–95, esp. 393.

32. See, for example, L. Michael White's critique of Harnack's *Ausbreitung*, "Adolf Harnack and the 'Expansion' of Early Christianity: A Reappraisal of Social History," *The Second Century* 5/2 (1985/86): 97–127.

33. See Garth Fowden's review of Robin Lane Fox, "Between Pagans and Christians," *JRS* 78 (1988): 173–82 and 176; and Peter Brown's chapter "The Limits of Intolerance" in his *Authority and the Sacred: Aspects of the Christianization of the Roman World* (Cambridge: Cambridge University Press, 1995).

34. See Peter Lampe and Ulrich Luz, "Post-Pauline Christianity and Pagan Society," in *Christian Beginnings*, ed. Jürgen Becker (Louisville, KY: Westminster John Knox, 1993), 242–80, esp. 270–71.

35. Of course, Luke did not know the word "pagan." *Pagani*, insofar as we know, came into existence only in the fourth century and was used to mean either "rustics" or "civilians." On this point, see Robin Lane Fox, *Pagans and Christians* (New York: Knopf, 1986), 30–31. On the problem of defining paganism, see also Ramsay MacMullen, *Christianizing the Roman Empire A.D. 100–400* (New Haven, CT: Yale University Press, 1984), 8; idem, *Paganism in the Roman Empire* (New Haven, CT: Yale University Press, 1981), 1–18; Nock, *Conversion: The Old and New in Religion from Alexander the Great to Augustine of Hippo* (Baltimore: The Johns Hopkins University Press, 1998), 5 and 10; Simon Price, *Religions of the Ancient Greeks* (Cambridge: Cambridge University Press, 1999), 3 passim and where the plural in the title is analytically significant.

36. See his highly stimulating work, *On Suicide Bombing* (New York: Columbia University Press, 2007).

37. Philip F. Esler's "Christ-follower" is exactly what *Christianus* means in Latin, the language in which the term was coined. See, for example, his *Conflict and Identity in Romans: The Social Setting of Paul's Letter* (Minneapolis, MN: Fortress, 2003). If by "Christ-follower" we are to understand "follower of a/the Jewish Messiah," then we will have to mediate our understanding through Hebrew. On this, see n. 186 in chap. 4.

38. The term "long march" is Charles Taylor's in his book *A Secular Age* (Cambridge, MA: Harvard University Press, 2007) and is a particularly useful way to signal the need for caution in tracing the roots of our present situation and to object to reductive accounts of how we have arrived on these shores. In this space, it is impossible to name the ways in which such movement has taken place. I simply refer the reader to Taylor's book as an entre into the wider discussion. Recognizing the depth of these shifts renders the attempt to develop "a method" intellectually comical. Even Taylor himself, for example, may underestimate the hermeneutical shifts that accompany the digital age.

39. In his brief introduction to biblical interpretation, Manfred Oeming, *Biblische Hermeneutik: Eine Einführung* (Darmstadt: Primus, 1998), deals with no less than seventeen different interpretive methods. That the past decade has added even more hardly requires comment.

40. See especially Markus Bockmuehl, *Seeing the Word: Refocusing New Testament Studies* (Grand Rapids, MI: Baker Academic, 2006), who insightfully elucidates the discipline's disarray. Though Bockmuehl employs the vocabulary of "methodological suggestions" and the like, I take his proposal to be more of an attempt to redirect our thinking toward the kind of fruitful interpretation that reception history fosters than a manifesto that treats all our intellectual difficulties with a particular methodological salve.

CHAPTER 2

1. This theme is central to Barth's theology; it is difficult, therefore, to know where to point the reader. But see, for example, Karl Barth, *Church Dogmatics* (Edinburgh: T. & T. Clark, 1958), II/1 § 26, esp. 76, 117; § 28, esp. 312–13; § 31, 562; or III/1 §§ 40–41, esp. 5–7, 11–13.

2. Cf., for example, Barth's statement in *Dogmatics in Outline* (New York: Harper and Row, 1959), 50: "[E]verything that is said about creation depends absolutely upon this Subject [i.e., God the Creator]."

3. There has long been phenomenological difficulty in identifying "paganism" as one "thing." Yet linguistic alternatives create more problems than they solve; traditional usage is thus best retained so long as it is not understood to describe a monolithic religion, culture, power structure, and so forth. See Robin Lane Fox, *Pagans and Christians* (New York: Knopf, 1987), 33, for a brief and lucid statement of the problem.

4. Lane Fox is again concise on the problem of speaking of paganism as a single "religion;" it is, he argues, more like a pattern of religiousness. Still, this pattern displays enough of a common core and broad similarity that we can speak of it in something of a holistic way. See *Pagans and Christians*, 31–38, 90 passim. In addition, I take it now for granted that religion in pagan antiquity was a public and political affair, that the attempt to privatize beliefs or piety perpetuates a modern mistake in the study of antiquity, and that these matters have been amply demonstrated in recent study. See, for example, Simon Price, *Rituals and Power: The Roman Imperial Cult in Asia Minor* (Cambridge: Cambridge University Press, 1984), 15–16; 234–48; Robert Louis Wilken,

The Christians as the Romans Saw Them, 2nd ed. (New Haven, CT: Yale University Press, 2003), x. Cf. the concluding section to this chapter.

5. This is not necessarily to say, however, that in the early periods "Christian" is the word that would have been used. In many cases the Jewish Christian missionaries (Paul, etc.) would simply have been "Jews" to the outsiders (as in Acts 16:20, for example). It is also noteworthy that Tertullus presents Paul to Felix as a ringleader of a Jewish sect (αἵρεσις), the Nazarenes (24:5). Yet, once gentiles are in the picture, the word χριστιανοί is doubtless there soon, too: there is a community of Jews and gentiles that behaves socially like Jews in some very important ways (one God, no sacrifice to pagan gods, etc.) but differs visibly from other Jews in some very important ways (the absence for the most part of dietary restrictions, no circumcision, no rigorous Sabbath keeping, the claim to follow Jesus as the Messiah, etc.). Acts 11:26; 26:28; 1 Pet 4:16 all suggest that χριστιανός was first coined by outsiders. On this important issue, see David Horrell, "The Label Χριστιανός: 1 Pt 4:16 and the Formation of Christian Identity," *JBL* 126 (2007): 361–81.

6. For the OT echoes in this phrasing, see Nils A. Dahl, "A People for His Name (Acts 15:14)," *NTS* 4 (1957/58): 319–27. Though Dahl settles on Zech 2:15 (LXX) as the "most interesting parallel" to Acts 15:14, he also notes that "the number of similar [LXX] texts indicates that Acts 15:14 is modeled upon the general pattern rather than upon any individual passage" (323). In my judgment, Dahl is correct to say that Luke's formulation in Acts 15:14 depends upon a larger reading of the OT (including Zech 2:14–17) in which "the conversion of the Gentiles is seen as a fulfilment of God's promises to Israel: Luke ii. 29–32; Acts ii. 39; iii. 25; xiii. 47, etc." (327). As these remarks indicate, my way of putting the issue of a formation of a people (main text, above) hardly intends to say that Acts is unconcerned with Judaism and Jewish traditions (cf. n. 4 in chap. 1).

7. In theological terms: theology proper is distinct but never separate from ecclesiology. God's revelation and the formation of a people are in fact one theological movement.

8. Lane Fox, *Pagans and Christians,* 140.

9. The parallel to Peter's act of healing in Acts 3:1–10 and Jesus's in Luke 5:17–26 has long been observed, as has the connection to Jesus's programmatic reading of Isa 61 in the synagogue in Nazareth (Luke 4:18–19). Cf. Luke 7:22.

10. Acts 14:4, 14, the only time Paul and Barnabas are called ἀπόστολοι in Acts.

11. Many scholars note that this detail helps to explain why the sacrificial act progressed as far as it did without Paul and Barnabas's interference. See, for example, Henry J. Cadbury, *The Book of Acts in History* (Eugene, OR: Wipf and Stock, 2004), 22.

12. There is a marked emphasis upon the ὄχλοι. The word occurs five times in ten verses (14:11, 13, 14, 18, and 19).

13. Ramsey MacMullen, *Christianizing the Roman Empire: AD 100–400* (New Haven, CT: Yale University Press, 1984), 25–42, for example, strongly argues for the importance of Christian "wonder-working" as a major factor in the story of how Christianity won the battle of religions in the empire (cf. his *Paganism in the Roman Empire* (New Haven, CT: Yale University Press, 1981), 96–97.).

14. The phrase "spell of Homer" is taken from Walter Burkert's treatment of that theme in his classic study, *Greek Religion* (Cambridge, MA: Harvard University Press, 1985), 119–25. Burkert speaks of a "common Homeric literary culture" from the "eighth century onwards" (8). The judgment about the importance of Homer's influence is ubiquitous among classicists. See, for example, Lane Fox, *Pagans and Christians*, 110; Arthur Darby Nock, "Religious Attitudes of the Ancient Greeks," in *Essays on Religion and the Ancient World* (Oxford: Clarendon, 1972), 534–50, esp. 543, 550; Simon Price, *Religions of the Ancient Greeks* (Cambridge: Cambridge University Press, 1999), 3.

15. Homer, *Od.* 17.485–6 (LCL trans.). Cf. Lane Fox, *Pagans and Christians*, 119: "Greek votive reliefs of all periods owe a large debt to sightings of their gods." For this theme in the apocryphal Acts, see Rosa Söder, *Die apokyrphen Apostelgeschichten und die romanhafte Literatur der Antike* (Stuttgart: Kohlhammer Verlag, 1969 [original 1932]), 95–98. Margaret M. Mitchell discusses briefly Luke's possible allusion to this Homeric text in her lengthy (and highly critical) review of Dennis MacDonald's *The Homeric Epics and the Gospel of Mark* ("Homer in the New Testament?" *JR* 83 (2003): 244–60 [257–58]).

16. Lane Fox, *Pagans and Christians*, 110. For a concise treatment of the excerpts from Homer (and other ancient material) that circulated in the ancient world, see Henry Chadwick, "Florilegium," in *Reallexikon für Antike und Christentum* 7.1131–1160.

17. For a helpful starting point, see Price's chapter on "Greek Thinkers" in *Religions of the Ancient Greeks*. Harold W. Attridge, "The Philosophical Critique of Religion under the Early Empire," *ANRW* II.16.1: 45–78, provides a significant overview of the discussion during the time of the NT. See also Daniel Babut, *La religion des philosophes grecs: de Thalès aux Stoïciens* (Paris: Presses Universitaires de France, 1974), who discerns a broad unity in the focus of the critique despite considerable historical development and points of material disagreement within such a focus (esp. 204–5).

18. Aristotle here holds that the mythology (gods in the shape of humans or other animals) was developed to "influence the vulgar and as a constitutional and utilitarian expedient" (*Metaphy.*, 12.8.18 [1074B], LCL).

19. Jos., *C. Ap.* 2.239–242 (LCL trans. altered).

20. Lane Fox, *Pagans and Christians*, 115. I take it that one of the outstanding merits of Lane Fox's study is that, in terms of historical perception, he refuses simply to adopt the more sophisticated philosophical perspectives that are frequently the viewpoint of the literary sources and, instead, attempts to correlate more closely the views presupposed by those sources with other types of evidence (e.g., inscriptions, statues, etc.). Cf. the insightful remarks of Ramsay MacMullen, *Paganism in the Roman Empire*, esp. 77–79; and, G. E. M. de Ste. Croix, "Why Were the Early Christians Persecuted?" *Past and Present* 26 (1963): 6–38: "Whatever view we may hold about the mentality of the educated, upper-class intellectuals, we must admit that the great mass of the population of the Roman empire, in both East and West, were at least what we should call deeply superstitious; and I see not the least reason why we should deny them genuine religious feeling." (24). On Socratic criticism as the cause of an Athenian "religious crisis," see the judicious discussion by Robert Parker, *Athenian Religion: A History* (Oxford: Clarendon, 1996), esp. 199–217, who notes that Socrates' criticism

of the gods was taken to be socially dangerous only because of its (perceived) necessary link to a moral relativism (esp. 212).

21. Lucian, *Alexander the False Prophet*, 13–14 (LCL trans., slightly altered).

22. Ibid.

23. Lane Fox, *Pagans and Christians*, 242. Lane Fox's discussion of the cult is concise and excellent for the way in which he situates it within the overall cultic practice of the empire (241–50).

24. They are first unrecognized in their human form and rejected: "To a thousand homes they came, seeking a place for rest; a thousand homes were barred against them" (VIII.628–29).

25. Luke Johnson, for example, remarks that "Luke may well be playing off a literary motif concerning the hospitality shown to the gods Zeus and Hermes by residents of Phrygia.... These folk do not want to miss the chance to be the next Baucis and Philemon!" (*The Acts of the Apostles*, SacPag 5; [Collegeville, MN: Liturgical Press, 1992], 251; cf. his earlier remark: "It is difficult to avoid the suspicion that Luke's account plays off such a tradition" [248]). Cf., for example, Barrett, *Acts*, 2 vols., ICC (London: T. & T. Clark, 1994/1998), 1.677; Klauck, *Magic and Paganism*, 59.

26. Cf. Cilliers Breytenbach, "Zeus und der lebendige Gott: Anmerkungen zu Apostelgeschichte 14.11–17," *NTS* 39 (1993): 396–413, who argues that both Ovid and Luke draw upon local traditions (403).

27. See the text in Carl Holladay, *Fragments from Hellenistic Jewish Authors: Vol. I: Historians* (Chico, CA: Scholars Press, 1983), 210–11, fragment 3, lns. 10–13 (in Eusebius, *Praep. Evang.* 9.27.6; Eusebius quotes at this point from Alexander Polyhistor). Due to his theological "synchronism," whether Artapanus was Jewish or pagan has been a point of contention, but the consensus now views him as a Jew (see Holladay, *Fragments*, 189–90).

28. Horace, *Odes*, 1.2, lns. 40–50 ("Or you come, o winged son of kindly Maia, if you take on the shape of a young man on earth and are willing to be called Caesar's avenger... may you be glad to be called Father and First Citizen... while you are our leader, Casear" LCL trans.). Noted also in Nock, *Conversion: The Old and New in Religion from Alexander the Great to Augustine of Hippo* (Baltimore: The Johns Hopkins University Press, 1998), 237.

29. Lane Fox, *Pagans and Christians*, 100.

30. Ernst Haenchen, *The Acts of the Apostles: A Commentary* (Philadelphia: Westminster, 1971), 432.

31. Klauck, *Magic*, 57, remarks: "Apparitions of gods on earth in human form are a stable element of hellenistic piety—assertions to the contrary in some commentaries are nothing more than a sign that their authors have never read the 'Bible of the Greeks,' Homer's epics." Klauck does not mention whom he has in mind, and it is difficult to believe that Haenchen never read Homer, but Klauck's general point is sound.

32. Johnson, *Acts*, 251. Cf. Nock, *Essays*, 2.549.

33. By the first century AD, this "refusal of divine honors" had become a highly complex, grand-scale political maneuver—specifically in relation to the Roman emperor—and varied as to its interpretation within the different parts of the empire.

See, for example, M. P. Charlesworth, "The Refusal of Divine Honours: An Augustan Formula," *PBSR* 15 (1939): 1–10; or Price, *Rituals and Power*, 72–77. Pseudo-Callisthenes' *Alexander Romance* is frequently cited in relation to Acts (e.g., Johnson, *Acts*, 249). See, for example, 12:22: "I beg off from such honors equal to the gods. For I am a mortal man and I fear such ceremonies. For they bring danger to the soul." But it should be acknowledged that (1) even in this work, Alexander does not always refuse the honors (1.22.7; 2.14), and (2) the third-century date and the weak historical core of the work make it difficult to relate to Acts.

34. On the complex associations surrounding this term and its cognates, which also occur in Acts 17:22 and 25:19, see P. J. Koets, Δεισιδαιμονία: *A Contribution to the Knowledge of the Religious Terminology in Greek* (Purmerend: J. Muusses, 1929).

35. Certain types of Cynics are the primary exceptions (e.g., Diogenes of Sinope and, if Eusebius is accurate, Oenomaus of Gadara). There were of course accusations leveled at Epicurus along these lines (recall, e.g., the linkage of Epicureans with Christians and atheists in Lucian, *Alexander the False Prophet*, 38), but we must remember that Philodemus's *On Piety* defended Epicurus with respect to traditional religious practice, claiming even that he was initiated into the Eleusinian Mysteries. Moreover, criticism of the Epicurean "hypocrisy" also presupposes their participation in traditional religious practice (e.g., Cotta's remark to Velleius in Cicero, *Nat. D.*, 1.115: "Epicurus actually wrote books about holiness and piety. But what is the language of these books? Such that you think you are listening to a Corcuncanius or a Scaevola, high priests, not to the man who destroyed the very foundations of religion, and overthrew—not by main force like Xerxes, but by argument—the temples and the altars of the immortal gods. Why, what reason have you for maintaining that men owe worship to the gods?"). On this point in general, see Attridge, "Philosophical Critique," and Price, *Religions of the Ancient Greeks*, 135–37.

36. See, too, of course, his *On the Laws*—modeled on Plato's similarly titled work—in which he argues for the necessity of religious practice for the good of Roman society; indeed, the "rites shall ever be preserved and continuously handed down in families, and . . . they must be continued forever" (*Leg.*, 2.19.47). On Plato as the "first political thinker to argue that matters of belief can be criminal offences," see Price, *Religions of the Ancient Greeks*, 133–34.

37. Plutarch, *De Stoicorum Repug.*, 1034B.

38. See, for example, Cicero, *Nat. D.*, 2.76; and, Lucian, *Alex.*, 38.

39. Plutarch, *De Stoicorum Repug.*, 1034C; cf. Cicero, *Nat. D.*, 1.85, 123; 3.3.

40. The relevant occurrences are plentiful. See, for example, Lev 17:7; Amos 2:4; Isa 32:6; Jer 10:3, 15; Ezek 8:10. See also BDAG3, 621.

41. Though it may well be that "Halb nackt mit zerrissenen Kleidern (vgl. *Appian*, Bell Civ I, 66,300) man kaum noch für einen Gott gehalten werden [kann]" (Pesch, *Apostelgeschichte*, 2.58), the more likely point for the narrative audience is similar to what one sees in the OT or, better, in Matt 26:65 // Mark 14:63 when the high priest tears his clothes at the perceived blasphemy. Cf., from a later period, *m.Sanh.*7.5.

42. Reading diachronically, the crowd in Lystra would hardly have heard μάταια with its larger biblical resonance (false god). Yet, at the level of the narrative audience,

Luke shapes the auditor's perception by the use of this theologically freighted word from the LXX.

43. Acts 15:3 ("the conversion of the gentiles"); 26:20 ("I declared to the gentiles that they should repent and convert/turn to God"). Of course pagans, too, could speak of ἐπιστροφή (Plato, *Resp.*, VII.517Cff. of the task of educating the soul) or *conversio* (Cicero, *Nat. D.*, 1.77, of the philosophers' attempt with the masses), but the point here is that (1) such "turning" was compatible with traditional cultic practice, whereas for Luke it clearly is not, and (2) the ultimate object toward which one is to turn is clearly different.

44. Barrett, *Acts*, 1.680, is right to note of ἐπιστρέφειν that "the verb has so fully taken on the sense of proclamation that it means almost *to command: telling you to turn.*" The relationship to 1 Thess 1:9 has often been discussed. See, for example, Ulrich Wilckens, *Die Missionsreden der Apostelgeschichte* (Neukirchen: Neukirchener Verlag, 1961), 81–82, esp. 86–87.

45. On this point, see C. Kavin Rowe, "Luke–Acts and the Imperial Cult: A Way through the Conundrum?" *JSNT* 27 (2005): 279–300, esp. 290. Cf. Barrett, *Acts*, 1.665, who notes that the "denial that apostles and evangelists are anything other than human is another Lucan theme."

46. Cf. Josephus's criticism in *Ap.* 2.251 (§35).

47. Barrett, *Acts*, 1.680.

48. Cf. Breytenbach, "Zeus und der lebendige Gott: 396–413, who notes the OT and early Jewish link between ὁ θεὸς ζῶν and his status as creator (esp. 397). See, too, Mark J. Goodwin, *Paul: Apostle of the Living God: Kerygma and Conversion in 2 Corinthians* (Harrisburg, PA: Trinity Press International, 2001), esp. 105–8, who notes the connection in Jewish traditions between the "living God" and the criticism of idols.

49. Pausanias, *Description of Greece*, 8.9.2, here of Zeus in Mantineia ("for indeed he gives good things to humankind").

50. *Description of Greece*, 1.32.2. "Averter of ills" can be read as the obverse of one who brings good. See ἀπήμιος and its cognates in Liddell and Scott rev. ed., 188 (cf. ἀπήμων as "kindly" or "propitious" in *Od.*, 7.266). For the ancient altar on Parnes, see Robert Parker, *Athenian Religion*, 30–31. Breytenbach, "Zeus und der lebendige Gott," 399–403, provides an excellent summary of the relevant material for Zeus and Hermes in relation to Lystra in particular.

51. See the pertinent material in Arthur Bernard Cook's monumental study, *Zeus: A Study in Ancient Religion*, 3 vols. (Cambridge: Cambridge University Press, 1914–1940).

52. In citing the opening lines of Aratus's *Phaenomena*, Aristobulus simply substitutes θεός for Ζεύς/Δίς: "we have signified [that the power of θεός permeates all things] by removing the divine names Δίς and Ζεύς used throughout the verses; for their inherent meaning relates to θεός" (in Eusebius, *Praep. Evang.* 13.12). For the text and translation of Aristobulus, see Carl R. Holladay, *Fragments from Hellenistic Jewish Authors: Volume III: Aristobulus* (Atlanta, GA: Scholars Press, 1995), 171–3. The interchangeability of divine names was of course a commonplace in the Graeco-Roman

world at both the popular and philosophical levels: one may think readily, for example, of the closing hymn to Apollo in the first book of Statius, *Thebaid*, in which Apollo is asked for his blessings "whether 'tis right to call thee rosy Titan . . . or Osiris . . . or Mithras" (I.696–720, LCL trans.); or of Lucius's opening prayer to Isis in Apuleius's *Metamorphoses:* "O Queen of heaven—whether you are bountiful Ceres . . . or heavenly Venus . . . or Phoebus' sister . . . or dreaded Proserpina." (11.2; LCL); or, in a more philosophical vein, of Pseudo-Aristotle: "God being one has many names . . ." (*Mund.*, 401A; LCL); and Diogenes Laertius, *Lives*, 7.135: "God is one and the same with Reason, Fate, and Zeus; he is also called by many other names" (LCL trans.).

53. "*Dis pater Veiovis Manes, sive vos quo alio nomine fas est nominare*" ran an ancient Roman prayer ("Dis pater, Veiovis, Manes, or by whatever other name it is allowed to address you"; preserved in Macrobius, *Saturnalia*, 3.9.10 [this text was made known to me by P. W. van der Horst, "The Unknown God," in *Knowledge of God in the Graeco-Roman World*, ed. R. van den Broek et al. (Leiden: Brill, 1998), 19–42, 39]). Apuleius, *Met.*, 11.22, to take another example almost at random, speaks of Isis as "the goddess of many names" (and of course "myrionyma is a regular epithet for her," as Nock, *Conversion*, 150, notes). Divine names could also be referred to specific potencies or attributes of the one god atop the Greek metaphysical ladder, as the Stoics recognized: they give to God "the name Dia (*Δία*) because all things are due to (*διά*) him; Zeus (*Ζῆνα*) in so far as he is the cause of life (*ζῆν*) . . . ; the name Athena is given because the ruling part of the divinity extends to the aether; the name Hera marks its extension to the air; he is called Hephaestus since it spreads to the creative fire; Poseidon, since it stretches to the sea; Demeter; since it reaches to the earth. Similarly humans have given the deity his other titles, fastening, as best they can, on some one or other of his peculiar attributes" (Diogenes Laertius, *Lives*, 7.147, LCL).

54. Breytenbach, "Zeus und der lebendige Gott," 397. For a list of the allusions to the OT in 14:15–18, see esp. Gustav Stählin, *Die Apostelgeschichte*, NTD 5 (Göttingen: Vandenhoeck & Ruprecht, 1962), 193–94, who lists nine principal areas—with about twenty texts—that demonstrate the OT theological roots of Paul's exclamation.

55. Taking the pl. λιθάσαντες in v. 19 to include the crowds (in light of πείσαντες— what else would be its purpose?). So, rightly, Jacob Jervell, *Die Apostelgeschichte* (Göttingen: Vandenhoeck & Ruprecht, 1998), 379 n. 607; and Gerhard Schneider, *Die Apostelgeschichte* (2 vols.; Freiburg: Herder, 1980, 1982), 2.162. Contra Klauck, *Magic and Paganism*, 59–60, who thinks (1) that Luke includes only the Jews from Iconium, and (2) that Luke needs correction—Paul would not have survived a Jewish stoning—so that a gentile mob is in view. If one takes λιθάσαντες to include the crowds, Klauck's problem simply disappears. With respect to the content of the Jewish persuasion, Luke does not narrate it explicitly, but from the rest of Acts such content is not hard to discern: in essence the gentiles are told that the missionaries "advocate customs which it is not lawful for us Romans to accept or practice" (16:21), or "are acting against the decrees of Caesar, saying there is another King, Jesus" (17:7), or "persuade people to worship God contrary to the law" (18:13), or cause στάσις (24:5), and so forth.

56. So, rightly, Pesch, *Apostelgeschichte*, 2.59–60. Johnson, *Acts*, 251, forces the passage in a positive direction when he writes that this scene shows how God "is

opening a door of faith for the Gentiles." Johnson is correct that the gentiles are not simply condemned for their idolatry. In an important sense, they are open to divine visitation. However, to read the passage as something of a commendation of the gentile impulse toward idolatry ("Luke portrays these rustics as having precisely the conditions for genuine faith") goes too far and makes unintelligible the concluding evangelistic disaster. If God is opening a door for the gentiles in Lystra (see μαθηταί in 14:22), it would seem to be based on Paul's preaching (14:7) rather than this healing in particular (indeed, as Haenchen, *Acts*, 431, noted, the mention of πίστιν τοῦ σωθῆναι in 14:9 presupposes Paul's preaching). Moreover, the exhortation in 14:22 to the disciples in Lystra, Iconium, and Antioch seems to point to some level of persecution in these locations (παρακαλοῦντες ἐμμένειν τῇ πίστει καὶ ὅτι διὰ πολλῶν θλίψεων δεῖ ἡμᾶς εἰσελθεῖν εἰς τὴν βασιλείαν τοῦ θεοῦ). That "much suffering / many tribulations" could be the life of the disciples in Lystra is of course narratively compelling in light of the proximity of 14:22 to the Lystra story, though it could easily pertain also to the missionaries' prior experience in Pisidian Antioch and Iconium (13:50–14:6).

57. Jacob Jervell, *The Theology of the Acts of the Apostles* (Cambridge: Cambridge University Press, 1996), 19, takes v. 16 as a statement about God's absence from the history of gentiles. Perhaps this is to go too far, but the narrative contrast with the description of God's continuous activity in Israel is certainly striking.

58. Moshe Halbertal and Avishai Margalit, *Idolatry*, trans. Naomi Goldblum (Cambridge, MA: Harvard University Press, 1992), 163.

59. Lane Fox, *Pagans and Christians*, 208.

60. Cf. Luke 8:28 where the Gerasene demoniac cries out in a great voice ἀνακράξας . . . φωνῇ μεγάλῃ: "What have you to do with me, Jesus, Son τοῦ θεοῦ τοῦ ὑψίστου?" In this pericope Luke speaks both of demons (pl., δαιμόνια) and of an unclean spirit (sg., τὸ πνεῦμα τὸ ἀκάθαρτον). These two different ways of speaking are presumably unified in the single name "Legion," which stands for the man's possession by many demons.

61. Nock, *Essays*, 1.425. Cf. Barrett, *Acts*, 2.786, for other literature on this point.

62. So, rightly, Barrett, *Acts*, 2.786 et al.

63. See Stephen Mitchell, "The Cult of Theos Hypsistos," in *Pagan Monotheism in Late Antiquity*, ed. Polymnia Athanassiadi and Michael Frede (Oxford: Clarendon, 1999), 81–148 (110; cf. 115–121). A cultic sight has yet to be found in Philippi in particular. Mitchell's suggestion depends upon (1) a coordination of Luke's use of προσευχή (Acts 16:13, 16) with the terminology of other known Theos Hypsistos "shrines," (2) the possibility that Lydia—as a godfearer—would have already been involved in the worship of Theos Hypsistos, and (3) the widespread finds mentioned in the citation above in the main text of this essay. Mitchell notes that the cult of Theos Hypsistos "from the Hellenistic period until the fifth century was found in town and country across the entire eastern Mediterranean and the Near East" (125–26). See, too, the concise treatment by Paul R. Trebilco, *Jewish Communities in Asia Minor*, SNTSMS 69 (Cambridge: Cambridge University Press, 1991), 127–44, esp. 143, for this context.

64. In Origen, *C. Cel.*, 5.41 (trans. Chadwick). The identification of Jupiter/Zeus ὕψιστος with the God of the Jews was of course present already in Varro (see collection

of texts in Menahem Stern, *Greek and Latin Authors on Jews and Judaism*, 3 vols. [Jerusalem: The Israel Academy of Sciences and Humanities, 1974–1984], 1.210–211) and continued through late antiquity. See, for example, Damascius, *Isid.*, 141 (in Photius, *Bibliotheca*): "[Isidorus wrote] that on this mountain there is a most holy sanctuary of Zeus ὕψιστος to whom Abraham the father of the old Hebrews consecrated himself" (cited in Stern, *Greek and Latin Authors*, 2.674). One does not have to argue that the populus was consciously aware of the Platonic or Stoic philosophical pressure toward one supreme being—refracted differently through different (local) gods—to note the intermingling of divine names (Zeus Sarapis/Attis/Dionysius, etc.).

65. For Luke's use of καταγγέλλω, see esp. Acts 4:2; 13:38; 16:21 (!); 17:3, 18, 23; 26:23.

66. On the non-eschatological meaning of σωτηρία for pagans, Nock, *Conversion*, 9, is concise.

67. Klauck, *Magic and Paganism*, 69.

68. Werner Foerster, "πύθων," *TDNT*, 6.917–20.

69. See, too, the still-relevant critique of ventriloquism in general as a way to explain the phenomena of divination, prophecy, and so forth in E. R. Dodds, *The Greeks and the Irrational* (Berkeley: University of California Press, 1951), 71–2, with notes.

70. Barrett, *Acts*, 2.785.

71. The girl, that is, has "a spirit, a pythian/pythonic one," taking the accusatives in apposition. Though a larger resonance with the official priestess (πυθία or πυθιάς) in Delphi or its mythological prehistory could well be intended (Gaventa, *Acts*, 238), "official" cultic religion is not primarily in view here. In the first instance, πύθων is used at this point, rather, in a more general sense of one of the many and various fortune-tellers of the ancient world. See, for example, the tale of the nameless but influential wanderer in Plutarch, *De def. or.*, 421A–E; Lucian, *Alex.*, 9, which mentions traveling mantics (μαντεύεσθαι) as if they were a commonplace; and Dio Chrysostom, *Or.*, 1.56, who contrasts a true mantic with the οἱ πολλοὶ τῶν λεγομένων ἐνθέων ἀνδρῶν καὶ γυναικῶν—the many men and women who are only *said* to be inspired. Cf., too, the plural "pythons" in the (Pseudo) *Clementine Homilies*, 9.16.3: ὅτι καὶ πύθωνες μαντεύονται ἀλλ' ὑφ' ἡμῶν ὡς δαίμονες ὁρκιζόμενοι φυγαδεύονται ("for even pythons prophesy, but they are cast out by us as demons, and put to flight"). Klauck, *Magic and Paganism*, 66, takes πύθων as a proper name, "a spirit named Python." This is an attractive translation in view of the emphasis upon the πνεῦμα in v. 18; yet, in light of Lukan style, it is probably better to retain the adjectival sense (see BDF §242).

72. On μαντεία κτλ. as oracle, and so forth, see LSJ, 1079–80. We may also note that μαντεύεσθαι is used only here in NT and thus never of Christian prophets. Luke's usage follows that of the LXX, where μαντεύεσθαι κτλ. are uniformly employed in a critical sense and not of Israel's prophets.

73. See *De def. or.*, 417 passim.

74. Cf. Plutarch, *De Pyth. or.*, 402BC, who notes the worry about the πυθία that "the spirit [πνεῦμα] has been completely quenched and her powers have forsaken her" (LCL trans.), or *De def. or.*, 418D, where Cleombrotus speaks, for the moment, for those who believe that the defection of the oracles should be attributed to the departure of the δαίμονες (cf. also, e.g., ibid, 438C–D).

75. Of course it is entirely possible that 16:19 simply means that the masters become aware that the oracles will stop. But in light of the "form" of exorcism stories in general, it would not be out of character for there to be a demonstration of the spirit's departure. See, for example, Rudolf Bultmann, *History of the Synoptic Tradition*, trans. John Marsh (Oxford: Basil Blackwell, 1963), 218–32, esp. 225.

76. Cicero mentions Xenophanes and Panaetius. See also Dodds, *The Greeks and the Irrational*, 190, who makes reference to Cicero's work along with other evidence. Cf. Attridge, "Philosophical Critique," 54, on the fragments of the Epicurean Diogenianos (preserved in Eusebius).

77. See citation of Lane Fox in n. 144.

78. In addition to this passage itself, see, for example, Cicero, *Div.*, 2.132–33, who mentions diviners who "prophesy for money" and "beg for a coin": "I [Ennius] do not recognize fortune-tellers, or those who prophesy for money, or necromancers, or mediums, whom your friend Appius makes it a practice to consult . . . for they are not diviners either by knowledge or skill. . . . From those to whom they promise wealth they beg a coin" (LCL trans.); and Plato, *Resp.*, 2.364B–C, who knows of nonprofessional diviners that are the equivalent of door-to-door religious salesmen.

79. Lane Fox, *Pagans and Christians*, 207. See, too, the remark of Gaius Velleius, the representative Epicurean in Cicero's *Nat. D.*, who mentions various "prophetic persons" in his criticism of the Stoics' belief in μαντική: "if we consented to listen to you . . . we should be the devotees of soothsayers, augurs, oracle-mongers, seers, and interpreters of dreams" (1.55–56); and Plutarch's chiding of the superstitious people who put "themselves in the hands of conjurors and imposters" (*De Superstitione*, 166). Cf. Ramsey MacMullen, *Enemies of the Roman Order: Treason, Unrest, and Alienation in the Empire* (Cambridge, MA: Harvard University Press, 1966), 128: "In the Roman empire, a universal confidence that the future could be known either through rites of official priests on public occasions, or privately, produced an infinitely combustible audience for predictions." At the level of more official oracles, scholars have long noted that Plutarch's *de defectu oraculorum* is not the final word on the subject. Business in Delphi may have slowed, but it was booming in Abonuteichos. See, for example, MacMullen, *Paganism in the Roman Empire*, 61–62 and 175–76 n. 55.

80. MacMullen, *Christianizing the Roman Empire*, 108–9 (emphasis original).

81. For a compendium of ancient attitudes toward Jews, see Stern, *Greek and Latin Authors*. Roman citizenship is obviously an important aspect of this passage (cf. 16:37–38), particularly because of Philippi's status as a *colonia*, but the issues involved regrettably cannot be treated here (see chap. 3).

82. A handful of influential exegetes have identified the Areopagus speech as the "high point" of Luke's second volume (Philipp Vielhauer, "On the 'Paulinism' of Acts," in *Studies in Luke–Acts*, ed. L. E. Keck and J. L. Martyn (Mifflintown, PA: Sigler, 1999), 33–50 [34]). Cf., among others, Paul Schubert, "The Place of the Areopagus Speech in the Composition of Acts," in *Transitions in Biblical Scholarship*, ed. J. Coert Rylaarsdam (Chicago: University of Chicago Press, 1968), 235–61, esp. 261. Despite the learning of these scholars, it is exceedingly difficult to understand their readings at this point. Nothing in the narrative suggests that Luke has shaped Acts to build to this

moment or that the story comes down afterward as if from a pinnacle. One suspects, rather, that it is the academic inclination of the interpreters in question that has led them to value the explicitly philosophical speech above other parts of the narrative.

83. This generalization is true of both the "literary" and "historical" lines of research (Schneider, *Apostelgeschichte*, 2.234), though of course there are considerable differences between the particular foci and the exegesis of individual scholars.

84. Martin Dibelius, "Paul on the Areopagus," in *The Book of Acts: Form, Style, and Theology*, ed. K. C. Hanson (Minneapolis, MN: Fortress, 2004), 95–128 (113 and 119, respectively). Many scholars would obviously take issue with Dibelius's statement, as did Gärtner, for example, who attempted to establish the biblical (i.e., Jewish) basis for the speech (Bertil Gärtner, *The Areopagus Speech and Natural Revelation* [Lund: C. W. K. Gleerup, 1955]). Alfons Weiser, *Die Apostelgeschichte*, ÖTKNT 5, 2 vols. (Gütersloh: Gerd Mohn, 1981/1985), 2.478–80, offers the most concise *Forschungsbericht* on this question and attempts a mediating position between Dibelius and those exegetes who would stress the (biblical or Hellenistic) Jewish content of Paul's speech: "Methodisch ist es erforderlich, den Text weder einseitig atl.-biblisch noch einseitig stoisch auszulegen, sondern gemäss des neuen Kontextes" (479). Drawing upon Haenchen, Gerhard Schneider, *Apostelgeschichte*, 2.234, holds that the speech reflects a specifically Christian tradition of preaching to the gentiles: practically speaking it would make no sense to begin with issues of the identity of the Messiah and Jesus's resurrection; for this reason it should occasion no surprise that Paul's *Ausgangspunkt* is different. Yet, there is no pre-Lukan evidence for such a tradition. It is difficult to see, therefore, how Schneider's point could amount to anything other than a restatement of a particular construal of Luke's intention with the passage (this is of course exegetically valuable, but it is not the same thing as an answer to the *traditionsgeschichtliche* question).

85. This would not, however, be true of some of the most recent commentators that display an awareness of the importance of narrative interpretation (e.g., Beverly Gaventa or Scott Spencer).

86. During Paul's day, Athens no longer enjoyed the status it once had and would again have in the so-called Second Sophistic (this is not to say that it was intellectually impoverished). By Luke's time, however, the city may have already begun to flourish again.

87. So, similarly, Barrett, *Acts*, 2.828; and Charles H. Talbert, *Reading Acts* (Macon, GA: Smyth & Helwys, 2005), 150.

88. R. E. Wycherley, "St. Paul at Athens," *JTS* 19 (1968): 619–21, on κατείδωλος (619). Wycherley's emphasis on the Herms in particular is, however, highly questionable (as Barrett, *Acts*, 2.827, also notes).

89. See, for example, Livy, 45.27.11; Pausanias, *Descr. Gr.*, 1.17.1; Strabo, *Geog.* 9.1.16, and so forth.

90. This interpretation of the end of 17:18 goes back at least to Chrysostom (τὴν ἀνάστασιν θεόν τινα εἶναι ἐνόμιζον, ἅτε εἰωθότες καὶ θηλείας σέβειν). See Émile Beurlier, "Saint Paul et L'Aréopage," *Rev. d'hist. et de litt. rel.* 1 (1896): 344–66 (344).

91. See Chadwick, "Florilegium."

92. It may be, as Abraham J. Malherbe, " 'Not in a Corner': Early Christian Apologetic in Acts 26:26," *The Second Century* 5/4 (1985/86): 193–210 (197–201), says, that σπερμολόγος is employed by Luke as part of his overall concern to present Paul as an "educated" preacher, but the immediate reach of the word pertains first of all to Athens.

93. The charge of ignorant babbling also prepares one not to be surprised that the philosophers are not easily won over by Paul's awareness of Stoic themes and citation of Aratus; indeed, reticence on the part of the philosophers is what should be expected in light of their evaluation of Paul's preaching. That some (τινὲς ἄνδρες, v. 34) should join and believe can then be read as a rather dramatic success. In phrasing things this way, I do not assume that the entirety of Paul's audience is portrayed as philosophers (Stoics and Epicureans). The Areopagus court in any case would not have been composed of philosophers alone (contra Cassiodorus et al.; see Beurlier, "Saint Paul" 345, 349). Yet, it seems clear from the content of the speech and from vv. 18, 21, and 32 that those with philosophical sophistication are primarily in view.

94. Barrett, *Acts*, 2.831, citing Acts 9:27 and 23:19. Whether or not the tribune's action in 23:19 is "well-intentioned" is disputable, but Barrett's general semantic point is sound (cf. Haenchen, *Acts*, 518).

95. Gärtner, *Areopagus Speech*, 54–55. Cf. Pesch, *Apostelgeschichte*, 2.135.

96. See the translation and commentary of Lake and Cadbury, *Beginnings*, 4.212.

97. For example, Weiser, *Apostelgeschichte*, 2.465–66; Klauck, *Magic and Paganism*, 79. This or a variation thereof was the official title of the council, though it could also be designated simply as the Ἄρειος πάγος ἐν Ἐλευσῖνι. On this latter point, see Timothy D. Barnes, "An Apostle on Trial," *JTS* 20 (1969): 407–19 (410). To question Luke's terminological accuracy here would be akin to questioning a future historian's accuracy in referring to the United States House of Representatives with the shorthand expression "the House" (e.g., the House failed to pass the bill). On the Areopagus in the Roman period, see esp. Daniel J. Geagan, *The Athenian Constitution after Sulla* (Buffalo, NY: Hein, 2004), 32–61.

98. This is not at all to say that the argument is circular. It is true for any interpretation of the passage—not just my particular interpretation—that the reading of a certain part is inextricably bound with an understanding of the other parts. The question is how best to put the total picture together. In this case, to read ἐπιλαμβάνομαι in a mild sense is already to presuppose a certain understanding of the Areopagus that ignores its well-known function in the ancient world and renders irrelevant the echoes of Socrates' trial.

99. Though they are speaking of an earlier period, A. A. Long and D. N. Sedley illustrate well the importance of the agora for philosophical discussion and debate: the agora "was the one area toward which any philosopher staying in Athens could be expected to gravitate" (*The Hellenistic Philosophers*, 2 vols. [Cambridge: Cambridge University Press, 1987], 1.3).

100. Nock, *Essays*, 2.831.

101. Beurlier, "Saint Paul," 344–46. Interestingly, as Haenchen and others have noted, Origen reflects the belief that Socrates' trial was before the Areopagus, which

it was not. Such a belief is indubitably founded on the loud echoes of Socrates' trial in Luke's Areopagus scene.

102. See esp. Acts 27:21: σταθεὶς ὁ Παῦλος ἐν μέσῳ αὐτῶν εἶπεν ἔδει μέν ὦ ἄνδρες.

103. So Gärtner, *Areopagus Speech*, 55–56. Contra Haenchen, *Acts*, 520, who asserts somewhat bizarrely: "The words 'in the midst of the Areopagus' . . . suggest that the narrator is thinking about Mars' hill."

104. Of which Διονύσιος ὁ Ἀρεοπαγίτης was a member (17:34). Barrett, *Acts*, 2.885, asserts that this designation "confirms that, in Luke's view, the Areopagus was a body of men, not a place." Attending to the full verse, however, exposes the weakness of Barrett's assertion. Luke writes: "Some men believed and joined him [Paul], among whom was Dionysius the Areopagite, and a woman named Damaris, and others with them." Thus it is unclear that Luke does anything more than mention the status or identifying feature of a particular convert subsequent to Paul's encounter with the Areopagus. Cf. Clayton Croy, "Hellenistic Philosophies and the Preaching of the Resurrection (Acts 17:18, 32)," *NovT* 39 (1997): 21–39, who recognizes the interpretive difficulty in v. 32: "whether Luke meant these persons to be included among the *hoi de* of 32b, or whether their conversions occurred on a later occasion is uncertain" (28).

105. Barnes, "An Apostle on Trial," 414.

106. Ibid., esp. 408–9; Haenchen, *Acts*, 518, and Cadbury, *Book of Acts*, 52, assume that the council met in the στοά βασίλειος (cf. Klauck, *Magic and Paganism*, 79), a view that derives ultimately from a single statement in Ps–Demosthenes and that was advanced by Nock, *Essays*, 2.831–32, esp. n. 51 (in fairness to Cadbury, he does "leave open" the possibility that the council met on the hill, 67). Barnes, however, shows convincingly that the Ps–Demosthenes passage cannot possibly be used to support their view, and, moreover, that Aelius Aristides, Pausanias, and Lucian all attest to the meeting of the council on the hill.

107. Barnes, "An Apostle on Trial," 410.

108. For example, Nock, *Essays*, 2.831: Luke "may not have realized the two senses of the word Areopagus." This problem is acute in Barrett's commentary just at this point: "Luke may have meant both [hill and council], but if he intended to *say* both he should have done so explicitly" (*Acts*, 2.832; emphasis original).

109. The Areopagus appears not infrequently as a "high court" in Lucian's writings. See, for example, *Timon, or The Misanthrope*, 46; *Philosophies for Sale*, 7; *Hermotimus, or Concerning the Sects*, 64; *The Dance*, 39, and so forth. Indeed the authority of the court was well known. See, for example, Cicero, who assumes its authority when he says in another context: "As a matter of fact, 'providence' is an elliptical expression; when one says 'the Athenian state is ruled by the council,' the words 'of the Areopagus' are omitted" (*Nat.D.*, 2.74).

110. Barnes, "An Apostle on Trial," 413. Part of Barnes's critical point here is in response to those scholars who seek to delimit the authority of the Areopagus (to education, to religion, etc.). Barnes shows concisely and convincingly that such attempts run aground on the various pieces of contrary evidence that complicate the attempt to tie the Areopagus to one particular function.

111. Barrett, *Acts*, 2.832, with no argumentation.

112. LSJ, 452. See Paul's remark to Festus in Acts 25:11: οὐδείς με δύναται αὐτοῖς χαρίσασθαι ("no one has the legal right to hand me over to them"). On this passage, see chap. 3.

113. The other charge usually mentioned was that he corrupted the youth. On this charge as a political one—that is, Socrates educated traitors such as Critias and Alcibiades—see Peter Garnsey, "Religious Toleration in Classical Antiquity," in *Persecution and Toleration*, ed. W. J. Sheils (London: Basil Blackwell, 1984), 1–27, esp. 3. Of course, Socrates' trial and death as a whole played a large role in the self-understanding of many philosophers in antiquity. Seneca, for example, had hemlock prepared for his own suicide/execution, though the poison was administered too late to take effect (Tacitus, *Ann.*, 15.64). On this point in general, see Ramsay MacMullen, *Enemies of the Roman Order: Treason, Unrest, and Alienation in the Empire* (Cambridge, MA: Harvard University Press, 1966), 75.

114. Trans. LCL, altered (LCL, not without reason, translates ἕτερα δὲ καινὰ δαιμόνια as "strange deities"). Xenophon continues by saying that it was well known that Socrates claimed to be guided by τὸ δαιμόνιον and this claim was the likely cause for the charge that he was bringing in new deities (1.1.2: καινὰ δαιμόνια εἰσφέρειν). Cf. Plato, *Apol.*, 28E–30E, 37E; *Euthyphr.*, 3B.

115. Trans. LCL, altered. Cf. the statement in Euripides' *Bacchae* where Pentheus accuses Teiresias of having introduced Dionysus: "This is all your doing, Teiresias: you want to introduce this new divinity to humans [θέλεις τὸν δαίμον ἀνθρώποισιν ἐσφέρων νέον] and read his bird signs and entrails and take fees! If you weren't protected by your gray hair, you would be sitting in prison surrounded by bacchants for introducing these wicked rites" (lns. 255–59; LCL).

116. My translation (see, too, *Apol.*, 26C; 29A; 30A–D; 31A; 37E). Cf. *Euthyphr.*, 3B (καινοὺς ποιοῦντα θεούς, τοὺς δ᾽ ἀρχαίους οὐ νομίζοντα).

117. Justin Martyr, for example, in defending Christians against the accusation of atheism, cites the charge brought against Socrates that resulted in capital punishment: "he brings in new deities" (*1 Apol.* 5.4: καινὰ εἰσφερειν αὐτὸν δαιμόνια). And Diogenes Laertius insists that the affidavit of Socrates' case still existed (ἀνάκειται γὰρ ἔτι καὶ νῦν). Socrates is guilty because he does not acknowledge the gods recognized by the polis but instead brings in other, new deities (ἕτερα δὲ καινὰ δαιμόνια εἰσηγούμενος; *Lives*, 2.40). Josephus knew this aspect of Athenian history well, too. Though the charge against Socrates is stated in slightly different form, the substance is the same. Socrates was put to death "because he used to swear strange oaths [καινοὺς ὅρκους] and give out . . . that he received communications from a certain deity" (τι δαιμόνιον; *C. Ap.*, 2.263 [trans. LCL, altered]). Furthermore, continues Josephus, the Athenians did not hesitate to put to death "Ninus the priestess because someone accused her of initiating people into the mysteries of foreign gods [ξένους θεούς]. This was forbidden by their law, and the penalty decreed for any who introduced a foreign god was death" (*C. Ap.* 2.267–268: τιμωρία κατὰ τῶν ξένον εἰσαγόντων θεὸν ὥριστο θάνατος). Cf. Cassius Dio, *Hist. Rom.* 52.36.1–2, who notes Maecenas's recommendation that Augustus should (1) "force" ἀναγκάζω all people to honor τὸ θεῖον and (2) despise and punish those who "attempt to distort our religion with strange rites

(τοὺς . . . ξενίζοντας)." Maecenas grounds his advice in the ultimate political danger involved in allowing new deities to be brought in: "such men, by bringing in new divinities in place of the old [καὶ καινά τινα δαιμόνια . . . ἀντεσφέροντες], persuade many to adopt foreign practices, from which spring up conspiracies, factions, and cabals, which are far from profitable to monarchy" (trans. LCL). For the reputation of classical Athens even before Socrates, cf. the statement in Euripides' *Bacchae* mentioned above in n. 115. On the virtual synonymy of καινός and ξένος, see LSJ, 858; and, Eduard Norden, *Agnostos Theos: Untersuchungen zur Formengeschichte religiöser Rede* (Berlin: B.G. Teubner, 1913), 53 n. 3. To this day, these are the charges classical scholars accept, though more attention has also been paid to Socrates' political alignments.

118. Of interest is the fact that καινότερον occurs only here in the NT and that it does not occur at all in the LXX. See, however, Demosthenes, *Orat.*, 4.10 (43), who, in chastising the inaction of the Athenians, asks, "Or tell me, are you content to run round and ask one another, 'What's new?' Could there be anything newer than that a Macedonian is triumphing over Athenians and settling the destiny of Greece?" (LCL trans., altered: λέγεταί τι καινόν; γένοιτο γὰρ ἄν τι καινότερον ἢ Μακεδὼν ἀνήρ).

119. Though he speaks primarily about the charge of corrupting the youth, Apuleius, *Met.*, 10.33, notes that the Athenian action against Socrates resulted in the city's perpetual ignominy, or "stain of eternal disgrace" (LCL; *ignominae perpetuae maculam*). Cf., too, the remark of Josephus in n. 117 above.

120. What is significant, of course, about Socrates' trial for all the above-mentioned authors is not so much that Socrates was tried but that the trial led to his demise. In Athens, bringing in new deities could result in death. On the issue of the need to receive permission from the Athenian council to introduce a new cult, Price, *Religions of the Ancient Greeks*, 76–78, is concise (cf. Parker, *Athenian Religion*, 199–200). With respect to the public sphere, such permission makes intelligible remarks that we see, for example, in Strabo, *Geog.*, 10.3.18: "Just as in all other respects the Athenians continue to be hospitable to things foreign, so also in their worship of the gods; for they welcomed so many of the foreign rites that they were ridiculed by comic writers [Plato, Demosthenes]" (LCL trans.; περὶ τοὺς θεούς. πολλὰ γὰρ τῶν ξενικῶν ἱερῶν παρεδέξατο). It should be noted, too, that Strabo here refers to an earlier period of Athenian history (pre-Plato) and that, as with the entirety of the *Geography*, serious caution must be exercised in applying his descriptions to the concrete realities of particular locations.

121. Though Luke does not have the Areopagus say explicitly that Paul "rejects the gods acknowledged by the state," it is distinctly possible that we are to discern this connection with Socrates' trial as well, especially given the complaint of Demetrius in Ephesus (Acts 19:26).

122. This is not to suggest that Socrates stood before the Areopagus (see n. 101 above) but rather simply to note the general shape of the analogy.

123. Hans Conzelmann, *Acts of the Apostles* (Philadelphia: Fortress, 1987), 140 (among others), and Haenchen, *Acts*, 520, respectively. The motive of the Areopagus was given in vv. 19–20: to know if in fact Paul is bringing in new, strange deities.

124. Cf., inter alios, Nock, *Essays*, 2.831. The text would make excellent narrative sense without v. 21.

125. The comparative καινότερον has occasionally been thought to carry a superlative sense (e.g., Haenchen, *Acts*, 520), but the discussion of Norden, *Agnostos Theos*, 333–35, on Attic words in Acts 17 has largely remained persuasive (see, e.g., BDF § 244.2; Jervell, *Apostelgeschichte*, 445, n. 223; Schneider, *Apostelgeschichte*, 2.237 passim). Norden notes: "[D]ie Bemerkung im Wendtschen Kommentar: τι καινότερον "etwas Allerneuestes." 'Der Komparativ hat hier, wie sonst oft im nt. Sprachgebrauch, superlative Bedeutung' ist unrichtig. Dieser Komparativ ist mit der Spracherscheinung der Vulgärsprache . . . keineswegs zu identifizieren, sondern ein gerade bei dem Begriffe der 'Neuheit' typisches Spezifikum des Attischen: wenn ich frage: 'gibt es etwas Neue?,' so ist dies Neue, das ich zu erfahren wünsche, im Verhältnis zu dem Stande meines gegenwärtigen Wissens immer ein Plus" (333).

126. The citation derives from Malherbe, "Not in a Corner," 199.

127. "Paul" here refers to Luke's character who gives the speech; questions of the correspondence of Luke's presentation to the historical Paul are, alas, for another time.

128. For example, Haenchen, *Acts*, 520; Pesch, *Apostelgeschichte*, 2.136; Schneider, *Apostelgeschichte*, 2.237. Lucian, *Anacharsis, or Athletics*, 19, says through the mouth of Solon that the Areopagus will hear only of the facts of the case before it, and "if anyone prefaces his speech with an introduction in order to make the court more favourable, or brings emotion of exaggeration into the case—tricks that are often devised by the disciples of rhetoric to influence the judges—then the crier appears and silences them at once, preventing them from talking nonsense to the court." And Apuleius, while telling of a murder trial, notes that "the defendant was summoned and brought in, and, in accordance with Attic law and the Areopagus court, the herald forbade the advocates in the case to speak prefaces or to try to arouse pity" (*Met.* 10.7). One should note, too, as a possible continuation of the resonance of his trial, Socrates' repeated address to the "men of Athens" in Plato's *Apol.* (ὦ ἄνδρες Ἀθηναῖοι; see e.g., 28A, D; 29D; 30C, etc.).

129. See, among many others, Conzelmann, *Acts of the Apostles*, 140; and, Gaventa, *Acts*, 250. On the range of meanings of δεισιδαίμων, see Koets, Δεισιδαιμονία.

130. The piety of the Athenians was well known in the ancient world. See, for example, Sophocles, *Oedipus Coloneus*, 260: of all the states, "Athens is said to be the most pious" (τὰς γ᾿ Ἀθήνας φασὶ θεοσεβεστάτας εἶναι); Jos., *C. Ap.* 2.130: "by common consent [Athens] is the most pious of the Greeks" (εὐσεβεστάτους τῶν Ἑλλήνων ἅπαντες λέγουσιν); and the works cited above (Livy, Pausanias, etc. on idols).

131. Barrett, *Acts*, 2.836, is therefore right to reverse Conzelmann's logic: the latter's argument that "δεισιδαιμονέστερος must be understood *sensu bono* because it occurs in a *captatio benevolentiae* is invalid: Paul's words are to be understood as a *captatio benevolentiae* only if we know that δεισιδαιμονέστερος is intended *sensu bono*." Johnson, *Acts*, 314, also follows the Conzelmann line.

132. For example, Jervell, *Apostelgeschichte*, 445.

133. Klauck, *Magic and Paganism*, 81–82, though the distinction between "narrated communication" (story-world: Paul and the Athenians) and "communication via narration" (the author and his readers) is terminologically problematic inasmuch as narrated communication is communicated only via the narration.

134. The reader knows, that is, that theologically speaking Luke is not commending idolatry, while historically speaking Paul does not simply insult them right out of the gates, as it were. That Luke is a master of dramatic irony emerges clearly in a consideration of his use of the vocative κύριε in the Gospel. On this point, see C. Kavin Rowe, *Early Narrative Christology: The Lord in the Gospel of Luke*, BZNW 139 (Berlin: Walter de Gruyter, 2006).

135. There are of course several references to the plural "unknown gods" (ἀγνώστοις θεοῖς, etc.). So far, the only strong possibility for the singular form occurs in Diogenes Laertius's account of Epimenides. Epimenides freed the Athenians from a plague by offering sacrifice to the "local god" (θύειν τῷ προσήκοντι θεῷ) upon the Areopagus wherever the sheep brought in for the occasion happened to lay down (*Lives*, I.110). For a thorough review of the literary and inscriptional evidence, see esp. P. W. van der Horst, "The Unknown God," 19–42. Altars to the unknown gods are usually interpreted as evidence of pagan anxiety not to neglect—and thereby anger—any god whatsoever. See Van der Horst, "The Unknown God," 27, for example, and Lane Fox, *Pagans and Christians*, 38 passim, for the general context of "the gods' own anger at their neglect." From a different angle, Stephen Mitchell, "Cult of Theos Hypsistos," 122, has noted that if—following Barnes—Paul stood trial on the Areopagus, "he was standing directly in front of the cult place of Theos Hypsistos, the God 'not admitting of a name, known by many names.'" Mitchell's quotation refers of course to the famous oracle inscription from Oenoanda (northern Lycia).

136. Pagan philosophy, too, could speak of divine "making" in relation to the cosmos. One thinks naturally of Plato's *Timaeus* or other statements we find, for example, in Epictetus, *Discourses*, 4.7.6: "God has made all things that are in the world—and, indeed, the whole world itself—to be unhindered and to contain its telos in itself" (trans. LCL, altered: ὁ θεὸς πάντα πεποίηκεν τὰ ἐν τῷ κόσμῳ καὶ αὐτὸν τὸν κόσμον ὅλον μὲν ἀκώλυτον καὶ αὐτοτελῆ). Yet such similarities to the Jewish view of creation should not be overdrawn inasmuch as the pagan conception retained room for the human creation of divine images whereas the Jewish one did not (cf., among many possible texts for comparison, Gen 1:1; Isa 42:5; Wis 9:1, 9; 4 Macc 5:25, etc.). The Jewish boundary corresponds, to put it in contemporary terms, to an ontological distinction between God and the world that is, insofar as we can discern, theologically of a fundamentally different order than that of a pagan continuum of being.

137. Here the translation of *vaoí* as "shrines" (location within the temple where the images were) rather than "temples" is to be preferred in light of the end of v. 25, which refers clearly to the treatment of the images of pagan gods. Among others, Pausanias affords numerous examples of caring for images of the gods. To take one virtually at random, see his mention of the treatment of Athena's statue in Athens and Asclepius in Epidaurus: "On the Athenian Acropolis the ivory of the image they call the Virgin is benefited not by olive oil [as is the image of Zeus at Olympus] but by water. For the Acropolis ... is over-dry, so that the image ... needs water or dampness. When I asked at Epidaurus why they pour neither water nor olive oil on the image of Asclepius ... [they] informed me that both the image of the god and the throne were built over a cistern" (*Descr. Gr.*, 5.11.10–11).

138. For those who knew the LXX, however, χειροποίητος would evoke the biblical prohibitions and criticisms of idolatry (e.g., Lev 26:1; Isa 31:7; 46:6, etc.). See also Luke's use of χειροποίητος in an explicitly Jewish setting (Acts 7:48). On this notion in the *Fourth Epistle of Heraclitus*, see the discussion of Harold W. Attridge, *First-Century Cynicism in the Epistles of Heraclitus*, HTS 29 (Missoula, MT: Scholars Press, 1976), 13–23.

139. In Augustine, *De Civ. D.*, 4.31. On the aniconism of the ancient Romans, cf. also Plutarch, *Num.*, 8.7–8: "Numa forbade the Romans to revere an image of god which had the form of man or beast. Nor was there among them in this earlier time any painted or graven likeness of deity, but while for the first hundred and seventy years they were continually establishing sacred shrines, they made no statues in bodily form for them, convinced that it was impious to liken higher things to lower, and that it is impossible to apprehend Deity except by intellect."

140. *Ep.*, 95.47. Seneca's criticism could also be rather sharp: "To beings who are sacred, immortal and inviolable, [people] consecrate images of the cheapest inert material. [These images] are called divinities, but if they were suddenly brought to life and encountered, they would be regarded as monsters" (*De Superst.* [in Augustine, *De Civ. D.*, VI.10]). Cf., *Ep.*, 31.11, where he cites Virgil's *Aeneid* (8:364: "And mould thyself to kinship with thy God") and remarks: "This molding will not be done in gold or silver; an image that is to be the likeness of God cannot be fashioned of such materials; remember that the gods, when they were kind unto men, were moulded in clay" (trans. LCL). Cf., to take another obvious example, Plutarch's remark in *De Superst.*, 167: the superstitious "give credence to workers in metal stone, or wax, who make their images of gods in the likeness of human beings, and they have such images fashioned, and dress them up, and worship them."

141. Cf. Epictetus, *Discourses*, 2.8.11–29, or the teaching of Zeno mentioned by Plutarch: "It is a doctrine of Zeno's not to build temples of the gods, because a temple not worth much is also not sacred and no work of builders or mechanics is worth much" (*De Stoicorum Repug.* 6 [1034B]). The Epicureans, of course, went further in their criticism and would have no problem, therefore, asserting that one "cannot believe that the holy abodes [*sanctas*] of the gods are in any region of our world" (Lucretius, *De Rer. Nat.*, 5.146 [cited in Long and Sedley, *The Hellenistic Philosophers*, 2.144]). What the Epicureans would mean positively by the "holy abodes" of the gods is highly complex. On this point, see the discussion in *Long and Sedley*, ibid., 145–49.

142. Price, *Religions of the Ancient Greeks*, 57. On the wide range of possible construals of the precise relation between gods and their images (from "fetish" to "dead wood," as in the OT critiques), see Halbertal and Margalit, *Idolatry*, 37–66, esp. 39–45.

143. See, for example, the relevant portions of Jaś Elsner's work: for example, *Imperial Rome and Christian Triumph: The Art of the Roman Empire AD 100–450* (Oxford: Oxford University Press, 1998); *Art and the Roman Viewer: The Transformation of Art from the Pagan World to Christianity* (Cambridge: Cambridge University Press, 1995); "Image and Ritual: Reflections on the Religious Appreciation of Classical Art," *CQ* 46 (1996): 515–31. Cf. Lane Fox, *Pagans and Christians*, 27: "The argument from tradition continued to outweigh the scepticism which was sometimes expressed by members of the educated class"; or MacMullen, *Paganism in the Roman Empire*, 59.

144. Lane Fox, *Pagans and Christians*, 134 (cf. 117). Affirming the accuracy of this statement does not require a "hard sense" of identification but simply that identification was made at various levels. For a sophisticated account that seeks to show how the ancients "at once assert and deny that statues or painted figures are alive," see Richard L. Gordon, "The Real and the Imaginary: Production and Religion in the Graeco-Roman World," in *Image and Value in the Graeco-Roman World: Studies in Mithraism and Religious Art* (Brookfield, VT: Ashgate, 1996), 5–34 (10).

145. Pausanias, *Descr. Gr.*, 9.38.5 (trans. LCL). On the phenomenon of chaining divinities as a whole, see Reinhold Merkelbach, "Gefesselte Götter," *Antaios* 12 (1971): 549–65.

146. Pausanias, *Descr. Gr.*, 6.11.6–9 (trans. LCL).

147. Lucian, *De Syr. Dea*, 36–37. Lucian writes, "And I shall tell you one other thing which he did in my presence: when the priests picked him up and bore him about, he left them upon the ground and flew in the air alone" (LCL, altered). Admittedly, it may be that—if Lucian did in fact write *De Dea Syria*—the entire work is satire, but this hypothesis is by no means free of problems. For a balanced discussion of Lucian authorship, as well as a treatment of the issues involved in understanding this complex text, see the hefty work of J. L. Lightfoot, *Lucian: On the Syrian Goddess* (Oxford: Oxford University Press, 2003). Lightfoot also provides a fresh translation.

148. Elsner, "Image and Ritual," 529. Elsner's article is remarkably stimulating particularly with respect to its articulation of the "visual theology" of the ancients, that is, "thinking about one's gods through their images" (518).

149. Lane Fox, *Pagans and Christians*, 135 passim.

150. Ibid., 134.

151. See, for example, the reference to Mercury in Apuleius, *Apol.*, 63.

152. For a fascinating account of the religious/political crisis in Athens brought about by the defamation of the Herms, see Parker, *Athenian Religion*, 200 passim.

153. Here, too, it must be remembered that, with few exceptions, even the philosophers commended traditional religious rites. See n. 35.

154. Luke cleverly leaves out the name Adam—though this is clearly whom Luke means—which would have been meaningless to the Areopagus (the story-world) and obvious to readers familiar with the OT (level of auditors). He thereby allows a (momentary) connection to Stoic "oneness" doctrine. By mentioning that all humanity springs from "one," Luke also skillfully frames his charge of idolatry—he is able thereby to narrate the history of humanity in terms of a group that should know better but went astray into ignorance.

155. Despite the RSV et al., Acts 17:27 does not say that the gentiles have found God. The optative mood of ψηλαφήσειαν and εὕροιεν expresses the wish or hope embedded in God's creative purpose but not the fact that the gentiles have "touched and found." Indeed, Luke's point is that *despite* such a hope the gentiles have remained ignorant of God (i.e., they have *not* touched or found him). This much is clear from the καί γε that begins the next sentence.

156. Barrett, *Acts*, 2.846, is therefore right to distrust the dichotomy constructed by modern scholars between a biblical ("will") and philosophical ("mind") search. For

Luke the point is, rather, that the biblical text illumines the places where philosophy has something true to say, even as—at least narratively—the latter is fitted into the former.

157. See Norden, *Agnostos Theos*, 19 n. 2.

158. With respect to this passage in Dio, David L. Balch, "The Areopagus Speech: An Appeal to the Stoic Historian Posidonius against Later Stoics and the Epicureans," in *Greeks, Romans, and Christians: Essays in Honor of Abraham J. Malherbe*, ed. David L. Balch et al. (Minneapolis, MN: Fortress, 1990), 52–79, notes that "all interpreters see . . . a parallel" (77).

159. See, for example, H. Hommel, "Platonisches bei Lukas. Zu Acta 17.28a (Leben-Bewegung-Sein)," *ZNW* 48 (1957): 193–200; Kirsopp Lake, " 'Your Own Poets,' " *Beginnings of Christianity*, 5.246–51; Balch, "Areopagus Speech," 78, respectively. Cf., inter alios, Epictetus, *Discourses*, 1.14.6; 2.8.11–29.

160. For the critical edition, see that of Douglas Kidd, with translation and commentary: Aratus, *Phaen.*, ed. and trans. Douglas Kidd (Cambridge: Cambridge University Press, 1997). We would be remiss not to mention that within the world of the story Paul—by citing one of "their" poets—has entered a further argument before the Areopagus that his preaching is not "new"; indeed, Aratus himself testifies to the truth of Paul's message.

161. Aratus, *Phaen.* 166.

162. Trans. Long and Sedley, *Hellenistic Philosophers*, 1.326 (text, 2.326). Though the specific terminology is lacking in the text, Barrett, *Acts*, 2.849, also cites as an important parallel *Orphic Fragment* 164, which he takes to be pre-Stoic.

163. "If what is said by the philosophers regarding the kinship of God and men be true." (*Discourses*, 1.9.1, LCL; cf. 1.9.6–34; 2.8.11–12 etc.).

164. Pindar, *Nem.*, 6.1–5, is occasionally mentioned as support for the idea that gods and humans have a common γένος. Ultimately, this text does support the notion that the gods and humans have a common ancestry, but this common ancestry is traced behind the two *different* γένοι (gods and humans) to "one mother": ἕν ἀνδρῶν ἕν γένος ἐκ μιᾶς δὲ πνέομεν ματρὸς ἀμφότεροι.

165. See n. 53.

166. Balch, "Areopagus Speech," 78, is right to note that "the common γένος between God and humanity is that both are 'living.' " See also Gärtner, *Areopagus Speech*, 193.

167. *Acts*, 2.850–51. Contra Paul Schubert, "Areopagus Speech," 235–61, who misses the significance of Luke's critique: "the Areopagus speech stresses (with great emphasis) the unity of a theology of nature and of history" (261).

168. It is by missing this reversal in theological direction that the otherwise illuminating discussion—particularly with respect to Wis 15:16–17—in Klauck, *Magic and Paganism*, 90, goes astray: "The logic of Luke's argument remains somewhat unclear, since from the fact that the human person is related or similar to God it is possible to infer that an anthropomorphic portrayal of the divine would be particularly appropriate." The expression "visual theology" derives from the important work of J. Elsner (see n. 143).

169. The oft-noted stress on τὰ νῦν is correct. See, for example, Gaventa, *Acts*, 252.

170. Schubert, "Areopagus Speech," 261, notes the use of "eight adjectival and adverbial forms of πᾶς in the last eight verses of the Areopagus speech."

171. Cf. Conzelmann, *Acts*, 146: "The whole of world history is viewed from the perspective of the one, decisive turning point that occurred in the resurrection of Christ."

172. For the reader of Acts, that the ἀνήρ is Jesus is obvious. But so, too, on the basis of 17:18 we may reasonably assume that in the story-world Jesus was also known as the one of whom Paul speaks.

173. Some scholars attempt to coordinate the response to Paul with particular groups (given their philosophical positions, disdain for Paul's speech could be characteristic of the Epicureans, while interest in further discussion might fit with a Stoic reaction). See, for example, N. Clayton Croy, "Hellenistic Philosophies," esp. 32, 39. The problem with such specificity of course is that Luke introduces other people (οἱ δέ, 17:18) into the scene in addition to Stoics and Epicureans and thereby makes it impossible—without further elaboration—to pin the responses to particular groups. Moreover, contra Croy (32), both the Stoics and the Epicureans think of Paul as a babbler (17:18, τινες ἔλεγον refers not to the Epicureans alone but to both parties). Finally, Paul stands before the Areopagus; though the reader is doubtless to remember their importance for the scene, the philosophical schools are not mentioned again.

174. Cf. Barnes, "An Apostle on Trial," 417: "The speech can be construed as an effective answer to the charge of introducing a new religion."

175. Johnson, *Acts*, 319.

176. As does Plutarch, for example, in his works against the Stoics. Plutarch also wrote a work entitled *On Epicurean Self-Contradictions*, but it has not survived.

177. *Ep.* 88.28: *Philosophia nil ab alio petit, totum opus a solo excitat.* In this section of his letter on "liberal studies," Seneca cites Posidonius. However, contra Long and Sedley, *Hellenistic Philosophers*, 159–60, who appear to include this phrase within the fragments that can be attributed to Posidonius, it is Seneca rather than Posidonius who speaks at this particular moment. See, I. G. Kidd, *Posidonius II. The Commentary: (i) Testimonia and Fragments 1–149* (Cambridge: Cambridge University Press, 1988), 359–65.

178. Cf. Gaventa, *Acts*, 254.

179. See Alasdair MacIntyre, *Whose Justice? Which Rationality?* (Notre Dame, IN: University of Notre Dame Press, 1988), esp. chap. 19. To translate the Christian faith into pagan philosophy is to posit a conceptual equivalence between these two different "languages" that allows them to say basically the same thing: the gospel and pagan philosophy speak ultimately about the same subject matter and mean ultimately the same thing, but they use different languages—the latter, a philosophical system; the former, a story about God, Jesus, resurrection, and so forth. But this is precisely the move that Luke does *not* make. He does not put the gospel into the language of a pagan philosophical system but instead rejects pagan wisdom as leading to idolatry. Luke takes the terms of pagan discourse but in so doing strips them of their philosophical or

theological content by transforming them into terms that, in Luke's view, simultaneously criticize pagan philosophy and point toward the truth of Paul's preaching.

180. Cf. Karl Barth, *Church Dogmatics* II/1, 123: if one of the pagan philosophers "now knows about the God proclaimed to them by Paul, it is definitely not in confirmation of what he knew before, perhaps as a member of a sect that worshipped the unknown God, or as a reader of Aratus. It is in a quite new knowledge of his previous complete ignorance."

181. This is true also in the Corinthian scene immediately following Paul's stay in Athens. "The Jews" haul Paul before the βῆμα of the Achaian proconsul Gallio and accuse Paul of "persuading people to worship God παρὰ τὸν νόμον" (Acts 18:13). Before Paul can speak, Gallio responds with a refusal to be a judge in the dispute since it is a matter concerning words, names, and the νόμος of the Jews. Though νόμος could mean Torah in each case (the charge would then be that Paul was creating the possibility of serious disorder among the Jews), it is also possible to take the first use of νόμος to mean Roman provincial law. In this case, Gallio quickly turns the issue back on the Jews: this is not a problem of Roman law (νόμος) but of piddly words, names, and the Jewish law (νόμος). Gallio's curtness has long been noted as displaying rather well the pagan attitude toward Jews. On this passage as a whole, see the exegesis in chap. 3.

182. Pliny the Younger to the Emperor Trajan, ca. 112 (*Ep.*, 10.96).

183. Still, as Fergus Millar says of the Ephesus material, "No text illustrates better the city life of the Greek East, its passionate local loyalties, its potential violence precariously held in check by the city officials, and the overshadowing presence of the Roman governor" (*The Roman Empire and Its Neighbors* [New York: Dell, 1967], 199).

184. On Acts 19:13–16, see Scott Shauf, *Theology as History, History as Theology: Paul in Ephesus in Acts 19*, BZNW 133 (Berlin/New York: Walter de Gruyter, 2005). Interpreters have frequently worried over the nonexistence of a Jewish "High Priest" named Sceva. However, in context ἀρχιερεύς need not mean more than leading or chief priest (cf. esp. the characteristically Lukan use of τις—a certain Jewish leading/chief priest).

185. Fritz Graf, *Magic in the Ancient World* (Cambridge, MA: Harvard University Press, 1997), 1.

186. See Chester C. McGown, "The Ephesia Grammata in Popular Belief," *Transactions and Proceedings of the American Philological Association* 54 (1923): 128–40.

187. Plutarch, *Quast. Conv.* 706D.

188. See Lampe, "Acta 19," 69.

189. Barrett, *Acts*, 2.901 (emphasis added). Pliny the Elder, *NH* 30.11, for example, notes the "recent" development of a branch of magic in Cyprus. Cf. Acts 13:6–12 in relation to Pliny's remark.

190. See, for example, Graf, *Magic in the Ancient World*, esp. 61–117.

191. MacMullen, *Enemies of the Roman Order*, is perceptive on the apparent legal contradiction: the practice of magic was both prohibited and allowed. He argues that the ancients resolved this tension through the attempt to distinguish between "good" and "bad" magic. The latter was magic that was intended to do harm to other people. Obviously measures such as the *lex Cornelia*, and so forth, were only somewhat successful: scores of curse tablets survive.

192. On book burning in general, see the concise piece by Arthur Stanley Pease, "Notes on Book-Burning," in *Munera Studiosa*, ed. M. H. Shepherd Jr., and S. E. Johnson (Cambridge, MA: Episcopal Theological School, 1946), 145–160, here 146.

193. Livy, 39.16.8; Suetonius, *Aug.*, 31.1 The line between prophecy/divination and magic was not clear, as is implied by Pease, "Notes," 155.

194. There is in this passage an emphasis upon the public nature of the mission in Ephesus: a form of πᾶς occurs in 19:10, 17 (2x), 19.

195. So Barrett, *Acts*, 2.913.

196. The omission of the unity of currency with ἀργυρίου is not unusual. See, for example, Plutarch, *Galb.*, 17; and Jos., *AJ*, 17.189 (noted by Barrett, *Acts*, 2.913).

197. So, too, Klauck, *Magic and Paganism*, 102.

198. That magic as a whole is something with which Luke is deeply concerned has long been noted by Lukan scholars. See esp. the treatments of Simon Magus in Acts 8:9–24 (Samaria) and Elymas in Acts 13:4–12 (Cyprus). For a helpful discussion of these passages see, for example, the work of Susan R. Garrett, *The Demise of the Devil: Magic and the Demonic in Luke's Writings* (Minneapolis, MN: Fortress, 1989).

199. MacMullen, *Enemies of the Roman Order*, 103.

200. Further instances of all of these examples—and dozens more—can be seen even with a cursory glance at the PGM (Betz) table of contents.

201. See also Elias J. Bickerman, "Trajan, Hadrian, and the Christians," *Rivista di filologia classica* 96 (1968): 290–318, for an excellent discussion of the economic interconnection between the rescripts of Trajan and Hadrian and their willingness to persecute Christians.

202. See Lampe, "Acta 19," 65, who mentions terra-cotta; and Floyd V. Filson, "Ephesus and the New Testament," *Biblical Archaeologist* 8/3 (1945): 73–80, who mentions marble (76).

203. Pesch, *Apostelgeschichte*, 2.180.

204. See the findings of G. K. Boyce, *Corpus of the Lararia of Pompeii* (Memoirs of the Academy of Rome, 1937), with plates. Cf. Helmut Koester, "Ephesos in Early Christian Literature," in *Ephesos: Metropolis of Asia: An Interdisciplinary Approach to its Archaeology, Religion, and Culture* (HTS 41; ed. Helmut Koester; Valley Forge, PA: Trinity Press International, 1995), 130 n. 4, who conjectures: "It is unlikely that the designation 'silver shrines' . . . refers to small-scale models of the entire temple of Artemis; rather, the silversmith probably produced statues standing in a simple, small naiskos."

205. Lampe, "Acta 19," 65. Statuettes of various gods and goddesses inside the houses have also been discovered in Pompeii. See the picture in Boyce, *Corpus of the Lararia of Pompeii*, plate 31. On statuettes of Artemis in particular, see LIMC 2.2.442–628 (564–73 for images of Artemis Ephesia).

206. The πείσας μετέστησεν resists somewhat felicitous translation. One might simply say "converted," or, in light of the overall concern of this book, "persuaded and taken out/removed, etc."

207. Cf. Lily Ross Taylor, "Artemis of Ephesus," *Beginnings* I/5, 251–56 (251). Artemis of the Ephesians has been the topic of extensive research (e.g., the thorough study of Robert Fleischer, *Artemis von Ephesos und verwandte Kultstatuen aus Anatolien*

und Syrien, EPRO 35 [Leiden: Brill, 1973]). In relation to Acts in particular, see the concise article of Richard Oster, "The Ephesian Artemis as an Opponent of Early Christianity," *Jahrbuch für Antike und Christentum* 19 (1976): 24–44, which is excellent for its condensation and clear presentation of a vast amount of relevant material, both literary and archaeological.

208. Pausanias, *Descr. Gr.*, 4.31.8. Pausanias mentions Artemis of the Ephesians/ the Artemesium multiple times, often in connection to the economic success of the cult or of Ephesus more generally. See, for example, 7.5.4: "The land of the Ionians has ... temples such as are to be found nowhere else. First among them is that of the Ephesians because of its size and wealth ... " (LCL, altered).

209. The translation is that of Lampe, "Acta 19," 63. For the text of the inscription, see no. 18b (lns. 1–2) in *Die Inschriften von Ephesos, Teil 1a*, ed. Hermann Wankel (Bonn: Rudolf Habelt Verlag, 1979), 101. The inscription is dated to ca. AD 44.

210. Taylor, "Artemis of Ephesus," 252.

211. This is not to say that the temple always worked as well as it could or that everyone respected, for example, the asylum it offered. On this latter point, Christine M. Thomas, "At Home in the City of Artemis," in *Ephesos: Metropolis of Asia*, 82–117, esp. 98–106, is particularly instructive.

212. Oster, "Ephesian Artemis," 34. Cf. Lampe, "Acta 19," 65 passim.

213. See Nock, *Conversion*, 90 and 287. Nock also lists multiple "great" acclamations in *Essays*, I.36.

214. Lane Fox, *Pagans and Christians*, 54. Cf. MacMullen, *Enemies of the Roman Order*, 167–69, 185–88, who can speak of "the extraordinary aggressive value placed on the possession of an amphitheater bigger than anyone else's" (185).

215. Lane Fox, *Pagans and Christians*, 54.

216. In the theologically elaborate and dramatic scene in the *Acts of John*, 38–44, Artemis is vanquished, her temple destroyed, her priest killed, and her people converted. That the scene in the *Acts of John* depends heavily both on Acts 19 and on Elijah's contest with the prophets of Baal is self-evident. On the history of the city, see Peter Scherrer, "The City of Ephesos from the Roman Period to Late Antiquity," in *Ephesos: Metropolis of Asia*, 1–25.

217. The best discussion is Steven J. Friesen, *Twice Neokoros: Ephesus, Asia and the Cult of the Flavian Imperial Family* (Leiden: Brill, 1993), 92–113, who rejects the traditional understanding of Asiarch as simply another name for provincial high priest. Neither were the Asiarchs directly related to the provincial imperial cults. Their positive role, however, is much more difficult to identify with precision; it seems to have consisted in various public services that were related to municipal life (which could of course include priestly service).

218. Whether or not the Asiarchs were Christians is finally unclear: the word φίλοι does not ultimately push one way rather than another (i.e., it may mean that they are Christians, or it may mean that they have somehow come to know Paul during his time in Ephesus). Klauck, *Magic and Paganism*, 106, suggests that the Asiarchs portray "the

support of philosophically educated and enlightened Gentiles" whose viewpoint would place them in "a position of solidarity with the Christians, against the fanatical busybodies in their own ranks." This suggestion is plausible; it depends, however, upon a simple identification between the Asiarchs and a philosophical viewpoint. In general, civic leaders may well have been more "enlightened" than the populus, but this connection should not necessarily be assumed. Not only might the "educated" have similar worries as the artisans of their city, they might also turn out to be superstitious. One remembers, for example, Lucian's opening characterization of Rutilianus, "who, though a man of birth and good breeding, put to the proof in many Roman offices, nevertheless in all that concerned the gods was very infirm and held strange beliefs about them" (*Alex.*, 30). For other important pagan officials who are well disposed toward Christianity, one may think readily of the convert Sergius Paulus, the proconsul of Cyprus (Acts 13:7, 12). Another proconsul, Gallio (of Achaia), is indifferent (18:12–16), while the centurions in Luke–Acts are manifestly well disposed: see, for example, Cornelius (10:1–8, 17–48), Julius (27:1, 3), and the unidentified donor in Luke 7:1–10.

219. Haenchen, *Acts*, 574; cf. Barrett, *Acts*, 2.932: "It remains quite unclear who Alexander was, why he was chosen, and what he was expected to do or to say."

220. Klauck, *Magic and Paganism*, 107, sets out concisely the basic alternatives. Broadly speaking, the second of these two options—that Alexander was a Jewish Christian—makes far better sense of the narrative and provides an entirely plausible ground for why he would be called on to speak. See also Lampe, "Acta 19," 71–75.

221. Barrett, *Acts*, 2.935–36, thinks that to supply "image" to $\tau o\hat{v}$ $\delta\iota o\pi\epsilon\tau o\hat{v}s$ (he chooses $\check{a}\gamma a\lambda\mu a$) is to be "over-precise." But surely this is just the point the clerk is making: Artemis's image is obviously not "made with hands."

222. Koester, "Ephesos in Early Christian Literature," 130.

223. Many commentators point out that the object in question must be a meteorite and that such objects were also revered elsewhere (see, e.g., Cook, *Zeus* III, 12, 881–942, on meteorites as cultic objects). Barrett, *Acts*, 2.935–36, however, is correct to take seriously the reference to Zeus in $\delta\iota o\pi\epsilon\tau\acute{\eta}s$. From the pagan perspective, the object is a divine gift rather than a piece of astronomical phenomena known as a meteorite.

224. One might wonder how the town clerk knows Paul's criticism. Acts 19:17, 20, 26, and the explicit mention of Demetrius and the $\tau\epsilon\chi\nu\hat{\iota}\tau a\iota$ in 19:38 all suggest that—in terms of the story-world—the clerk would certainly know Paul's preaching.

225. Lampe, "Acta 19," 60, notes the occurrence of $\nu\acute{o}\mu\iota\mu os$ $\acute{\epsilon}\kappa\kappa\lambda\eta\sigma\acute{\iota}a$ for the legal assembly of Ephesus.

226. MacMullen, *Enemies of the Roman Order*, 163. MacMullen here refers to the development of skilled detective forces. For an attempt to relate uprisings to the beating of Sosthenes in Acts 18:17, see Moyer V. Hubbard, "Urban Uprisings in the Roman World: The Social Setting of the Mobbing of Sosthenes," *NTS* 51 (2005): 416–28.

227. Jos., *AJ*, 19.24–26; Cf. Cassius Dio, *Hist. Rom.*, 59.28.11. Dio also writes of Claudius's action against the Lycians "who had revolted [$\sigma\tau a\sigma\iota\acute{a}\sigma a\nu\tau\epsilon s$] and slain some Romans." As a punishment, they were reduced to slavery [$\tau o\grave{v}s\ldots\acute{\epsilon}\delta o\upsilon\lambda\acute{\omega}\sigma a\tau o$] and incorporated into the prefecture of Pamphylia (ibid., 60.17.3).

228. On the riot in Pompeii, see MacMullen, *Enemies of the Roman Order*, 169, with notes (338–39). Typically, scholars have viewed the "mob" through the lens of the authors who write about riotous action. This manner of investigation inevitably results in a treatment of the mob from the perspective of the elite. For a thought-provoking challenge to this way of reading the mob, see Thomas W. Africa, "Urban Violence in Imperial Rome," *Journal of Interdisciplinary History* 2 (1971): 3–21, who argues that mob violence often occurred as a protest against deeply unjust practices of the Roman government. Africa may overstate his case—there is a considerable amount of violence in relation to sporting events, for example—but his observation that not infrequently the people involved in mob violence were involved as groups "who had grievances to air" ("shopkeepers, craftsmen, and workers'") is worth serious consideration (4).

229. Robert F. Stoops, "Riot and Assembly: The Social Context of Acts 19:23–41," *JBL* 108 (1989): 73–91 (89 and 88, respectively). Stoops represents the long-established trend in Lukan scholarship that sees Luke's politics as an apology to Rome on behalf of the church (see, too, Haenchen, *Acts*, 102).

230. Jos., *AJ*, 4.207: βλασφημείτω δὲ μηδεὶς θεοὺς οὓς πόλεις ἄλλαι νομίζουσι· μηδὲ συλᾶν ἱερὰ ξενικά, μηδ' ἂν ἐπωνομασμένον ᾖ τινι θεῷ κειμήλιον λαμβάνειν. Josephus gives his reason for this reading of the Decalogue in *C. Ap.*, 2.237: "Our legislator has expressly forbidden us to deride or blaspheme the gods recognized by others, out of respect for the very word θεός." Josephus's exegesis here of Exod 22:28—"you shall not revile *Elohim*'—reflects the LXX translation of Elohim as θεοί. Philo shares this interpretation (see *De Vita Mosis*, 2.205; and *De Spec. Leg.*, 1.9.53). Of course, in practice Josephus does criticize pagan religion, as in the paragraph directly following the one just cited: "But since our accusers expect to confute us by a comparison of the rival religions, it is impossible to remain silent." (*C. Ap.*, 2.238). Whether or not Jews actually avoided robbing temples was evidently up for debate, at least from the Egyptian perspective. See, for example, Josephus's treatment of "Egyptian gossip" in *C. Ap.*, 1.248–51 and 1.304–11.

231. Barrett, *Acts*, 2.925.

232. Such a role had a long and distinguished pedigree, as is evident from the observations of MacMullen, *Paganism in the Roman Empire*, 57: "It was certainly recognized throughout antiquity, at least by people able to look at their world with any detachment, that religion served to strengthen the existing social order." As evidence for this statement, MacMullen cites Plutarch and states that Plutarch's views "represent the end of a string of statements on the social usefulness of religious faith, going back to the fifth century BC" (58). Though MacMullen's language here leans too far in the direction of detaching religion from the rest of ancient culture, his basic point about the interconnection between religious stability and the status quo is correct. See also n. 36.

233. F. G. Downing, "Common Ground with Paganism in Luke and Josephus," *NTS* 28 (1982): 546–59 (557).

234. Because of the inherent complexity involved in the notion of idolatry, Halbertal and Margalit, *Idolatry*, 234, speak of it "as a range of gestures exclusive to God" that should not be "transferred to any other being." My language of "range of practices and convictions" owes much to their discussion.

235. Nock, *Conversion*, 272; cf., inter alios, Price, *Rituals and Powers*, 15–16, 234–48; and the review essay of J. A. North, "Religion and Politics, from Republic to Principate," *JRS* 76 (1986): 251–58. For a succinct appreciation within NT studies of the methodological significance of this point, see Wayne A. Meeks, *The Origins of Christian Morality: The First Two Centuries* (New Haven, CT: Yale University Press, 1993), esp. 10–11.

236. Young, *Biblical Exegesis*, 50.

237. Price, *Religions of the Ancient Greeks*, 83. Price speaks here more generally, but his point is particularly apropos of ancient Athens.

238. Peter R. L. Brown, "Art and Society in Late Antiquity," in *An Age of Spirituality: A Symposium*, ed. Kurt Weitzmann (Princeton, NJ: Princeton University Press, 1980), 17–27 (23). One does not have to stop using wood for fires, for example, just making fires as a part of pagan sacrifice rituals.

CHAPTER 3

1. C. A. Heumann, "Dissertatio de Theophilo: Cui Lucas Historiam Sacram Inscripsit," *BHPT*, classis IV, Bremen (1720): 483–505. Heumann argues that Luke wrote the *historiam Christi & Apostolorum* for the Roman official Theophilus as a response—an *apologia pro Christiana religione*—to particular charges brought against the early Christians (see esp. §§1, 10–11). It is important to note, as Alexandru Neagoe, *The Trial of the Gospel: An Apologetic Reading of Luke's Trial Narratives*, SNTSMS 116 (Cambridge: Cambridge University Press, 2002), points out, that focusing on "Rome" is not necessarily the same thing as asking after Luke's "purpose" in writing Acts (or Luke–Acts). It may be that one discovers the latter in seeking to understand the former, but in my judgment that is unlikely and has been proven so by the remarkably different answers given in the history of NT scholarship to the question of Luke's purpose. Focusing on Roman officials, therefore, provides a particular angle of vision that is needed to see the overall picture of Acts displayed in the present book.

2. For example, Friedrich W. Horn, "Die Haltung des Lukas zum römischen Staat im Evangelium und in der Apostelgeschichte," in *The Unity of Luke–Acts*, ed. J. Verheyden (Leuven: Leuven University Press, 1999), 203–24; Alexandru Neagoe, *The Trial of the Gospel*, 3–24; and Steve Walton, "The State They Were In: Luke's View of the Roman Empire," in *Rome in the Bible and the Early Church*, ed. Peter Oakes (Grand Rapids, MI: Baker Academic, 2002), 1–41. As Neagoe's survey demonstrates with admirable concision, the secondary literature on this topic is extensive. Despite the continuing study of this theme, however, in terms of exegetical sophistication, research as a whole has not moved much past Conzelmann and Haenchen. Moreover, with the possible exception of Gary Gilbert's essay ("Roman Propaganda and Christian Identity in the Worldview of Luke–Acts," in *Contextualizing Acts: Lukan Narrative and Greco-Roman Discourse*, eds. Todd Penner and Caroline Vander Stichele [Atlanta, GA: Society of Biblical Literature], 233–56), reappraisals of Lukan politics have not scrutinized the conception of politics itself that underwrites the exegetical trends in past discussion. So, too, in relation to the Graeco-Roman world, conversation partners from the post-WWII era are better drawn from the field of classics. There are, of course, exceptions to

this observation as well (e.g., Brian Rapske, *The Book of Acts and Paul in Roman Custody*, vol. 3 of *The Book of Acts in Its First Century Setting* [Grand Rapids, MI: Eerdmans, 1994]).

3. In putting it this way, I do not intend to suggest that this is the way the majority of Acts commentators have seen or still see the purpose of Acts as a whole. I mean simply to say that when the question of Lukan politics arises, this manner of reading is the way it has been answered most frequently. Rudolf Pesch's commentary in the EKK series is a good example. In the introduction to the commentary, Pesch clearly rejects the idea that the *Abfassungszweck* and *theologische Intention* of Acts can be identified with a "Nachweis gegenüber römischen Behörden," which attempts to say that "die Kirche keine staatsgefährdende Bewegung [ist] und wie das Judentum als 'religio licita' zu tolerieren sei" (29). Yet, when it comes to the exegesis in the commentary, Pesch consistently follows the dominant reading of Lukan politics (e.g., see esp. his treatment of the Claudius Lysias material).

4. Johannes Weiss, *Über die Absicht und den literarischen Charakter der Apostelgeschichte* (Göttingen: Vandenhoeck & Ruprecht, 1897); Henry Joel Cadbury, *The Making of Luke–Acts* (London: SPCK, 1927), esp. 308–15.

5. The two outstanding figures are of course Ernst Haenchen, *The Acts of the Apostles: A Commentary* (Philadelphia: Westminster, 1971) and Hans Conzelmann, *The Theology of St. Luke* (New York: Harper and Row, 1961). But one sees this position in countless secondary works as well. To take only one particularly clear example, see Harry W. Tajra, *The Trial of St. Paul: A Juridical Exegesis of the Second Half of the Acts of the Apostles*, WUNT 2/35 (Tübingen: Mohr Siebeck, 1989), esp. 199: "Luke tries hard to cast the Roman authorities in as favorable a light as possible"; "Luke tries to show the basic tolerance (or at worst indifference) which Rome had for the Christian message"; "Luke's marked pro-Roman stance is meant to counterbalance certain anti-Roman tendencies present in the Church in the wake of the savage Neronian persecution," and so forth.

6. See, for example, Martin Meiser, "Lukas und die römische Staatsmacht," in *Zwischen den Reichen: Neues Testament und Römische Herrschaft*, TANZ 36 (Tübingen: Franke Verlag, 2002), 175–93. Erika Heusler, *Kapitalprozesse im lukanischen Doppelwerk: Die Verfahren gegen Jesus und Paulus in exegetischer und rechtshistorischer Analyse*, NTA 38 (Münster: Aschendorff, 2000), 259–60, takes it as an established fact of NT scholarship: "Lukas schreibt seine Prozessdarstellungen und weitere Abschnitte seines Doppelwerks als Apologie gegenüber Rom, dem für ihn nach Jerusalem neuen Zentrum und Brennpunkt des Christentums—darauf hat sich die neutestamentliche Exegese weithin verständigt."

7. Paul W. Walaskay, *"And So We Came to Rome": The Political Perspective of St Luke* (Cambridge: Cambridge University Press, 1983). Walaskay has also recently written a commentary on Acts in which he both reiterates certain parts of his *pro imperio* thesis and seems to accept the possibility of the earlier *pro ecclesia* hypothesis (*Acts* [Louisville, KY: Westminster John Knox, 1998], e.g., 13–14).

8. Walaskay, for example, plays the common tune in reverse. On a more nuanced level of discussion, where Haenchen argues that Luke presents Christianity as a *religio quasi licita* (thus acknowledging the difficulties with the traditional religio licita theory),

Conzelmann rejects such terminology altogether. Yet, in substance, there is little difference between their proposals about Lukan politics.

9. See the discussion later in this chapter in "Festus and Agrippa II."

10. The most succinct summary of this position is Robert F. O'Toole, "Luke's Position on Politics and Society," in *Political Issues in Luke–Acts*, eds. Richard J. Cassidy and Philip J. Scharper (Maryknoll, NY: Orbis, 1983), 1–17 (8).

11. See, for example, Richard J. Cassidy, *Society and Politics in the Acts of the Apostles* (Maryknoll, NY: Orbis, 1987), 148–55.

12. See, for example, Richard A. Horsley, *The Liberation of Christmas: The Infancy Narratives in Social Context* (New York: Crossroad, 1989), esp. 107–23.

13. For δίκη as a term for a Roman (in this case, imperial) court, see, for example, Cassius Dio, *Hist. Rom.* 60.28.6.

14. C. Kavin Rowe, "Luke–Acts and the Imperial Cult: A Way through the Conundrum?" *JSNT* 27 (2005): 279–300, esp. 287–88.

15. See the discussion in chapter 2 of the riot in Ephesus.

16. Indeed, the clerk actually undermines long-term interests where Demetrius seeks to protect them.

17. Against the common thesis that "From now on I will go to the Gentiles" indicates Luke's view that the mission to the Jews has been abandoned, has been a failure, and so forth (Haenchen, Tyson, Sanders, Wilson, et al.), we may note that such a thesis not only overlooks the immediate context of this statement but also the fact that after Paul says something very similar in 13:45–47, we find him again in the synagogue. Things are no different after this statement in Corinth. He leaves Corinth, goes to Ephesus, and goes straight to the synagogue (19:8).

18. See the concise discussion of Kirsopp Lake in his article, "The Chronology of Acts," *Beginnings* 5.460–64.

19. Indeed, the importance of this one piece of material evidence for the reconstructions of Pauline chronology has often been emphasized. See, for example, Rainer Riesner, *Paul's Early Period: Chronology, Mission Strategy, Theology*, trans. Doug Stott (Grand Rapids, MI: Eerdmans, 1998 [1994]), 202–11; also Robert Jewett, *A Chronology of Paul's Life* (Philadelphia: Fortress, 1979), 38–40. Thanks are due here to Douglas A. Campbell for a brief discussion of this matter.

20. Haenchen, *Acts*, 538.

21. Schneider, *Apostelgeschichte*, 2 vols. (Freiberg: Herder, 1980/1082), 2.252 and n. 54. So, too, for example, Cassidy, *Society and Politics in the Acts of the Apostles*, 92.

22. G. E. M. de Ste. Croix, "Why Were the Early Christians Persecuted?" *Past and Present* 26 (1963): 6–38, also cites this passage from Paul, though he dismisses it as irrelevant for his question (14). It may well be that we cannot read the legal developments from Paul's time back into the earliest period, but the similarity in the charges should not for this reason be obscured. Walaskay, *Acts*, 171, also knows this text from the *Sententiae*.

23. Jervell, *Apostelgeschichte* (Göttingen: Vandenhoeck & Ruprecht, 1998), 461: "Das kaiserliche Gesetz wird nicht berührt, denn dann ware die Antwort des Gallio

unverständlich." Cf. Pilate's response to the Jews in John 18:31: λάβετε αὐτὸν [Jesus] ὑμεῖς καὶ κατὰ τὸν νόμον ὑμῶν κρίνατε αὐτόν.

24. Contra the RSV et al. λόγος is of course singular. Might it refer here to "resurrection"? See esp. Acts 25:19.

25. On "gap-filling," readerly competence, and the host of hermeneutical questions associated therewith, see the discussion in C. Kavin Rowe, *Early Narrative Christology: The Lord in the Gospel of Luke*, BZNW 139 (Berlin: Walter de Gruyter, 2006), esp. 37–38 with notes.

26. Conzelmann, *Theology of St. Luke*, 143. Cf. Conzelmann, *Acts*, 153.

27. Noted also by Johnson, *Acts*, 328, among others.

28. Gallio might ask, "Has this man defiled the temple of so and so?" "Has he defiled the images?" One can easily grasp the potential for official redress by recalling that one of the greatest "religious" crises of Greek history occurred when the Herms in Athens were defiled.

29. On this point, see Fergus Millar's classic essay, "The Emperor, the Senate and the Provinces," *JRS* 56 (1966): 156–66.

30. On the evidence from the Julio-Claudian and Flavian periods, Millar, "The Emperor, the Senate and the Provinces," 164, is concise. According to Millar, the issue of the senate's authority over proconsuls can be handled rather easily: "What evidence is there for either instructions of the Senate to proconsuls or specific communications from the Senate to individual proconsuls while in their provinces? The answer is simple—none" (159). With respect to communication with Rome from imperial *legati*, we need do no more than mention the name of Pliny.

31. Petronius, *Saty.*, 111, in the famous (Milesian) tale of the "Widow of Ephesus." Elias Bickerman also notes this remark from Petronius in discussing the power of a provincial governor (see the response and discussion section to Fergus Millar, "The Imperial Cult and the Persecutions," in *Le culte des souverains dans l'empire romain*, ed. W. den Boer (Geneva: Foundation Hardt, 1973), 145–65 [166–75, 171]).

32. Millar, "The Emperor, the Senate and the Provinces," 165.

33. A. N. Sherwin-White, *Roman Society and Roman Law in the New Testament* (Oxford: Clarendon, 1963), 2. For practical limitations to a proconsul's ability to govern—in particular the custom of touring the province and holding court in so-called assize centers rather than in a centralized location—see G. P. Burton's interesting analysis, "Proconsuls, Assizes and the Administration of Justice Under the Empire," *JRS* 65 (1975): 92–106: "the assize-tour provided the real historical framework within which the proconsul not only dispensed justice, but also conducted his administrative duties. Consequently, vast though the powers of the proconsul were in theory, there were severe physical restraints upon the manner in which he could exercise them" (106).

34. Sherwin-White, *Roman Society and Roman Law in the New Testament*, 13. See also the perceptive piece by de Ste. Croix, "Why Were the Early Christians Persecuted?"; the response by Sherwin-White, "Why Were the Early Christians Persecuted?—An Amendment," *Past and Present* 27 (1964): 23–27; and the reply by de Ste. Croix, "Why Were the Early Christians Persecuted?—A Rejoinder," *Past and Present* 27 (1964): 28–33.

35. How frequently such situations arose is unknown. However, it is doubtless reasonable to surmise that the highest official in the province "left a great deal of minor jurisdiction to the local municipal courts" and focused "his special concern . . . [on] matters affecting public order" (Sherwin-White, *Roman Society and Roman Law*, 14).

36. Cf. de Ste. Croix, "Why Were the Early Christians Persecuted?" 13, who says with respect to "how things might work in practice": "A governor exercising *cognitio extraordinaria* in a criminal case was bound (for all practical purposes) only by those imperial *constitutiones* and *mandata* which were relevant in his particular area and were still in force." "Unfortunately," he continues with reference to Pliny's correspondence with Trajan, "official publication of imperial constitutiones seems to have been an extremely inefficient and haphazard process." There was also the possibility that the proconsul or governor could consult with his advisory council (*consilium*), as we see with Festus, for example (see below). But such consultation was not a necessity. On this point, see Sherwin-White, *Roman Society and Roman Law*, 17–18.

37. Contra Conzelmann, *Theology of St. Luke*, 143, who thinks the Jews are intentionally deceiving Gallio, the narrative provides ample clues that the Jews in Corinth could have seen Paul's mission as threatening (e.g., the belief of Crispus, the ἀρχισυνάγωγος). See 18:4, 6, 8, and 17.

38. To take one of many possible examples, see the list of decrees in Josephus, *AJ*, 14.190–265 [10.2–25].

39. See the relevant texts in n. 217 (Stern). Sergius Paulus is also a proconsul (of Cyprus), but he does not speak (Acts 13:4–12).

40. Bruce W. Winter, "Gallio's Ruling on the Legal Status of Early Christianity," *TynB* 50 (1999): 213–24, translates ἀδίκημα as "felony" and ῥᾳδιούργημα πονηρόν as "political misdemeanor" (cf. Conzelmann, *Theology of St. Luke*, 143). Despite some of the more tenuous historical proposals (e.g., the connection of Claudius's expulsion of the Jews), Winter's article is helpful both for its clear attention to the legal terminology of the passage and for its realization that Gallio draws a distinction between the Roman and Jewish law (esp. 220). Yet, even here Winter fails to realize that λόγου, ὀνομάτων, and νόμου are all objects of the preposition περί (v. 15). He thus mistakenly specifies λόγος and ὄνομα in a Roman sense while treating νόμος in a Jewish sense—even though Gallio has clearly signaled that these are all three Jewish matters (ζητήματα).

41. Both this and the citation in the previous sentence are from Sherwin-White, *Roman Society and Roman Law*, 102.

42. Sherwin-White, *Roman Society and Roman Law*, 102. The formula of the edict from Nazareth runs: τοῦτον κεφαλῆς κατάκριτον θέλω γένεσθαι. The full text—"Edictum (Augusti?) De Violatione Sepulc[r]orum"—can be found in *Fontes Ivris Romani Antejvstiniani* 69, ed. Salvator Riccobono (Florentiae: S. A. G. Barbèra, 1941), 414–16.

43. Jos., *AJ*, 14.195 (LCL altered).

44. Conzelmann, *Theology of St. Luke*, 142.

45. Ibid., 153.

46. The term *religio licita* has of course seen much debate. It never occurs in the ancient sources, though its obverse does (*religio illicita*).

47. Cassidy, *Society and Politics in the Acts of the Apostles*, 92–93. Cassidy here also overlooks the information Luke assumes that the reader can fill in based on Gallio's response; that is, it is not merely Gallio's bias but also the content that he hears in the accusation that leads him to dismiss the Jews.

48. Cassidy, *Society and Politics in the Acts of the Apostles*, 93.

49. For ἄξιον θανάτου as Roman legal terminology, cf. Acts 23:29; 25:11, 25; and 26:31. See, too, Pilate's remarks in John 18:38; 19:4, 6 (cf. Mark 15:14 // Matt 27:23, and Matt 27:19, 24). For those who worry here about the status of Judaea as a province, I would simply note the following: (1) it is true that its governor was called a prefect (prior to AD 41) and procurator (after AD 44), but (2) "the term *provincia* is relevant to a man, not a territory. When Judaea is administered by Augustus or his prefect, it is his *provincia*" (Sherwin-White, *Roman Society and Roman Law*, 12; see his discussion, 5–12). In practice, that is, the man who lived in Caesarea Maritima was more or less in charge of Judaea in the same way that Gallio was in charge of Achaea—"more or less" because of the imperial legate of Syria, who was superior in power to the governor of Judaea (see also Heusler, *Kapitalprozesse*, 204 n. 35). Cadbury, "Roman Law and the Trial of Paul," *Beginnings*, 5.307, writes that "[t]he authority of the procurators of Judea is apparently like that of the proconsuls in senatorial provinces, of *legati* in imperial provinces, and of the prefects of Egypt." Bearing in mind the *legatus* of Syria, Cadbury's point is basically correct.

50. One may rightly question whether or not the character Gallio speaks "for Luke." People in narratives can obviously speak in ways that reflect "character-appropriate" speech; yet such speech may or may not express the author's own opinion, as it were. In Gallio's case, however, we can confirm his speech with attention to the speech of a reliable character, Paul: "I have done nothing against . . . Caesar" (Acts 25:8). We shall return later to what Paul's statement means for our interpretation of Acts.

51. Conzelmann, *Theology of St. Luke*, 143.

52. Ibid., 142: "The State can declare that it has no interest in the controversy between Jews and Christians, for its Law is not affected by it."

53. See the discussion on p. 149ff. above.

54. The tablets have been discussed many times. See, for example, Elias J. Bickerman, "The Warning Inscriptions of Herod's Temple," *JQR* 37 (1947): 387–405. Bickerman translates the tablets as follows: "No alien [ἀλλογενῆ] may enter within the balustrade around the sanctuary and the enclosure. Whoever is caught, on himself shall he put blame for the death which will ensue" (388). Cf., for example, Jos., *AJ*, 15.417; *BJ*, 5.193; 6.124; Philo, *Leg.*, 31.

55. Bickerman, "Warning Inscriptions," 394–401, esp. 401. A lack of sufficient historical contextualizing plagues commentators at this point. To take but one example, see Walaskay, *Acts*, 201: "[T]he scene depicts a mob wildly out of control, rather than a rational proceeding in which the truth of the matter might be discerned." While it is certainly true that Luke paints a picture of public disturbance, he also provides a much more nuanced account of the problem than Walaskay allows (i.e., the whole scene—esp. 21:29—shows that Luke well understands that one who violated the temple proscription could reasonably expect death).

56. Precise troop numbers of a cohort (*speira*) differed, particularly with respect to the "first" cohort of a legion. Roman military organization is of course a highly complex topic, as even its greatest ancient scholar seemed to think: "I will explain the organization for the ancient legion according to the norm of military law. If this description should seem a bit obscure and unpolished, this is to be attributed not to me, but to the difficulty of the material itself" (Vegetius, *De Re Mil.* 2.4). For the Latin text and translation of Vegetius's classic work on the military, see Flavius Vegetius Renatus, *Epitoma Rei Militaris,* ed. and trans. Leo F. Stelten (New York: Peter Lang, 1990). For an excellent contemporary study on military structure and terminology, see Yann le Bohec, *The Imperial Roman Army,* trans. R. Bate (London Routledge, 2000).

57. See E. Mary Smallwood, *The Jews Under Roman Rule: From Pompey to Diocletian: A Study in Political Relations* (Leiden: Brill, 1981). One may recall, for example, the gruesome situation in Jerusalem under Florus (Jos., *BJ,* 2.297–332).

58. Jos., *BJ,* 7.83, of the Roman suppression of a German revolt in the 60s. The Germans were "forced to abandon their folly and learn prudence."

59. That the use of ἐπιλαμβάνομαι is a Lukan way of signaling danger for Paul at this juncture hardly requires comment.

60. See Rapske, *The Book of Acts and Paul in Roman Custody;* Richard J. Cassidy, *Paul in Chains: Roman Imprisonment and the Letters of St. Paul* (New York: Crossroad, 2001), 211–34; and the careful excursus by Matthew L. Skinner, *Locating Paul: Places of Custody as Narrative Settings in Acts 21—28* (Atlanta, GA: Society of Biblical Literature, 2003), 139–41, on the vocabulary of binding in Luke–Acts.

61. See Justinian's *Digest,* 48.3.8, noted by Fergus Millar, "Condemnation to Hard Labour in the Roman Empire, from the Julio-Claudians to Constantine," *PBSR* 52 (1984): 124–47 (132).

62. *Toxaris,* 29 (ὁ κλοιὸς ἤρκει καὶ ἡ ἑτέρα χεὶρ πεπεδημένη). "Guilty" is in quotation marks above because in the story Antiphilus is wrongly considered to be guilty and, therefore, wrongly in prison.

63. For example, Bruce, *The Book of the Acts,* 435.

64. See Rapske, *The Book of Acts and Paul in Roman Custody,* 283–312.

65. See Ramsay MacMullen, *Enemies of the Roman Order;* idem, "Judicial Savagery in the Roman Empire," *Chron* 16 (1986): 147–66. Cf. the discussion in de Ste. Croix, "Why Were the Early Christians Persecuted?" 16.

66. *Digest,* 1.18.3. I owe this reference to de Ste. Croix, "Why Were the Early Christians Persecuted?," 16 n. 75.

67. Walaskay, *Acts,* 201–2. Haenchen, *Acts,* 634 n. 4, is only slightly better. He asserts, with reference to Cadbury's article in *Beginnings* 5.297–338, that the legal situation "is unfortunately by no means clear. . . . Whether this was a case of protective custody or the arrest of a disturber of the public peace could only be decided when the reason for the lynch attempt was clarified—inter alia by an examination of Paul." Insofar as the subsequent and precise course of action is concerned, Haenchen is correct (this will depend upon Lysias's judgment). However, at this moment in the narrative, the ambiguity does not exist with respect to the issue of "protective custody," which emerges properly only in 23:23ff.

68. See, for example, Peter Garnsey, *Social Status and Legal Privilege in the Roman Empire* (Oxford: Clarendon, 1970); and Peter Brunt, "Evidence Given under Torture in the Principate," *Zeitschrift der Savigny-Stiftung für Rechtsgeschichte* 97 (1980): 257–63: Roman laws "did not protect the persons of free peregrini.... There is no known procedure under which an official could have been prosecuted for cruel treatment of peregrini unless in the pursuit of his own gains" (259).

69. Cf. Bruce, *The Book of the Acts*, 435, where Bruce understands that Paul is a "criminal" in Lysias's perspective.

70. "Get rid of him!" translates αἶρε αὐτόν (cf. 22:22). "Take him away!" is also possibility (RSV etc.), as is "Take him up!" with reference to the two flights of stairs from the temple to the barracks. "Get rid of him!" attempts to take account of the fact that it is very difficult to understand the tumult of the crowd as an attempt to wrest Paul from the hands of the Romans in order to kill him themselves, especially in light of their action in 21:32 and the dramatic request in 22:22–23. Βία in 21:35 is not "violence" but "force," in the sense of the tumultuous and physically jarring or pressing manner in which a multitude (τὸ πλῆθος) of agitated people move.

71. So, rightly, Cassidy, *Society and Politics in the Acts of the Apostles*, 97.

72. Johnson, *Acts*, 381. Cf., among others, Haenchen, *Acts*, 619.

73. Modern scholars who are aware that almost all of our Greek papyri come from Egypt should also not be surprised. To support a reading similar to Haenchen's and Johnson's, Conzelmann, *Acts*, 183, cleverly adduces Lucian, *Navig.* 2, where it is said of an Egyptian youth that he "spoke in a slovenly manner, one long continuous prattle; he spoke Greek, but his accent and intonation pointed to his native-land" (LCL trans.). Yet even here the emphasis is upon the way in which he spoke Greek rather than that he spoke Greek *simpliciter*. That dialect and tone could differ between native and nonnative speakers should not surprise. Indeed, linguistic differences even among native Greek speakers within various parts of the empire should be no more surprising than the fact that English sounds different, say, in Durham, North Carolina, than it does in Boston, Massachusetts.

74. I. Howard Marshall, *Acts* (Grand Rapids, MI, Eerdmans, 1980), 352.

75. C. K. Barrett, *Acts*, 2. vols. (London: T. & T. Clark, 1994/1998), 2.1024. With the use of "dramatic flare," I do not mean to suggest that this should be a principle for translation but rather only that it fits well the dramatic tension of the scene under discussion.

76. The Greek is emphatic: ἐγὼ ἄνθρωπος μέν εἰμι Ἰουδαῖος.

77. Indeed, Luke has already mentioned both Theudas and Judas the Galilean (Acts 5:36–37). One may think, for example, the unnamed "deceivers and imposters" who led the multitude (τὸ πλῆθος) into the desert in the hopes of a divinely backed revolution—with the result that Felix took military action and "put a large number to the sword" (Jos., *BJ*, 2.258–60; cf. *AJ*, 20.168, where Josephus relates that πολλοί were deceived and that the offenders were brought before Felix and punished). Of figures whose names we know, we may simply mention in addition to Theudas and Judas the Galilean, Jesus son of Sapphias, John of Gischala, Menahem son of Judas the Galilean, and so forth. Cf., too, Matt 24:26: "If they say to you, 'behold, he is in the wilderness,' do

not go out"; and Mark 13:22: "False messiahs and false prophets will arise and show signs and wonders to lead astray, if possible, the elect."

78. Richard A. Horsley and John S. Hanson, *Bandits, Prophets, and Messiahs: Popular Movements in the Time of Jesus* (Minneapolis, MN: Winston, 1985), 170. They attempt to justify this view with reference to Josephus's account of the Egyptian in *AJ*, 20.169–72, where Josephus writes that at the Mount of Olives the Egyptian wished "to demonstrate from there that at his command Jerusalem's walls would fall down, through which he promised to provide them an entrance into the city" (2.170). Horsley and Hanson are of course right in that the version in *AJ* fails to mention the Egyptian's planned tyranny and defeat of the Roman garrison, but it is hard to know what to think will happen once the walls fall down if it is not a battle (or rout). More importantly, in relating the disappearance of the Egyptian, Josephus says explicitly that he escaped from the fight or battle (μάχη) with the Roman army.

79. For example, Conzelmann, *Acts*, 184; Horsley and Hanson, *Bandits, Prophets, and Messiahs*, 170.

80. In *AJ*, 20.169–72, Josephus relates the story of the Egyptian, which concludes: ὁ δ' Αἰγύπτιος αὐτὸς διαδρὰς ἐκ τῆς μάχης ἀφανὴς ἐγένετο. Whether or not the next sentence πάλιν δ' οἱ λῃσταί begins a description of a different group is the point at issue. It is conceivable that here Josephus names the "brigands" as those who were associated with the Egyptian, but it is perhaps more likely that with the destruction of the Egyptian's movement and the vanishing of its leader Josephus now shifts groups to a favorite target of blame for the war.

81. *BJ*, 2.254–57 (Sicarii, λῃσταί); 261–63 (Egyptian); 264–65 (Sicarii?, λῃσταί); *AJ*, 20.162–67 (Sicarii, though not named explicitly as such); 169–72 (Egyptian); 172 (Sicarii).

82. One need think only of Pilate, Cornelius, Gallio, Festus, and so forth. For Luke's accuracy in character-speech, see briefly Rowe, *Early Narrative Christology*, 238–40.

83. That our readerly expectations are in line with Luke's development of Lysias as a character is confirmed by the ensuing narrative in which Lysias has no understanding of the debate at the Sanhedrin and in which his letter reflects a genuine puzzlement (cf. "Gallio" in this chapter).

84. The "Indeed!" here is an attempt to render the force of the μέν (see, e.g., Barrett, *Acts*, 2.1026). Tarsus had of course been a free city from the time of Pompey; it became the provincial capital of Cilicia in AD 72. Paul's move here may thus also be read as an attempt to anticipate and thus influence Lysias's decision about what to do with Paul, that is, return him to his place of origin.

85. Johnson, *Acts*, 391, rightly notes the similarity in the reaction of the crowd to others in Acts.

86. Cf. here the *Apol.* of Apuleius, who was of course a considerably lettered person. Johnson, *Acts*, 392, speaks of a culture "fundamentally shaped by forensics." This may be somewhat of an exaggeration, but it nevertheless gets at the point.

87. See, for example, Johnson, *Acts*, 387–95.

88. "The Nazarene," following Johnson, *Acts*, 389.

89. See K. M. Coleman, "Fatal Charades: Roman Executions Staged as Mythological Enactments," *JRS* 80 (1990): 44–73 (with plates).

90. Cicero, *Rab. Post.*, 4.12 (cf. 3.8). See also Livy, 10.9.4.

91. Sherwin-White, *Roman Society and Roman Law*, 57. Cf. Paulus the Jurist, *Sent.*, 5.26.1.

92. Ulpian in the *Digest*, 48.6.7.

93. For a Roman legal scholar who sees clearly this narrative dynamic, see A. H. M. Jones, "I Appeal Unto Caesar," in *Studies in Roman Government and Law* (Oxford: Basil Blackwell, 1960), 53–65 (54–55). Occasionally the question is raised as to whether or not Jews could be Roman citizens. The answer is not hard to find: Josephus records at least two official decrees—from Ephesus and Delos, respectively—from the 40s BC that explicitly state that Jews who were Roman citizens were exempt from military service (see *AJ*, 14.228 and 232). The ground given is the same in each case: Jewish δεισιδαιμονία.

94. As Sherwin-White, *Roman Society and Roman Law*, 77, notes, there is a line in the *Sententiae Pauli* that describes well the incident in Philippi. Indeed, it is "the only precise parallel to the affair at Philippi." With respect to fortune-tellers it reads, "The custom is to give them a beating and drive them out of the city" (5.21.1).

95. This reading seems also to be confirmed by 22:29, where Lysias is afraid because he "had bound Paul." The text, that is, refers only to the binding infraction and not to any torture.

96. See discussion in section above.

97. Skinner, *Locating Paul*, 139, rightly notes that δέω in 22:29 refers to the action τοῖς ἱμᾶσιν.

98. Cf., among other NT scholars, Conzelmann, *Acts*, 189, who makes reference to Cicero's statement. In citing this statement to "prove" that Romans citizens could not be bound, and so forth, NT scholars as learned as Haenchen, Johnson, and others have unfortunately overlooked the actual context of Cicero's statement: it is his prosecutorial speech against the once governor of Sicily (Verres) for the latter's reckless disregard of the Roman citizenship of one of his victims (Publius Gavius): Gavius was "dragged off to be crucified in spite of his proclaiming himself a Roman citizen." Cicero presses on: "this mention of his citizenship had not even so much effect upon you as to produce a little hesitation, or to delay, even for a little, the infliction of that cruel and disgusting penalty" (*Verr.*, 2.5.64 §165). It is right to note that Verres was prosecuted but important also to point out that the presupposition of his trial is the flagrant disregard for precisely the kind of thing that Cicero upholds. Even in the Republican period, the provinces could be dangerous places for Roman citizens.

99. See. n. 98 and n. 111.

100. Garnsey, "Legal Privilege in the Roman Empire," in *Social Status and Legal Privilege*, 9. Cf. MacMullen, "Judicial Savagery," 165: "Definition of citizenship in terms of culture rather than according to the letter of the law seems to me the best explanation, over most of the Principate, for the denying of rights to a person having technical title to them."

101. See Garnsey, "Legal Privilege," 19–24, for a refutation of the older view (e.g., Sherwin-White and A. H. M. Jones) that the distinction between *honestiores* and *humiliores* simply replaced the distinction between citizen and alien. Cf. Garnsey, *Social*

Status, 260–71; and the remarks on status in MacMullen, "Judicial Savagery," 147; and Millar, "Condemnation to Hard Labour," 125. Garnsey, *Social Status,* 223, admits that the terms *honestiores* and *humiliores* do not occur together in the pre-Severan or Severan period, but his investigation is hardly marred by this fact: where one sees, for example, legislation prohibiting this or that as it applies to the *honestiores,* one may reasonably surmise that the people to whom such legislation does *not* apply are the *humiliores.*

102. Garnsey, *Social Status,* 266.

103. *De Ira* 3.18.3. For further discussion, see Garnsey, *Social Status,* 144.

104. Through Suetonius's gossip about Claudius, one can easily detect the Emperor's ruthlessness in putting opponents to death (see esp. *Claud.,* 34–37, and 39).

105. Tacitus, *Ann.,* 15.60. Neither Scaevinus nor Natalis were actually tortured because "at the sight and threat of torture they broke down." The rank of Scaevinus is given in *Ann.* 15.49 and that of Natalis in 15.50. In relation to this overall topic, one may think particularly of one finding of Brunt's: to surmount the problem that a slave could not testify against a master, Augustus ruled that whenever the charge of *maiestas* was at issue, "the slave should be sold either to the state or to himself, in order that [the slave] might be examined as being then no longer the property of the master" ("Evidence Given under Torture," 257).

106. On this material as a whole, see esp. Garnsey, *Social Status,* 144–45; 213–18.; Theodor Mommsen, *Römisches Strafrecht* (Leipzig: Duncker & Humbolt, 1899), 406–18; and Rapske, *Paul in Roman Custody,* 53–55.

107. The decree presupposes the practice. See MacMullen, "Judicial Savagery," 153. The larger point of MacMullen's article is that there was an increase in both the manner and reach of brutality as one moves through the empire from the first to the fourth centuries. Mommsen, *Strafrecht,* 405–6, sees a major difference in the shift from republic to empire in terms of the Roman willingness to use torture as a method of coercion in the "magistratischen Strafprozess." The "Ausschliessung der Folter in republikanischer Zeit" is not intended to speak of unofficial methods of coercion. With respect to physical brutality, perhaps Richard A. Bauman put it best in the conclusion to his study *Crime and Punishment in Ancient Rome* (London: Routledge, 1996): regardless of the variation that one finds in attitudes toward and methods of punishment, "[t]he bottom line is that there were very few bleeding hearts in Ancient Rome" (163).

108. Garnsey, *Social Status,* 141.

109. The narrative fulfillment of Agabus's prophecy is one more example of how Luke does not think or write about prophecy in any kind of wooden manner. On this point, see Rowe, *Early Narrative Christology,* 32–34.

110. Sherwin-White, *Roman Society and Roman Law,* 54, notes that as a tribune Lysias does not have the *imperium* formally to try provincials once order is restored. Yet by this time, Lysias knows that Paul is not only a citizen of Tarsus but also of Rome.

111. Suetonius, *Galb.,* 9.1 (LCL). Cf. Garnsey, "Legal Privilege," 19, who notes that in the late-second century "some peasants on an Imperial estate in Africa protested to the Emperor Commodus (AD 180–93) that, even though some of them were Roman citizens, they had been beaten by a procurator and various overseers of the estate." Nor were such problems restricted to the imperial period. Pollio's quaestor in Spain, for

example, threw Roman citizens to the beasts and buried in the ground and burned alive a Roman citizen named Fadius. "While this was going on, Balbus walked up and down after lunch barefoot, his tunic loose and his hands behind his back. [Fadius] kept crying out, 'I am born a Roman citizen.' 'Off you go then!' responded Balbus. 'Appeal to the people'" (Cicero, *Fam.* 10.32 [415], LCL altered). In contrast to Verres (see above n. 98), who lived in exile after Cicero's prosecution, Balbus was not even reprimanded; indeed, he went on to a highly successful political career.

112. Jos., *BJ*, 2.308 (LCL). Josephus writes that Florus's action was something that "none had ever done before." Whether or not Florus's action can be construed as legal on grounds of Roman law is a matter of some debate. Drawing on the work of A. H. M. Jones, Sherwin-White, *Roman Society and Roman Law*, 61–62, observes that provincial governors by Florus's time may have had the authority to deal with certain crimes of Roman citizens covered by the *ordo* (i.e., the citizens could be executed for "active sedition," *maiestas*). Sherwin-White thus concludes that while Josephus may have "disapproved of Gessius Florus for executing for active sedition Jews who were Roman citizens," this disapproval "does not prove that the action was illegal." Jones himself, however, is more doubtful and, as Sherwin-White admits, sees Florus's action as an abuse of power. The problem is not easily solved, inasmuch as it is bound up with larger views about the development of the appeal system (*provocatio/appellatio*) and the differences between the early and later empire.

113. See esp. Charles H. Cosgrove, "The Divine *ΔΕΙ* in Luke–Acts: Investigations into the Lukan Understanding of God's Providence," *NovT* 26 (1984): 168–90.

114. In many contemporary Bibles, there is a break between 23:11 and 23:12. This is unfortunate given the clear signal in both 23:11 and 23:12 that they should be read together (τῇ δὲ ἐπιούσῃ νυκτί . . . γενομένης δὲ ἡμέρας). If there is a break, it should occur between 23:10 and 23:11.

115. For example, Cassidy, *Society and Politics in the Acts of the Apostles*, 99–100.

116. Despite their status in the military, tribunes were obviously not beyond severe reproach. In a much-publicized case during the governorship of Cumanus, the Syrian legate Quadratus sent a military tribune to Rome—along with Cumanus himself, and leading Jews and Samaritans—to obtain a decision in the court of the emperor concerning the party at fault in the war between the Jews and Samaritans. The Emperor Claudius decided in favor of the Jews: the Samaritans were promptly executed, Cumanus was exiled, and Celer the tribune was to be "taken to Jerusalem, where he was to be dragged around the whole city in a public spectacle and then put to death" (Jos., *AJ*, 20.134–46; *BJ*, 2.245–46). Cf. Tacitus, *Ann.* 12.54, for a different account of the general problem (he does not mention Celer).

117. To take but one more salient example: Lysias says that he rescued Paul *after* learning that the latter was a Roman citizen.

118. Though Christian readers of Acts doubtless know the general outcome of Paul's various trials, in the world of the narrative, of course, this information is new.

119. For a brief compilation of the legal terminology in Acts, see Allison A. Trites, "The Importance of Legal Scenes and Language in the Book of Acts," *NovT* 16 (1974): 278–84.

120. As Pesch, *Apostelgeschichte*, 2.250, notes, Felix is named Antonius by Tacitus (*Ann.* 12.54; *Hist.* 5.9) and Claudius by Josephus (*AJ*, 20.37).

121. Tacitus, *Ann.* 12.54 and *Hist.* 5.9, respectively.

122. Jos., *AJ*, 20.162.

123. Upon Felix's recall an embassy of the leading Jews from Caesarea traveled to Rome to accuse him before Nero for his ἀδικήματα toward the Jews. Nero, however, was persuaded by Beryllus/Burrus not to punish Felix but instead authorized a rescript that revoked "the grant of equal civic rights to the Jews" (Jos., *AJ*, 20.182–84).

124. See, for example, Sherwin-White, *Roman Society and Roman Law*, 55–57, who attempts to answer the question with reference to the changing provincial status of Cilicia. Peter Garnsey, "The Criminal Jurisdiction of Governors," *JRS* 58 (1968), 51–59, shows, however, that the governor could simply judge his prisoner without such extradition (esp. 52–55, 57–59).

125. See n. 33.

126. Sherwin-White, *Roman Society and Roman Law*, 51 (with Mommsen before him). As we will see, however, in contrast to the situation with Gallio, as the scene here moves forward it becomes apparent that there is some difficulty in specifying the charges against Paul before Felix as those which fall *extra ordinem*. Indeed, if *maiestas* is the principal legal charge levied by Tertullus (see below), it may be that the (alleged) crime would technically fall within the normal *ordo*. This is in fact the argument of Heusler, *Kapitalprozesse*, passim (cf. Sherwin-White, *Roman Society and Roman Law*, 62). Even so, Sherwin-White, *Roman Law and Society*, 62, claims that the "treason law" was "not left to the authority of the provincial governors." If this remark is taken to apply to active sedition (*maiestas*), then it is a strange remark indeed. Jones, "I Appeal," upon whom Sherwin-White draws heavily, knows better: despite the differences in system of appeals for which Jones argues (*provocatio/appellatio*), the exception to the rule of appeal in various times seems to have been "notable brigands, ringleaders of sedition...leaders of faction...threat[s] to public order"; these were to be dealt with by the governor (57). As Ulpian's student Modestinus put it: "it is in the public interest to punish [such persons] immediately on condemnation" (*Digest*, 49.1.16). The critical point here, as the work of Peter Garnsey in particular has made clear, is to recognize amidst the legal tangles the de facto power of the provincial governor. Among other things, Garnsey's work has exposed a subtle romanticizing of Roman law by Sherwin-White et al. in which their legal vision has been blind to the dynamics on the ground, as it were. One sees this tendency in other discussions as well. For example, Robert Samuel Rogers, "Treason in the Early Empire," *JRS* 49 (1959): 90–94, esp. 92, on the emperor as "bound by every law which did not itself provide for his exemption from it"; and 94: "The Empire *was* a reign of law...for *Law* was Rome's contribution to civilization" (emphasis original); or Hugh Last, "Rome and the Druids: A Note," *JRS* 39 (1949): 1–5, in which Rome's action against the Druids is seen as a key episode in the larger story of western European "civilization"; even Ramsay MacMullen once generalized in this way: "No strength was more characteristic of Roman civilization than law" (*Roman Government's Response to Crisis A.D. 235–337* [New Haven, CT: Yale University Press, 1976], 201).

127. Who was not a popular figure, at least according to the treatment he receives in Josephus. On this material, see Sanders, *Judaism: Practice and Belief 63 BCE–66 CE* (Philadelphia: Trinity Press International, 1992), passim.

128. That Tertullus's brief speech is well crafted—in light of ancient rhetorical conventions—has been amply demonstrated. See, for example, Stephan Lösch, "Die Dankesrede des Tertullus; Apg 21, 1–4," *TQ* 112 (1931): 295–315; Jerome Neyrey, "The Forensic Defense Speech and Paul's Trial Speeches in Acts 22–26: Form and Function," in *Luke–Acts: New Perspectives from the Society of Biblical Literature Seminar*, ed. Charles H. Talbert, (New York: Crossroad, 1984), 210–24; Bruce W. Winter, "The Importance of the Captatio Benevolentiae in the Speeches of Tertullus and Paul in Acts 24:1–21," *JTS* 42 (1991): 505–31. Heusler, *Kapitalprozesse*, 68, notes that Tertullus's portraits of Felix and Paul are mirror images of each other: "Das Auftreten des Paulus steht . . . in genauem Gegensatz zum Wirken des Präses und wird an diesem gemessen. Stelle Felix seine Kräfte in den Dienst der pax Romana, tue Paulus alles, um diese Politik des Ausgleichs und der Entspannung zu untergraben und Unruhen zu provozieren und zu schüren—so das Plädoyer des Tertullus."

129. Haenchen, *Acts*, 650: "Anyone who simply presupposes in Luke the portrait of Felix painted by Tacitus and Josephus misinterprets the scene." Cf. Conzelmann, *Acts*, 198, who softens the point: "[I]t is unnecessary to explain [Tertullus's] praise of Felix by appeal to contemporary events."

130. Though Quintilian attributes Athenaeus's definition of rhetoric to a misreading of Plato's *Gorgias*, it is not without reason that Athenaeus defined rhetoric as "the art of deceiving" (Quintilian, *Inst.*, 2.15.23–32). As Quintilian's cataloguing of various definitions of rhetoric shows, Athenaeus is hardly alone in his opinion of rhetoric. Indeed, this opinion expresses one side of a long tradition that criticizes rhetoric for divorcing the "good"—teleologically understood—of speaking well from the mere science of persuasion (as a whole, 2.15.1–36 offer a good summary of the deep conflict surrounding the proper use of rhetoric).

131. On πρωτοστάτης, see LSJ, 1545.

132. Sherwin-White's translation of κοινήν τινα τῆς οἰκουμενης νόσον ἐξεγείροντας—except that where I use "common" he employs "universal" (51). See H. Stuart Jones, "Claudius and the Jewish Question at Alexandria," *JRS* 16 (1926): 17–35.

133. Πάντα τρόπον αὐτοὺς ἐπεξελεύσομαι ("I will take vengeance on them in every way"). The letter can be found in M. P. Charlesworth, *Documents Illustrating the Reigns of Claudius and Nero* (Cambridge: Cambridge University Press, 1939), nos. 1 and 2, 3–5. For ἐπεξέρχομαι as "take vengeance," see LSJ, 617. The verb can also mean attack, punish, march out against, and so forth. Cf. the similar accusation against the Jews in P. Berol. 8877, col. 2., lns. 20–24 (text: "Acta Isidori," Recension C, p. 23; trans. p. 25 in Herbert A. Musurillo, *The Acts of the Pagan Martyrs: Acta Alexandrinorum* [Oxford: Clarendon, 1954]). Musurillo also has an informative discussion on the debate that surrounds how to relate this papyrus to Claudius's letters (esp. 118–24).

134. As Franz Cumont, "La lettre de Claude aux Alexandrins," *Rev. Hist. Rel.* 91 (1925): 3–6, notes, "La formule est assez vague pour se prêter à plusieurs applications.

Néamoins, l'analogie est telle qu'on ne peut écarter le soupcon de quelque relation entre les deux documents" (4). Cumont remains agnostic about his own proposal, which is that of an indirect connection between Acts 24:5 and Claudius's letter. Such a connection rests ultimately on the supposition of a centralized response of Rome to the "agitation" of Jewish synagogues (4–6).

135. See Alfred Loisy, *Les Actes des Apôtres* (Paris: Émile Nourry, 1920), 852, for a brief but suggestive reflection on the possible connection of λοιμός to 1 Macc 15:21, in which the renewal of the alliance with Rome results in the handing over of "pests" to the High Priest Simon "so that he may punish them according to their law" (15:21).

136. Johnson, *Acts*, 411.

137. It should not go unnoticed: Barabbas is only one of the στασιασταί who were in prison for murder ἐν τῇ στάσει (15:7).

138. Cf. de Ste. Croix, "Why Were the Early Christians Persecuted?" 12.

139. See, for example, Theodor Mommsen, "Die Rechtsverhältnisse des Apostels Paulus," *ZNW* 2 (1901): 81–96; and Sherwin-White, "The Early Persecutions and Roman Law Again," *JTS* 3 (1952): 199–213; and Sherwin-White, *Roman Society and Roman Law.*

140. Mommsen, *Strafrecht*, 340 (cited also in de Ste. Croix, "Why Were the Early Christians Persecuted?" 12).

141. So, rightly, Conzelmann, Haenchen, Pesch, Preuschen, Schneider, *Beginnings*, 4.308, et al.

142. Tacitus, *Ann.*, 1.72. Classical scholars debate vigorously the line of development of this notion from the Republican period through the Principate. See, for example, the critical reviews by Peter Garnsey (*JRS* 59 [1969]: 282–84) and Ramsey MacMullen (*AJP* 91 [1970]: 117–18) of R. A. Bauman, *The Crimen Maiestatis in the Roman Republic and Augustan Principate* (Johannesburg: Witwatersrand University Press, 1967). For a concise treatment of the difference between the notion of *maiestas populi Romani* ("the majesty or superiority of the Roman people over all others") in the republican and the early imperial periods—especially how this notion gets transferred to the emperor—see Nicola Mackie, "Ovid and the Birth of Maiestas," in *Roman Poetry and Propaganda in the Age of Augustus*, ed. Anton Powell (London: Bristol Classical Press, 1992), 83–97, esp. 88–91. As is well known Tertullian, *Apol.* 2.8; 10.1–2; 28.1–2; 35.5, mentions that Christians were thought of as *maiestatis rei*. Sherwin-White, "Early Persecutions," 203, asserts that this description does not fit well the situation reflected in Pliny's famous epistle to Trajan (10.96), where it cannot be that "provincial *peregrini* were accused directly on the grounds of *maiestas*." Without further argument, it is not clear why Sherwin-White dismisses this possibility out of hand. To the extent that refusal to sacrifice to the gods could be connected to basic matters of the Roman state (e.g., *ius divinarum* as a way to keep the *pax deorum*; cf. de Ste Croix, "Why Were the Early Christians Persecuted?"), it seems that *maiestas* remains a distinct possibility. In any event, that such a charge fits Paul's context much better than Pliny's is not to be doubted.

143. For example, Garnsey, *Social Status and Legal Privilege*, passim. For example: "virtually from the beginning of the Empire, death sentences were expected to follow

convictions for *maiestas*, whatever the status of the defendant. This was the situation not only in the case of conspiracies and plots, but also in the case of less serious, but still treasonable, acts (*facta*), and treasonable words (*dicta*)" (105); "[A]rmed rebellion against the state and violation of the Emperor's *maiestas* were never included in the practical immunity of senators from execution" (236). On the situation during Hadrian's reign, Garnsey is concise (107 passim).

144. The fact that the *crux* was supposedly reserved for slaves did not do much to prevent its use. In addition to Jesus himself of course, for the penalty of death by *crux*, see Josephus's description of Florus in *BJ*, 2.301; of Quadratus, the legate of Syria, who executed Jewish rebels in *AJ*, 20.129 during the governorship of Cumanus; and of Felix in *BJ*, 2.253. For the penalty of death by *bestiae* (*damnatio ad bestias*), see, for example, Tacitus, *Ann.*, 15.44, with reference to the Christians.

145. The word αἵρεσις does of course mean "school" as in "school of thought" or "philosophy" (see, e.g., Jos., *BJ*, 2.118; or Diogenes Laertius, *Lives*, 7.191; indeed, Chrysippus wrote a work with this title). Yet in this context it undoubtedly has a negative connotation. In his speech to Felix, for example, Paul repeats the term but in a manner that distances the Christians from it: "which *they* call a sect" (24:14). Cf. αἵρεσις elsewhere in Acts: of Christians by Jews (28:22); and of Sadducees and Pharisees (5:17; 15:5; 26:5).

146. Cf. esp. Pesch, *Apostelgeschichte*, 256.

147. I use the term zealot here in its more general sense. On the need to keep clear about the terminology for specific Jewish groups, see E. P. Sanders, *Judaism*, esp. 281.

148. Tacitus, *Hist.* 5.1 (*Sed quoniam famosae urbis supremum diem tradituri sumus, congruens videtur primordial eius aperire*); cf. 5.12, where Tacitus remarks that from the time of Claudius Jewish *seditio* in Jerusalem was "the more rife" (due to an influx of "rabble").

149. Including the Roman procurator Cumanus. See n. 144.

150. Jos., *AJ*, 20.125–36; *BJ*, 2.240–46.

151. Jos., *BJ*, 2.232 (a Galilean pilgrim); *AJ*, 20.118 (several pilgrims).

152. Jos., *AJ*, 18; *BJ*, 2.169–74.

153. Sanders, *Judaism*, 242 passim.

154. Ibid.

155. Jos., *AJ*, 18.257–309; *BJ*, 2.184–203. If Josephus's narratives are near the mark, Petronius was indeed a remarkable diplomat. Tacitus, *Hist.* 5.9, knows a different version of the incident under Gaius: "[W]hen Caligula ordered the Jews to set up his statue in their temple, they chose rather to resort to arms, but the emperor's death put an end to their uprising."

156. Cf. the list of ancient chroniclers who comment upon Antiochus's desecration of the temple in *C. Ap.* 2.83–85.

157. Some scholars would argue that Tertullus puts three charges forward. For example, Heusler, *Kapitalprozesse*, 69–70. So, too, Bruce, *The Book of the Acts*, 464–66, for example, holds that Tertullus's claim that Paul is the leader of the Nazarenes is itself a separate charge. Yet, as Bruce himself virtually acknowledges (465), this charge

would have been meaningless in itself. It needs a wider context for it to have any legal purchase. It is better, therefore, to view it as part of the first charge. Moreover, whether there is even more than one charge is debatable. It is possible, that is, to read the statement about Paul's attempt to defile the temple as an illustration of or support for the initial statement regarding his seditious activity rather than as a separate charge in itself (so the argument above).

158. Lest it go unnoticed: both Mark and Matthew illustrate the importance of the association between the temple and "physical insurrection" in their renditions of the charges that were brought against Jesus (Mark 14:57–58; Matt 26.60–61). On this point, see E. P. Sanders, *Jesus and Judaism* (Philadelphia: Fortress, 1985), esp. 71–72. Sanders speaks of the "physical insurrection" that is implied in the charge. Luke, however, eliminates this charge—though neither the "cleansing" (19:45–46) nor the "prediction" (21:5–6)—in his gospel. The likely reason for Luke's omission is bound up with his desire to distance Jesus from any seditious banditry in the final portion of the gospel; Luke can thereby proclaim Jesus' innocence.

159. Schneider, *Apostelgeschichte*, 2.346. Cited in part also by Pesch, *Apostelgeschichte*, 2.256. Cf. also Sherwin-White, *Roman Society and Roman Law*, 64.

160. On the hermeneutical problems involved in confusing the different levels at which Luke's narratives may be read, see Rowe, *Early Narrative Christology*, esp. 208–16.

161. Jos., *BJ*, 6.124–28.

162. Tertullus's statement reverses the historical sequence so that the Jews now prevent the desecration rather than react to it: κρατέω here is not "seize" in order to put to death, but "seize" or "restrain" in order to prevent pollution.

163. Barrett, *Acts*, 2.1093–94, summarizes well the arguments on both sides of this old problem. He concludes that it is impossible to be sure one way or the other (e.g., the "we" in ἐκρατήσαμεν is balanced by the fact that a lawyer may well identify with his clients, etc.).

164. Cf. Barrett, *Acts*, 2.1092, who notes, that "the Jews seem to be playing down the theological issue; wisely, for it would not interest Romans, who would not be likely to condemn a man simply as an erring theologian."

165. "Die Religionsfrevel nach römischem Recht," in *Gesammelte Schriften III* (Berlin: Weidmannsche Buchhandlung, 1907), 389–422.

166. See, for example, Hugh Last, "The Study of the Persecutions," *JRS* 27 (1937): 80–92, esp. 81; and, Sherwin-White, "Early Persecutions and Roman Law Again," 203–4.

167. For a discussion of the range of crimes that could be construed as treason ("high treason," etc.) as well as a brief treatment of the changes in treason law, see C. W. Chilton, "The Roman Law of Treason under the Early Principate," *JRS* 45 (1955): 73–81, and the rejoinder by Rogers, "Treason in the Early Empire." Whether or not the laws against treason changed over time (and they doubtless did; cf. the policy of Hadrian), the critical point for our chapter remains the same, that *maiestas* in the first and early second centuries was a capital crime.

168. Because of Paul's status as a *civis Romanus*, the mode of execution would have normally been decapitation. However, as mentioned above, governors did not

always adhere to the law with utmost scrupulousness, and citizens were crucified, thrown to the beasts, burned alive, and so forth.

169. For the *captatio* as a standard feature of the defense speeches found in the ancient sources, see, for example, Fred Veltman, "The Defense Speeches of Paul in Acts," in *Perspectives on Luke–Acts*, ed. Charles Talbert (Danville, VA: Association of Baptist Professors in Religion, 1978), 242–56.

170. So, for example, Jervell, *Apostelgeschichte*, 569.

171. Cf., among others, Jervell, *Apostelgeschichte*, 570; Pesch, *Apostelgeschichte*, 2.258; Roloff, *Apostelgeschichte*, 337.

172. Acts scholars have often noted the awkward Greek of 24:17. See, for example, Johnson, *Acts*, 413–14, for a clear discussion. In particular, the verb παραγίνομαι is placed so as to render the interpretation of προσφοραί somewhat difficult. Yet the immediate reference to the temple in the following sentence (24:18) makes it reasonably certain that Paul speaks here in 24:17 of offerings he intended to make in the temple.

173. Θόρυβος is used also of the riot in Ephesus (20:1) and of the crowd in Jerusalem (21:34).

174. Sherwin-White, *Roman Society and Roman Law*, 53 (cf. 52).

175. Pliny, *Ep.*, 6.31.12, here of Trajan's threat to the heirs of Julius Tiro regarding the dispute over the latter's will.

176. Sherwin-White, *Roman Society and Roman Law*, 51.

177. Ibid., 53.

178. Several NT exegetes note the oddness of Felix's judicial move given his possession of the tribune's letter. See, for example, Talbert, *Reading Acts* (Macon, GA: Smyth & Helwys, 2005), 202.

179. It is only by overlooking the narrative importance of 24:17 that Haenchen, *Acts*, 662–63, can portray Felix as genuinely interested in the content of the Christian faith. Furthermore, Luke's διό in 24:26 is an unambiguous mark of Felix's purpose in his repeated summoning of Paul. With reference to Paul's particular type of *custodia*, Conzelmann, *Acts*, 200, rightly notes Paul's ability to receive care from "his own" certainly does not mean that one should regard his conditions as "idyllic." For Christian ministry to those in prison, cf. from a pagan perspective, Lucian, *De Mort Peregr.*, 13. According to Lucian, Peregrinus was of course a rather insincere Christian at best. Nevertheless, when he was thrown into prison, the Christians—severely duped in Lucian's view—ministered to him: "[M]uch money came to [Peregrinus] from [the Christians] by reason of his imprisonment, and he procured not a little revenue from it."

180. See, for example, *Digest*, 48.11. On the *Lex Repetundarum* in particular, see Sherwin-White, "The Date of the *Lex Repetundarum* and Its Consequences," *JRS* 62 (1972): 83–99.

181. *Vesp.*, 16.

182. See Cicero, *Caecin.*, 73; and Pliny, *Ep.*, 2.11. Of interest is Pliny's indication that the charge against the proconsul Marius Priscus, brought by the province of Africa, had in part to do with the fact that "Priscus had taken bribes to sentence innocent persons to punishment and even to death." Talbert, *Reading Acts*, 203, has a brief and excellent treatment of bribery that notes several important texts.

183. Jos., *BJ*, 2.273 (cf. *AJ*, 20.215).

184. It was also well aimed toward the governor's lack of δικαιοσύνη and ἐγκράτεια (24:25). In addition to the ancient literature on Felix's reputation cited above, Josephus also tells us about his willingness to hire "a Cyprian Jew named Atomus, who pretended to be a magician" to seduce Drusilla away from her husband Azizus. Drusilla "was persuaded to transgress the ancestral laws and marry Felix" (*AJ*, 20.141–44).

185. According to Sherwin-White, *Roman Society and Roman Law*, 53 (with reference to Josephus and Mommsen), leaving a prisoner for one's successor "creates no difficulty" from a legal or procedural point of view.

186. Cf. Luke's use of αἴτιος as "crime" in Luke 23:4 and 14—of which, by Pilate's declaration, Jesus is innocent.

187. So, too, for example, Bruce, *The Book of the Acts*, 476–77; and, Jervell, *Apostelgeschichte*, 579.

188. Bruce, *The Book of the Acts*, 476.

189. It is this change in the approach to Felix and Festus that creates the difficulty for scholars such as Sherwin-White, who want to treat the charges brought before both Felix and Festus under the same legal heading (*extra ordinem*). It is not that such a hypothesis is impossible, but rather that Tertullus's charges before Felix might fit well within the traditional *ordo* (cf. Heusler in n. 126); yet before Festus, it seems clear that they do not (hence Festus's puzzlement). The legal sophistication of Paul's accusers seems to have regressed through the time he was imprisoned.

190. See below on the significance of δεισιδαιμονία.

191. That the hermeneutical and political importance of Paul's statement in 25:8 is for Luke ultimately grounded in the life of Jesus should be obvious to any attentive reader of the final chapters of Luke's gospel. Christianity, it may be said, is christological in shape.

192. Indeed, over a century later in Lyons, despite a direct imperial *mandatum* not to throw Roman citizens to the beasts, another provincial governor did just that to a Christian named Attalus. His reason: to satisfy the mob. See Eusebius, *Eccl. Hist.* 5.1.43–52. This passage is cited also by Jones, "I Appeal Unto Caesar," 55–56. So, too, Sherwin-White, *Roman Society and Roman Law*, 70 n. 1, notes this incident but fails to comment on the most startling fact for his topic, namely, that a provincial governor simply ignored a mandate from the emperor and had a Roman citizen killed like an alien (*bestiae*). De Ste. Croix, "Why Were the Early Christians Persecuted?" 15, includes the Attalus text in his discussion of the power of the provincial governor, but then goes on to note that even the governor's "attitude might be less important than what I must call 'public opinion.' If the state of local feeling was such that no one particularly wanted to take upon himself the onus of prosecuting Christians, very few governors would have any desire to instigate a persecution." De Ste. Croix's remarks here are self-evidently perceptive with respect to the time of Pliny through later antiquity, but they are also relevant to the narrative dynamics of Acts. One may think not only of the situation in Jerusalem, but also of that in Ephesus, for example.

193. On the legal specifications of *reiectio* in the early empire, see esp. Garnsey, "Criminal Jurisdiction," 56–57.

194. See Garnsey, "Criminal Jurisdiction of Governors," 57.

195. In addition to the studies by Skinner and Rapske already mentioned, see John Layton Lentz, *Luke's Portrait of Paul*, SNTSMS 77 (Cambridge: Cambridge University Press, 1993), 139–70; Heiki Omerzu, *Der Prozess des Paulus: Eine Exegetische und Rechtshistorische Untersuchung*, BNZW 115 (Berlin: Walter de Gruyter, 2002); Heusler, *Kapitalprozesse*; Tajra, *The Trial of St. Paul*.

196. Mommsen, "Die Rechtsverhältnisse des Apostels Paulus," 81: "Wenn ich einer Aufforderung des Herausgebers dieser Zeitschrift entsprechend in derselben die Rechtsverhältnisse und insbesondere den Prozess des Apostels Paulus vom römischen Standpunkt aus erörtere, so geschieht es nicht, als ob ich darüber viel Besonderes und Neues zu sagen wüsste. Dem Juristen wird die folgende Auseinandersetzung, wie ich hoffe, meistenteils als selbstverständlich erscheinen. Aber für den Theologen mag eine derartige Darlegung nicht überflüssig sein."

197. See Cadbury, "Roman Law and the Trial of Paul," *Beginnings* 5.297–338, et al.

198. In addition to Sherwin-White's *Roman Society and Roman Law*, we can mention once again the highly influential article of Jones, "I Appeal Unto Caesar."

199. This is not to say, of course, that classical scholars have been unaware of the counter-examples (Galba et al. above). It is rather the case that the scholars who hold Mommsenian-like positions tend to see these examples as "illegal" or, at best, as "exceptions" to the otherwise clear legal picture. See, for example, Sherwin-White, *Roman Society and Roman Law*, 60–62.

200. Sherwin-White, *Roman Society and Roman Law*, 63. Sherwin-White here overreads Cadbury, who does not offer this as a theory or explanation but rather as a question (based on the text of Acts, it might be said).

201. See, for example, Tacitus, *Ann.* 14.28, where *provocatio* and *appellatio* appear to be synonymous: "[Nero] also added to the dignity of the Fathers by ruling that litigants appealing [*provocavissent*] from civil tribunals to the senate must risk the same deposit as those who appealed [*appellarent*] to the Emperor" (LCL, altered; noted by Garnsey, "The *Lex Iulia* and Appeal Under the Empire," 182 n. 147; Mommsen, of course, was not unaware of the terminological issues [*Strafrecht*, 473 n. 4]). Haenchen, *Acts*, 669–70, argues that at the historical level of Paul's ministry the appeal makes sense only on the supposition that Paul was convicted by Festus (i.e., Luke has reversed this verdict for his apologetic purpose). This argument, however, presupposes a fixity in the Roman legal system of appeals that is simply not there (i.e., it is never the case that a citizen can appeal prior to sentence; Garnsey's analysis of *reiectio* clearly shows otherwise).

202. Garnsey also criticizes the circularity involved in the arguments of Jones and Sherwin-White, due to the fact that Acts is really the only indisputable piece of first-century evidence in favor of their theory: "If Paul's appeal is '*provocatio-before-trial*' in the sense assumed by Jones and Sherwin-White, there is no parallel which is of any use, and consequently the case has to be explained in the light of itself" (*Social Status and Legal Privilege*, 75 n. 4). This point has not always been appreciated by Acts scholars, even among those who are somewhat aware of the legal issues involved (an exception is

Lentz, *Luke's Portrait of Paul*, 145–53, who is appreciative of Garnsey's efforts). See, for example, Heusler, *Kapitalprozesse*, 235–36, who does not know Garnsey's work. Ben Witherington, *The Acts of the Apostles: A Socio-Rhetorical Commentary* (Grand Rapids, MI: Eerdmans, 1998), 723–26, appears to know Garnsey's book but simply incorporates him into a thesis that Garnsey's work clearly opposes (e.g., 723: "What we are dealing with here is a case of *provocatio*, not *appellatio*"). And Rapske, *Paul in Roman Custody*, 186–88, has obviously read Garnsey, too, but seems to set him against Lintott's rejection of a clear *provocatio/appellatio* distinction—the same position for which Garnsey himself actually argued (see Andrew W. Lintott, "Provocatio: From the Struggle of the Orders to the Principate," *ANRW* I.2.226–67, esp. 233–34). Moreover, as Rapske presents it (perhaps following the mistake of Lintott, 264), Garnsey denies that Paul's appeal is an actual appeal—it is instead a rejection of the court—but Garnsey's argument as a whole is that Paul's appeal and rejection are the same thing (*provocatio/appellatio* in Paul's case = *reiectio*). It is true that Paul's appeal is not "a case of appeal *proper* at all," but by this Garnsey means to point to the fact that proper appeals were after sentencing whereas Paul's is obviously before (Garnsey, "The *Lex Iulia* and Appeal Under the Empire," 185; [emphasis mine]). But that Paul actually appealed to Caesar Garnsey does not deny. Whether or not in so doing Paul usurped a legal right granted *only* after sentencing (so Garnsey contra Jones, Sherwin-White, et al.) is a question that needs further attention from specialists in the field of Roman legal history. Indeed, the entire debate illustrates well the need for NT exegetes to think more deeply about the intersection of Roman law and the NT. Bruce Winter, "Roman Law and Society in Romans 12–15," in *Rome in the Bible and the Early Church*, ed. Peter Oakes (Grand Rapids, MI: Baker Academic, 2002), 67–102, esp. 68, is therefore right indeed to encourage NT scholars to take "cognisance of the wider nexus between Roman law and Roman society." Winter's study, though of a different topic than the present one, is excellent for the way in which it attempts to deal interpretively with the legal underpinnings of Roman society (in dependence upon Crook's insights in *Law and Life of Rome* [Ithaca, NY: Cornell University Press, 1967], Winter reverses Sherwin-White's book title).

203. See esp. Garnsey, "Criminal Jurisdiction of Governors," 53–55.

204. The issue here likely goes somewhat deeper methodologically and turns on the perspectival difference between a more Rome-centered way of looking at things and one that begins from the provinces. See, for example, the critical remarks of Fergus Millar in his lengthy review of Sherwin-White's translation of and commentary on Pliny's letters. Of the commentary, Millar remarks, "In a way not easy to define, the book still reflects the outlook on this period current a generation ago, the assumptions, one might put it, of the *CAH* rather than Syme's *Tacitus*. That is to say, [the book] is the product of that firmly 'constitutionalist,' Rome-based, tradition in the study of Roman history as studied in England, which goes back to Mommsen . . . and by-passes both Syme and Rostovtzeff" (*JRS* 58 [1968]: 218–24, 224).

205. Garnsey, "The *Lex Iulia* and Appeal Under the Empire," 183.

206. Jos., *AJ*, 18.2—including the power to impose the death penalty (μέχρι τοῦ κτείνειν, *BJ*, 2.117). On these and like passages, see Garnsey, "Criminal Jurisdiction of Governors," 52.

207. That in rejecting the court in Caesarea Paul availed himself of a formal legal right is yet another side to Garnsey's proposals (i.e., the appeal constituted a rejection of the courts; see "The *Lex Iulia* and Appeal Under the Empire," 182). Yet, in suggesting that the "system of the *quaestiones perpetuae* at Rome" applies directly to Paul, Garnsey may have pushed the evidence beyond its reach (see, e.g., Lintott, "Provocatio," 265, on Garnsey's invocation of *reiectio* Roman in *Social Status and Legal Privilege*, 76). That Paul's appeal, however, is simultaneously a rejection of the court in Caesarea seems beyond dispute—at least as Luke tells it.

208. Sherwin-White, *Roman Society and Roman Law*, 17 passim, esp. 23 ("more a body of assessors than of jurors").

209. Cf. Paul's later statement about the Jewish response to the Roman wish to free Paul: "But when the Jews objected..." (Acts 28:19a).

210. Haenchen, *Acts*, 677–78, following Loisy, thinks Festus has enough material to write his report (with reference to Acts 25:26). But the issue is not the amount of knowledge Festus needs or has but the fact that he cannot understand what to do with what he has. Ζητήματα within the Jewish δεισιδαιμονία are scarcely standard legal fare. Conzelmann, *Acts*, 207, cites Ulpian's remark that "after an appeal has been entered, records must be furnished by the one who made the appeal to the person who is going to conduct the examination" (*Digest*, 49.6.1). It may well be that, given the debate over the procedure of appeal in the early/late empire, we should be cautious in applying Ulpian's text either to Paul's or Luke's time, but the prima facie relevance is nevertheless striking.

211. David C. Braund's article "Agrippa," ABD 1.98–101, is concise, though there are inaccuracies (e.g., Agrippa II's praise for Josephus's works occurs in *Vit.*, 364–66 and *C. Ap.*, 1.51). Braund's book on the so-called client kings also has a nice discussion of the function of the various Herodian kings within the Roman Empire: though not technically Roman officials, since "the king needed Roman recognition and operated, once recognized, within the Roman sphere, he was a Roman appointee." See Braund, *Rome and the Friendly King: The Character of Client Kingship* (New York: St. Martin's, 1984), 85 (cf., too, esp. 116).

212. See esp. Jos., *Vit.*, 364–66.

213. Jos., *BJ*, 2.345–401.

214. For example, Jos., *BJ*, 2.500–506. At the end of his speech mentioned above, he states clearly his position: "as for you, if you decide aright, you will enjoy with me the blessings of peace, but, if you let yourselves be carried away by your passion, you will face—without me—this tremendous peril" (*BJ*, 2.401).

215. Jos., *BJ*, 2.360 (LCL, altered).

216. It is significant for readers' understanding of Agrippa's Romanism, as it were, that Festus says to him *their own* δεισιδαιμονία rather than *your* θρησκεία/εὐσέβεια (*religio*).

217. Tacitus, *Hist.* 5.8. Menahem Stern, *Greek and Latin Authors on Jews and Judaism*, collects the most relevant texts. See nos. 30b (Agatharchides); 115 (Strabo); 128 (Horace); 230 (Quintilian); 255–56 (Plutarch); 281 (Tacitus); 302, 306 (Suetonius); 341 (Fronto); 362 (Apuleius). Such language was also used in official imperial decrees.

See those transmitted, for example, in Jos., *AJ*, 14.228–30 and 231–32. Once more we may observe Luke's care in constructing the right speech for his characters. Of course, one also recalls the famous texts about the *Christiani* from Tacitus (*Ann.*, 15.44) and Suetonius (*Nero*, 16.2) that characterize Christianity as a *superstitio* (see chap. 4).

218. Barrett, *Acts*, 2.1167, is right to caution against Festus's use of μανία as pointing to "philosophic madness." It may well be that those familiar with the charge often thrown at Cynics would hear in Festus's exclamation a resonance with criticism of philosophers. Abraham J. Malherbe, "Not in a Corner": Early Christian Apologetic in Acts 26:26," *The Second Century* 5 (1985/86): 193–210, for example, argues forcefully for this position (esp. 206–7). Malherbe's larger point, that Luke here presents Paul as a legitimate "public" philosopher as a way to respond to then-current pagan criticisms of Christianity, works well as a tool for investigation if one presupposes the philosophical problem Malherbe addresses. And perhaps such a presupposition does in fact help us to dig more deeply and uncover yet another layer of Luke's narrative. But the foreground of the text, so to speak, seems indisputably to be about the *legal-political* issues involved in Paul's trial (the Roman and Jewish νόμος, στάσις, *maiestas*, the death penalty, and the like). My interpretive suggestion is thus that Festus does not so much accuse Paul of being Cynic-like as he does express his astonishment and incomprehension: Paul's speech may work well as an exposition of his Pharisaic learning, but as a forensic defense speech to avoid the charge of *maiestas* and subsequent death, the speech is sheer nonsense. Festus does not, that is, have the framework to understand how this narrative of salvation constitutes a genuine *apologia*.

219. See Jos., *BJ*, 2.217; *AJ*, 20.145; cf. Juvenal, *Sat.* 6.156–60, who writes of Agrippa and Berenice when speaking of a legendary diamond whose "value was enhanced by Berenice's finger." This diamond "was once given by the barbarian Agrippa to his incestuous sister to wear, in the place where barefooted kings keep the Sabbath as their feast day and their traditional mercy is kind to elderly pigs."

220. For an exegetical study that emphasizes the typology of Paul and Jesus at this point in the Acts narrative, see Robert F. O'Toole, *Acts 26: The Christological Climax of Paul's Defense (Ac 22:1–26:32)* (Rome: Biblical Institute, 1978). Occasionally NT scholars worry about the precision of the typology (see, e.g., Skinner, *Locating Paul*, 159–60, who issues several cautions against "pushing the notion of parallels too far"). But in practice this worry does not do much more than point to the importance of the typology itself.

221. On the significance of this use of κύριος for the Roman Emperor, see C. Kavin Rowe, "Luke–Acts and the Imperial Cult: A Way through the Conundrum?" *JSNT* 27 (2005): 279–300. In addition, we should remark that in juxtaposing κύριος to βασιλεύς, Festus keeps clear the power relations of the "client King" and Rome. King Agrippa, too, has a κύριος.

222. See, for example, Apuleius, *Met.*, 2.21.

223. Barrett's clever translation of the singular τὸ δωδεκάφυλον (*Acts*, 2.1152).

224. We shall return to this theme in the next chapter.

225. For example, as Millar, "The Emperor, the Senate and the Provinces," 157–58, notes, the one imperial *mandatum* that Pliny incorporated into the edict issued upon his

arrival in Bithynia was that forbidding the formation of *hetairiae*. Robert Louis Wilken, *The Christians as the Romans Saw Them*, 2nd ed. (New Haven, CT: Yale University Press, 2003), 12–47, is particularly clear and concise on the political issues that surround the perception of Christianity as a "society," "club," "association," and so forth.

226. Malherbe, "Not in a Corner," 210, also notes the emphasis in Luke's presentation upon the "public character of the church."

227. The sentence resists entirely felicitous translation. It is not without good reason that mss. *E Ψ* et al. substitute γενέσθαι for ποιῆσαι. On Χριστιανός in Acts, see the discussion in chapter 4; for an overview of the term, see David G. Horrell, "The Label Χριστιανός: 1 Peter 4:16 and the Formation of Christian Identity," *JBL* 126 (2007): 361–81. Paul's response to Agrippa has drawn much attention because of the phrase παρεκτὸς τῶν δεσμῶν, which, on a certain reading of how Paul was chained, appears to stand in contradiction to 26:1 where Paul stretches out his hand (see Haenchen, *Acts*, 682, for example). But as Skinner, *Locating Paul*, 139–41, 148 n. 106, has pointed out, it is by no means clear that δεσμός here means chain rather than simply "imprisonment." Moreover, Luke does not give the precise manner in which Paul was chained.

228. It is for this reason that Conzelmann's strange assertion that the trial before Festus "concerns the specific charge against Paul, and not the general legal status of Christianity" (*Acts*, 203) is ultimately to be rejected. Moreover, literarily speaking, that the character Paul is meant to represent Christianity has long been known and is beyond dispute. For a recent book that works with this feature of Acts, see Alexandru Neagoe, *The Trial of the Gospel*. See chap. 4 of the present book for a discussion of the narrative significance of the word "Christian" in Acts.

229. Garnsey, "The *Lex Iulia* and Appeal Under the Empire," 184. Garnsey's "half-truth" remark pertains to the process of appeal. Agrippa's remark is half-true, that is, because Festus had the authority to deny Paul's appeal. This is, however, a somewhat different question than that of the interpretive function of the statement at this point in the Acts story.

230. Walaskay, *Acts*, 15.

231. Tajra, *The Trial of St. Paul*, 201.

232. Heusler, *Kapitalprozesse*, 262.

233. O'Toole, "Luke's Position on Politics and Society," 8.

234. Heusler, *Kapitalprozesse*, 266.

235. See Carl Schmitt, *Political Theology: Four Chapters on the Concept of Sovereignty*, trans. George Schwab (Chicago: University of Chicago Press, 1985).

236. That the way in which "the state itself" operates is through its officials scarcely needs comment. Here, too, lies the ultimate ground for Luke's careful attention to matters of Roman law: Luke's presentation of the state's findings could appear realistic only if it follows the legal path the state itself would (or did) follow. Perhaps it is overstated, but it is not without reason that Walter Radl, *Paulus und Jesus im lukanischen Doppelwerk* (Frankfurt: Peter Lang, 1975), 336 n. 4, says "Statt Arzt könnte Lukas eher Jurist gewesen sein" (cited also—as the last line of the book—in Heusler, *Kapitalprozesse*, 266).

237. See, for example, the discussion in Daniel Marguerat, "The End of Acts (28.16–31) and the Rhetoric of Silence," in *Rhetoric and the New Testament: Essays from*

the 1992 Heidelberg Conference, eds. Stanley E. Porter and Thomas H. Olbricht, JSNTSup 90 (Sheffield: JSOT Press, 1993), 74–89.

238. See Marguerat, "The End of Acts," 74–89; and esp. Talbert, *Reading Acts*, 231. In *The Sense of an Ending: Studies in the Theory of Fiction* (Oxford: Oxford University Press, 1966), literary critic Frank Kermode argues that the need to supply endings is actually a kind of interpretive defect, one which cannot handle openness but must instead opt for "closure." But of course to be good readers of *Acts*, we must follow the clues of that work, which point the reader toward completing the ending.

239. For a brief discussion of a Pauline mission to Spain, see Philip Towner, *The Letters to Timothy and Titus* (Grand Rapids, MI: Eerdmans, 2006), 11–12.

240. Lest it need pointing out: the point of constructing a literary typology is not to achieve a one-to-one correspondence but to suggest an outgrowth in the life of Paul of what Jesus was all about. On Luke as an emphatically un-wooden writer, see Rowe, *Early Narrative Christology*, 32–34; 117–21; 123–27.

241. Talbert, *Reading Acts*, 231; cf., in his own way, Cadbury, "Roman Law and the Trial of St. Paul," *Beginnings* 5.338. Conzelmann, *Theology of St. Luke*, 144, could hardly be wider of the literary mark: "In the end it is confidence in the justice of the Emperor that forms the great climax of the narrative. There is no suggestion whatever of any weakening of this confidence" (cf. Radl, *Paulus und Jesus*, esp. 344). Talbert goes on to suggest that the reader would also attribute Paul's death to corrupt Roman officials. If Jews were involved "it would probably have been those from the Aegean basin." In any event, Paul's death "was not due to Roman Jewry." That the reader is to attribute Paul's death to Roman officials seems as likely as not in light of Pilate's role in Jesus's death; yet Felix, as corrupt as he was, still knew Paul could not be killed then and there. That the Jewish leadership would be involved seems also to be required of the reader, at least of an ancient one aware of the legal matters involved. As mentioned earlier, the accusers' absence from the trial could have considerable negative consequences. By the time we reach the end of Acts, the accusers are no longer simply the Jews from Asia but now include the Jerusalem leadership, which could easily appear in Rome either in the person of their lawyer or through another representative. How King Agrippa II would fit into this scenario is a complicated and, in my view, ultimately unanswerable question. Finally, on a somewhat different note, that Eusebius, Tertullian, and others (e.g., the *Acts of Paul* and *Acts of Peter*) know a tradition in which Paul was beheaded may be significant inasmuch as beheading was the legally accepted punishment for Roman *cives* convicted of *maiestas*. Such a tradition in itself obviously does not mean that Paul was convicted; he may well have still been found innocent (as was Jesus). But it is intriguing for the possible connection with Paul's status as a Roman citizen, something that plays a significant role in the Acts narrative.

CHAPTER 4

1. On these three practices as "core practices," see below.

2. Acts 17:2 ("three sabbaths"). The Thessalonian correspondence may presuppose a much longer stay.

3. Plutarch, *Aem.*, 38: "Appius saw Scipio rushing into the agora attended by me who were of low birth and had lately been slaves, but who were frequenters of the agora and able to gather a mob and force all issues by means of solicitations and shouting." Cf. Demosthenes, *De Cor.*, 18.127 (269), cited in chap. 2.

4. A. N. Sherwin-White, *Roman Society and Roman Law in the New Testament*, (Oxford: Clarendon Press, 1963), 96. The free city status did not mean, however, that the Romans did not interfere (see note directly following).

5. A. H. M. Jones, *The Greek City from Alexander to Justinian*, for example, 132: "the scope for Roman interference was enormous." Yet, as Jones also notes, even though the number of free cities declined in the imperial period, the "constitutional status of free cities was on the whole more scrupulously observed under the principate than it had been under the republic, when governors had ridden roughshod over their privileges" (ibid.).

6. Cf. Sherwin-White, *Roman Society and Roman Law*, 96: "Acts is particular and well informed about Thessalonica." Many other commentators (e.g., C. K. Barrett, *Acts*, 2 vols. [London, T. & T. Clark, 1994/1998], 2.807) also note Luke's accuracy, especially in relation to his term πολιτάρχαι. As noted in relation to the Ephesus material in particular, Luke is a master at creating "Lokalkolorit."

7. Cf. the remark of Winfried Elliger, *Paulus in Griechenland: Philippi, Thessaloniki, Athen, Korinth* (Stuttgart: Katholisches Bibelwerk, 1987), 93: "Die wichtigste Aufgabe dieser Beamten war die Rechtsprechung."

8. Sherwin-White, *Roman Society and Roman Law*, 96. Cf. F. F. Bruce, *The Acts of the Apostles: The Greek Text with Introduction and Commentary* (London, Tyndale, 1951), 326.

9. Barrett, *Acts*, 2.814. Cf. Conzelmann, *Acts of the Apostles*, (Philadelphia, Fortress, 1987), 135, who takes δῆμος here to be synonymous with ὄχλος.

10. Though of course the assembly is an unlawful one.

11. Why Jason and the others were not lynched in Paul's and Silas' place is not revealed; yet we may reasonably surmise that being a citizen of Thessalonica had at least this advantage (Jason's name is known to the attackers and perhaps even to the magistrates, v. 7). Ernst Haenchen, *Acts: A Commentary* (Philadelphia: Westminster, 1971), 506, states that the Christians are "accidentally met." This statement appears incorrect in light of the fact that the accusers know Jason is the host of the Christians— and it is to his house that they go.

12. Sherwin-White, *Roman Society and Roman Law*, 96. Whether Luke means for his readers to assume that Jason and the others were *peregrini* or Roman citizens is not evident from the narrative. But the very fact that Jason and the Christians are hauled before the magistrates suggests that they are likely provincials.

13. See Sherwin-White, *Roman Society and Roman Law*, 95, and the discussion there of the practice of *satis accipere/dare* that is reflected here in Acts 17:9 (λαβόντες τὸ ἱκανόν). Cf. Bruce, *Acts of the Apostles* (Greek text), 327. The giving of security hardly means, however, that the host is out of danger. Paulus the Jurist, *Sent.*, 5.4, would later put the main threat into a legal formula: "Those who harbor the aggressors [specifically, a crowd that is responsible for assault and robbery] are punished with the same penalty as the robbers [i.e., death]."

14. Cf. Jacob Jervell, *Die Apostelgeschichte* (Göttingen: Vandenhoeck & Ruprecht, 1998), 435, who notes the accusers' skillful use of the tumult before the city authorities. Talbert, *Reading Acts*, 149, notes the deep irony of the scene.

15. Sherwin-White, *Roman Society and Roman Law*, 103. Cf. his earlier remark that the charges are "somewhat obscure, and possibly garbled" (96). For a criticism of Sherwin-White's position, see E. A. Judge, "The Decrees of Caesar at Thessalonica," *RTR* 30/1 (1971): 1–7.

16. Moreover, as will be seen, the charges actually do make good sense historically.

17. Even among those commentators who are interested in separating older material (sources/tradition) from Lukan formulation, the point is frequently made that the scene in Thessalonica appears to be a Lukan construction. See, for example, Rudolf Pesch, *Die Apostelgeschichte*, 2 vols. (Neukirchener-Vluyn: Neukirchener Verlag, 1986), 2.120.

18. Sherwin-White, *Roman Society and Roman Law*, 103.

19. So, too, Barrett, *Acts*, 2.816. For an essay that reads "upside down" in relation to more traditionally Jewish concerns (Torah, purity, etc.), see Jerome H. Neyrey, "The Symbolic Universe of Luke-Acts: 'They Turn the World Upside Down,'" in *The Social World of Luke–Acts: Models for Interpretation*, ed. idem (Peabody, MA: Hendrickson, 1991), 271–304. Neyrey's essay is commendable for its recognition that the "doctrine of God" is bound up with Luke's social construals (296–9), but the literary context of Acts 17:1–9, which presses for a more specific relation to Roman law, is by and large ignored.

20. Cf. Barrett, *Acts*, 2.815. This important intranarrative point is overlooked by Justin Hardin, "Decrees and Drachmas at Thessalonica: An Illegal Assembly in Jason's House (Acts 17.1–10a)," *NTS* 52 (1996): 29–49. At times, Hardin's essay also stretches the limits of Graeco-Roman evidence (e.g., in drawing on a text from a municipality in Spain) but as a whole, it adds another important layer to the passage: the Christians in Thessalonica may well have been seen as an illegal political club ("assembly"). At one point (n. 61), Hardin seems to recognize that this fact only strengthens the charge of sedition—the organizing content of the club is what makes it politically problematic in the first place (Jesus is King)—but he then retreats from his observation into historical speculation on matters about which neither Acts nor 1 and 2 Thessalonians have much to say.

21. See chap. 3 for a discussion of the charges and the citation of Claudius' letter.

22. Barrett, *Acts*, 2.8.15.

23. Judge, "The Decrees of Caesar," 1.

24. See esp. 1 Thess 4:2–3; 2 Thess 2:3; 4:8.

25. Paulus, *Sent.*, 5.21.3 (trans. Scott).

26. The point here is not to challenge Judge's project of historical reconstruction—that is, using 1 and 2 Thessalonians to explain Acts—as it is to note that nothing whatever is said in the Acts text about predictions, diviners, and so forth.

27. Judge, "The Decrees of Caesar," 5–7.

28. The Cypriot inscription does not actually say anything about the local magistrates administering the oath, but it is as clear an example of a loyalty oath to

the Roman emperor (Tiberius) as one could hope to find. Judge must interpret the inscription from Cyprus as the kind of thing the magistrates from Samos were to administer. Cf. Karl P. Donfried, "The Cults of Thessalonica and the Thessalonian Correspondence," *NTS* 31 (1985): 336–56 (esp. 343–44). On imperial oaths, see Franz Bömer, "Der Eid beim Genius des Kaisers," *Athanaeum* 44 (1966): 77–133; and Stefan Weinstock, "Treueid und Kaiserkult," in *Mitteilungen des Deutschen Archäologischen Instituts: Athenische Abteilung* 77 (Berlin: Gebr. Mann Verlag, 1962), 306–27.

29. Judge, "The Decrees of Caesar," 7, worries that oaths would not have been considered "decrees." This is semantic quibbling. As both Luke and Josephus show elsewhere, one can use δόγματα to refer both to empire-wide *edicta* (see Luke 2:1, for example) and to more local decrees that affect particular cities (see list of decrees in Jos., *AJ*, 14). Barrett, *Acts*, 2.815, asserts that imperial decrees would not have been binding on a *civitas libera* (referring to Sherwin-White, *Roman Society and Roman Law*, 96, who notes that the court of Thessalonica was technically not under direct Roman jurisdiction). Once again, the brushstroke is too broad. Despite the legal terminology or technical niceties of being a free city, certain things were simply not allowed by Rome: rebellion and sedition, for example, or—to come directly to the text in question— setting up a rival to the imperial throne that would itself lead to sedition. Free cities did not have the kind of jurisdiction that would allow them to sanction such action. In truth, the "court" of the free cities (i.e., the aristocracy), as in any other city, was expected to be Rome's power broker and keep things in order. The consequences of not doing so were severe. This is, incidentally, why the accusers do not in practice need to go directly to the proconsul for charges of treason or sedition. Moreover, if Donfried is correct about the local magistrates' role in administering the oath of loyalty to the emperor (see previous note), it would also be reasonable to assume that they played a role in seeing that it was upheld. When Donfried asserts, therefore, that the charges cannot be treason because treason "was founded on public law, not Caesarian decree" (here citing Sherwin-White), he grants too much to Sherwin-White's observations and forces an otherwise readable text into an unaccommodating legal grid. Neither philological nor jurisprudential nor exegetical concerns cause difficulty for what the Acts text presents rather clearly. What else other than "traitor"— or some version thereof—would one call a person who violated the oath of loyalty to the emperor by proclaiming another King?

30. The Greek after all is one continuous sentence. Cf. Barrett, *Acts*, 2.816: "λέγοντες is probably to be taken as explanatory of πράσσουσιν."

31. Conzelmann, *Acts*, 135.

32. See esp. the well-known passage from book 2.52: "Now after these two hundred and forty years of monarchy... when Tarquinius had been banished, the title of rex came to be as bitterly hated by the Romans as it had been longingly desired after the death, or rather departure, of Romulus. Hence, just as then they could not bear to be without a king, so now, after the banishment of Tarquinius, they could not bear even to hear the title of rex mentioned" (LCL trans.). Cf. the report of the popularity of Caesar's repeated refusal to be βασιλεύς in Plutarch, *Caes.*, 60–2.

33. Millar, *The Emperor in the Roman World*, 613.

34. We might recall Josephus' statement in *C. Ap.* 2.134: "[W]hen war had been declared by the Romans on all the monarchs of the world, our kings alone, by reason of their fidelity, remained their allies and friends."

35. For a study of the phenomenon of "client kingship" during the republic and principate (through the Severans), see David Braund, *Rome and the Friendly King: The Character of Client Kingship* (New York: St. Martin's Press, 1984). As Braund notes, with the change from republic to empire, the number of kings was obviously reduced since—through a variety of means—kingdoms became provinces (and were thus under the authority of the proconsuls/legates). Yet he also cautions against the simplistic view that the phenomenon of client kings ceased to exist altogether, which it did not (esp. 187–8). Our main evidence for how kingship worked during the early empire is of course the situation in Palestine.

36. Conzelmann, *Acts*, 135. For the text, see Herbert Musurillo, *Acts of the Pagan Martyrs*, vol. 1 (Oxford: Oxford University Press, 2000), 18–19, recension A, col. 3, ln. 5. Musurillo translates βασιλεύς as "emperor" (25).

37. See Winfried Elliger, *Paulus in Griechenland*, 96 n. 27.

38. Cf. from somewhat later, Herodian, *History of the Empire*, 2.4.4.

39. Dio Chrysostom, *Or.*, 1–4 and 62. Due to its brevity and style, *Or.*, 62 is harder to see as a work actually composed for delivery to Trajan. The translator/editor of the LCL edition is right also to note that Dio mentions that he used to repeat to others his speeches before the emperor and, therefore, that it is not unreasonable to surmise that *Or.* 62 is an excerpt of a speech.

40. Dio Chrysostom, *Or.* 3.134–5 (the other king—the flute player—is Ptolemy "Auletes").

41. See Erwin R. Goodenough, "The Political Philosophy of Hellenistic Kingship," *Yale Classical Studies* 1 (1928): 55–102.

42. Seneca, *De Clem.*, 1.4.1, citing Virgil, *Georg.*, 4.212: *Rege incolumi mens omnibus una; amisso rupere fidem* (the translation here is a slight alteration of that given by Fairclough and Gould in the LCL edition of the *Georgics*). The image of the "king" bee was frequently employed in the ancient world—obviously they did not know it was the queen bee!

43. Millar, *The Emperor in the Roman World*, 615. Though we might recall Ovid, *Pont.*, 1.8.21, which speaks of Augustus as "the bravest *rex* of our time."

44. Stefan Weinstock, *Divus Julius* (Oxford: Clarendon Press, 1971), esp. 13, "Kingship and Divinity" (see 40–53 on the present statue). The citation derives from the review of Weinstock's book by A. H. McDonald, "Caesar's Ruler Cult?" *Classical Review* 26/2 (1976): 222–5 (223). Among many other interesting pieces of evidence Weinstock produces, it is worth mentioning that Caesar's throne was "without republican precedent and against tradition: it is clear that it...was to be a regal privilege" (273). On this topic, see also the interesting article by Elizabeth Rawson, "Caesar's Heritage: Hellenistic Kings and Their Roman Equals," *JRS* 65 (1975): 148–59 and Josephus, *BJ*, 3.350, who writes of "the destinies of the Roman kings" (τὰ περὶ τοὺς Ῥωμαίων βασιλεῖς ἐσόμενα).

45. Josephus, *BJ*, 2.434.

46. Josephus, *BJ*, 7.29–31. For a discussion of Simon bar Giora as "king," see Horsley, *Bandits, Prophets, and Messiahs*, 119–27.

47. Millar, *The Emperor in the Roman World*, 615.

48. So, rightly, Bruce, *Acts* (Greek text), 327.

49. Judge, "The Decrees of Caesar," 1. Cf. Donfried, "The Cults of Thessalonica and the Thessalonian Correspondence," esp. 343.

50. Given the official imperial policy of not taking the title *rex*, we should probably not expect such a decree to turn up. We do, however, have the intriguing text in John 19:15: "We have no βασιλεύς except Caesar." It should not be controversial, however, to observe that if the Romans did not have official *edicta* saying "no King other than Caesar," this was at least basic to the notion of Roman law, of treason, of border control, and so forth.

51. See, for example, Jervell, *Apostelgeschichte*, 435, or, to take another prominent example, Wayne Meeks, *The Origins of Christian Morality*, 168: "As the author of Acts recalled, Christians were sometimes accused of 'acting contrary to the decrees of Caesar and saying that there is another king, Jesus' (17:7). However, that author is at pains to show that the accusation was really false; the Christians were not subversive at all."

52. Mark 11:9 (though v. 10 does speak about the coming kingdom of our father David—and this might perhaps be what Luke transposes as "King"); cf. Matthew 21:9. If Luke also knew Matthew's text, he ignores that version, too. John 12:12 is similar to Luke, though John even adds "of Israel" ("blessed is the one who comes in the name of the Lord, [even] the King of Israel").

53. Bruce, *Acts* (Greek text), 327.

54. Barrett, *Acts*, 2.808.

55. Eusebius, *Eccl. Hist.*, 3.20 (cited also in Talbert, *Reading Acts*, 149).

56. Ibid. This stands in stark contrast to a Christian text such as the Acts of Paul (ca. AD 200), for example, whose drama hinges on the fact that the Emperor Nero interprets Jesus's kingship as a direct "royal" challenge. The dialogue makes clear that Nero perceives himself to be profoundly threatened by the disciples of the "King of Ages"—indeed, he has them tortured and subsequently executed.

57. Justin Martyr, *Apol.* 11. For the critical edition, see Miroslav Marcovich, *Iustini Martyris Apologiae pro Christianis*, Patristische Texte und Studien 38 (Berlin: Walter de Gruyter, 1994).

58. Cf. n. 226 in chap 3.

59. This approach has a long pedigree in Lukan studies. To take only one well-known example, see Helmut Flender, *St. Luke: Theologian of Redemptive History* (Philadelphia: Fortress, 1967).

60. Whether σχολή is "lecture hall" or "building" or simply "gathering" is not certain (see Barrett, *Acts*, 2.904–5). I include it here for good measure.

61. Moreover, as we shall see, other aspects of church life in Acts are traceable to one or more of these three more basic matters. Baptism and the Eucharist, for example, are markers of the people set apart, even as they attest to the Lordship of Jesus and exist as church practices from place to place because of the traveling missionaries. Care for the widows is an economic outworking of the character of humility and service that constitutes what it means to be Lord. And so on.

62. Cf. the redistribution of property in Acts 4 and 5 (esp. Ananias and Saphira) and in Qumran (e.g., 1 QS 6.24–5).

63. On this matter, see Charles Taylor, *A Secular Age* (Cambridge, MA: Harvard University Press, 2007).

64. Thus the focus here is not on early Christian practice in abstraction from the narrative of Acts—as best as we can reconstruct it historically from all available sources—but practice according to the narrative of Acts. Of course knowing something about the former can help us to see the more distinctive features of the latter, but the focus of our vision nevertheless remains on the latter. Speaking of narrativized practices should indicate that I think Alasdair MacIntyre's influential description of practices in *After Virtue*, 3rd ed. (Notre Dame, IN: University of Notre Dame Press, 2007), esp. 187–203, needs serious qualification at two important points: (1) practices are not self-authenticating; they are always embedded within a wider narrative that provides the telos of the practice—and therefore its meaning and justification; (2) institutions are not opposed to practices but in fact engage in them. It is of considerable significance, to put the points in relation to this study, that Acts is a narrative of the church. The focus on practices is not without precedent in New Testament or ancient historical scholarship. See, for example, Nock's section on "The Practice of Christianity" in *Early Gentile Christianity and Its Hellenistic Background* (New York: Harper and Row, 1964).

65. See Rowe, *Early Narrative Christology: The Lord in the Gospel of Luke*.

66. "Luke–Acts and the Imperial Cult: A Way through the Conundrum?" *JSNT* 27 (2005): 279–300. There is, however, much more to be said about this passage, as Justin R. Howell has amply demonstrated in his recent piece "The Imperial Authority and Benefaction of Centurions and Acts 10.34–43: A Response to C. Kavin Rowe," *JSNT* 31 (2008): 25–51. While Howell's piece may not take sufficient account of the many difficulties involved in trying to locate Acts in a specific place on a Mediterranean map, it does make multiple important observations to which we should attend. His close and careful analysis develops considerably my initial suggestion that this passage in Acts in particular would have been heard in connection with the imperial cult/Roman religio-political claims.

67. Cf. Paul's preaching in Damascus: "and [he went] immediately into the synagogues and preached Jesus—this one is the Son of God!" (9:20: ἐκήρυσσεν τὸν Ἰησοῦν ὅτι οὗτός ἐστιν ὁ υἱὸς τοῦ θεοῦ, taking ὅτι here as a marker of direct speech).

68. W. H. Roscher, *Ausführliches Lexikon der griechischen und römischen Mythologie*, II/1, 1755–69.

69. It is worth noting that Luke himself does not employ κύριος for any pagan divinity.

70. In terms of minor officials that had contact with imperial administration, one could think of Isidorus, gymnasiarch in Alexandria during the reign of Claudius, who in his trial addresses the emperor as κύριέ μου Καῖσαρ. See Damascius, *Isid.*, Rec. A, col. ii, ln. 10; Rec. B, col. I, ln. 17 [and supplied in ln. 6], in Musurillo, *Acts of the Pagan Martyrs*, 18–26 (Isidorus was of course executed). Interestingly, Claudius is also referred to as Βασιλεύς (Rec. A, ln. 5).

71. Ditt., Syll³ II.814, lns. 30–1.

72. Of course Lucan may here simply be reflecting the practice of the mid-first century rather than a habitual manner of referring to Caesar and/or Pompey the Great. Inasmuch as Acts was written after Nero's reign, however, this point is immaterial to our reading of Acts.

73. *Off.*, 3.83: Speaking of Julius Caesar, Cicero says, "Behold, here you have a man who was ambitious to be King [*rex*] of the Roman People and Lord of the whole world, and he achieved it!"

74. Polybius was the first to see that Roman domination amounted to "universal" rule. See esp. the opening of his famous work: "For who is so worthless or indolent as not to wish to know by what means and under system of polity the Romans in less than fifty-three years have succeeded in subjecting almost all things in the world to their sole dominion—a thing unique in history (*Hist.*, 1.1.5, LCL altered; cf. 1.63.9 on Roman "universal hegemony"). On this point, see Susan P. Mattern, *Rome and the Enemy: Imperial Strategy in the Principate* (Berkeley: University of California Press, 1999), 212.

75. One should not lightly express puzzlement at the findings of a scholar such as Nock. Yet in light of the contrast illustrated above, it remains puzzling how he could say "it may be doubted whether there is in the use of Kyrios any conscious contrast or *anything that would be felt as such* between Jesus and the Emperor" (*Early Gentile Christianity*, 34; emphasis added).

76. Price, *Rituals and Power*, 181–3.

77. Steven J. Friesen, *Imperial Cults and the Apocalypse of John: Reading Revelation in the Ruins* (New York: Oxford University Press, 2001), 62.

78. For a concise treatment of how the Forum of Augustus articulated his relation to the gods—including Mars Ultor—see Mary Beard et al. *Religions of Rome*, 2 vols. (Cambridge: Cambridge University Press, 1998), 1.198–201; 2.80. The emperor was of course also associated with other gods, especially Jupiter. Clauss is right to say that it is impossible—even in such a thorough study as his—to list all the gods with whom the emperor was associated in practice ("Kaiser und Gott," 247).

79. Mattern, *Rome and the Enemy*, xii. Indeed, in her final chapter, which focuses on Roman "strategy"—especially in its psychological form—in and after the Punic wars, Mattern concludes that with respect to Roman imperialism, "we find a system that is not describable in terms of aggression and defense as easily as it is described in terms of insult and revenge, terror and deference" (222).

80. This has long been recognized. See, for example, Klaus Wengst, *Pax Romana and the Peace of Jesus Christ* (Philadelphia: Fortress, 1987).

81. Tacitus, *Agr.*, 30 (LCL, altered). Calgacus' reference to "the contamination of dominatio" occurs just prior to the section of his speech cited above.

82. That Augustus' accomplishments were spread publicly in the empire is without doubt, though the inscriptional remains are less than we would desire. See the concise discussion by Frederick W. Shipley in the LCL, 332–340.

83. *Et superos quid prodest poscere finem? Cum domino pax ista venit. Duc, Roma, malorum, Continuam seriem clademque in tempora multa, Extrahe, civili tantum iam libera*

bello (Lucan, *Phar.*, 1.669–72). This translation owes more to Quint than to the LCL or Leigh.

84. As Michael Ginsburg put it in his review of Syme's famous book on the Roman revolution, "[w]hen peace came, it was the peace of despotism" (*American Historical Review* 46 [1940]: 106–8, 108).

85. See, for example, David Quint, *Epic and Empire: Politics and Generic Form from Virgil to Milton* (Princeton, NJ: Princeton University Press, 1993), 147–8, and, Matthew Leigh, *Lucan: Spectacle and Engagement* (New York: Oxford University Press, 1997), 26.

86. Sheldon S. Wolin, *Politics and Vision: Continuity and Innovation in Western Political Thought*, expanded edition (Princeton, NJ: Princeton University Press, 2004), 82.

87. These are obviously not the only problems in the study of the divinity of the Roman emperor, but they are among those that have received significant attention in much of the recent literature.

88. "Power," as Price learned from Foucault, is never uni-directional but is always and ever something inherently relational.

89. Clifford Ando, *Imperial Ideology and Provincial Loyalty in the Roman Empire* (Berkeley: University of California Press, 2000), 407. Ando's point is of course not to deny that many people worshipped Zeus, for example, or Apollo, but simply to point to the fact that to an unprecedented degree the emperor served in many ways as the focal point of an entire culture irrespective of the profound differences in local knowledge, religious praxis, city politics, and so on. To speak of the theological reading of the emperor is not, however, to return to an older mode of analysis wherein the focus was on the typical pagan's religious "thoughts" or "emotions" or "feelings"—in short, how the typical pagan experienced the emperor in a romantic or religious sense. Price, among others, has been rightly critical of an earlier generation of scholars (Dodds, Nock, et al.) who unwittingly betray the influence of Liberal Protestant conceptions about "religion."

90. See, for example, Justin Meggitt, "Taking the Emperor's Clothes Seriously: The New Testament and the Roman Emperor," in *The Quest for Wisdom: Essays in Honour of Philip Budd*, ed. Christine E. Joynes (Cambridge: Orchard Academic, 2002) 143–68: "[I]n crude terms we can say that the cult, although varying significantly in its form over time, and from location to location, claimed that the emperors, as rulers and benefactors of the world, were worthy of worship" (144). As Meggitt also notes, the "buildings and statues were not static but dynamic in the consciousness of the inhabitants of the first-century world" (147). In my judgment, Meggitt's article—unknown to me until recently—is the best concise overview written by a NT scholar of the importance of the Roman emperor for interpreting the NT.

91. Price, "Gods and Emperors: The Greek Language of the Roman Imperial Cult," *JHS* 104 (1984): 79–93, notes that, perhaps better than anything else, the practice of simultaneous prayer to and on behalf of the emperor captures well the ambiguity that attended his divinity (92–4).

92. The inscription can be found in *IGR* 4.145. The translation is Price's (*Rituals and Power*, 244).

93. For example, Price, *Rituals and Power*, 220; and idem, "Gods and Emperors." Somewhat against the scholarly stream, Ittai Gradel, *Emperor Worship and Roman Religion* (Oxford: Clarendon Press, 2002), argues for the primary importance of *divus* (see his chap. 3).

94. See, for example, the discussion of *deus* and *divus* in Gradel, *Emperor Worship and Roman Religion*, 54–72.

95. See the list of inscriptions in Appendix 3 "Gottheiten als divi," in Clauss, *Kaiser und Gott*, 522.

96. *Pan.*, 94.1–5.

97. See the still important article of Kenneth Scott, "Emperor Worship in Ovid," *Transactions and Proceedings of the American Philological Association* 61 (1930), 43–69.

98. Even in Vespasian's famous joke about his impending death—"Woe is me. I think I'm turning into a god!"—Suetonius makes use of *deus* where, in accordance with "official" usage, we would naturally expect *divus* (*Vae . . . puto deus fio*). Of course, these are hardly Vespasian's *ipsissima verba*. But the use of *deus* is not for that reason any less significant for the point made here (*Vesp.*, 33).

99. As Weinstock, *Divus Iulius*, 391, notes, even Julius Caesar was called *Deus Invictus* during his lifetime.

100. See, e.g., Price, *Rituals and Power*, 232–3.

101. Suetonius, *Dom.*, 13. There is of course some debate about Domitian's willingness to allow these terms. On this point see Rowe, "Luke–Acts and the Imperial Cult," 292–3, n. 49. Among other things, we should not forget the story in Cassius Dio, *Hist. Rom.*, 67.13.4, where a conspirator against Domitian "saved his life in a remarkable way. When he was on the point of being condemned, he begged that he might speak to the emperor in private, and thereupon did obeisance before him [προσκυνήσας αὐτῷ]" and repeatedly "called him δεσπότης and θεός (terms that were already being applied to him by others)."

102. Cf. *P. Oxy* 1143 (ca. AD 1), which speaks of a sacrifice and libation for the Emperor Augustus, "God and Lord" (ὑπὲρ τοῦ θεοῦ καὶ κυρίου αὐτοκράτορος). See the brief discussion by Nock in Colin Roberts, Theodore C. Skeat, and Arthur Darby Nock, "The Gild of Zeus Hypsistos," *HTR* 29 (1936): 39–88 (50). The significance of the Egyptian origin of this (and other) papyrus should not be overlooked, of course, but neither should the similarity to later imperial language. Lest it go unremarked, Zeus, too, was addressed as "God and Lord" and even "God and Lord, King" (see ln. 10 of *P. Lond* 2710, discussed by Nock in the same article).

103. Agamben, *State of Exception*, 60. By coupling Schmitt with Agamben, I do not intend to minimize the differences between them. In fact, much of Agamben's *State of Exception* is a quarrel with Schmitt. Yet they both recognize that notions of ultimate authority—such as that involved with the Roman emperor, for example— trade inescapably on theological or metaphysical conceptions of God/the divine, and so forth. One might also recall Hobbes' naming of the absolute sovereign as "an earthly God." On the "theological" vision of Hobbes' Leviathan, see recently Mark Lilla's stimulating book, *The Stillborn God: Religion, Politics, and the Modern West* (New York: Knopf, 2007) here, 86–103. Sheldon Wolin, *Politics and Vision*, xviii, claims that the names "behemoth" and "leviathan" have (rather recently) become

anachronistic terms; that is, they no longer represent well the modes of power we see in postmodern politics in which the traditional role of the nation-state as the sole arbiter of power (violence) is increasingly dwindling in the face of global capitalism, terrorism, and so forth. For similar reflections on the changing role of the nation-state, see Philip Bobbitt, *Terror and Consent* (New York: Knopf, 2008). These arguments do not lessen the point made above, namely, that whatever mode of political being we adopt, it will inevitably trade heavily on theological conceptions and that those conceptions, when scrutinized, will offer up something like "God"—a justification for the particular mode of political being that is extrinsic to that mode itself—whenever questions of ultimate authority/sovereignty (even of "the people") are put to the test.

104. See, for example, Agamben's brilliant discussion of the ancient Roman practice of *iustitium* in *State of Exception*, esp. 41–51 and 60, 68–70.

105. Gradel, *Emperor Worship and Roman Religion*, 71–2, comes close to this point when he says that "absolute power entailed divinity and vice versa."

106. Price, *Rituals and Power*, 233. Note once again the importance of οὗτος in Acts 17:24.

107. See C. Kavin Rowe, "Romans 10:13: What Is the Name of the Lord?" *Horizons in Biblical Theology* 22/2 (2000): 135–173.

108. Precisely because it is explicitly marked as a citation of the OT!

109. Cf. Acts 2:20.

110. By translating προορώμην as "I saw," the RSV et al. obscure Luke's reading of the Psalm as prophecy (the point of the prefix προ–).

111. Perhaps looking ahead to the λέγει κύριος at the end of the citation.

112. On this point, see Rowe, *Early Narrative Christology*, esp. 202–7.

113. One could here easily recall the political context for the Barmen Declaration (Nazi Germany 1934). The work of Halbertal and Margalit—and, perhaps somewhat ironically, that of Carl Schmitt—helps us to understand why loosing the category of "idolatry" is a political no less than a theological mistake: it robs us of our ability to see the full depth of the problem of dictatorship/tyranny: it is a idolatrous challenge to God, and as such it will wreak havoc in the world. To be able to name political configurations as idolatry is to be able to get down to the bottom of illegitimate outworkings of human community.

114. See, for example, the argument of John Milbank, *Theology and Social Theory* (esp. 417).

115. Cassius Dio, *Hist. Rom.*, 44.49.2: ὁ εἰρηνοποιός of Julius Caesar.

116. Ulrich Mauser, *The Gospel of Peace: A Scriptural Message for Today's World* (Louisville, KY: Westminster John Knox, 1992). Among other solid treatments, see Willard M. Swartley, "Politics and Peace (Eirēnē) in Luke's Gospel," in *Political Issues in Luke-Acts*, eds. Richard J. Cassidy and Philip J. Scharper (Maryknoll, NY: Orbis Books, 1983), 18–37.

117. Mauser, *Gospel of Peace*, 46–50, 83–103 (here, 46).

118. Ibid., 46.

119. Ibid.

120. Ibid., 85. Thus, while I agree with Mauser about the necessity to read Luke–Acts in relation to the Pax Romana, I take Luke to be much more critical of this notion than Mauser does.

121. The linguistic connections to the rest of Acts and to the larger Mediterranean world should be obvious, but we shall list them for good measure: βασιλεῖς τῶν ἐθνῶν, κυριεύουσιν, ἐξουσιάζοντες, εὐεργέται, ἡγούμενος.

122. On the use of κύριος in parables to refer to God/Jesus in Luke's Gospel, see Rowe, *Early Narrative Christology*, 151–57.

123. Mauser, *Gospel of Peace*, 85, is right to say that for Luke both "the life on earth of Jesus of Nazareth and the life of his growing community" are "taken together...the history of Jesus Christ." It would indeed be difficult to formulate more precisely the ultimate theological unity of Luke and Acts. The quotation marks around Paul are not meant to argue against historicity so much as they are intended to draw the reader's attention to the symbolic or paradigmatic significance of the character Paul as Luke portrays him. Rather, that is, than simply thinking that Luke's picture of Paul is about Paul *simpliciter*, I want to suggest that Luke means for the readers to see their own Christian lives figured forth, even foreshadowed, in Paul's, even as they are meant to find this same element of readerly participation in the life of Jesus in the Gospel. Such is the larger point—or certainly at least part of it—of Luke's "typological" characterization (Jesus, Peter, Paul) noted long ago by no less a mind than that of Austin Farrer: "The Ministry in the New Testament," in *The Apostolic Ministry: Essays on the History and the Doctrine of the Episcopacy*, ed. Kenneth E. Kirk (New York: Morehouse-Gorham, 1946), 113–82.

124. For a concise treatment of this matter, see David G. Horrell, *1 Peter* (Edinburgh: T. & T. Clark, 2008), 45–60.

125. This topic is too large to treat here. I will note only one point that should not be overlooked. It is frequently assumed that Pliny is our earliest witness to the first real trials of Christians (outside of the NT). But this position can be held only by ignoring Pliny's first sentence in the body of his famous letter to Trajan: "I have never been present at a trial of Christians." This sentence, with its official language (*cognitio*), presupposes the practice of trials prior to Pliny's involvement. Whether these trials were strictly legal or not is disputed. For a brief discussion of these points, see Joachim Molthagen, *Der römische Staat und die Christen im zweiten und dritten Jahrhundert* (Göttingen: Vandenhoeck & Ruprecht, 1970), 14–15.

126. The classic study is Adolf von Harnack, *Die Mission und Ausbreitung des Christentums in den ersten drei Jahrhunderten* (Leipzig: Hinrichs, 1915).

127. See, for example, John North, "The *Development of Religious Pluralism*," in *The Jews among Pagans and Christians in the Roman Empire*, ed. Judith Lieu et al. (London: Routledge, 1992), 174–93: "It is easy to forget how unusual is [the Christian] enthusiasm to persuade outsiders into the fold and to slip into the assumption that some explanation must be offered for those who do not engage in the same recruiting" (187). It is also true, of course, that because of Christianity's dominance in the West we may have forgotten its original missionary impulse. See, for example, the opening remarks of Elizabeth Schüssler Fiorenza, "Miracles, Mission, and Apologetics: An Introduction,"

in *Aspects of Religious Propaganda in Judaism and Early Christianity,* ed. Elizabeth Schüssler Fiorenza (Notre Dame, IN: University of Notre Dame Press, 1976), 1–25.

128. Lane Fox, *Pagans and Christians,* 36. Cf. the description of Nock, *Conversion,* 93, who noted that pagan cults were "spread by the obscure activity of scattered individuals." One does occasionally find the language of "mission" in the scholarly literature. See, for example, Burkert, *Greek Religion,* 143, on Apollo: "a peculiarity of the Apollo cult is that it has two supra-regional centres, which exert nothing short of a missionary influence: Delos and Pytho-Delphi, sanctuaries dedicated specifically to the Delian or the Pythian god are found in many places, often even next to one another. Festal envoys were regularly dispatched from these to the central sanctuary... Delos, a small island without springs, was the central market and common sanctuary of the Cyclades; Delphi, with its out-of-the-way location, owed its popularity to the oracle." Yet it seems clear—not least from the rest of Burkert's discussion—that his description simply reflects the importance of Delos and Delphi as cultic sites rather than an actual mission in the name of the Delian god or the missionary activity of the Pythian priests.

129. It may be, too, that some would want to see a missionary movement in Alexander's effort to draw people to Abonuteichos. If Lucian is to be taken seriously, it seems that Alexander sent "oracle-mongers"—we might say evangelists in a loose sense—around to cities to prophesy their doom. He also posted various assistants in Rome and elsewhere to help keep him abreast of current events so that he might issue an oracle on target, as it were. And during the plague of Galen, he evidently sent around an oracle that could be found over many doors. In short, Alexander was remarkably adept at drumming up business for his site (*Alex.,* 36).

130. Meeks is typical: "Being or becoming religious in the Greco-Roman world did not entail either moral transformation or sectarian resocialization" (*The Origins of Christian Morality,* 28). Epicurus is perhaps our best chance at finding an exception, but—as we have seen in chap. 2—Epicureans themselves denied that their philosophy entailed the cessation of traditional forms of religious life. In this they may or may not have disagreed with the *populus.* Goodman, *Mission and Conversion,* 34–7, is concise on this matter.

131. Goodman, *Mission and Conversion,* for example, treats the philosophers under the heading of "educational mission," but this could be further subdivided or rightly contested. James Carleton Paget, "Jewish Proselytism at the Time of Christian Origins: Chimera or Reality?" *JSNT* 62 (1996): 65–103, for example, objects to Goodman's overall three-part definitional schema.

132. See, for example, the relevant portions of the three chapters in Louis H. Feldman, *Jew and Gentile in the Ancient World: Attitudes and Interactions from Alexander* (Princeton, NJ: Princeton University Press, 1993), that deal with the "Attractions of the Jews" (their "Antiquity," "Cardinal Virtues," and "Ideal Leader, Moses," respectively). Indeed, this is part of the deeper theological logic of Israel's role as a "light to the nations."

133. Goodman, *Mission and Conversion,* 32. Cf. North, "Development of Religions Pluralism," 187: the Christians "take on... from the very beginning a missionary character, quite unlike the traditions of any of their competitors at the time."

134. See, for example, Jervell, *Apostelgeschichte*, 380, who can speak of the similarity of Acts 14:8–20 to Jewish "Missionsliteratur," or 453, n. 274, where he debates Nauck's proposed threefold "Schema" that allegedly structured Jewish missionary literature. In terms of the Areopagus speech, we are—*selbstverständlich*—dealing with a *"jüdisch-hellenistischen Tradition"* that has a body of missionary literature out of which Luke has drawn (directly or indirectly?) several elements for Paul's speech (*"Lukas kennt Einzelheiten aus der Missionsliteratur dieser Kriese,"* 453). This is little more than speculation.

135. As Shaye J. D. Cohen, "Was Judaism in Antiquity a Missionary Religion?" in *Jewish Assimilation, Acculturation and Accommodation: Past Traditions, Current Issues and Future Prospects*, ed. Menachem Mor (Lanham, MD: University Press of America, 1992), 14–23, correctly notes, Matt 23:15 is "the only ancient source that explicitly ascribes a missionary policy to a Jewish group" (18). The interpretation of this verse is hotly contested: it is unclear, for example, whether Jesus's words should be taken literally (the Pharisees actually travel—unlikely in my judgment) or metaphorically (they go to very great lengths) or hyperbolically (Jesus exaggerates for rhetorical effect). It is also unclear whether the object of the "mission" is other Jews (i.e., non-Pharisees are encouraged to become Pharisees) or non-Jews (pagans are encouraged to become Jews or even Pharisaic Jews). These questions are further complicated of course by the debate surrounding the precise meaning of προσήλυτος.

136. See Carleton Paget, "Jewish Proselytism at the Time of Christian Origins," and Rainer Riesner, "A Pre-Christian Jewish Mission?" in *The Mission of the Early Church to Jews and Gentiles*, eds. Jostein Ådna and Hans Kvalbein (Tübingen: Mohr Siebeck, 2000), 211–50, for *Forschungsberichten*. This scholarly trend was presaged by the learned appendix to Amy-Jill Levine's Duke dissertation, "The Matthean Program of Salvation History: A Contextual Analysis of the Exclusivity Logia," (Ph.D. diss., Duke University, 1984). The appendix was unfortunately not published in the revised version of this work.

137. Carleton Paget, "Jewish Proselytism at the Time of Christian Origins," 65.

138. Ibid., 75–77; and Riesner, "A Pre-Christian Jewish Mission?" 221–23.

139. Harnack, *Mission and Expansion*, 1 (trans. alt.). One does not have to agree with Harnack's use of the term "new religion" nor with the Marcionite theological consequence he would draw from the Jewish presupposition (that they can perhaps be discarded) to see the practical importance and accuracy of his statement.

140. That the Jewish synagogue was the first place Paul would go upon arriving in a new town is confirmed on page after page in Acts, not least in the passage with which we began the current chapter (Thessalonica). For a provocative exploration of the significance of such networks, see Rodney Stark's sociological treatment in *The Rise of Christianity* (Princeton, NJ: Princeton University Press, 1996).

141. For an exploration of the significance of this fact for questions of jurisprudential policy, see G. E. M. de Ste. Croix, "Why Were the Early Christians Persecuted?" *Past and Present* 26 (1963): 6–38.

142. Goodman, *Mission and Conversion*, 83–4, speaks of the "unique" circumstances in the early church.

143. Carleton Paget, "Jewish Proselytism at the Time of Christian Origins," 99, n. 130.

144. Taking Acts 1:8 as "programmatic" for the narrative is an exegetical commonplace. But in this case it is nevertheless correct. Some scholars have seen in Acts' missionary "summaries of success" (6:7; 9:31; 12:24; 16:5; 19:20; 28:31) a key to the structure of the book as a whole (e.g., Richard N. Longenecker, *Acts* [Grand Rapids, MI: Zondervan, 1981], 234), though most attempts at a comprehensive structure are fraught with difficulties of one kind or another.

145. E. Earl Ellis, "The End of the Earth (Acts 1:8)," *BBR* 1 (1991): 123–32; On Luke's geographical horizon in general, see the extensive article by James M. Scott, "Luke's Geographical Horizon," in *The Book of Acts, Vol. 2: Greco-Roman Setting*, 483–544.

146. So correctly Talbert, *Reading Acts*, 9, among others. For the view that the phrase "end of the earth" also carries "ethnic" weight (i.e., the gentile world), see Thomas S. Moore, "'To the End of the Earth': The Geographical and Ethnic Universalism of Acts 1:8 in Light of Isaianic Influence on Luke," *JETS* 40 (1997): 389–99.

147. Barrett, *Acts*, 1.79. See, too, the recent piece by Michael Goheen, "A Critical Examination of David Bosch's Missional Reading of Luke," in *Reading Luke: Interpretation, Reflection, Formation*, eds. Craig G. Bartholomew, Joel B. Green, and Anthony C. Thiselton, SHS 7 (Grand Rapids, MI: Zondervan, 2005), 230–64: "Mission is not just one of the many things Luke talks about, but it undergirds and shapes the text so that to read Luke in a non-missional way is to misread Luke and misunderstand what God is saying" (229). That this is so makes it difficult to discuss "mission" in Acts inasmuch as to do it adequately one must discuss the entirety of the narrative. Obviously that is beyond the scope of this (or any) book. The hope is simply to point toward a few constitutive features of mission that will help to illumine why Luke's vision turns the world upside down.

148. See Acts 1:8, 22; 2:32; 3:15; 4:33; 5:32; 8:25; 10:39, 41, 42, 43; 13:31; 18:5; 20:21, 24; 22:15, 18, 20; 23:11 [2]; 26:16, 22; 28:23.

149. See, for example, W. H. C. Frend, *Martyrdom and Persecution in the Early Church: A Study of Conflict from the Maccabees to the Donatus* (Oxford: Basil Blackwell, 1965), 85. Contra Bolt, "Mission and Witness," in *Witness to the Gospel: The Theology of Acts*, eds. I. Howard Marshall and David Peterson (Grand Rapids, MI: Eerdmans, 1998), 191–214, whose dismissal of the importance of μάρτυς for Stephen can only be seen as an unsuccessful attempt to save the word-study method with which he began (192–3).

150. See Frend, *Martyrdom*, 87–91.

151. Haenchen, *Acts*, 146. There are some modern readers—even confessed demythologizers—who would want to draw the theological lines with a little more precision of course. "The Lord" may not be on the same plane as "a vision," for example. But the drift of Haenchen's remarks is clear enough.

152. Ibid., just prior to his remark cited above. Whether Haenchen means to identify theologically or philosophically with his "modern reader" is a question for a different day.

153. Cf. Hans-Georg Gadamer, *Truth and Method* (New York: Seabury Press, 1975) on interpretive sympathy as a requisite posture for adequate understanding.

154. On the phrase *Missio Dei*, see Stephen B. Chapman and Laceye C. Warner, "Jonah and the Imitation of God: Rethinking Evangelism and the Old Testament," *JTI* 2 (2008): 43–69, n. 67.

155. See, among others, John Nolland, "Salvation-History and Eschatology," in *Witness to the Gospel*, 63–81.

156. As I have recently argued elsewhere, when seen in the hermeneutical context of Luke's literary project Acts 2:36 is not about the time at which Jesus became something he was not before (Lord and Christ) but about the confirmation of Jesus's identity by God in the face of death. See C. Kavin Rowe, "Acts 2.36 and the Continuity of Lukan Christology," *NTS* 53 (2007): 37–56.

157. See the five essays in *Witness to the Gospel*, eds. Marshall and Peterson, that deal with salvation in Luke and/or Acts (63–166). To take an obvious example: when, in the midst of a violent storm, Paul says to his fellow sailors that their food will be their σωτηρία, the characters in the story may understand little more than that they will not die in the storm (27:34). The reader, of course, understands a good deal more than the characters in the story because of the ability to hear the theological overtones in this use of salvation. This is yet another example of the Lukan use of dramatic irony.

158. See Green's essay, "God as Savior." It is often thought that salvation in Acts is tied closely to the "forgiveness of sins." And it is (see, e.g., 2:38; cf. 3:19; 5:31, etc.). Indeed, as Green points out, "'forgiveness' can appear in balanced apposition with 'salvation' in Acts, or as a synecdoche for 'salvation' " (91). However, as Green labors to make clear, if we want to remain close to Luke and Acts, forgiveness of sins should not be thought of exclusively in metaphysical terms (the God-human relation alone) but in deeply social ones as well (restoration to God's people of the outcast). Luke obviously does not deny the former but his emphasis is on the latter.

159. Green, "God as Savior," 91. Green's phrase occurs in the first part of his treatment of "salvation" but is relevant to his entire discussion.

160. On New Testament anthropology in general, see Udo Schnelle, "Neutestamentliche Anthropologie: Ein Forschungsbericht," *ANRW* 2.26.3: 2658–2714.

161. Well known is the essay by Jack T. Sanders, "The Salvation of the Jews in Luke-Acts," in *Luke-Acts: New Perspectives from the SBL Seminar*, ed. Charles Talbert (New York: Crossroad, 1984), 104–28. One could also see, for example, the relevant remarks of John G. Gager, "Jews, Gentiles, and Synagogues in the Book of Acts," *HTR* 79 (1986): 91–99 (esp. 99).

162. See, for example, Stenschke, "The Need for Salvation," in *Witness to the Gospel: The Theology of Acts*, ed. I. Howard Marshall and David Peterson (Grand Rapids, MI: Eerdmans, 1998), 142.

163. Even Luke's language of "this crooked generation" (Acts 2:40; or "this generation" in the Gospel) should not be taken rigidly, as if it referred to a particular group of wicked people over against others who somehow are not. The expression, rather, names the fact that "people need to be saved because they are part of one of the many generations that have failed or is presently failing before God and thus

constitute a corrupt humankind" (see idem, 140). Paul's explanation to the Ephesian elders in Acts 20:21 is materially the same: the Christian mission proclaims the need for "repentance toward God and faith in our Lord Jesus Christ" not to select portions of the human population but "both to Jews and Greeks," that is, everyone.

164. Cf. Jacques Dupont, *The Salvation of the Gentiles: Studies in the Acts of the Apostles* (New York: Paulist Press, 1979), 16: "the history that Luke wishes to trace is the history of the revelation of God's salvation to all flesh." Dupont's remark remains important not only because he sees the interconnection in Acts between God's revelation and salvation (the link between God *in se* and *pro nobis*) but also because his way of putting this matter reminds us—as do the other essays in this volume—of the necessity to think of "history" in explicitly theological terms when reading Acts.

165. One thinks, for example, of Nock's opinion that the one really striking difference between the early Christian view of Jesus's resurrection and the Graeco-Roman stories of Osiris, and so forth, had to do with historical particularity: "In Christianity everything is made to turn on a dated experience of a historical Person" (*Early Gentile Christianity*, 107). There has been some debate about whether pagans possessed a concept of "sin." This is less complicated than it appears. If the concept of "sin" means an awareness that there are dire problems in the world that need addressing, or that human beings are complex entities with competing and frequently injurious desires, then—other than a few naves—it would probably be hard to find people who were not aware of sin. If, however, "sin" is taken in its specifically Jewish/ Christian sense as distorted worship of the God of Israel and all the consequences that come therewith, then obviously the pagans did not think about human problems in these terms (this applies *a fortiori* to Pauline notions of sin as an apocalyptic power or as something related to the Mosaic law).

166. Lane Fox, *Pagans and Christians*, 299. Cf. the classic statement of this position by Ernst Troeltsch, *The Social Teaching of the Christian Churches*, vol. 1, trans. Olive Wyon (London: Allen & Unwin, 1931), 61: "It is . . . clear that the message of Jesus is not a programme of social reform. It is rather the summons to prepare for the coming of the Kingdom of God; the preparation, however, is to take place quietly within the framework of the present world-order, in a purely religious fellowship of love, with an earnest endeavor to conquer self and cultivate the Christian virtues. Even the Kingdom of God itself is not (for its part at least) the new social order founded by God. It creates a new order upon earth, but it is an order which is not concerned with the State, with Society, or with the family at all. How this will work out in detail is God's affair; man's duty is simply to prepare for it."

167. Given the obvious importance of the term from Ignatius in the second century down to the present day, its extraordinary paucity in the New Testament should at least arouse our interest (two of the three total references in the NT occur in Acts; cf. 1 Ptr 4:16). And indeed it has. The study of the term has been extensive, though, as David Horrell points out, not much of it has been recent. See Horrell's learned piece, "The Label Χριστιανός: 1 Peter 4:16 and the Formation of Christian Identity," *JBL* 126/2 (2007): 361–81. Despite the plethora of studies on the term's origins, I am unaware of any study of the term that analyzes its narratively shaped use in Acts.

168. Considerable attention has been given to the almost twenty different ways Luke speaks of the early Christians, especially "the Way" and "*ecclesia*." Cadbury's survey in *Beginnings*, 5.375–92, remains a valuable introduction.

169. Preferring ἔλληνας here to ἑλληνιστάς. Johnson, *Acts*, 203, offers an excellent and concise explanation for this preference.

170. Pesch, *Apostelgeschichte*, 1.352.

171. This matter—how the early Christians preached efficaciously—should not be confused with the question of the origin of κύριος (where they learned to call Jesus κύριος). Contra Bousset et al., the term's origin is fully Jewish. See Joseph A. Fitzmyer, "New Testament Kyrios and Maranatha and their Aramaic Background," in *To Advance the Gospel: New Testament Studies*, 2nd ed. (Grand Rapids, MI: Eerdmans, 1998), 218–35; and, idem, "The Semitic Background to the New Testament Kyrios-Title," in *The Semitic Background to the New Testament* (Grand Rapids, MI: Eerdmans, 1997), 115–42.

172. Of course, for those who have ears to hear—and perhaps Cornelius should be included here—Peter does speak of Jesus's messianic identity: God anointed him (ἔχρισεν); he is the one to whom the prophets bear witness, and so on.

173. For a brief survey that links ancient pagan religion to the material remains of Syrian Antioch, see Sarolta A. Takács, "Pagan Cults at Antioch," in the splendidly done book *Antioch: The Lost Ancient City*, ed. Christine Kondoleon (Princeton, NJ: Princeton University Press, 2000), 198–216.

174. Haenchen, *Acts*, 366; Johnson, *Acts*, 203; BAGD 382. For χεὶρ κυρίου in Acts, see also 13:1; for ἐπιστρέφειν, see 3:19; 9:35; 14:15; 26:18, 20; 28:27 (!).

175. It might also be claimed that the anarthrous use of κύριος always refers to God (as did Moule, for example). This is incorrect, however, as well-known passages such as Acts 2:36 and 10:36 immediately make clear. On this point, see Rowe, *Early Narrative Christology*, 211–13.

176. Determining the referent of κύριος in vv. 23 and 24 is materially the same matter as it is in vs. 20 and 21 (e.g., in vs. 23 the expression τὴν χάριν τοῦ θεοῦ could be used to argue equally well both that the ensuing κύριος refers to God and that it refers to Jesus).

177. See Rowe, *Early Narrative Christology*, passim.

178. The singular participle makes clear that it is the great number that turns, not merely some of them.

179. Meeks, *Origins of Christian Morality*, 42–43.

180. Luke does not need to repeat for the reader what the practical shape of Christian community is: he has given ample example at the beginning of Acts (sharing possessions, feeding the widows, etc.). Readers who have been paying attention should easily be able to create the necessary picture. We may, however, note that many of the basic practices such as economic redistribution, meeting together, and so on, would not have been well received in a typical Graeco-Roman city, at least if the remarks of Jones, *The Greek City*, 134, are on target: "The system of control employed by the imperial government was in its general lines the same as that invented by the republic—to maintain the ascendency of the wealthier classes. As before, the

constitutions of the cities were so arranged as to give the control to the rich, and any attempts to upset this arrangement were severely checked. Left-wing politicians found themselves relegated to islands. If the assembly proved too active its meetings were suspended. Above all the formation of clubs which might organize the voting power of the lower orders was strictly supervised and often prohibited." On early Christian economics—especially vis-à-vis Roman imperial practices—see the excellent essay of Peter Lampe and Ulrich Luz, "Post-Pauline Christianity and Pagan Society," in *Christian Beginnings*, ed. Jürgen Becker, esp. 252–5, 270–1.

181. Elias Bickerman, "The Name of Christians," repr. in *Studies in Jewish and Christian History*, 3.137–51.

182. So, rightly, David G. Horrell, "The Label," 362–3. Cf., for example, the essay of Judith M. Lieu, " 'I am a Christian': Martyrdom and the Beginning of 'Christian' Identity," in *Neither Jew Nor Greek? Constructing Early Christianity* (Edinburgh: T. & T. Clark, 2002), esp. 212.

183. For the patristic testimony, see Bickerman, "The Name of Christians," 142–43.

184. Erik Peterson, "Christianus," repr. in *Frühkirche, Judentum und Gnosis: Studien und Untersuchungen* (Freiburg: Herder, 1959), 64–87 (66–68), with multiple examples. Cf. the convincing criticisms of Bickerman's unnecessary philological worries by Justin Taylor, "Why Were the Disciples First Called 'Christians' at Antioch?" *RB* 101 (1994): 75–94 (esp. 82–83). Conzelmann, too, notes the occurrence of χρηματίζειν with a passive meaning (*Acts*, 88).

185. Against this reading Conzelmann, *Acts*, 88 cites Jos. *AJ*, 8.157, where χρηματίζειν seems unofficial (the names of future emperor's were not randomly chosen) and καλεῖν certainly is official (they were "designated" as Caesar). But Peterson's claim is hardly that every occurrence of χρηματίζειν in the ancient world is within the legal sphere; moreover, one example from Josephus does not outweigh the multiplicity of examples given by Peterson and their prima facie relevance to Acts 11. (Conzelmann also cites Rom 7:3, which is somewhat bizarre given that the legal connotations of the word—even though transposed here into the Jewish realm—are hard to miss: according to the νόμος, "she will be designated [χρηματίσει] an adulteress.") Conzelmann's real objection, however, is something else: "Those who interpret the phrase as official language view our sentence as the report of a definite event, faithfully recorded in official minutes. But Luke would not have recorded an official action against Christians in this way, because it did not fit in with his apologetic intention." Two points are in order: (1) In no way are those who recognize the official overtones of χρηματίζειν necessarily committed to a wooden historicist reading of the passage. The key interpretive point is not that Luke records an event from "official minutes" but that he presents the naming of the Christians in one way rather than another. That is, taking χρηματίζειν seriously as a historiographical choice corresponds necessarily to the hermeneutical direction of the narrative (whether or not that direction is exactly concomitant with the Antiochene *Sitz im Leben* in the late 30s/early 40s is yet a further layer of inquiry—Conzelmann conflates the two). (2) While allegedly based on philological considerations, the center of Conzelmann's objection rests in his overall

theory of Luke's apologetic purpose. If Conzelmann's proposal about Luke's purpose is off the mark (and it is), then his objection disappears.

186. See the judicious discussion by Horrell, "The Label," 365–7. See Peterson, "Christianus," 68, for the further "juristic" significance of πρώτως. Johnson, Acts, 205, suggests that for Χριστιανός "the translation 'Messianist' would also be appropriate in English." The translation "Messianist" assumes philological analysis and perhaps even wordplay on the part of the coiners: these are the Christ-followers, the Messianists. The problem, however, is that the word Χριστιανός is a Latinism (-ianus), which not only speaks again to its Roman origin but also to the fact that it is unlikely that those among whom the term originated would have intended the wordplay. The simpler explanation is that offered by Peterson and Molthagen among others: Christianus/Χριστιανός means followers of the man named Christus (cf., e.g., Tacitus, who refers to Jesus as Christus: "Christus, the author of the name"). The wordplay between the name and their Messianism is a simple coincidence between the fact that Χριστός was not actually Jesus' name and the fact that the Romans did not know this.

187. The similarity to the situation reflected in Pliny's famous exchange with Trajan should not be overlooked: in both Acts and Pliny, the locals are the ones that sense the trouble the Christians bring and haul them before official Roman administration. There is no point in squabbling over whether the very first use of the term was in the mouth of an Antiochene gentile simpliciter or a Roman administrator. Luke does not give us such information.

188. See Fergus Millar, The Roman Near East, 87–90, for a concise discussion of Vespasian's major construction projects in the area (all of which required substantial military labor, e.g., four legions, twenty cohorts, etc.).

189. Haenchen, Acts, 367–8, n. 3, asserts that the term "Christian" could not come from the Romans because for the reader to sense this would imperil Luke's pro-Roman agenda. Haenchen's argument is circular in that it begins from his hypothesis regarding Luke's Tendenz and evaluates (or ignores) the data accordingly. The circularity itself does not make Haenchen's argument wrong (some circular arguments are right); it is rather because the analysis of the Tendenz is wrong that the circularity becomes de facto problematical.

190. As Cadbury noticed, πρώτως implies "that the same thing occurred again" (Beginnings, 5.386, n. 1, with reason to reject unfounded corrections to πρῶτον). Peterson is even stronger: we should understand πρώτως "im Sinne einer die Zukunft bestimmenden Norm" ("Christianus," 69, n. 10).

191. This text is noteworthy in that it is pagan testimony to the kind of people who could be Christian ministrae (slaves/women). LCL trans. "deaconesses."

192. Citations from Horrell, "The Label Χριστιανός," 369. In my judgment, contra John Elliott, for example, Horrell demonstrates beyond all reasonable doubt the fruitfulness of reading 1 Peter in relation to the Pliny/Trajan correspondence. Peterson and Taylor, among others, treat the highly problematic Testimonium Flavianum in Josephus, AJ, 18.3.3. (63/64). The central point to be taken from such attempts is that if Josephus discussed the followers of Jesus at all, he did so in the context of other θόρυβοι in the time of Pilate (though, as Norden pointed out, the

word θόρυβος need not have been used specifically in relation to the Christians inasmuch as the concept was already implicit in the latter term). See esp. Taylor, "Why Were the Disciples First Called 'Christians' at Antioch?" 85–6.

193. "Christianus," 78. Peterson does not, however, necessarily explain why the term would have been coined in Antioch ca. 40 in the sense that he does not provide a specific political problem that involved Christians and needed the action of the Roman administration. Taylor, "Why Were the Disciples First Called 'Christians' at Antioch?" attempts to coordinate the impact of "Christian propaganda" with Jewish unrest in Antioch, but this is little more than intriguing speculation. Cf. Botermann, *Judenedikt*, 155–7, who discusses our lack of historical evidence and Taylor's "somewhat confused line of thought" and "breakneck eclecticism" (154, 155, respectively).

194. For a compact discussion of Pliny's use of this term (including its significance in the context of forming political organizations), see Robert Louis Wilken, *The Christians as the Romans Saw Them*, 2nd ed. (New Haven, CT: Yale University Press, 2003), 12–15, 32–5. Cf. Jones, *The Greek City*, 134. Though the expulsion of the Jews under Claudius is a complicated topic in its own right, there may be an interesting coincidence between Claudius' forbidding of clubs/societies and the naming of "Christians" under Claudius (according to Acts): Cassius Dio, *Hist. Rom.*, notes that Claudius did not throw the Jews out but ordered them "while continuing their traditional mode of life, not to hold meetings" (60.6.6.; also disbanded clubs [*hetaeria*], which had been reintroduced by Gaius" (60.6.6).

195. Nevertheless, as Peterson, "Christianus," 78, notes, the *flagitia* "die den Christen vorgeworfen werden, gehören ja gerade zum Repertoire der politischen Propaganda."

196. Taylor, 84 (except for Josephus, all our sources derive from the second century, though they make reference to events of the first). Taylor's observation is noted also by Botermann, *Judenedikt*, 154. Botermann's work is concerned mainly with trying to pin down the date of the term's coinage, but in mounting her case she provides concise summaries of some of the more important work on Χριστιανός (141–88).

197. *Beginnings*, 5.385.

198. Had the early Christians coined this term in a positive self-affirmation of group identity, Luke (and the author of 1 Peter for that matter) may well have felt free to use it.

199. See Barrett, *Acts*, 2.1170–71, for a summary of the position that Agrippa is sincere (or close to it). Barrett himself seems to think that if we ask "what Luke intended" rather than "what happened," we will answer that Agrippa was sincere. But this is to reject the later, positive meaning of Christian as well as to ignore the fact that Luke does not so designate the followers of Jesus.

200. 25:23: Festus, tribunes, leading men of the city.

201. Lest the point be overlooked: I am not suggesting that the character Agrippa speaks out of a Roman perspective *simpliciter* (as, e.g., does Tacitus, Suetonius, etc.). He rather speaks for Luke speaking for Rome. That is, Luke's character Agrippa says what Luke wants him to say.

202. From the pagan side of things, we could think immediately of Pliny's use of both *hetaeria* and *superstitio* to describe the Christians.

203. See the discussion in Botermann, *Judenedikt*, 147–57 ("politische Interpretation"—the Χριστιανοί are political conspirators); 157–67 ("theologische Interpretation"—the Χριστιανοί are not Jews *simpliciter*). Botermann herself finds the theological interpretation implausible and opts resolutely for the political one. Though he initially admits the importance of the word *superstitio* in the Roman authors, Molthagen, *Der römische Staat und die Christen*, 32–3, tends in the same direction.

204. Thus is their task of witness a universal task. On this point, see Dietrich Bonhoeffer, *Ethics* (New York: Macmillan, 1962), 287–91.

205. I am obviously arguing against certain sociologically reductionist ways of construing the public visibility of early Christian communities. To those who remain committed to such reasoning, it can only be pointed out that they stand at odds with the phenomenon they are trying to describe. This is not a new problem—in the field of anthropology, for example, it is often referred to with the emic/etic distinction—but it is one that should be seen: the Christians claim that they are visible because of God's action in Jesus Christ. Any explanation of their visibility that ignores this claim would seem hard-pressed to do justice to the richness of the historical reality.

206. Though chronologically later than the period that most concerns us, Tertullian nevertheless sees clearly the unity of "religion" and "politics" both in Roman life and their accusations. Because the Christians will not sacrifice to the emperor, who is a god, "We are accused of sacrilege and treason at once" (*Apol.* 10.1–2: *itaque sacrilegii et maiestatis rei convenimur*).

207. *Über die Absicht und den literarischen Charakter der Apostelgeschichte* (Göttingen: Vandenhoeck & Ruprecht, 1897).

208. And, let it be said clearly, he had more good days than many a *Neutestamentler*.

209. *Acts*, 369–70.

210. One need think only of the frequent worries about "early Catholicism" in mid-twentieth-century German New Testament scholarship, or even of Nock's famous typology of individual conversion in the last chapter of *Conversion* (Justin, Arnobius, Augustine). Yet we would misread the nature of the Christian mission according to Acts were we to think only of the individual "heroes" of the story as the icons who best figure forth the missional identity of the church (e.g., Peter, Stephen, and Paul). Though Acts obviously focuses much attention on these characters, the modern individualism that has long ground the lenses of our interpretive perception can all too easily blind us to the fundamental importance of the communities and established networks that finally make sense of the main characters lives in the first place. Put more simply, for Luke the church is as important as Paul.

211. Both citations are from Haenchen, *Acts*, 370.

212. Haenchen, *Acts*, 370, believes that if Antioch had been presented as the "legitimate" outcome of Cornelius' conversion, "the opposition to the Gentile mission in chapter 15 would have become incomprehensible." But, again, the whole order of the narrative has been ignored: Cornelius prepares the way for Antioch, and

the Jerusalem council responds to events that arise out of the church Antioch. As Luke tells it, in Antioch we then see the creation of an actual community of gentiles and Jews. The Jerusalem council is not a response, that is, to the conversion of one pious gentile or his household but to the fact that the church at Antioch now commissions a mission to the gentiles (13:1–4). Whether or not Luke's version is exactly contiguous with the historical order is a different question (and is obviously bound up with one's reading of Galatians). But the narrative logic is clear.

213. One recalls Flannery O'Connor's purported gloss on John 8:32: "you shall know the truth and the truth shall make you odd."

214. Pagan philosophers knew the ideal of not owning property: Lucian, *The Wisdom of Nigrinus*, mentions how Nigrinus—a Platonist philosopher—"used to say that [his farm] was not his at all." Whether Lucian's subsequent interpretation of Nigrinus' statement is right or not, is immaterial. The most lucid treatment of "possessions" in Acts is still Luke T. Johnson, *The Literary Function of Possessions in Luke–Acts*, SBLDS 39 (Missoula, MT: Scholars Press, 1977). For a more recent treatment, see Reta Halteman Finger, *Of Widows and Meals: Communal Meals in the Book of Acts* (Grand Rapids, MI: Eerdmans, 2007).

215. The most convenient collection of evidence—common vocabulary, and so forth—remains Jacques Dupont, "Aequitas Romana: Notes sur Actes 25, 16," in idem, *Études sur les Actes des Apôtres*, 527–52. Positive judgments about Luke's legal knowledge were not unknown in antiquity. Assuming the text does not need amending, the Muratorian Fragment, for example, names Luke as a *iuris studiosis* (see Bruce Metzger, *The Canon of the New Testament*, 305, n. 2, on the difficulty of determining the meaning of the text).

216. Rainer Riesner, "James's Speech, Simeon's Hymn, and Luke's Sources," in *Jesus of Nazareth: Lord and Christ*, eds. Green and Turner, 263–78, discusses the possibility of a pre-Lukan source as the best explanation of the linguistic links between the Nunc Dimittis in the Gospel and James' speech in Acts. The interpretive conundrum is the alleged problem caused by Luke's use of the Semitic Συμεών (15:14). Despite Riesner's objection, however, this form of Peter's name (Πέτρος, 15:7!) can easily be taken as yet one more instance of Luke's skill in creating *Lokalkolorit*, as the majority of Acts commentators have held (Cadbury, Haenchen, Roloff, Schneider, et al.). Given Luke's literary style, moreover, it is not surprising that he would allow Simeon/Symeon to create a suggestive resonance between Peter and the speaker of the Nunc Dimittis. This does not altogether rule out the possibility that with Συμεών Luke intends to refer back to the elderly prophet Symeon rather than to Peter—a suggestion going back as far as John Chrysostom—but it makes it unnecessary.

217. Although, of course, Luke does see sin as a universal problem from which all humans need deliverance. Indeed, the differences between the thought of Luke and Paul have not infrequently been greatly overdrawn (e.g., Vielhauer). On this point see, for example, François Bovon, "The Law in Luke-Acts," in *Studies in Early Christianity*, WUNT 161 (Tübingen: Mohr Siebeck, 2003), 59–73, and Rowe, *Early Narrative Christology*, 219–31. The comparison between Luke and Paul is hardly meant to suggest that we should measure Luke by Paul. That time has long past. See, for

example, the remarks of Joseph A. Fitzmyer, *The Gospel according to Luke*, 2 vols., AB 28–28A (Garden City, NY: Doubleday, 1981/1985), 1.143–258 passim.

218. Cf. Dupont, "Le Salut des Gentils et la signification théologique du Livre des Actes," in *Études*, 393–419, who sees clearly the connection between Lukan historiography and God's salvific self-revelation: "l'histoire que Luc veut retracer se définit comme celle de la manifestation du salut de Dieu en faveur de toute chair" (401).

CHAPTER 5

1. Paul Minear, "Dear Theo: The Kerygmatic Intention and Claim of the Book of Acts," *Int* 27 (1973): 131–50.

2. To those who would worry that this way of putting it is Jewish but not specifically Christian (i.e., where is Jesus?), I can only respond by repeating that to think of God in Luke's terms just is to think of Jesus, and vice versa. The "God" who somehow exists in abstraction from Jesus has nothing to do with the God spoken of in the Gospel of Luke or Acts.

3. See chap. 2. For a brief discussion of the "objective" and "subjective" aspects of culture, see Robert Wuthnow, *Communities of Discourse: Ideology and Social Structure in the Reformation, the Enlightenment, and European Socialism* (Cambridge, MA: Harvard University Press, 1989), 537–58.

4. Taylor's discussion of this notion occurs primarily in two places: *Modern Social Imaginaries* (Durham, NC: Duke University Press, 2004), and, *A Secular Age* (Cambridge, MA: Harvard University Press, 2007), esp. 159–211, with some significant overlap.

5. Taylor, *Modern Social Imaginaries*, 23.

6. Ibid., 24 (emphasis added).

7. Ibid., 25; cf. *A Secular Age*, esp. 175.

8. Taylor, *A Secular Age*, 173–4.

9. Ibid., 174.

10. Ibid.

11. For the relevant philosophical background to the notion that an intelligible action is a more fundamental concept than action per se, see, for example, G. E. M. Anscombe, *Intention* (Ithaca, NY: Cornell University Press, 1957) and Alasdair MacIntyre, *After Virtue*, 3rd ed. (Notre Dame, IN: University of Notre Dame Press, 2007).

12. The disagreement about the proper form of magic still presupposes its importance and efficacy in certain spheres, and the disagreement about whether images should be taken care of physically (washed, etc.) still presupposes the web of practices surrounding the gods that is pagan religion. This is radically different from saying, for example, that (1) "magic" as a practice is wrongheaded *in toto*, or (2) caring for images is unnecessary because these gods are not God.

13. One of the advantages of Taylor's analysis is that it does not require people to be consciously aware of their social imaginary or the ways in which practices embody norms and moral/metaphysical orders. But precisely because the practices do embody norms and moral orders, the possibility for an intuitive grasp of the larger issues at stake

in any particular practice remains a live option for even the least reflective of human communities/individuals.

14. For a book that raises similar questions in a very different context, see Jonathan Lear, *Radical Hope: Ethics in the Face of Cultural Devastation* (Cambridge, MA: Harvard University Press, 2006). My discussion owes much to Lear's insights into the way a culture can collapse (in this case, the Native American Crow), though I remain thankful to my colleague Jay Carter for pointing out some of the book's problems. Prof. Carter's criticism of Lear's book was that it could appear as just one more instance of the dominant white man's attempt to understand himself ("human vulnerability," etc.) at the expense of those whom he has vanquished. This is hardly Lear's intention, as can be seen for the way in which he valorizes Chief Plenty Coups' ability to create a new life for his people, but his book is not for that reason delivered from Carter's criticism.

15. Another advantage that emerges from Taylor's notion is that it allows us to move well beyond the simplistic analyses of Acts and Graeco-Roman culture that attempt to get at Luke's posture vis-à-vis the wider Mediterranean world by focusing on isolated matters (e.g., how well did Luke know Homer?) while neglecting the "whole sense of things," the overall structure of perception as evidenced through the narrative of Acts. Let it be understood, however, that I am not suggesting that Taylor's work should be adopted uncritically or put to use anachronistically. For example, at times Taylor speaks of the social imaginary as "unstructured," but this seems impossible (what would an unstructured moral/metaphysical order, etc. be?), and indeed his examples and analysis display a discernable structure in the social imaginary (e.g., *Modern Social Imaginaries*, 25). For those who worry about anachronism: obviously the ancients did not analyze their *Sitz im Leben* in terms of social imaginaries, a deep background to social life, and so forth. But Taylor's claim is not that all ages have thought this way but rather that this is the way things are—that is, the notion or concept may be a recent addition to our intellectual horizon but the reality it attempts to describe is not. To object to my use of Taylor would be to object to his description of the way things are and thus to offer a counter-proposal about the complex reality he names "the social imaginary."

16. In relation to the coming discussion below, it makes sense to note now that this is perhaps the deepest problem in Locke's notion of "toleration" (*Letter Concerning Toleration*, 1689). In the end, it is the state that decides when religious practice has overstepped its proper bounds (and can thus be checked). The state thus turns out to be the epistemic—no less than the political—guarantor of the reach of any particular religious claim/practice. "Civil interest" ("life, liberty, health, idolency of body...possession of outward things, such as money, lands, houses, furniture, and the like") forms the boundary of religious claims. So, if the resurrection of Jesus suggests that we should think differently about property, for example, such thinking would always take place within the ambit of what the state thought was amenable to its civil interests; the reach of the meaning of Jesus' resurrection would thus be determined by the state's knowledge of its civil interests. How the state gains such theologically superior knowledge is not addressed, but that the epistemological prowess of the state is underwritten by its ability not only to instill "the fear of punishment" but

also actually to punish is unambiguous. As was the case with the "peace" of Rome, violence is ultimately that which grounds the Lockean vision of "tolerance": religious tolerance thus turns out to be defined by the epistemological parameters of the state. Cf., of course, the conclusion to chapter 8 of Rousseau's *Social Contract* (1762), in which the only "dogma" that is excluded from "civil religion" is "intolerance"; anyone who makes "intolerant" claims on behalf of the church "must be expelled by the state." The state is thus the organ of knowledge with respect to the proper reach of the church and its claims.

17. We might once again remember Tertullian, who did something similar. Of course law never speaks by or for itself. It must always be spoken by someone (judge, court, sovereign, etc.). Between law and its application, that is, stands a human presence, which functions irreducibly and necessarily as the authoritative mediator(s) of the law's "force." Someone must decide in each and every case that the law applies or does not apply (in this case it does apply; in that case it does not apply). For an exploration of the significance of this fact, see Carl Schmitt, *Political Theology* ("The Problem of Sovereignty"), esp. 30–35.

18. For an insightful essay that deals with this question, among others, see Cora Diamond, "Losing Your Concepts," *Ethics* 98 (1988): 255–77, esp. 264–66 on Tolstoy and Primo Levi.

19. Thus another layer to the argument behind the structure of chapter 4 is that more elaborate exegesis of particular passages will only continue to disclose further the depth of the tension. To see its generation, we must step back and attempt to view these core practices as a whole.

20. On this point as a whole, see Rowe, *Early Narrative Christology*.

21. Mauser, *The Gospel of Peace*, 46.

22. Recall chap. 4, in which we rejected a kind of thinking that would posit a "level playing field" on which Jesus and Caesar compete to rule.

23. Where many thinkers have located the rise of individualism in the Enlightenment, Taylor argues for the origin of certain key features of this self-understanding in the Reformation.

24. Luke is certainly aware of the term's circulation; his use of πρώτως in Acts 11:26 says as much.

25. To put it in terms of the narrative order of Acts: Cornelius leads to Antioch, which leads to the necessity to read the "Christian" social reality.

26. For a bracing statement of the "return" of the importance of political theology, see Mark Lilla's introduction to his *The Stillborn God*, 3–13.

27. Assmann was until recently Professor of Ancient History in the University of Heidelberg. He is a renowned Egyptologist, but his interests and publications are extraordinarily wide-ranging and sophisticated. He is perhaps best known—in terms of his theoretical contributions—for the articulation of "mnemohistory" as a way to think not only about historical study but also about the construction of cultures (what we remember constructs who we are). See, for example, the recently translated essays in *Religion and Cultural Memory*, trans. Rodney Livingstone (Stanford, CA: Stanford University Press, 2006).

28. Jan Assmann, *Moses the Egyptian: The Memory of Egypt in Western Monotheism* (Cambridge, MA: Harvard University Press, 1997), 1.

29. Ibid.

30. Ibid., 2.

31. This is his distinction between the "real" other and the "constructed" other (2ff.).

32. Ibid., 2. Assmann's argument that polytheism provides a religiously based context for cultural translation is more subtle than it might at first appear. Consider, for example, Samuel P. Huntington's *New York Times* best seller, *The Clash of Civilizations and the Remaking of World Order* (New York: Simon & Schuster, 1996), whose clunky argument typifies the modernist presumption that the "revitalization of religion" enhances rather than diminishes cultural misunderstanding (28–29 passim).

33. *Moses the Egyptian*, 217. Assmann's reason for our intellectual shortcoming in this regard has to do with cultural amnesia: the West's cultural memory is basically Jewish/Christian to the extent that we have almost entirely forgotten what polytheism could mean.

34. Cf. Assmann, *Die Mosaische Unterscheidung: Oder, der Preis des Monotheismus* (München: Carl Hanser Verlag, 2003), 33.

35. Assmann, *Moses the Egyptian*, 3 (cf. 6–8, 44–54 passim). Though he obviously does not mean to endorse "polytheism," Jürgen Moltmann, *The Trinity and the Kingdom: The Doctrine of God* (Minneapolis. MN: Fortress, 1993), esp. 190–202, is similarly concerned with the political destructiveness of "monotheism." Moltmann's discussion owes much to Erik Peterson's well-known work *Monotheismus als politisches Problem: Ein Beitrag zur Geschichte der politischen Theologie im Imperium Romanum* (Leipzig: Jacob Hegner, 1935). I do not speak of monotheism because I think the term is too weighted with modern philosophical conceptions that are more "monadic" or monolithic than anything else. The NT, of course, knows well the *monos theos* confession, but God is not a monad in either the OT or NT. In my view, the NT makes theological judgments about the identity of God that are more properly received within a Trinitarian framework (see, e.g., my "Biblical Pressure and Trinitarian Hermeneutics," *Pro Ecclesia* 11 [2002]: 295–312). That this framework makes a substantial difference in the politics of divine identity is Peterson's point (e.g., 96–97, where he argues that orthodox Trinitarian theology threatens the "political theology" of the Roman Empire, to which, of course, Christian argument was also susceptible—see, for example, pp. 82ff. on Eusebius of Caesarea and the history of the correlation between one God and one Monarch). Unfortunately, we do not have room in this single study on Acts to deal with the importance of this position—that would be at least a new book.

36. Assmann, *Moses the Egyptian*, 3. Cf. MacMullen, *Paganism in the Roman Empire*, 88 passim.

37. To say it only slightly differently, there is no general thing called "religion" of which particular religions such as Judaism, Christianity, and so forth, partake. Religion in general is an academic abstraction and corresponds to the working fiction of modern intellectuals. On this matter at least, Aristotle trumps Plato. For a concise exploration of this fact, see Paul Griffiths, "The Future of the Study of Religion in the Academy," *JAAR* 74 (2006), 66–78.

38. The issue is deeper here than the anthropologists' emic/etic distinction and turns in fact on comprehensive and incompatible claims about how to read the world, claims that cannot be reduced to mere distinctions within another allegedly more encompassing framework of interpretation (whether of another anthropological theory or something else).

39. Now in ET in Odo Marquard, *Farewell to Matters of Principle: Philosophical Studies* (New York: Oxford University Press, 1989). The philosophical discussion of the merits of polytheism goes back in the modern world at least to Hume's *The Natural History of Religion* (1757), who had plenty of criticism for its ancient form but also thought it to exhibit "tolerance" (esp. chap. 8). The whole discussion of course received new impetus from Nietzsche's repeated and philohellenic praise. Cf. Richard Rorty, "Pragmatism as Romantic Polytheism," in the *Revival of Pragmatism*, ed. Morris Dickstein; for a discussion of Marquard's essay, see Jacob Taubes, "Zur Konjunktur des Polytheismus," in *Mythos und Moderne*, ed. K. H. Bohrer (Frankfurt, 1983), 457–70. It is quite possible, as Erich Zenger notes, to read the theoretical edge of Assmann's theory as a particularly postmodern formulation, though Assmann's actual working procedure is much more that of the typical modernist historian—indeed, in its pristine German *wissenschaftlich* form. (See Zenger's response to Assmann in *Die Mosaische Untderscheidung*, "Was ist der Preis des Monotheismus?" 209–220).

40. Ibid., 98. To be fair to Assmann, we should note that since *Moses the Egyptian* he has sought to clarify his views and to argue that he is not out to overturn "monotheism," in which he is "geistig und seelisch" at home (*Die Mosaische Unterscheidung*, 18; cf., esp. 25 passim). Commendably, however, Assmann notes that he understands how interpreters of *Moses the Egyptian* could read him differently—as they indeed have (see the work of Regina Schwartz, as well as the responses of Klaus Koch, Rolf Rendtorff, et al. in *Die Mosaische Unterscheidung*, 193–286)—and even admits to seeing something of their interpretations in his book. How one is to deal with the gap between Assmann's theoretical articulations and his personal avowals does not concern us here. Suffice it to say that "Assmann" in the text above refers not so much to the man Jan Assmann as to a theoretical position(s) and that insofar as he extends his theoretical proposals in *Die Mosaische Unterscheidung*, he strengthens rather than weakens the political effect of the true/false distinction.

41. I am not suggesting, of course, that the majority of the religious studies establishment is polytheist but rather attempting to point toward (1) a deep-seated and widespread sense that the universal claims of early Christianity are fundamentally intolerant and, therefore, ethically problematic, and (2) the sense that tolerance of difference and openness to diversity should be the requisite hallmarks of our thinking about religious matters. On this point, see the essay by G. G. Stroumsa, "Early Christianity as a Radical Religion," in *Concepts of the Other in Near Eastern Religions*, IOS 14 (Leiden: Brill, 1994), 173–93.

42. On my meaning of "truth" see the discussion in this chapter.

43. Ithamar Gruenwald, "Intolerance and Martyrdom: From Socrates to Rabbi 'Aqiva," *Tolerance and Intolerance in Early Judaism and Christianity*, eds. Graham N. Stanton and Guy G. Stroumsa (Cambridge: Cambridge University Press, 1998), 7–29 (9).

44. Cf. G. G. Stroumsa's remarks in his postscript to *Tolerance and Intolerance in Early Judaism and Christianity*, 356–7.

45. For an account of truth in the smart sense, that is, with extensive reference to recent philosophical analyses and their relevance to theological exposition, see Bruce Marshall, *Trinity and Truth* (Cambridge: Cambridge University Press, 2000). For Jenson's "dumb sense" of truth, see his lecture, "What if It Were True?" (available online at the Center for Theological Inquiry in Princeton, New Jersey: http://www.ctinquiry.org, accessed July 25, 2008).

46. Along with his other correspondence about the youth conference in Fanö, Denmark, Bonhoeffer's letter is printed in Dietrich Bonhoeffer, *No Rusty Swords* (New York: Harper and Row, 1965), 286–87. For a discussion of this letter and its connection to Bonhoeffer's larger theological conception of truth, see Stanley Hauerwas, *Performing the Faith: Bonhoeffer and the Practice of Nonviolence* (Grand Rapids, MI: Brazos, 2004), esp. 60–72.

47. This way of conceiving the truth, it could be argued, underlies the whole of Bonhoeffer's essay "What Is Meant by Telling the Truth?" (*Ethics*), in which he seems to think of truth as the living out of a life in light of who God is: the life you are living helps you to know when you are telling the truth and how to do this from situation to situation.

48. Hence does Luke's language of ignorance, blindness, and darkness belong essentially to a vocabulary of "hermeneutical imagery" for a total pattern of life. That truth is a total pattern of life is the fundamental reason that, as Paul Griffiths observes, "no one can inhabit more than one form of religious life at a time" (*Problems of Religious Diversity* [Oxford: Blackwell, 2001], 34). Griffiths' discussion is weighted toward truth or true statements in their more directly cognitive senses, but it is an extremely valuable sketch of some of the main issues at stake in any attempt to deal with the question of truth.

49. See the discussion in Garnsey, "Religious Toleration in Classical Antiquity," in *Persecution and Toleration*, ed. W. J. Sheils (Oxford: Basil Blackwell, 1984), 1–27 (13–14).

50. The term is MacMullen's in *Paganism in the Roman Empire*, 90, with examples at hand—Zeus Helios Sarapis, and so forth. The intensity of the "mergers" was of course different in different parts of the Roman Empire (compare Egypt to Athens to points west of Italy, for example). On this point, see Mary Beard, John North, and Simon Price, *Religions of Rome*, 2 vols. (Cambridge: Cambridge University Press, 1998), 1.317 passim.

51. MacMullen, *Paganism in the Roman Empire*, 2. Cited in part also in Garnsey, "Religious Toleration," 25, as well as Beard, North, and Price, *Religions of Rome*, 1.212.

52. MacMullen, *Paganism in the Roman Empire*, 2 (emphasis added). It was MacMullen of course who wrote the book *Enemies of the Roman Order*.

53. Ibid., 93.

54. Ramsay MacMullen, "Conversion: A Historian's View," in *The Second Century* 5/2 (1985/86): 67–81 (71–71; emphasis original). MacMullen's remark about Judaism seems less true than it is about Christianity. At least pre-70, aside from the Qumranian vituperations and self-chosen abstention from participation in the temple cult, even the various disagreeing parties could all sacrifice at the temple.

55. Again, to be fair to Assmann, he admits in the introduction to *Die Mosaische Unterscheidung und des Monotheismus* that polytheistic cultures had their share of

violence. Yet the focus in this chapter is less on his admissions than on the intellectual and ethical grain or drift of his theoretical proposals.

56. See Garnsey, "Religious Toleration," esp. 25.

57. Beard, North, and Price, *Religions of Rome*, 1.212; cf. Price, *Religions of the Ancient Greeks*, 67. The modern notion of "tolerance" is but one particular way of working out this more basic religio-political relation of one people to another. If one defines tolerance in an overly strict, modern sense, then it is not surprising that such arguments do not turn up in the classical world (see Garnsey, "Religious Toleration," esp. 1, 6, 11, 25). If, however, one sees tolerance as a way to name a range of relations of one people to another—a range that receives its specific details from its embeddedness within particular historical contexts—then asking about tolerance in the ancient world is not an anachronistic mistake but the employment of a conceptual configuration basic to how we describe the relation between any groups whose views do not coincide.

58. Price, *Religions of the Ancient Greeks*, 67.

59. Cf. Parker, *Athenian Religion*: "no Greek surely would have supposed that an impious opinion should be permitted to circulate out of respect for freedom of speech" (209). With respect to Athenian polytheism in particular, "we are dealing not with principled tolerance but with a failure to live up to intolerant principles" (210).

60. *L'Intolérance religieuse et la politique* (Paris: Ernest Flammarion, 1917). Bouché-Leclercq is fairly uncritical of the *Tendenz* of the writers whom he consults, but his book is nevertheless a valuable compendium of many of the main incidents that occurred under the various emperors.

61. Beard, North, Price, *Religions of Rome*, 1.212.

62. Ibid.

63. Maecenas' well-known speech is cited also in *Religions of Rome*, 1.214. Cf. n. 117 in chap. 2 of this book.

64. For example, Kathryn Tanner, *Theories of Culture*, 157–9, mistakes "diversity" for something like a norm (the section is called "Interpretation of Diversity"); and Richard Rorty, "Universality and Truth," in *Rorty and His Critics*, ed. Robert B. Brandom (Oxford: Blackwell, 2000), 1–30, does something similar with "inclusivism" ("Given that we want to be ever more inclusivist" 23), even though he is willing to say explicitly that the views of "religious fundamentalists" are clearly to be discarded for the "benefits of secularization" (22). To take one more example almost at random, see George Carey's essay on "Tolerating Religion" in *The Politics of Toleration in Modern Life*, ed. Susan Mendus (Durham, NC: Duke University Press, 2000), 45–63. Mendus's introduction is also particularly revealing in that it demonstrates how "startling" MacIntyre's claim was that tolerance is not simply a normative virtue but can in fact become a "vice" (see the essay cited in the note below, which was originally the final piece in the Duke University Press collection).

65. Cf. Alasdair MacIntyre's opening question to his important essay on toleration as a virtue, "Toleration and the Goods of Conflict," in *Ethics and Politics: Selected Essays, Vol. 2* (Cambridge: Cambridge University Press, 2006), 205–23: "When ought we to be intolerant and why?" (205). MacIntyre's essay is of crucial importance for our discussion.

66. This way of phrasing it acknowledges that our imagined interlocutor may be a good Nietzschean and have attempted to do away with the concepts of good and evil altogether. We would thus not only be arguing about the necessity to think in terms of racism at all but also about good and evil.

67. The fact that most modern universities would in principle wholeheartedly embrace the latter kind of tolerance is something for which to be profoundly thankful. It is also evidence of a basic conflict that lies in the heart of the university's self-understanding, namely, that it is against racism but tolerant of all viewpoints. Whether this means that the university does not know why it is against racism is an important question, and the answer to this question will be linked to its ongoing ability to preclude—to be rightly intolerant of—racist ideologies even as it will determine its fidelity to the cultivation of students for the good.

68. For this reason Assmann's suggestion that instead of mono- and polytheism we should speak of "exclusive" and "inclusive" religion is but a semantically reframed version of the same basic problem (*Die Mosaische Unterscheidung*, 52–53). Of course, "in general" tolerance/translation does not exist. Even to argue that it does is already— conceptually, in any case—to be intolerant of the position that it does not. Assmann also attempts to distinguish between tolerance and cultural translation principally on grounds that ancient polytheisms could be intolerant (*Die Mosaische Unterscheidung*, 28, 31–32 passim). But his constructive point remains the same; indeed, this admission should have led him to a reevaluation of the conceptual basis of his historical narrative.

69. Polytheism could not of course translate Judaism either, but Jews and gentiles could coexist so long as the former did not actively missionize the latter—which the Christians did—and the latter did not seek to impose itself on the former. But such coexistence with Jews was fraught with problems whenever polytheism meant in practice anything other than a policy of leaving the Jews to their own ways (consider, e.g., the incident involving Caligula and the Syrian legate Petronius).

70. The terminology is Assmann's. Assmann argues that polytheism is not a regulative idea, that "polytheism" as a single thing comes into being as result of polemic of monotheism (*Die Mosaische Unterscheidung*, 54 passim).

71. The adjective "ancestral" in the sentence to which this note is appended is meant primarily to gesture toward the particular kind of polytheism we see in the Roman period, where the age/tradition/establishment of a deity or cult was directly germane to the Romans' ability to see its worth and thus to allow its existence (and here the Jews are of course the example par excellence).

72. Charles Taylor, "The Politics of Recognition," now in *Philosophical Arguments* (Cambridge, MA: Harvard University Press, 1995), 225–56: "Liberalism is not a possible meeting ground for all cultures; it is the political expression of one range of cultures, and quite incompatible with other ranges. . . . [L]iberalism can't and shouldn't claim complete cultural neutrality. Liberalism is also a fighting creed" (249). Whether or not the various forms of polytheistic religion were aware of themselves as making up something like a fighting creed would be hard to know prior to their confrontation with the Christian mission. But that does not lesson the truth of the fact. We are often unaware of "fighting creeds" until they are

brought to our attention by some external stimulus, particularly if they have existed unchallenged and been simply "assumed" as the way life is. In short, latency should not be confused with nonexistence.

73. Of course, some scholars would want to object that polytheism is not "one thing," that is has no one frame, and that one should therefore speak of polytheisms or polytheistic systems. Those who want to speak of polytheisms must at least acknowledge that whatever it would mean to speak of polytheisms, it would not mean that they could—together or individually—incorporate a metanarrative that would mean their extinction. In this sense, they are unified, and we may be justified in speaking of polytheism. With respect to their intolerance of Christian way of life, they are all united. They oppose it. What this turns out to mean is that the true/false distinction cannot be eliminated without making a true/false judgment about Christianity—that it is false. Thus any kind of polytheism already exists on basis of true/false distinction; it is this distinction that gets brought to the surface in the encounter with Christian mission.

74. This point is sometimes explicit (e.g., Marquard, Rorty), sometimes more implicit (e.g., Assmann).

75. Marquard, "Lob," 101.

76. Cf., for example, Stroumsa, "Early Christianity as Radical Religion," 184, on Gibbon's "paganophile" historiography.

77. William T. Cavanaugh, *Theopolitical Imagination: Discovering the Liturgy as a Political Act in an Age of Global Consumerism* (Edinburgh: T. & T. Clark, 2002).

78. Assmann, *Die Mosaische Unterscheidung*, 29 (cf. 37 passim). Assmann does not of course deny that there was abundant hate prior to the introduction of the true/false distinction. But his focus is on the energy, antagonism, and newness of the hate that comes with this distinction.

79. Stroumsa, "Early Christianity as Radical Religion," 175. Cf. Halbertal, "Jews and Pagans in the Mishnah," 161, for whom "universalism breeds intolerance." Lest this gone unmentioned: the claim to universal truth is not at all the same thing as saying that there is no truth to be known outside the pattern of life that is Christianity. On this point, see Griffiths, *Problems of Religious Diversity*, 60–65.

80. Lilla is right to draw attention to the newspaper headlines as evidence of the need for serious thought about the relation of politics and theology (8–9), not least because this move helps to make explicit the fact that "the grand tradition of thought"— the discourse of the Great Separation—is one of secularized eschatological hope. Cf. the opening paragraph of Rorty's "Universality and Truth."

81. Schmitt, "Political Theology," 51.

82. Schmitt's argument is also a good deal more specific than the idea that political discourse is always involved in theological questions, judgments, and so forth; he also thinks that it is possible to trace precise connections between theological concepts and their transformation—or "secularization"—into modern political ideas (e.g., the "exception in jurisprudence is analogous to the miracle in theology," 36; the monarch in seventeenth political theory occupies a "position in the state exactly analogous to that attributed to God in the Cartesian system of the world," 46, etc.). Moltmann, *The*

Trinity and the Kingdom, 193, misreads Schmitt here. The point is not that something called religion determines something else called politics but that they are always bound together, that so-called political notions are always and ever theological, too. This is incidentally why Schmitt's image of a "metaphysical kernel" is problematic even on his own terms: the image should not be that of kernel and husk, as if all politics grows from metaphysics; it is rather that politics are metaphysical even as metaphysical speculation is political.

83. Cf. Foucault's now famous analysis of a "regime of truth" in *Power/Knowledge: Selected Interviews and Other Writings 1972–77*, ed. Colin Gordon (New York: Pantheon, 1980), esp. 131. Foucault's point is not so much that truth claims can be used violently as it is that all claims to truth function within a more fundamental relation of power such that the particular power relation actually generates what "truth" is taken to be, enables one to know what truth is, forms the status of the persons who speak truth, and so forth. Particular power relations thus become "regimes of truth." For an appreciative and critical use of Foucault's theory in relation to a particular NT text, see Brian J. Walsh and Slyvia C. Keesmaat, *Colossians Remixed: Subverting the Empire* (Downers Grove, IL: IVP, 2004), 102–14. Aside from the insight that "power" is more a relation than a property, I confess that I do not find Foucault all that illuminating for the topic at hand for the simple reason that Foucault's version of things is but one more instance of a real truth claim: namely, that it is true that all truth is reducible to, or explicable in terms of, some version of a "regime" or power relation. That claims to truth involve power relations is not to be doubted—indeed, that is part of the subject of this last section—and even that comprehensive ways of knowing the truth determine what truth is (scheme of life, or regime) obviously appears reasonable, but that such schemes of life are themselves reducible to power relations is obviously contestable on theological grounds.

84. Stroumsa, "Early Christianity as Radical Religion" argues for the importance of examining the "foundational texts" (174 passim). His own analysis of the NT is limited to a couple of sayings from the Gospels (he examines Qumran as well), and his reading of the logia takes no account of the narrative contexts in which they occur. Nevertheless, his point that to speak of Christian intolerance one must think deeply about the normative texts that (at least nominally) fund the Christian theological imagination is exactly correct and its importance can hardly be overestimated. Cf., from a different angle, Averil Cameron's remark in his review article, "Redrawing the Map: Early Christian Territory after Foucault," *JRS* 76 (1986): 266–71: "The social origins of early Christianity have had a long run; it is time for the return of interpretation" (270).

85. See chap. 4, on σωτηρία in its Lukan sense.

86. I say "rage" not because I particularly enjoy opening the door to Hare Krishnas (or even the local Baptists) but rather because I do not know how we know exactly what proselytizing is, and, further, I doubt that we are against it at all (so "rage" gets at the incoherence that afflicts attempts to oppose proselytizing). In other words, it seems to me that there are all kinds of permissible proselytizing that are still proselytizing and some kinds that are impermissible but that are still proselytizing.

So what we are against is not proselytizing as such but a certain range of styles. But what is that range? I do not mean what are the particular behaviors within the range but the range itself. What is that? What would we name it? Moreover, the idea that we should be against proselytizing *tout court* is itself the proselytizing of an idea. So again, we cannot be against proselytizing *simpliciter*.

87. Moshe Halbertal, "Jews and Pagans in the Mishnah," 162 (emphasis added). Whether Halbertal's modifier "common" is accurate or not is debatable, but that the argument has occurred in the history of the church is not.

88. Still, it is important to remember that this literature is the literature of a stereotyped, persecuted (and soon to be persecuted even more) minority. We greatly misread Acts if we think of its author as a crusading noble in the Middle Ages or modern colonialist, or something of that nature. Cf. the Qumran community, which did not have much in the way of material resources for coercion but could conceive of fairly heinous consequences for those who did not accept their theology of the temple corruption, and so forth.

89. To put it in literary terms: in that it retells the story of Jesus's life as the life of the community called "Christians," Acts explicates the meaning of Lordship given by the Gospel of Luke.

90. By no means do I want to imply that other scriptural texts are unimportant for mission. But Acts is the only narrative the church selected to represent adequately and accurately its collective theological memory of its initial mission. To the extent that modern NT scholarship has helped to illuminate distinctive emphases within the NT, it has helped to recover aspects of scripture to which the church must attend.

91. One may "feel" indifferent. But this is not an indifferent response. It is implicit rejection of Acts' vision. Further, to say that we should be intolerant of Acts' intolerance is simply to replace one scheme of life with another (tolerance, remember, always gets its meaning from the larger schemes in which it occurs). What then is the justification for this intolerance? Presumably it would be the truth of the scheme. But that of course is just the point at issue. Acts confronts its readers with a claim to a total scheme. To confront Acts with a counter-claim is not to be more "tolerant" (this is an illusion) but to be intolerant in a different way, and to claim (a) that Acts is wrong, and (b) that the different scheme is right (the possibility that neither one is right is but a subset of (b)—you are right that Acts is not right, even if you are wrong about your own alternative). So it seems that we are left with the decision that Acts wants to enjoin us to make.

92. Alasdair MacIntyre, *Three Rival Versions of Moral Enquiry: Encyclopaedia, Genealogy, and Tradition* (Notre Dame, IN: University of Notre Dame Press, 1990). In my view, MacIntyre conclusively discredits this way of knowing. He also shows how it lives on in the university as if it were still viable. The parallels to NT studies should be obvious, especially because most Ph.D. granting institutions are modern research universities.

93. By "vast production" I have in mind something like the entire scholarly enterprise: from *JBL* "critical notes," to short reviews, to regular articles, to large commentaries, to series, to multivolume works and beyond.

94. That such a work could come into existence is easily imaginable, especially given the strong trend in academic book publishing toward dictionaries, encyclopedias, textbooks, "companions to" and so forth.

95. "Introduction," ABD, 1.xxxvii. The author of the Introduction is Gary Herrion, but presumably the Introduction is intended as the editors' hermeneutical preface to the work.

96. The primary differences between the ABD and the ninth edition of the *Encyclopaedia Britannica* discussed by MacIntyre are that by the time of the production of the ABD (ca. one century later) scholars were more aware of the multiplicity of methods by which particular subjects were examined and of the historical conditioning of various proposals. But the actual mode of knowing that makes the works intelligible is much the same in that it assumes general, unitary rationality and knowledge. Put otherwise, Lord Gifford's basic convictions about knowledge underwrite—provide the unity for—the ABD's methodological multiplicity and historical contingency. At a slightly deeper level, the best way to read the ABD may be to view it as a specimen whose form covers not one but two periods in (post)modern epistemology. The total content reflects the coming apart of the encyclopedic way of knowing in that the different articles clearly evidence different modes of rationality, but the work as a whole puts these articles together under one roof: in its particulars, therefore, the ABD sits squarely in the late twentieth century, but as a whole it embodies a nineteenth-century mode of thought. In other words, it is a living relic.

97. That postmodernists of all kinds have reacted to encyclopedic knowledge needs no great elaboration. As MacIntyre shows, it was Nietzsche above all others who made such reactions possible. In contradistinction to some forms of postmodern thinking, the belief in a single Reality is compatible with a rejection of the ultimate epistemological viability of the encyclopedic way of knowing. In short, that there is Reality is a conflictual claim that a specifically Christian way of knowing makes (i.e., "creation").

98. As we have said above, the attempt at a third way—say, a refusal of the terms of the choice—is in reality just one more version of contesting Acts' vision.

Select Bibliography

Africa, Thomas W. "Urban Violence in Imperial Rome." *Journal of Interdisciplinary History* 2 (1971): 3–21.

Agamben, Giorgio. *State of Exception.* Chicago: University of Chicago Press, 2005.

Alkier, Stefan. "Intertexualität–Annäherungen an ein texttheoretisches Paradigma." In *Heiligkeit und Herrschaft: Intertextuelle Studien zu Heiligkeitsvorstellungen und zu Psalm 110,* edited by Dieter Sänger, 1–26. Neukirchen-Vluyn: Neukirchener Verlag, 2003.

Ando, Clifford. *Imperial Ideology and Provincial Loyalty in the Roman Empire.* Berkeley: University of California Press, 2000.

Asad, Talal. *On Suicide Bombing.* New York: Columbia University Press, 2007.

Assmann, Jan. *Religion and Cultural Memory.* Translated by Rodney Livingstone. Stanford, CA: Stanford University Press, 2006.

———. *Die Mosaische Unterscheidung: Oder, der Preis des Monotheismus.* München: Carl Hanser Verlag, 2003.

———. *Moses the Egyptian: The Memory of Egypt in Western Monotheism.* Cambridge, MA: Harvard University Press, 1997.

Attridge, Harold W. "The Philosophical Critique of Religion under the Early Empire." *ANRW* II.16.1 (1978): 45–78.

———. *First-Century Cynicism in the Epistles of Heraclitus.* Harvard Theological Studies 29. Missoula, MT: Scholars Press, 1976.

Babut, Daniel. *La religion des philosophes grecs: de Thalès aux Stoïciens.* Paris: Presses Universitaires de France, 1974.

Balch, David L. "The Areopagus Speech: An Appeal to the Stoic Historian Posidonius against Later Stoics and the Epicureans." In *Greeks, Romans, and Christians: Essays in Honor of Abraham J. Malherbe,* edited by David L. Balch et al., 52–79. Minneapolis, MN: Fortress, 1990.

Barnes, Timothy D. "An Apostle on Trial." *JTS* 20 (1969): 407–19.

Barrett, C. K. *Acts.* 2 vols. International Critical Commentary. London: T. & T. Clark, 1994/1998.

Barth, Karl. *Church Dogmatics.* Edinburgh: T & T Clark, 1936–1970.

———. *Dogmatics in Outline.* New York: Harper and Row, 1959.

Bauman, Richard A. *Crime and Punishment in Ancient Rome.* London: Routledge, 1996.

———. *The* Crimen Maiestatis *in the Roman Republic and Augustan Principate.* Johannesburg: Witwatersrand University Press, 1967.

Beard, Mary, John North, and Simon Price. *Religions of Rome.* 2 vols. Cambridge: Cambridge University Press, 1998.

Bechard, Dean Philip. *Paul Outside the Walls: A Study of Luke's Socio-Geographical Universalism in Acts 14:8–20.* Analecta Biblica 143. Rome: Pontifical Biblical Institute, 2000.

Betz, Hans Dieter. *The Greek Magical Papyri in Translation, Including the Demotic Spells.* 2nd ed. Chicago: University of Chicago Press, 1992.

Beurlier, Émile. "Saint Paul et L'Aréopage." *Rev. d'hist. et de litt. rel.* 1 (1896): 344–66.

Bickerman, Elias J. "Trajan, Hadrian, and the Christians." *Rivista di filologia classica* 96 (1968): 290–318.

———. "The Warning Inscriptions of Herod's Temple." *JQR* 37 (1947): 387–405.

———. "The Name of Christians." Reprinted in *Studies in Jewish and Christian History,* 3.137–51. Leiden: Brill, 2007.

Bobbitt, Philip. *Terror and Consent.* New York: Knopf, 2008.

Bockmuehl, Markus. *Seeing the Word: Refocusing New Testament Studies.* Grand Rapids, MI: Baker Academic, 2006.

Bolt, Peter. "Mission and Witness." In *Witness to the Gospel: The Theology of Acts,* edited by I. Howard Marshall and David Peterson, 191–214. Grand Rapids, MI: Eerdmans, 1998.

Bömer, Franz. "Der Eid beim Genius des Kaisers." *Athanaeum* 44 (1966): 77–133.

Bonhoeffer, Dietrich. *No Rusty Swords.* New York: Harper and Row, 1965.

———. *Ethics.* New York: Macmillan, 1962.

Botermann, Helga. *Das Judenedikt des Kaisers Claudius.* Stuttgart: Steiner, 1996.

Bouché-Leclercq, Auguste. *L'Intolérance religieuse et la politique.* Paris: Flammarion, 1917.

Bovon, François. "The Law in Luke–Acts." In *Studies in Early Christianity.* WUNT 161, 59–73. Tübingen: Mohr Siebeck, 2003.

Boyce, G. K. *Corpus of the Lararia of Pompeii.* Memoirs of the American Academy of Rome 14. Rome, 1937.

Braund, David C. "Agrippa." In *Anchor Bible Dictionary,* edited by David Noel Freedman et al. 6 vols., 1: 98–101. New York: Doubleday, 1992.

———. *Rome and the Friendly King: The Character of Client Kingship.* New York: St. Martin's, 1984.

Breytenbach, Cilliers. "Zeus und der lebendige Gott: Anmerkungen zu Apostelgeschichte 14.11–17." *NTS* 39 (1993): 396–413.

Brown, Peter "The Limits of Intolerance." In *Authority and the Sacred: Aspects of the Christianization of the Roman World*. Cambridge: Cambridge University Press, 1995.

———. "Art and Society in Late Antiquity." In *An Age of Spirituality: A Symposium*, edited by Kurt Weitzmann, 17–27. Princeton, NJ: Princeton University Press, 1980.

Bruce, F. F. *The Acts of the Apostles: The Greek Text with Introduction and Commentary*. London: Tyndale, 1951.

Brunt, Peter. "Evidence Given under Torture in the Principate." *Zeitschrift der Savigny-Stiftung für Rechtsgeschichte* 97 (1980): 257–63.

Bultmann, Rudolf. *History of the Synoptic Tradition*. Translated by John Marsh. Oxford: Basil Blackwell, 1963.

Burkert, Walter. *Greek Religion*. Cambridge, MA: Harvard University Press, 1985.

Burton, G. P. "Proconsuls, Assizes and the Administration of Justice Under the Empire." *JRS* 65 (1975): 92–106.

Cadbury, Henry J. *The Book of Acts in History*. Eugene, OR: Wipf and Stock, 2004.

———. "Roman Law and the Trial of Paul." In *The Beginnings of Christianity*, edited by F. J. Foakes-Jackson, Kirsopp Lake, and Henry Cadbury. 5 vols., 5: 297–338. London: Macmillan, 1920–1933.

———. *The Making of Luke–Acts*. London: SPCK, 1927.

Cameron, Averil. "Redrawing the Map: Early Christian Territory after Foucault." *JRS* 76 (1986): 266–71.

Carey, George. "Tolerating Religion." In *The Politics of Toleration in Modern Life*, edited by Susan Mendus, 45–63. Durham, NC: Duke University Press, 2000.

Carleton Paget, James. "Jewish Proselytism at the Time of Christian Origins: Chimera or Reality?" *JSNT* 62 (1996): 65–103.

Cassidy, Richard. *Society and Politics in the Acts of the Apostles*. Maryknoll, NY: Orbis, 1987.

Cavanaugh, William T. *Theopolitical Imagination: Discovering the Liturgy as a Political Act in an Age of Global Consumerism*. Edinburgh: T. & T. Clark, 2002.

Chadwick, Henry. "Florilegium." In *Reallexikon für Antike und Christentum* 7: 1131–60.

Chapman, Stephen B. and Laceye C. Warner. "Jonah and the Imitation of God: Rethinking Evangelism and the Old Testament." *JTI* 2 (2008): 43–69.

Charlesworth, M. P. "The Refusal of Divine Honours: An Augustan Formula." *PBSR* 15 (1939): 1–10.

———. *Documents Illustrating the Reigns of Claudius and Nero*. Cambridge: Cambridge University Press, 1939.

Cherry, David. *Frontier and Society in Roman North Africa*. Oxford: Clarendon Press, 1998.

Chilton, C. W. "The Roman Law of Treason under the Early Principate." *JRS* 45 (1955): 73–81.

Clauss, Manfred. *Kaiser und Gott: Herrscherkult im römischen Reich*. Stuttgart: Teubner, 1999.

Cohen, Shaye J. D. "Was Judaism in Antiquity a Missionary Religion?" In *Jewish Assimilation, Acculturation and Accommodation: Past Traditions, Current Issues and*

Future Prospects, edited by Menachem Mor, 14–23. Lanham, MD: University Press of America, 1992.

Coleman, K. M. "Fatal Charades: Roman Executions Staged as Mythological Enactments." *JRS* 80 (1990): 44–73.

Conzelmann, Hans. *Acts of the Apostles.* Philadelphia: Fortress, 1987.

——— . *Theology of St. Luke.* New York: Harper and Row, 1961.

Cook, Arthur Bernard. *Zeus: A Study in Ancient Religion.* 3 vols. Cambridge: Cambridge University Press, 1914–1940.

Cosgrove, Charles H. "The Divine *ΔΕΙ* in Luke–Acts: Investigations into the Lukan Understanding of God's Providence." *NovT* 26 (1984): 168–90.

Crook, John. *Law and Life of Rome.* Ithaca, NY: Cornell University Press, 1967.

Croy, Clayton. "Hellenistic Philosophies and the Preaching of the Resurrection (Acts 17:18, 32)." *NovT* 39 (1997): 21–39.

Cumont, Franz. "La lettre de Claude aux Alexandrins." *Rev. Hist. Rel.* 91 (1925): 3–6.

Dahl, Nils A. "A People for His Name (Acts 15:14)." *NTS* 4 (1957/58): 319–27.

De Ste. Croix, G. E. M. "Why Were the Early Christians Persecuted?—A Rejoinder." *Past and Present* 27 (1964): 28–33.

——— . "Why Were the Early Christians Persecuted?" *Past and Present* 26 (1963): 6–38.

Diamond, Cora. "Losing Your Concepts." *Ethics* 98 (1988): 255–77.

Dibelius, Martin. "Paul on the Areopagus." In *The Book of Acts: Form, Style, and Theology,* edited by K. C. Hanson, 95–128. Minneapolis, MN: Fortress, 2004.

Dodds, E. R. *The Greeks and the Irrational.* Berkeley: University of California Press, 1951.

Donfried, Karl P. "The Cults of Thessalonica and the Thessalonian Correspondence." *NTS* 31 (1985): 336–56.

Downing, F. G. "Common Ground with Paganism in Luke and Josephus." *NTS* 28 (1982): 546–59.

Dupont, Jacques. *The Salvation of the Gentiles: Studies in the Acts of the Apostles.* New York: Paulist Press, 1979.

——— . "Aequitas Romana: Notes sur Actes 25, 16." In *Études sur les Actes des Apôtres,* 527–52. Paris: Cerf, 1967.

——— . "Le Salut des Gentils et la signification théologique du Livre des Actes." *Études,* 393–419. Paris: Cerf, 1967.

Elliger, Winfried. *Paulus in Griechenland: Philippi, Thessaloniki, Athen, Korinth.* Stuttgart: Katholisches Bibelwerk, 1987.

Ellis, E. Earl. "The End of the Earth (Acts 1:8)." *BBR* 1 (1991): 123–32.

Elsner, Jaś. *Imperial Rome and Christian Triumph: The Art of the Roman Empire AD 100–450.* Oxford: Oxford University Press, 1998.

——— . "Image and Ritual: Reflections on the Religious Appreciation of Classical Art." *CQ* 46 (1996): 515–31.

——— . *Art and the Roman Viewer: The Transformation of Art from the Pagan World to Christianity.* Cambridge: Cambridge University Press, 1995.

Esler, Philip F. *Conflict and Identity in Romans: The Social Setting of Paul's Letter.* Minneapolis, MN: Fortress, 2003.

Farrer, Austin. "The Ministry in the New Testament." In *The Apostolic Ministry: Essays on the History and the Doctrine of the Episcopacy*, edited by Kenneth E. Kirk, 113–82. New York: Morehouse-Gorham, 1946.

Foucault, Michel. *Power/Knowledge: Selected Interviews and Other Writings 1972–77*. Edited by Colin Gordon. New York: Pantheon, 1980.

Feldman, Louis H. *Jew and Gentile in the Ancient World: Attitudes and Interactions from Alexander to Justinian*. Princeton, NJ: Princeton University Press, 1993.

Fleischer, Robert. *Artemis von Ephesos und verwandte Kultstatuen aus Anatolien und Syrien*. EPRO 35. Leiden: Brill, 1973.

Flender, Helmut. *St. Luke: Theologian of Redemptive History*. Philadelphia: Fortress, 1967.

Fitzmyer, Joseph A. "New Testament Kyrios and Maranatha and Their Aramaic Background." In *To Advance the Gospel: New Testament Studies*, 2nd ed., 218–35. Grand Rapids, MI: Eerdmans, 1998.

——— . "The Semitic Background to the New Testament *Kyrios*-Title." In *The Semitic Background to the New Testament*, 115–42. Grand Rapids, MI: Eerdmans, 1997.

——— . *The Gospel according to Luke*. 2 vols. Anchor Bible 28–28A. Garden City, NY: Doubleday, 1985.

Foakes-Jackson, F. J., Kirsopp Lake, and Henry Cadbury, eds. *The Beginnings of Christianity*. 5 vols. London: Macmillan, 1920–1933.

Foerster, Werner. "πύθων." TDNT 6: 917–20.

Fowden, Garth. "Between Pagans and Christians." *JRS* 78 (1988): 173–82.

Frend, W. H. C. *Martyrdom and Persecution in the Early Church: A Study of Conflict from the Maccabees to Donatus*. Oxford: Blackwell, 1965.

Friesen, Steven J. *Imperial Cults and the Apocalypse of John: Reading Revelation in the Ruins*. New York: Oxford University Press, 2001.

——— . *Twice Neokoros: Ephesus, Asia and the Cult of the Flavian Imperial Family*. Leiden: Brill, 1993.

Gadamer, Hans-Georg. *Truth and Method*. New York: Seabury Press, 1975.

Gager, John G. "Jews, Gentiles, and Synagogues in the Book of Acts." *HTR* 79 (1986): 91–99.

Garnsey, Peter "Religious Toleration in Classical Antiquity." In *Persecution and Toleration*, edited by W. J. Sheils. London: Basil Blackwell, 1984.

——— . *Social Status and Legal Privilege in the Roman Empire*. Oxford: Clarendon, 1970.

——— . Review of *The Crimen Maiestatis in the Roman Republic and Augustan Principate*, by R. A. Bauman. *JRS* 59 (1969): 282–4.

——— ."The Criminal Jurisdiction of Governors." *JRS* 58 (1968): 51–59.

Gärtner, Bertil. *The Areopagus Speech and Natural Revelation*. Lund: Gleerup, 1955.

Garrett, Susan R. *The Demise of the Devil: Magic and the Demonic in Luke's Writings*. Minneapolis, MN: Fortress, 1989.

Gaventa, Beverly Roberts. *The Acts of the Apostles*. Nashville, TN: Abingdon, 2003.

Geagan, Daniel J. *The Athenian Constitution after Sulla*. Buffalo, NY: Hein, 2004.

Gilbert, Gary. "Roman Propaganda and Christian Identity in the Worldview of Luke–Acts." In *Contextualizing Acts: Lukan Narrative and Greco-Roman Discourse*,

edited by Todd Penner and Caroline Vander Stichele, 233–56. SBJSS 20. Atlanta,
GA: Society of Biblical Literature, 2003.

Ginsburg, Michael. Review of *Roman Revolution*, by Ronald Syme. Oxford: Oxford
University Press, 1939. *American Historical Review* 46 (1940): 106–8.

Goheen, Michael. "A Critical Examination of David Bosch's Missional Reading of Luke."
In *Reading Luke: Interpretation, Reflection, Formation*, edited by Craig
G. Bartholomew, Joel B. Green, and Anthony C. Thiselton, 230–64. SHS 7.
Grand Rapids, MI: Zondervan, 2005.

Goodenough, Erwin R. "The Political Philosophy of Hellenistic Kingship." *Yale
Classical Studies* 1 (1928): 55–102.

Goodwin, Mark J. *Paul: Apostle of the Living God: Kerygma and Conversion in
2 Corinthians*. Harrisburg, PA: Trinity Press International, 2001.

Gordon, Richard L. "The Real and the Imaginary: Production and Religion in the
Graeco-Roman World." In *Image and Value in the Graeco-Roman World: Studies
in Mithraism and Religious Art*, 5–34. Brookfield, VT: Ashgate, 1996.

Gradel, Ittai. *Emperor Worship and Roman Religion*. Oxford: Clarendon Press, 2002.

Graf, Fritz. *Magic in the Ancient World*. Cambridge, MA: Harvard University Press, 1997.

Griffiths, Paul. "The Future of the Study of Religion in the Academy." *JAAR* 74
(2006): 66–78.

———. *Problems of Religious Diversity*. Oxford: Blackwell, 2001.

Gruenwald, Ithamar. "Intolerance and Martyrdom: From Socrates to Rabbi Aqiva."
Tolerance and Intolerance in Early Judaism and Christianity, edited by Graham N. Stanton
and Guy G. Stroumsa, 7–29. Cambridge: Cambridge University Press, 1998.

Haenchen, Ernst. *The Acts of the Apostles: A Commentary*. Philadelphia: Westminster,
1971.

Halbertal, Moshe, and Avishai Margalit. *Idolatry*. Translated by Naomi Goldblum.
Cambridge, MA: Harvard University Press, 1992.

Halteman Finger, Reta. *Of Widows and Meals: Communal Meals in the Book of Acts*.
Grand Rapids, MI: Eerdmans, 2007.

Hardin, Justin. "Decrees and Drachmas at Thessalonica: An Illegal Assembly in
Jason's House (Acts 17.1–10a)." *NTS* 52 (1996): 29–49.

Harnack, Adolf von. *Die Mission und Ausbreitung des Christentums in den ersten drei
Jahrhunderten*. Leipzig: Hinrichs, 1915.

Hauerwas, Stanley. *Performing the Faith: Bonhoeffer and the Practice of Nonviolence*.
Grand Rapids, MI: Brazos, 2004.

Heumann, C. A. "Dissertatio de Theophilo: Cui Lucas Historiam Sacram Inscripsit."
BHPT, classis IV, Bremen (1720): 483–505.

Heusler, Erika. *Kapitalprozesse im lukanischen Doppelwerk: Die Verfahren gegen Jesus
und Paulus in exegetischer und rechtshistorischer Analyse*. NTA 38. Münster:
Aschendorff, 2000.

Holladay, Carl. *Fragments from Hellenistic Jewish Authors: Volume III: Aristobulus*, 171–73.
Atlanta, GA: Scholars Press, 1995.

———. *Fragments from Hellenistic Jewish Authors: Vol. I: Historians*. Chico, CA: Scholars
Press, 1983.

Hommel, H. "Platonisches bei Lukas. Zu Acta 17.28a (Leben-Bewegung-Sein)." *ZNW* 48 (1957): 193–200.

Horn, Friedrich W. "Die Haltung des Lukas zum römischen Staat im Evangelium und in der Apostelgeschichte." In *The Unity of Luke–Acts*, edited by J. Verheyden, 203–24. Leuven: Leuven University Press, 1999.

Horrell, David. *1 Peter.* Edinburgh: T. & T. Clark, 2008.

――― . "The Label Χριστιανός: 1 Pt 4:16 and the Formation of Christian Identity." *JBL* 126 (2007): 361–81.

――― . "Introduction." *JSNT* 27/3 (March 2005): 251–55.

Horsley, Richard A. "Paul's Assembly in Corinth: An Alternative Society." In *Urban Religion in Roman Corinth: Interdisciplinary Approaches*, edited by D. N. Schowalter and S. J. Friesen. HTS 53, 371–95. Cambridge, MA: Harvard University Press, 2005.

――― . *The Liberation of Christmas: The Infancy Narratives in Social Context.* New York: Crossroad, 1989.

――― and John S. Hanson. *Bandits, Prophets, and Messiahs: Popular Movements in the Time of Jesus.* Minneapolis, MN: Winston, 1985.

Horst, P. W. van der. "The Unknown God." In *Knowledge of God in the Graeco-Roman World*, edited by R. van den Broek et al., 19–42. Leiden: Brill, 1998.

Howell, Justin R. "The Imperial Authority and Benefaction of Centurions and Acts 10.34–43: A Response to C. Kavin Rowe." *JSNT* 31 (2008): 25–51.

Huntington, Samuel P. *The Clash of Civilizations and the Remaking of World Order.* New York: Simon & Schuster, 1996.

Jenson, Robert. "What if It Were True?" Center for Theological Inquiry in Princeton, New Jersey. Online. Available: www.ctinquiry.org. July 25, 2008.

Jervell, Jacob. *Die Apostelgeschichte.* Göttingen: Vandenhoeck & Ruprecht, 1998.

――― . *The Theology of the Acts of the Apostles.* Cambridge: Cambridge University Press, 1996.

Jewett, Robert. *A Chronology of Paul's Life.* Philadelphia: Fortress, 1979.

Johnson, Luke Timothy. *The Acts of the Apostles.* SacPag 5. Collegeville, MN: Liturgical Press, 1992.

――― . *The Literary Function of Possessions in Luke–Acts.* SBLDS 39. Missoula, MT: Scholars Press, 1977.

Jones, A. H. M. "I Appeal Unto Caesar." In *Studies in Roman Government and Law*, 53–65. Oxford: Blackwell, 1960.

――― . *The Greek City from Alexander to Justinian.* Oxford: Clarendon, 1940.

Jones, H. Stuart. "Claudius and the Jewish Question at Alexandria." *JRS* 16 (1926): 17–35.

Judge, E. A. "The Decrees of Caesar at Thessalonica." *RTR* 30/1 (1971): 1–7.

Kermode, Frank. *The Sense of an Ending: Studies in the Theory of Fiction.* Oxford: Oxford University Press, 1966.

Kidd, I. G. *Posidonius II. The Commentary: (i) Testimonia and Fragments 1–149.* Cambridge: Cambridge University Press, 1988.

Klauck, Hans-Josef. *Magic and Paganism in Early Christianity: The World of the Acts of the Apostles.* Edinburgh: T. & T. Clark, 1999.

Koester, Helmut. "Ephesos in Early Christian Literature." In *Ephesos: Metropolis of Asia: An Interdisciplinary Approach to Its Archaeology, Religion, and Culture*, edited by Helmut Koester. HTS 41. Valley Forge, PA: Trinity Press International, 1995.

Koets, P. J. Δεισιδαιμονία: *A Contribution to the Knowledge of the Religious Terminology in Greek*. Purmerend: J. Muusses, 1929.

Lake, Kirsopp. "'Your Own Poets.'" In *The Beginnings of Christianity*, edited by F. J. Foakes-Jackson, Kirsopp Lake, and Henry Cadbury. 5 vols., 5: 246–51. London: Macmillan, 1920–1933.

——— . "The Chronology of Acts." In *The Beginnings of Christianity*, edited by F. J. Foakes-Jackson, Kirsopp Lake, and Henry Cadbury. 5 vols., 5: 460–64. London: Macmillan, 1920–1933.

Lampe, Peter, and Ulrich Luz. "Post-Pauline Christianity and Pagan Society." In *Christian Beginnings*, edited by Jürgen Becker, 242–80. Louisville, KY: Westminster John Knox, 1993.

Lane Fox, Robin. *Pagans and Christians*. New York: Knopf, 1986.

Last, Hugh. "Rome and the Druids: A Note." *JRS* 39 (1949): 1–5.

——— . "The Study of the Persecutions." *JRS* 27 (1937): 80–92.

Le Bohec, Yann. *The Imperial Roman Army*. Translated by R. Bate. New York: Routledge, 2000.

Lear, Jonathan. *Radical Hope: Ethics in the Face of Cultural Devastation*. Cambridge, MA: Harvard University Press, 2006.

Leigh, Matthew. *Lucan: Spectacle and Engagement*. New York: Oxford University Press, 1997.

Lentz, John Layton. *Luke's Portrait of Paul*. SNTSMS 77. Cambridge: Cambridge University Press, 1993.

Levine, Amy-Jill. "The Matthean Program of Salvation History: A Contextual Analysis of the Exclusivity Logia." Ph.D. diss., Duke University, 1984.

Lieu, Judith M. "'I am a Christian': Martyrdom and the Beginning of 'Christian' Identity." In *Neither Jew Nor Greek? Constructing Early Christianity*, 211–31. Edinburgh: T. & T. Clark, 2002.

Lightfoot, J. L. *Lucian: On the Syrian Goddess*. Oxford: Oxford University Press, 2003.

Lilla, Mark. *The Stillborn God: Religion, Politics, and the Modern West*. New York: Knopf, 2007.

Lintott, Andrew W. "Provocatio: From the Struggle of the Orders to the Principate." *ANRW* I.2 (1972): 226–67.

Loisy, Alfred. *Les Actes des Apôtres*. Paris: Émile Nourry, 1920.

Long, A. A. and D. N. Sedley. *The Hellenistic Philosophers*. 2 vols. Cambridge: Cambridge University Press, 1987.

Longenecker, Richard N. *Acts*. Grand Rapids, MI: Zondervan, 1981.

Lösch, Stephan. "Die Dankesrede des Tertullus; Apg 21, 1–4." *TQ* 112 (1931): 295–315.

Marguerat, Daniel. "The End of Acts (28.16–31) and the Rhetoric of Silence." In *Rhetoric and the New Testament: Essays from the 1992 Heidelberg Conference*, edited by Stanley E. Porter and Thomas H. Olbricht, 74–89. JSNTSup 90. Sheffield: JSOT Press, 1993.

Marquard, Odo. *Farewell to Matters of Principle: Philosophical Studies*. New York: Oxford University Press, 1989.

MacIntyre, Alasdair. *After Virtue*, 3rd ed. Notre Dame, IN: University of Notre Dame Press, 2007.

——— . "Toleration and the Goods of Conflict." In *Ethics and Politics: Selected Essays, Volume 2*, 205–23. Cambridge: Cambridge University Press, 2006.

——— . *Three Rival Versions of Moral Enquiry: Encyclopaedia, Genealogy, and Tradition*. Notre Dame, IN: University of Notre Dame Press, 1990.

——— . *Whose Justice? Which Rationality?* Notre Dame, IN: University of Notre Dame Press, 1988.

Mackie, Nicola. "Ovid and the Birth of Maiestas." In *Roman Poetry and Propaganda in the Age of Augustus*, edited by Anton Powell, 83–97. London: Bristol Classical Press, 1992.

MacMullen, Ramsay. "Judicial Savagery in the Roman Empire." *Chiron* 16 (1986): 147–66.

——— . "Conversion: A Historian's View." *The Second Century* 5/2 (1985/86): 67–81.

——— . *Christianizing the Roman Empire A.D. 100–400*. New Haven, CT: Yale University Press, 1984.

——— . *Paganism in the Roman Empire*. New Haven, CT: Yale University Press, 1981.

——— . Review of *The* Crimen Maiestatis *in the Roman Republic and Augustan Principate*, by R. A. Bauman. *AJP* 91 (1970): 117–18.

——— . *Roman Government's Response to Crisis A.D. 235–337*. New Haven, CT: Yale University Press, 1976.

——— . *Enemies of the Roman Order: Treason, Unrest, and Alienation in the Empire*. Cambridge, MA: Harvard University Press, 1966.

Malherbe, Abraham J. "'Not in a Corner': Early Christian Apologetic in Acts 26:26." *The Second Century* 5/4 (1985/86): 193–210.

Marcovich, Miroslav. *Iustini Martyris Apologiae pro Christianis*. Patristische Texte und Studien 38. Berlin: Walter de Gruyter, 1994.

Marshall, Bruce. *Trinity and Truth*. Cambridge: Cambridge University Press, 2000.

Mattern, Susan P. *Rome and the Enemy: Imperial Strategy in the Principate*. Berkeley: University of California Press, 1999.

Mauser, Ulrich. *The Gospel of Peace: A Scriptural Message for Today's World*. Louisville, KY: Westminster John Knox, 1992.

McClendon, James Wm. Jr. *Systematic Theology: Witness, Volume 3*. Nashville, TN: Abingdon, 2000.

McDonald, A. H. "Caesar's Ruler Cult?" *Classical Review* 26/2 (1976): 222–25.

McGown, Chester C. "The Ephesia Grammata in Popular Belief." *Transactions and Proceedings of the American Philological Association* 54 (1923): 128–40.

Meeks, Wayne A. *The Origins of Christian Morality: The First Two Centuries*. New Haven, CT: Yale University Press, 1993.

Meggitt, Justin. "Taking the Emperor's Clothes Seriously: The New Testament and the Roman Emperor." In *The Quest for Wisdom: Essays in Honour of Philip Budd*, edited by Christine E. Joynes, 143–68. Cambridge: Orchard Academic, 2002.

Meiser, Martin. "Lukas und die römische Staatsmacht." In *Zwischen den Reichen: Neues Testament und Römische Herrschaft,* edited by Michael Labahn and Jürgen Zangenberg 166–83. TANZ 36. Tübingen: Franke Verlag, 2002.

Merkelbach, Reinhold. "Gefesselte Götter." *Antaios* 12 (1971): 549–65.

Metzger, Bruce. *The Canon of the New Testament: Its Origin, Development, and Significance.* Oxford: Clarendon, 1997.

Milbank, John. *Theology and Social Theory: Beyond Secular Reason.* Oxford: Blackwell, 1990.

Millar, Fergus. *Rome, the Greek World, and the East.* 3 vols. Edited by Hannah M. Cotton and Guy M. Rogers. Chapel Hill: University of North Carolina Press, 2002–06.

——— . *The Roman Near East 31 BC–AD 337.* Cambridge, MA: Harvard University Press, 1993.

——— . *The Emperor in the Roman World (31 BC–AD 337),* 2nd ed. London: Duckworth, 1992.

——— . "Condemnation to Hard Labour in the Roman Empire, From the Julio-Claudians to Constantine." *PBSR* 52 (1984): 124–47.

——— . "The Imperial Cult and the Persecutions." In *Le culte des souverains dans l'empire romain,* edited by W. den Boer, 145–65. Geneva: Foundation Hardt, 1973.

——— . *The Roman Empire and Its Neighbors.* New York: Dell, 1967.

——— . "The Emperor, the Senate and the Provinces." *JRS* 56 (1966): 156–66.

Minear, Paul. "Dear Theo: The Kerygmatic Intention and Claim of the Book of Acts." *Int* 27 (1973): 131–50.

Mitchell, Margaret M. "Homer in the New Testament?" *JR* 83 (2003): 244–60.

Mitchell, Stephen. "The Cult of Theos Hypsistos." In *Pagan Monotheism in Late Antiquity,* edited by Polymnia Athanassiadi and Michael Frede. Oxford: Clarendon, 1999.

Molthagen, Joachim. *Der römische Staat und die Christen im zweiten und dritten Jahrhundert.* Göttingen: Vandenhoeck & Ruprecht, 1970.

Moltmann, Jürgen. *The Trinity and the Kingdom: The Doctrine of God.* Minneapolis, MN: Fortress, 1993.

Mommsen, Theodor. "Die Rechtsverhältnisse des Apostels Paulus." *ZNW* 2 (1901): 81–96.

——— . "Die Religionsfrevel nach römischem Recht," in *Gesammelte Schriften III,* 389–422. Weidmannsche Buchhandlung, 1907.

——— . *Römisches Strafrecht.* Leipzig: Duncker & Humbolt, 1899.

Moore, Thomas S. " 'To the End of the Earth': The Geographical and Ethnic Universalism of Acts 1: 8 in Light of Isaianic Influence on Luke." *JETS* 40 (1997): 389–99.

Musurillo, Herbert A. *Acts of the Christian Martyrs.* Oxford: Clarendon, 1972.

——— . *The Acts of the Pagan Martyrs: Acta Alexandrinorum.* Oxford: Clarendon, 1954.

Neagoe, Alexandru. *The Trial of the Gospel: An Apologetic Reading of Luke's Trial Narratives.* SNTSMS 116. Cambridge: Cambridge University Press, 2002.

Neyrey, Jerome. "The Symbolic Universe of Luke–Acts: 'They Turn the World Upside Down.'" In *The Social World of Luke–Acts: Models for Interpretation*, edited idem, 271–304. Peabody, MA: Hendrickson, 1991.

———. "The Forensic Defense Speech and Paul's Trial Speeches in Acts 22–26: Form and Function." In *Luke–Acts: New Perspectives from the Society of Biblical Literature Seminar*, edited by Charles H. Talbert, 210–24. New York: Crossroad, 1984.

Nicolet, Claude. *Space, Geography, and Politics in the Early Roman Empire*. Ann Arbor: University of Michigan Press, 1991.

Nilsson, Martin P. *Greek Popular Religion*. New York: Columbia University Press, 1940.

Nock, A. D. *Conversion: The Old and New in Religion from Alexander the Great to Augustine of Hippo*. Baltimore: The Johns Hopkins University Press, 1998.

———. "Religious Attitudes of the Ancient Greeks." Reprinted in *Essays on Religion and the Ancient World*. 2 vols., 2:534–50. Oxford: Clarendon, 1972.

———. *Early Gentile Christianity and Its Hellenistic Background*. New York: Harper and Row, 1964.

Nolland, John. "Salvation-History and Eschatology." In *Witness to the Gospel: The Theology of Acts*, edited by I. Howard Marshall and David Peterson, 63–81. Grand Rapids, MI: Eerdmans, 1998.

Norden, Eduard. *Agnostos Theos: Untersuchungen zur Formengeschichte religiöser Rede*. Berlin: B. G. Teubner, 1913.

North, J. A. "The Development of Religious Pluralism." In *The Jews among Pagans and Christians in the Roman Empire*, edited by Judith Lieu et al., 174–93. London: Routledge, 1992.

———. "Religion and Politics, From Republic to Principate." *JRS* 76 (1986): 251–58.

Oeming, Manfred. *Biblische Hermeneutik: Eine Einführung*. Darmstadt: Primus, 1998.

Omerzu, Heiki. *Der Prozess des Paulus: Eine Exegetische und Rechtshistorische Untersuchung der Apostelgeschichte*. BZNW 115. Berlin: Walter de Gruyter, 2002.

Oster, Richard. "The Ephesian Artemis as an Opponent of Early Christianity." *Jahrbuch für Antike und Christentum* 19 (1976): 24–44.

O'Toole, Robert F. "Luke's Position on Politics and Society." In *Political Issues in Luke–Acts*, edited by Richard J. Cassidy and Philip J. Scharper. Maryknoll, NY: Orbis Books, 1983.

———. *Acts 26: The Christological Climax of Paul's Defense (Ac 22:1–26:32)*. Rome: Biblical Institute, 1978.

Owens, E. J. *The City in the Greek and Roman World*. London: Routledge, 1991.

Parker, Robert. *Athenian Religion: A History*. Oxford: Clarendon, 1996.

Pease, Arthur Stanley. "Notes on Book-Burning." In *Munera Studiosa*, edited by M. H. Shepherd Jr., and S. E. Johnson, 145–160. Cambridge, MA: Episcopal Theological School, 1946.

Penner, Todd. *In Praise of Christian Origins: Stephen and the Hellenists in Lukan Apologetic Historiography*. London: Continuum, 2004.

———. "Madness in the Method? The Acts of the Apostles in Current Study." *CBR* 2.2 (2004): 223–93.

Pesch, Rudolf. *Die Apostelgeschichte.* 2 vols. Neukirchener-Vluyn: Neukirchener Verlag, 1986.

Peterson, Erik. "Christianus." Repinted in *Frühkirche, Judentum und Gnosis: Studien und Untersuchungen,* 64–87. Freiburg: Herder, 1959.

———. *Monotheismus als politisches Problem: Ein Beitrag zur Geschichte der politischen Theologie im Imperium Romanum.* Leipzig: Jacob Hegner, 1935.

Price, Simon. *Religions of the Ancient Greeks.* Cambridge: Cambridge University Press, 1999.

———. "The Roman Mind." In *The World of Rome: An Introduction to Roman Culture,* edited by Peter Jones and Keith Sidwell, 235–61. Cambridge: Cambridge University Press, 1997.

———. "Gods and Emperors: The Greek Language of the Roman Imperial Cult." *JHS* 104 (1984): 79–93.

———. *Rituals and Power: The Roman Imperial Cult in Asia Minor.* Cambridge: Cambridge University Press, 1984.

Quint, David. *Epic and Empire: Politics and Generic Form from Virgil to Milton.* Princeton, NJ: Princeton University Press, 1993.

Radl, Walter. *Paulus und Jesus im lukanischen Doppelwerk.* Frankfurt: Peter Lang, 1975.

Rapske, Brian. *The Book of Acts and Paul in Roman Custody,* vol. 3. In *The Book of Acts in Its First Century Setting.* Grand Rapids, MI: Eerdmans, 1994.

Rawson, Elizabeth. "Caesar's Heritage: Hellenistic Kings and Their Roman Equals." *JRS* 65 (1975): 148–59.

Riccobono, Salvator, ed. *Fontes Ivris Romani Antejvstiniani* 69. Florentiae: S. A. G. Barbèra, 1941.

Riesner, Rainer. "A Pre-Christian Jewish Mission?" In *The Mission of the Early Church to Jews and Gentiles,* edited by Jostein dna and Hans Kvalbein, 211–50. Tübingen: Mohr Siebeck, 2000.

———. *Paul's Early Period: Chronology, Mission Strategy, Theology.* Translated by Doug Stott. Grand Rapids, MI: Eerdmans, 1998.

———. "James's Speech, Simeon's Hymn, and Luke's Sources." In *Jesus of Nazareth: Lord and Christ: Essays on the Historical Jesus and New Testament Christology,* edited by Joel B. Green and Max Turner, 263–78. Grand Rapids, MI: Eerdmans, 1994.

Roberts, Colin, Theodore C. Skeat, and Arthur Darby Nock. "The Gild of Zeus Hypsistos." *HTR* 29 (1936): 39–88.

Rogers, Robert Samuel. "Treason in the Early Empire." *JRS* 49 (1959): 90–94.

Rorty, Richard. "Universality and Truth." In *Rorty and His Critics,* edited by Robert B. Brandom, 1–30. Oxford: Blackwell, 2000.

———. "Pragmatism as Romantic Polytheism." In the *Revival of Pragmatism: New Essays on Social Thought, Law, and Culture,* edited by Morris Dickstein, 21–36. Durham, NC: Duke University Press, 1998.

Roscher, W. H. *Ausführliches Lexikon der griechischen und römischen Mythologie.* II/1, 1755–69.

Rowe, C. Kavin. "Acts 2:36 and the Continuity of Lukan Christology." *NTS* 53 (2007): 37–56.

———— . *Early Narrative Christology: The Lord in the Gospel of Luke*. BZNW 139. Berlin: Walter de Gruyter, 2006; Grand Rapids, MI: Baker Academic, 2009.

———— . "Luke–Acts and the Imperial Cult: A Way through the Conundrum?" *JSNT* 27 (2005): 279–300.

———— . "Biblical Pressure and Trinitarian Hermeneutics," *Pro Ecclesia* 11 (2002): 295–312.

———— . "Romans 10:13: What Is the Name of the Lord?" *Horizons in Biblical Theology* 22/2 (2000): 135–73.

Sanders, E. P. *Judaism: Practice and Belief 63 BCE–66 CE*. Philadelphia: Trinity Press International, 1992.

———— . *Jesus and Judaism*. Philadelphia: Fortress, 1985.

Sanders, Jack T. "The Salvation of the Jews in Luke–Acts." In *Luke–Acts: New Perspectives from the SBL Seminar*, edited by Charles Talbert, 104–28. New York: Crossroad, 1984.

Scherrer, Peter. "The City of Ephesos from the Roman Period to Late Antiquity." In *Ephesos: Metropolis of Asia: An Interdisciplinary Approach to Its Archaeology, Religion, and Culture*, edited by Helmut Koester, HTS 41, 1–25. Valley Forge, PA: Trinity Press International, 1995.

Schmitt, Carl. *Political Theology: Four Chapters on the Concept of Sovereignty*. Translated by George Schwab. Chicago: University of Chicago Press, 1985.

Schneider, Gerhard. *Die Apostelgeschichte*. 2 vols. Freiburg: Herder, 1980/1982.

Schnelle, Udo. "Neutestamentliche Anthropologie: Ein Forschungsbericht." *ANRW* II.26 (1996): 2658–2714.

Schubert, Paul. "The Place of the Areopagus Speech in the Composition of Acts." In *Transitions in Biblical Scholarship*, edited by J. Coert Rylaarsdam, 235–61. Chicago: University of Chicago Press, 1968.

Schüssler Fiorenza, Elizabeth. "Miracles, Mission, and Apologetics: An Introduction." In *Aspects of Religious Propaganda in Judaism and Early Christianity*, edited by Elizabeth Schüssler Fiorenza, 1–25. Notre Dame, IN: University of Notre Dame Press, 1976.

Scott, James M. "Luke's Geographical Horizon." *The Book of Acts, vol. 2: Greco-Roman Setting*, edited by David. W. J. Gill and Conrad Gempf, 483–544. Grand Rapids, MI: Eerdmans, 1994.

Scott, Kenneth. "Emperor Worship in Ovid." *Transactions and Proceedings of the American Philological Association* 61 (1930): 43–69.

Shauf, Scott. *Theology as History, History as Theology: Paul in Ephesus in Acts 19*. BZNW 133. Berlin: Walter de Gruyter, 2005.

Sherwin-White, A. N. "The Date of the *Lex Repetundarum* and Its Consequences." *JRS* 62 (1972): 83–99.

———— . "Why Were the Early Christians Persecuted?—An Amendment." *Past and Present* 27 (1964): 23–27.

———— . *Roman Society and Roman Law in the New Testament*. Oxford: Clarendon Press, 1963.

———— . "The Early Persecutions and Roman Law Again." *JTS* 3 (1952): 199–213.

———— . *The Roman Citizenship*. Oxford: Clarendon, 1939.

Skinner, Matthew L. *Locating Paul: Places of Custody as Narrative Settings in Acts 21–28.* Atlanta, GA: Society of Biblical Literature, 2003.

Smallwood, E. Mary. *The Jews Under Roman Rule: From Pompey to Diocletian: A Study in Political Relations.* Leiden: Brill, 1981.

Stählin, Gustav. *Die Apostelgeschichte.* NTD 5. Göttingen: Vandenhoeck & Ruprecht, 1962.

Stark, Rodney. *The Rise of Christianity.* Princeton, NJ: Princeton University Press, 1996.

Stenschke, Christoph W. *Luke's Portrait of the Gentiles Prior to Their Coming to Faith.* WUNT 2/108. Tübingen: Mohr Siebeck, 1999.

———. "The Need for Salvation." In *Witness to the Gospel: The Theology of Acts,* edited by I. Howard Marshall and David Peterson, 125–44. Grand Rapids, MI: Eerdmans, 1998.

Stern, Menahem. *Greek and Latin Authors on Jews and Judaism.* 3 vols. Jerusalem: The Israel Academy of Sciences and Humanities, 1974–1984.

Stoops, Robert F. "Riot and Assembly: The Social Context of Acts 19: 23–41." *JBL* 108 (1989): 73–91.

Stroumsa, G. G. "Early Christianity as a Radical Religion." In *Concepts of the Other in Near Eastern Religions.* IOS 14, 173–93. Leiden: Brill, 1994.

———. "Postscript." In *Tolerance and Intolerance in Early Judaism and Christianity,* edited by Graham N. Stanton and Guy G. Stroumsa, 356–7. Cambridge: Cambridge University Press, 1998.

Swartley, Willard M. "Politics and Peace (Eirēnē) in Luke's Gospel." In *Political Issues in Luke–Acts,* edited by Richard J. Cassidy and Philip J. Scharper, 18–37. Maryknoll, NY: Orbis Books, 1983.

Takács, Sarolta A. "Pagan Cults at Antioch." In *Antioch: The Lost Ancient City,* edited by Christine Kondoleon, 198–216. Princeton, NJ: Princeton University Press, 2000.

Tajra, Harry W. *The Trial of St. Paul: A Juridical Exegesis of the Second Half of the Acts of the Apostles.* WUNT 2/35. Tübingen: Mohr Siebeck, 1989.

Talbert, Charles H. *Reading Acts.* Macon, GA: Smyth & Helwys, 2005.

Tanner, Kathryn. *Theories of Culture: A New Agenda for Theology.* Minneapolis, MN: Fortress, 1997.

Taubes, Jacob. "Zur Konjunktur des Polytheismus." In *Mythos und Moderne,* edited by K. H. Bohrer, 457–70. Frankfurt: Suhrkamp, 1983.

Taylor, Charles. *A Secular Age.* Cambridge, MA: Harvard University Press, 2007.

———. *Modern Social Imaginaries.* Durham, NC: Duke University Press, 2004.

———. "The Politics of Recognition." In *Philosophical Arguments,* 225–56. Cambridge, MA: Harvard University Press, 1995.

Taylor, Justin. "Why Were the Disciples First Called 'Christians' at Antioch?" *RB* 101 (1994): 75–94.

Taylor, Lily Ross. "Artemis of Ephesus." In *The Beginnings of Christianity,* edited by F. J. Foakes-Jackson, Kirsopp Lake, and Henry Cadbury. 5 vols., 5: 251–56. London: Macmillan, 1920–1933.

Thomas, Christine M. "At Home in the City of Artemis." In *Ephesos: Metropolis of Asia*, edited by Helmut Koester, 82–117.

Towner, Philip. *The Letters to Timothy and Titus*. Grand Rapids, MI: Eerdmans, 2006.

Trebilco, Paul R. *Jewish Communities in Asia Minor*. SNTSMS 69. Cambridge: Cambridge University Press, 1991.

Trites, Allison A. "The Importance of Legal Scenes and Language in the Book of Acts." *NovT* 16 (1974): 278–84.

Troeltsch, Ernst. *The Social Teaching of the Christian Churches*, vol. 1. Translated by Olive Wyon. London: Allen & Unwin, 1931.

Tyson, Joseph. "Jews and Judaism in Luke–Acts: Reading as a Godfearer." *NTS* 41 (1995): 19–38.

Veltman, Fred. "The Defense Speeches of Paul in Acts." In *Perspectives on Luke–Acts*, edited by Charles Talbert, 242–56. Danville, VA: Association of Baptist Professors in Religion, 1978.

Vielhauer, Philipp. "On the 'Paulinism' of Acts." In *Studies in Luke–Acts*, edited by L. E. Keck and J. L. Martyn, 33–50. Mifflintown, PA: Sigler, 1999.

Wainwright, Geoffrey. *Lesslie Newbigin: A Theological Life*. New York: Oxford University Press, 2000.

Walaskay, Paul. *Acts*. Louisville, KY: Westminster John Knox, 1998.

———. *"And so we came to Rome": The Political Perspective of St Luke*. Cambridge: Cambridge University Press, 1983.

Walsh, Brian J. and Slyvia C. Keesmaat. *Colossians Remixed: Subverting the Empire*. Downers Grove, IL: IVP, 2004.

Walton, Steve. "The State They Were In: Luke's View of the Roman Empire." In *Rome in the Bible and the Early Church*, edited by Peter Oakes, 1–41. Grand Rapids, MI: Baker Academic, 2002.

Wankel, Hermann, ed. *Die Inschriften von Ephesos, Teil 1a*. Bonn: Rudolf Habelt Verlag, 1979.

Weinstock, Stefan. *Divus Julius*. Oxford: Clarendon Press, 1971.

———. "Treueid und Kaiserkult." In *Mitteilungen des Deutschen Archäologischen Instituts: Athenische Abteilung* 77. Berlin: Gebr. Mann Verlag, 1962.

Weiser, Alfons. *Die Apostelgeschichte*. ÖTKNT 5. 2 vols. Gütersloh: Gerd Mohn, 1981/1985.

Weiss, Johannes. *Über die Absicht und den literarischen Charakter der Apostelgeschichte*. Göttingen: Vandenhoeck & Ruprecht, 1897.

Wengst, Klaus. *Pax Romana and the Peace of Jesus Christ*. Philadelphia: Fortress, 1987.

White, L. Michael. "Adolf Harnack and the 'Expansion' of Early Christianity: A Reappraisal of Social History." *The Second Century* 5/2 (1985/86): 97–127.

Wilckens, Ulrich. *Die Missionsreden der Apostelgeschichte*. Neukirchen: Neukirchener Verlag, 1961.

Wilken, Robert Louis. *The Christians as the Romans Saw Them*. 2nd ed. New Haven, CT: Yale University Press, 2003.

Williams, Raymond. *Keywords: A Vocabulary of Culture and Society*. New York: Oxford University Press, 1976.

Winter, Bruce W. "Roman Law and Society in Romans 12–15." In *Rome in the Bible and the Early Church*, edited by Peter Oakes, 67–102. Grand Rapids, MI: Baker Academic, 2002.

———. "Gallio's Ruling on the Legal Status of Early Christianity." *TynB* 50 (1999): 213–24.

———. "The Importance of the Captatio Benevolentiae in the Speeches of Tertullus and Paul in Acts 24:1–21." *JTS* 42 (1991): 505–31.

Witherington, Ben. *The Acts of the Apostles: A Socio-Rhetorical Commentary*. Grand Rapids, MI: Eerdmans, 1998.

Wolin, Sheldon S. *Politics and Vision: Continuity and Innovation in Western Political Thought*, expanded edition. Princeton, NJ: Princeton University Press, 2004.

Wuthnow, Robert. *Communities of Discourse: Ideology and Social Structure in the Reformation, the Enlightenment, and European Socialism*. Cambridge, MA: Harvard University Press, 1989.

Wycherley, R. E. "St. Paul at Athens." *JTS* 19 (1968): 619–21.

Young, Frances. *Biblical Exegesis and the Formation of Christian Culture*. Cambridge: Cambridge University Press, 1997.

Zanker, Paul. *The Power of Images in the Age of Augustus*. Translated by Alan Shapiro. Ann Arbor: University of Michigan Press, 1988.

Index of Scripture Citations

Index of Ancient Sources

Index of Modern Authors

CPSIA information can be obtained at www.ICGtesting.com
Printed in the USA
BVOW08s0913150415

396252BV00003B/9/P